MW00805989

FROM EVERY STORMY
WIND THAT BLOWS

FROM EVERY STORMY WIND THAT BLOWS

THE IDEA OF
HOWARD COLLEGE
AND THE ORIGINS OF
SAMFORD UNIVERSITY

S. JONATHAN BASS

LOUISIANA STATE UNIVERSITY PRESS   BATON ROUGE

Published with the generous support of the William E. and Wylodine H. Hull
Research Fellowship, Provost's Office, Samford University.

Published by Louisiana State University Press
lsupress.org

Manufactured in the United States of America
First printing

Designer: Barbara Neely Bourgoyne
Typeface: Arno Pro
Printer and binder: Sheridan Books

Jacket photograph: Howard College in 1876. Courtesy of Samford University,
Special Collection and University Archives.

Cataloging-in-Publication Data are available from the Library of Congress.
ISBN 978-0-8071-8177-5 (cloth: alk. paper)
ISBN 978-0-8071-8209-3 (pdf)
ISBN 978-0-8071-8208-6 (epub)

For my students

CONTENTS

ILLUSTRATIONS

PREFACE AND ACKNOWLEDGMENTS

While growing up in a smoke-filled industrial town west of Birmingham, I knew little about Samford University. It was beyond my reach—a private Baptist school that was unaffordable to working-class Baptists. During the 1920s, some of my grandfather's well-to-do cousins attended Howard College, but the only time he visited campus was to deliver a fresh supply of milk from a local dairy. Most of my knowledge of the institution came when I joined the faculty in the late 1990s and listened to several of my colleagues describe old Howard College as a fundamentalist-controlled Bible college and a "Baptist Preacher Boy's School." I soon realized it was neither and that these erstwhile colleagues were just imagining how unenlightened the institution was before their rapturous arrivals. The historical evidence revealed that Howard was a top-notch school with a capable faculty committed to rigorous learning in the liberating arts.

While Howard produced a fair share of ministers, most graduates entered successful middle-class careers. Of those graduating in the nineteenth century, several alumni rose to the top of their professions, including James R. Sampey, an Old Testament scholar who served as president of the Southern Baptist Theological Seminary during the Great Depression, and David Gordon Lyon who, as a young college student, rediscovered his father's Jewish roots en route to becoming a professor and one of the world's leading authorities on Semitic languages at Harvard University. And then, there was William Garrott Brown who had the distinction of being the first modern historian of the South. He graduated from Howard College in 1886, earned additional degrees from Harvard, and then worked at the Ivy League institution as a librarian, instructor, and writer. Long before the iconic works of U. B. Phillips, Wilber J. Cash, Robert Penn Warren, and C. Vann Woodward, Brown was writing lyrical prose about how race was the central theme of southern history, how southerners had no mind, and how he, along with every other resident from the region, carried the burden of southern history.

Brown was a native of Marion, Alabama (then home to Howard College), and his essays on Alabama and the "lower" South provided key interpretive elements for this book. So too did the writings, musings, and elucidations of my hunkered-down, bulldog dissertation advisor, James C. Cobb. I also must recognize the additional intellectual influences of Professors David E. "Ed" Harrell and David Bebbington. Many years ago, during my master's studies, the duo team-taught a course on "Evangelical Protestantism in Great Britain and America" that provided me with a grounding in American and British evangelical history. A few years ago, when I discussed this project with Professor Bebbington, he encouraged me to be factual, contextual, and at the most, only mildly celebratory. I strove to meet that standard.

Fifty years ago, historian David B. Potts called for a new approach to institutional histories of colleges and universities that focused on the "intersection between institution and society." For Howard College, that intersection stood at the crossroads of the Second Great Awakening. The three major strains of revivalism (Timothy Dwight, Charles G. Finney, and the Revival in the West) converged on Marion, Alabama, in 1841 and 1842. Few, if any, antebellum towns had similar experiences. The founding of Howard College must be understood within the context of the historiography of American revivalism and religious history, including works by George Marsden, Mark Noll, Nathan Hatch, and Perry Miller. In addition, important books on Alabama Baptists by Hosea Holcombe, Benjamin Franklin Riley, Lee Allen, Wayne Flynt, and Avery Hamilton Reid provided rich resources to explore Howard as part of the history of the state and the denomination.

Exploring the college's nineteenth-century history proved to be a more daunting task than I first realized. Most of the primary sources from the era were burned, lost, unpreserved, or discarded. When the college moved to East Lake in 1887, the school's records that made the trip were stored in an old outhouse. Much later, Howard/Samford archivists did remarkable work in preserving what was left and adding to the collection bit-by-bit. In Samford University's Special Collection, Elizabeth Wells and Jennifer Taylor provided access to all their archival materials and guided me through every step of this project. I also recognize the valuable support of Burns Kennedy and Becky Hyde in Special Collection and Kim Herndon and the staff of Harwell G. Davis Library.

In addition, archivists at other repositories provided key materials and information, including the Hargrett Rare Book and Manuscript Library at the

University of Georgia (Athens), Harvard University Library (Cambridge, MA), Library of Congress (Washington, DC), Morgan Library and Museum (New York), Judson College Archives (now located in Samford University Special Collection), Southern Baptist Theological Seminary Archives and Special Collections (Louisville, KY), Tennessee Department of Archives (Nashville), University of Alabama Libraries Special Collections (Tuscaloosa), University of North Carolina, Wilson Special Collection Library (Chapel Hill), Yale University Divinity School Library (New Haven, CT), University of South Carolina Libraries Special Collections (Columbia), Wake Forest University Special Collections and Archives (Winston-Salem, NC), and Virginia Military Institute Archives (Lynchburg). I also acknowledge the assistance of Lora Davis at Colgate University Archives, Geri Solomon at Hofstra University Special Collections (Hempstead, NY), Julia Cowart at Furman University Special Collections and Archives (Greenville, SC), Kristy Vanderpool at Henderson County (KY) Public Library, and Vanessa Nicholson at the Marion Military Institute Archives (Marion, AL). Thanks as well to Lonette Berg, executive director of the Alabama Baptist Historical Commission.

Special words of appreciation go out to Meredith McDonough and Haley Aaron at the Alabama Department of Archives and History, Jim Baggett, Catherine Oseas, and Don Veasey at the Department of Archives and Manuscripts at the Birmingham Public Library, and Mary Beth Newbill and Elizabeth Veatch in the Southern History Department at the Birmingham Public Library.

Those who also undertook the expedition for research sources included the crew in the Office of University Historian: Claire Davis, Jessica Davis, Holly Howell, Kerry Joiner, Blakely Lloyd, Clay Mapp, Evan Musgraves, Jenesia Porter, Mary Hailey Sinyard, Keely Smith, Christopher Taunton, Cameron Teaney, Chase Trautwein, Holly Vlach, Emily Wood, and Emily Youree.

Two indispensable people made this book a reality. The multitalented Michelle Little created and sustained both the Office of University Historian and the Oral History Program. She supervised research assistants, collected multiple oral history interviews, and organized and digitized over seventy-five linear feet of research materials. She also developed all the online materials that complement this book. In addition, Ivy Alexander gave rock-solid assistance and friendship from the beginning to the end of this project. She shouldered a myriad of duties and eased my heavy workload of serving as both chair of the Department of History and university historian.

Immeasurable guidance came from historian Jason Wallace, who provided resources and dispensed advice on American intellectual history, western thought, and theological interpretations. Thanks also to classics colleagues Doug Clapp, Andy Montgomery, and Randy Todd, who translated essential Latin and Greek phrases and taught me key interpretations of the classical world. Erin Stewart Mauldin provided indispensable assistance in several areas: research, analysis, and teaching. John Mayfield introduced me to frontier humor and essential readings in antebellum history. Other colleagues in the Department of History (past and present) offered support: James Brown, Jonathan Den Hartog, Annie DeVries, Brian Hamm, LeeAnn Reynolds, Marlene Rikard, Delane Tew, and Donald Wilson.

Additional Samford coworkers and friends (current and former) have my gratitude: Don Bradley, Kevin Blackwell, David Chapman, Roy Ciampa, William Collins, Timothy George, Scott Guffin, Glenda Martin, Chris Peters, Dennis Sansom, Jennifer Speights-Binet. I also offer praise to two remarkable comrades, Emily Hynds and Kelly Jenson, who both offered steady friendship, wise counsel, and occasional pep talks. Thanks to Andy Westmoreland for giving me a free hand in writing this project. I am also grateful to Howard Finch, P. J. Hughes, Michael Morgan, Beck Taylor, Tom Wooley, and Clark Watson.

The two biggest champions of this endeavor have been Provost Mike Hardin and Dean Timothy Hall. They gave me ample support and the encouragement that I needed to complete this project. I am grateful for their understanding of the importance of the original "idea of Howard College." In addition, the William E. and Wylodine H. Hull Research Fellowship from the Provost's Office provided additional funds for the university history.

A man of many hats (historian, preacher, attorney, librarian, politician) and tales, Chriss H. Doss laid the groundwork for this project. His research on Howard College's original charter, first Board of Trustees, and serious financial crises was critical for this book. He also spent hours regaling me with detailed anecdotes, legends, and facts about his alma mater. Harriet Amos-Doss has been a supportive friend and advisor for the last forty years.

Several former students and a host of friends who provided support, friendship, and laughter included: Chase Trautwein, Ryan Lally, Joe Hurtado, Max Lattermann, Yorgo Sarris, Noah Stewart, Tristan Mullen, Anna Beth Mason, Katie Graham, Ellen Davis, Sylvia Frank Rodrigue, Chris Shaeffer, Kitty Rogers Brown, Charlie Graham, Jerrod Williams, Kathleen Zebley Liulevicius, Jodi

Newton, Ashley Grantham Martin, Toney Wanamaker, Brad Walker, Gretchen Reynolds, Ken Reynolds, Mark Reynolds, Scott Reynolds, Susan Connor, Naomi Connor, Maude Tyler, and Ralph Henderson.

For almost forty years, Tennant S. McWilliams walked with me on my academic journey. As an undergraduate, I wandered pointlessly through various academic disciplines until the semester I took his class, "The Historian's Craft." Tennant opened a broader historical world for an aimless teenager—one that focused on ideas, interpretations, and deep questions. We read C. Vann Woodward and pondered the burden of southern history and made a rigorous study of Robert Penn Warren's *All the King's Men*. I was fascinated by Warren's rudderless character, Jack Burden, who bore the burden of history, took refuge in the past, and proclaimed, "If you could not accept the past and its burden there was no future . . . for only out of the past can you make the future." I was hooked. Tennant gave me the first A that I received in college, but he gave me more than a grade. He gave me hope. When he asked me to think about graduate studies and a career as a historian, he gave me direction. He showed me how I had a future in studying the past and helped me realize that a passion for history was there all along—I just needed someone to encourage me and point the way.

Tennant not only opened my mind to historical ideas but also provided the model for the type of professor and mentor that I wanted to be—someone who made lifelong investments in the lives of his students. When I asked Tennant to write an endorsement of this book, he had just received word of a terminal cancer diagnosis, but he was determined to fulfill my request. "I was just in awe," his wife Susan wrote me, "that after getting our feared news, he wanted to work." Several days later, he passed away. As I read what he wrote about this book, I was also in awe, not because of his generous endorsement, but because of how his words reflected the life and legacy of a teacher, scholar, mentor, and friend.

I also acknowledge the 2020 passing of a great friend and mentor from the University of Tennessee, Paul H. Bergeron, who taught me the history and historiography of the Age of Jackson, challenged me to be a rigorous scholar, forced me to become a better writer, and drove me to work harder, think deeper, and communicate clearer. He also cared for me more than I ever deserved.

I am indebted to Rand Dotson at Louisiana State University Press for his patience, guidance, and support as I completed this book. My personal and professional thanks go out to LSU Press for publishing my first book in 2001, the anniversary edition in 2021, and now this volume in 2024. I also recognize the important editorial work of Stan Ivester and Catherine L. Kadair in strengthening this manuscript.

This book would not have been completed without the support of my family, especially my in-laws, Lee and Donna Synnott. My Pentecostal-raised, charismatic Baptist mother passed away in 2019 and left an unfillable void. I am grateful for the countless hours that she prayed for me and my family. When I think of her, I'm often reminded of the Hank and Audrey Williams lyrics from the old country song: "I read the Bible on into the night / And soon began to see the light / And now at last my soul is free / Thank God, my mother prayed for me."

I am blessed that my three incredible children—Kathleen, Caroline, and Nathaniel—have all reached adulthood and are following God's calling in their lives. And, as always, I stand in awe of the love and grace I receive from my wife, Jennifer.

Finally, after twenty-five years of teaching and mentoring undergraduates at Samford University, I am grateful to be part of their lives—some for a semester and others for a lifetime. My life is richer, and I am a better person because of my interactions with each of them. With sincere admiration and humility, I dedicate this book to my students—past, present, and future.

FROM EVERY STORMY
WIND THAT BLOWS

INTRODUCTION
Useful and Enlightened Christian Citizens

From every stormy wind that blows;
From every swelling tide of woes.

—HUGH STOWELL

During the 1820s, James Harvey DeVotie was a sinful child of New York's western frontier. Before he turned ten, DeVotie rebelled against his mother's pious biblical instruction and became irreligious, rowdy, and a self-described "eager learner of wickedness." He joined other wild-eyed boys chasing mischief and sin in the tiny hamlet of Vernon, located in Oneida County. Other residents, however, chose a different path and pursued righteousness and redemption at ongoing revivals in the local Presbyterian church. But as the converts increased, so did the opponents—a noisy group of roughneck hedonists who resented the pious criticism of their sinful rabble-rousing. For months, they badgered church members, hurled obscene "Billingsgate language," and threatened to horsewhip the pastor. "It seems as though," a parishioner wrote in 1826, that Satan had "centered his legions" in Oneida County to end the revivals. The saints persevered, however, and the "anxious meetings" continued. Soon, as a neighboring Utica minister observed, the "sweet saving influence" of Christ came down and gave "holy hearts" to those same ramblers, gamblers, drunkards, cursers, liars, and Sabbath breakers; and also, to the self-righteous pharisees, skeptics, deists, and universalists.[1]

James H. DeVotie also received this "saving influence" during a quiet revival prayer meeting. His mother invited him to the gathering, he recalled, and after a scripture reading from the Book of John, DeVotie recognized his total depravity, confessed his wicked ways, and opened his "hardened heart" to redemption.

At that moment, he believed that God "strangely plucked" him like a "firebrand from the flames" and gave him peace and "unspeakable joy." He likened his conversion experience to the lyrics of a John Newton hymn from the eighteenth century: "In evil long I took delight / Unawed by shame or fear / Till a new object struck my sight / And stopped my wild career."[2]

DeVotie's conversion narrative was just one of thousands of similar re-demption stories told during the Second Great Awakening revivals throughout the United States between 1795 and 1865. These types of revivals occurred, as scholar David Bebbington wrote, when a group of concerned Christians felt the "stirrings" of spiritual renewal and the community's nonbelievers converted on a mass scale. These revivals were so widespread and impactful that historian Perry Miller concluded that *the* "dominant theme" in America during these years was the "invincible, persistence of the revival technique." In Connecticut at the turn of the nineteenth century, Yale College president Timothy Dwight sparked a campus revival that inspired a zealous generation of New England's educated elites to evangelize the West (and the globe), initiate moral reforms, create benevolent societies, and establish colleges—the latter of which, author George Marsden wrote, safeguarded "Protestant dominance over the mind ... heart and conscience of the nation." In Kentucky, the Scots-Irish settlers living in the frontier wilderness experienced spiritual renewal at rural camp meetings reminiscent of century-old Scottish "Holy Fairs." This awakening climaxed with the 1801 "Great Revival" in Cane Ridge that perhaps attracted as many as twenty-five thousand people to the ecumenical gathering. "Never before," one writer observed, "had religious piety and fervor been so openly expressed or conver-sions so numerous." The camp meetings served as a guide for future outdoor revivals in the West, including those in Alabama two decades later.[3]

In the 1820s and 1830s, another thread of Second Great Awakening revivalism began with recurring "protracted meetings" in established churches throughout western New York. Charles Grandison Finney emerged as the most recognized leader of the fiery revivals that swept the area so often that it was nicknamed the "Burned Over District." Thousands of residents, like James H. DeVotie, converted to Christianity and were encouraged by Reverend Finney to go forth and become "useful in the highest degree possible." Finney's revivalism spurred DeVotie's ministerial interests, one scholar observed, and provided him with an "early blueprint" of how institution building served as a natural outgrowth of organized revivals.[4]

With an unclear route to usefulness, James DeVotie accepted a job offer from his uncle in Savannah, Georgia. The young New Yorker moved to the thriving southern seaport, learned the shoe business, and attended his uncle's Baptist church—pastored by Henry Otis Wyer. A fervent revivalist from Massachusetts, Wyer most likely influenced DeVotie as he rejected Presbyterian doctrine on baptism, accepted Baptist beliefs, and joined the church. On December 2, 1831, Wyer baptized him in the Savannah River, and DeVotie arose from the waters shouting the gospel message to the people who stood along the riverbank. His brief, impromptu sermon made clear DeVotie's path to a useful life, and he embraced a self-described "divinely mandated duty" to evangelize the lost, to reform a sinful culture, and to build Christian institutions to further both. This was part of a providential plan for his life, DeVotie believed, because God chose an evangelizer whose last name derived from Latin words meaning devote, vow, devout, and pious. "The vows of God are upon us," he later wrote, and "we have promised to be the Lord's forever. I trust our name, and deportment may ever be in agreement."[5]

DeVotie left Savannah, enrolled at Furman Theological Institute in South Carolina, and served as a part-time preacher at the nearby Baptist Church of Camden. DeVotie, however, failed to understand the cultural decorum expected by well-educated southern elites. To his professors at Furman, he appeared arrogant, impulsive, and combative, which resulted in his decision to leave the institute before the end of the academic year. Even with this setback, DeVotie accepted a full-time pastorate at Camden, and one of his former professors, Jesse Hartwell, performed his ordination service. Although he was popular with the congregation, he left the church after another former professor, Samuel B. Furman, encouraged him to move to Alabama, where he "might be more useful" in ministry.[6]

In 1834, DeVotie took a stagecoach to Montgomery, a cotton-and-slave town in the heart of Alabama's agrarian Black Belt. He served as an occasional preacher at the Baptist church, but after his sermons impressed the church leadership, they offered him the full-time pastorate. Most likely, DeVotie noticed the parallels between central Alabama and western New York: rapid population gains, economic expansions, frontier rowdies, and recurring revivals. DeVotie reached Alabama in the 1830s just as revivals spread across the state like a "fire from heaven." A few months after DeVotie became pastor, a revival started at First Baptist and at least fifty-five new members joined the church. Despite his success as a preacher, DeVotie's boorish temperament alienated several church members and just weeks after the revival, the congregation terminated his contract. Although the Montgomery church later reconciled with DeVotie, he refused their offer to return to the pulpit.[7]

DeVotie left Montgomery despondent and uncertain of his calling. He became convinced that he "rushed into the ministry uncalled and now my feet were snared, and God was punishing my presumption, and I was . . . utterly unworthy to be a minister of Jesus Christ." He decided to leave the ministry and return to Savannah, but an encounter with Baptist missionary stalwart Luther Rice convinced him otherwise. With newfound confidence, DeVotie returned to Alabama and accepted the pastorate of Tuscaloosa Baptist Church in 1836. The following year, revivals at a small Baptist church west of town soon spread to the Presbyterian, Methodist, and Baptist churches in Tuscaloosa. DeVotie became a fixture at revival meetings throughout the region, including two at his own church in 1838 and 1839. By most measures, his ministry in Tuscaloosa was successful. DeVotie possessed a formidable pulpit presence, and his evangelistic zeal resulted in both new converts and members. Some in the congregation, however, found DeVotie's sermons little more than "eloquent nothings" that were short of theological depth and long on emotional appeal. The young minister's harshest criticism came from University of Alabama president Basil Manly, who disliked him, nitpicked every aspect of his ministry, and blasted DeVotie for "throwing himself into revivalism" to the detriment of the church. But those same revivals gave him an avenue to escape from Manly's grumbling. In 1839 and 1840, DeVotie held revival services in Marion, Alabama, a small town of about a thousand residents to the south of Tuscaloosa, and an emerging center of wealth, cotton, and slavery. As a result of his revivals, dozens converted to Christianity and scores became members at Siloam Baptist Church. In appreciation of DeVotie's evangelistic efforts, the congregation offered him their pastorate in 1840, and he accepted.[8]

In Marion, DeVotie moved beyond his youthful indiscretions and developed into one of the state's most respected preachers, organizers, and builders. At Siloam, the new minister discovered a like-minded group of members who previously helped establish the Marion Female Seminary and Judson Female Institute. When one church leader discussed building a school for young men in

British philanthropist John Howard embodied the college's founding principles of faith, intellect, benevolence, and virtue. (Samford University, Special Collection and University Archives)

Marion in 1841, DeVotie took the idea and made it a reality. In just a few months, the minister secured approval of the Alabama Baptist State Convention, obtained a suitable building, raised money from wealthy slaveowners, served as the leader of the initial Board of Trustees, hired the school's first leader, and gave the institution its name: Howard College, in honor of John Howard—a long-deceased reformer from Great Britain. For DeVotie and the board, John Howard embodied an enlightened Christian usefulness, exemplified a model moral agent, and demonstrated virtuous citizenship. Herein was the idea—the promise and the purpose—of Howard College: to liberate young men from the corrupting influences of frontier rowdyism, plantation hedonism, and cultural secularism and transform them into useful and enlightened Christian citizens.[9]

DeVotie and other Marion Baptists imagined that their new Christian college would become a community of learners who accepted and furthered the gospel message (faith), pursued a deeper understanding of God's universe (intellect), served their community and country (benevolence), and exemplified good moral character (virtue). Putting these four principles into action required a unifying curricular model that demonstrated Howard College's mission and identity. While James H. DeVotie played an indispensable role in founding Howard College, the minister was ill prepared to develop this type of curriculum for the students. Instead, he asked another young northern emigrant, Samuel Sterling Sherman, to design a course of study that allowed Howard College to become a beacon of both Christian *and* liberal learning.[10]

Samuel Sterling Sherman was a self-described industrious New Englander from Vermont who received a classical liberal arts education at Middlebury College in the 1830s. The college was a small Congregationalist school founded by citizens of Middlebury, Vermont, in 1800, and its curriculum was copied from Yale College and originally administered under the direction of Yale's president Timothy Dwight—the grandson of the First Great Awakening's Jonathan Edwards and the central figure in the New England strand of the Second Great Awakening. As student Lyman Beecher later wrote, when Dwight became Yale's president in 1795, he found a student body corrupted by "intemperance, gambling, licentiousness, profanity, and rowdyism." Dwight's enlightened sermons, however, awakened the students to the importance of personal character (wisdom, virtue, piety, and knowledge) in their quest to become godly citizens in a moral social order. For two decades, as student Heman Humphrey recalled, the revivals swept across campus like a "mighty rushing wind" that shook the college to its core. "It seemed for a time," he added, "as if the whole mass of students would press into the kingdom of God."[11]

Like Yale, Middlebury College experienced ongoing revivals both on campus and in the surrounding community between 1805 and 1835. A few months after Sherman entered the school in 1834, a "tenth season" of revivals broke out following the arrival of evangelist Jedediah Burchard. A former haberdasher, actor, and circus performer, Burchard was a former resident of western New York who worked with, and influenced, Charles G. Finney. In 1835, Burchard moved eastward and blanketed Vermont with revival meetings and emotional sermons—calling forward struggling sinners to sit on the "anxious seats," confess their sins, and find salvation. The minister elicited emotional responses by jumping out of the pulpit, executing acrobatic feats, and walking "among the people" by leaping from pew to pew. Sherman attended one of Burchard's services at the local Congregationalist church where he made a public profession of faith and later united with the Baptist church.[12]

During these years, Vermonters were the most "church going people" on earth, a writer once claimed, with at least 80 percent of the population attending church regularly. They were also impassioned reformers who viewed their efforts to change the world as a demonstration of their Christian faith and an opportunity to "renew their society spiritually and to live by Christian ideals." Following the tenth season of revivals, President Joshua Bates praised the spiritual awakenings on campus for gathering souls for the kingdom of God and for increasing happiness, liberty, and piety. Bates believed that the revivals and the "sanctified learning" at Middlebury (which combined Christianity, virtue, and knowledge) compelled students to serve the public good and have a "salutary influence" through teaching and other public professions. In other words, Bates believed that revivals and liberal education at the college produced generations of young men, like Samuel Sterling Sherman, with "high intellectual and moral character" who served as guardians of free institutions, defenders of republicanism, and protectors of the union.[13]

In 1837, with salvation in his soul and a college diploma in his hand, Sherman moved to Alabama, seeking teaching opportunities in the warm climate. He took the arduous six-week journey from Vermont to Alabama via steamer ship, train, and stagecoach. Many northern emigrants like Sherman moved to the frontier, as historian George Marsden observed, bringing with them a Puritan heritage and a "missionary zeal" to evangelize and transform the West into "their own image." Graduates of New England colleges, especially Yale (and Middlebury), were "fertile breeders" of denominational colleges that were upstart versions of their alma maters. "Zeal for education," one observer wrote, "was strongest wherever New Englanders went." Sherman arrived in Alabama with a Middlebury-influenced education philosophy rooted in the Christian and Western intellectual traditions. Along with Aristotelian notions of happiness, virtue, and wisdom, Sherman embraced natural theology that emphasized the complexity of the natural world in proving God's existence, natural law that explored innate values of morality, and moral philosophy that served as a distillation of Scottish Common Sense Realism.[14]

Throughout higher education at the time, Common Sense was the predominant philosophy—the notion that all humans have universal common sense in perceiving the world. Author Alexander Broadie argued that this philosophy was based on universal principles of how the human mind functions. It was an inductive, scientific way of thinking on a broad range of subjects including ethics, theology, virtue, and morality. Common Sense provided the foundation for reasoning through self-evident perception. The philosophy originated in the ideas of eighteenth-century Scottish philosopher Thomas Reid and was spread by its proponents in American higher education like John Witherspoon and Timothy Dwight. Teachers throughout the new nation brought Common Sense ideas into classrooms along the frontier areas of the West and in the settled areas of the East. In addition, preachers communicated Common Sense notions to parishioners throughout the nation. A prominent Congregationalist theologian in New England encouraged believers to use the "bar of common sense" in resolving black-and-white moral problems. In New York, Charles G. Finney and other revivalists spoke of "intuitively evident" morality and Christianity based on the "changeless laws of our being." As historian Mark Noll argued, Americans (southerners in particular) were less interested in the philosophical arguments supporting Common Sense than the practical "habits of the mind and reassuring conventions of thought."[15]

For educators like Samuel Sterling Sherman, the clearest way to communicate Common Sense ideas to students was through a liberal arts curriculum. The term "liberal arts" comes from the original Latin phrase *artes libérales. Artes* translates as a learned and practiced skill. *Libérales* derives from *liber*, which means free. Therefore, *artes libérales* refers to skills learned and practiced by a person who is liberated (unbound or unconstrained). In other words, the tools and knowledge needed for a free citizen. In the fifteenth century, author and teacher Pier Paolo Vergerio wrote a treatise on education entitled "The Character and Studies Befitting a Free-Born Youth." In it he wrote: "We will call those studies liberal, then, which are worthy of a free man."[16]

Students at Howard College took liberal arts courses in natural philosophy, moral philosophy, metaphysics, history, grammar, mathematics, rhetoric, logic, Latin, and Greek—all part of a "common core of knowledge" that united them in a community of liberated learners. In other words, this was a required set of ideas that every learned person needed to understand to be free. For example, from a disciplined study of Greek and Roman thinkers (Homer, Plato, Livy, Cicero, and others), students gained an understanding of Western Civilization's founding ideas of morality, character, citizenship, democracy, and republicanism. In addition, Samuel Sterling Sherman believed that Howard's liberal arts curriculum helped students to identify and eliminate vice and crime and to discover and embrace virtue, industriousness, uprightness, and happiness. The rigorous study of classical texts, he added, served as the guardian of free governments and the one "secure and unfailing hope" of republican institutions.[17]

Despite the importance of these writings, Sherman believed, an education at a Christian college was incomplete and illiberal without the Bible serving as the *sine qua non* of classical texts. Without the Bible, Sherman emphasized, a Howard College student's education was so "radically defective" that it rendered him unable to develop the physical, intellectual, and moral traits necessary to become a useful and enlightened Christian citizen. A person's "moral page," he added, was as much a blank slate (or in Lockean thought, *tabula rasa*) as the intellectual page, and it was the purpose of Howard's liberating Christian education to fill both. This enabled students to understand: (1) God's nature and characteristics, (2) his relationship to God and his neighbor, and (3) his duties as a "rational and accountable creature." Based on his experience at Middlebury, Sherman most likely emphasized these notions in chapel services, evening prayers, and through intensive studies and recitations in the Greek New Testament and the Latin Vulgate.[18]

While the liberal arts curriculum was inseparable from Howard College's Christian identity, the specifics of that identity—doctrinal standards and denominational affiliation—were purposely ambiguous. On the surface, this appears to be in keeping with Baptist educator and Brown University president Francis Wayland's opposition to all forms of confessions (or creeds) in favor of the Bible as the sole and "sufficient standard of faith and practice." Although Howard reflected the implicit Calvinist views of James H. DeVotie and most Alabama Baptists, the institution maintained an explicit nonsectarian policy that softened theological differences and allowed the school to compete for students within the free-enterprise system. This enabled Samuel Sterling Sherman to recruit young men from a broader Protestant constituency by emphasizing, as historian George Marsden wrote, the "socially unifying aspects of its Christian tradition, especially its moral benefits," rather than its denominational or "theological peculiarities." In Howard College's 1847 catalog, the institution recognized the rights of Christian students of all denominations to "enjoy without molestation" their specific "religious sentiments."[19]

Ties to the convention were less important, historian David Potts discovered, because institutions like Howard College were "local enterprises" and not denominational schools. Seen in this light, Baptist entrepreneurs in Marion created Howard and not the state convention. In 1841, the Alabama Baptist State Convention simply gave its blessing, and little else, to establish a college. As Potts emphasized, denominations in general provided "little more than sanction and verbal encouragement." For Howard College, most students and money came from Marion or adjacent communities. Combined with long-standing in-state sectional rivalries, most Alabamians from outside the Black Belt viewed Howard College not as an Alabama Baptist school, but the school of Marion's wealthy Baptists. This perception lasted until Howard College moved to the outskirts of Birmingham in 1887. Then the institution became the local enterprise of East Lake's prosperous New South boosters.[20]

At its inception, the college reflected the broad national trends of the era—reform, frontier settlement, democratization, economic expansion, slavery, and several others. The most important trend, however, was revivalism. As Perry Miller argued, the era should be seen as one "continuous, even though intermittent, revival." Howard College was established at the crossroads of the Second Great Awakening, where the revival influences of Timothy Dwight and Charles Grandison Finney converged during Alabama's Revival in the West. The college reflected the unique ideas and experiences of James Harvey DeVotie and Samuel Sterling Sherman. DeVotie brought a Charles Finney–inspired zeal for evangelism and a commitment to benevolent service and institution building. Sherman, a graduate of Middlebury College in Vermont, brought an educational philosophy reflecting Timothy Dwight's ideas on moral philosophy, personal character, and virtuous citizenry that combined Scottish Common Sense, classical liberal arts, and evangelical Christianity. From this context, the founders of Howard College emphasized four core values: Faith (rooted in Calvinism and revivalism), Intellect (guided by Common Sense philosophy), Benevolence (grounded in pious moral reforms), and Virtue (influenced by the Enlightenment in Great Britain). These four values worked together to fulfill the central task of the college: to create useful and enlightened Christian citizens.

James DeVotie and the first Board of Trustees named the institution after British moral agent John Howard because he embodied the four principles and served as a role model for students studying at Howard College.[21]

Educating students to become "responsible moral agents," philosopher Arthur F. Holmes wrote, demanded careful guidance of their thinking and values. For decades, Howard College maintained a unified sense of common purpose based on the four core values and the promise of educating the whole person. Holmes believed that Christian colleges combined the breadth of "life and learning" with the depth of a liberating education rooted in a clear Common Sense understanding that God was the ultimate source of truth. "We do not apologize for that conviction," another Christian liberal arts proponent wrote. "We find it not confining, but liberating, sparing us from the tyranny of momentary ideologues and the oppression of immediacy. It places us in an historic stream, and we do not wish to step outside of it." For an unapologetic Christian college or university to survive, the institution must maintain missional identity, unity of purpose, and a shared common experience through a curriculum rooted in the liberal arts.[22]

Throughout most of the first century of Howard College (now Samford University in Birmingham, Alabama), the stormy winds of impending financial ruin and the "tide of woes" from regional difficulties shaped the struggling institution's meager existence. Yet, the small Christian college endured these hardships by remaining true to its core values and focusing on the school's central idea of transforming young men (and later women) into useful and enlightened Christian citizens. Howard College endured the storms and woes by remaining steadfast to its missional identity and the guiding principles on which it was founded as it weathered the stormy burdens of southern history: from the rowdy Frontier South of drinking, fighting, and mayhem to the Old South of cotton, plantations, and slavery to the New South of iron, steel, and segregation. The institution survived fires, bankruptcies, southern nationalism, rebellions, Reconstruction, "Redemption," and relocation.

By the second decade of the twentieth century, however, the college lost much of its connection to the people, values, and ideas of the past—compelling one president of Howard to reject the idea that the institution was a liberal arts college. Over several years, Howard lost not only its history, but its unity and missional identity. Hence, the purpose of this book: to reconstruct the "idea" of Howard College and to recover the institution's history and original mission— all within the context of southern history. "It is a puzzle," W. B. Carnochan once wrote, "that universities charged with helping to preserve the past, know so little of their own."[23]

1

DUM VIVIMUS, VIVAMUS

The name above the tavern door was painted in big bright letters: *Dum Vivimus, Vivamus*. With an affinity for the classics, owner Billy Price chose the bold Latin phrase as the name for his establishment so that every parched and inquisitive "wayfaring man" would be compelled to step inside his door, ask for a drink, and inquire about the dram shop's odd name. Not a day went by when a customer, while nursing a pint of hooch, wouldn't lean across the hand-cut oak bar and ask Price, "Stranger, what do it mean?" In reality, Price chose a Latin Epicurean motto: "While we are alive, let us live," or as he interpreted the expression, "While we live, let's live it up"—a perfect phrase to describe the hedonistic environment in the Alabama frontier town of Marion in the 1820s, 1830s, and 1840s. As Howard College graduate William Garrott Brown wrote, patrons embraced the philosophy, although they "could only vaguely conjecture the meaning" of the classical sign. At Price's place assembled the "originators of all mischief perpetuated" in the town, a Marion resident explained, especially a thrill-seeking gang of idle young men that locals referred to as "the boys." A product of the frontier environment, these high-school and college-age boys, with no education and little hope of escaping the rugged frontier life, embraced a literal interpretation of Price's motto, endeavoring to "live it up" and raise hell at every possible occasion.[1]

In 1817, the first white settler in this isolated area was the wayfaring Michael Muckle (a garbled pronunciation of "McElroy"), who cleared trees, built a cabin, and squatted on land that was not his own. As one hyperbolic writer noted, "Romulus founded Rome; Dido built Carthage, but Providence decreed that Michael Muckle should settle Marion." Yet, there was nothing worth mentioning about the idle life of Muckle and, as more settlers arrived, he soon grew unhappy and grumbled about being "crowded" and wanting "elbow room." He packed up, abandoned "Muckle's Ridge," drifted over to Mississippi, and disappeared from recorded history.[2]

When Muckle's Ridge became the seat of government for the newly created Perry County, a few South Carolina migrants chose to rename the settlement for native son Francis "Swamp Fox" Marion—a wild-eyed Revolutionary War hero who used unorthodox guerrilla warfare tactics against the British and insisted on strict discipline from his rabble-rousing troops. Billy Price bought one of the first lots in Marion, built his saloon, and the town grew up around it; or as one observer noted, the bar was the "bung-hole" around which "the barrel would be built." As Marion's first business, Price's tavern provided an ironic start for a town that, a few short years later, declared itself the enlightened "Athens of the South" and the education capital of Alabama. Perhaps, as one Marion resident later speculated, a healthy measure of Latin was mixed with the homemade hooch and "infused itself into the heads and hearts" of the early settlers, while the mere contemplation of Price's motto inspired them to love the classics in such a tangible way that they embraced education with Epicurean delight.[3]

Nonetheless, during much of the two decades prior to the founding of Howard College, Marion was poor, sparsely settled, disease-ridden, and isolated from the East's civilizing influences of religion, education, and law. Few participated in any form of organized religion, and even fewer had any formal education. The only social outlet for the scattered settlers was drinking and fighting. The availability of cheap corn liquor and other intoxicating spirits, bought at one of the eleven establishments licensed to sell such rotgut, only fueled the violence. For over a decade, Price's place was the most popular, especially with "the boys" who spent their days and nights drinking, swearing, fighting, pranking, and most frequently, loafing. Dum Vivimus, Vivamus, served as the lounging spot for anyone seeking leisure and devilment.[4]

In establishments like Dum Vivimus, Vivamus, their brawny and competitive code of honor defined manhood and compelled the rugged individualism where frontier boys knew no restraint, flouted the law, and celebrated drunkenness that ended in a brutal fight. In Marion, the leader of "the boys" and the "pugilistic champion" of Perry County was Red Fox, who, in an epic fight in 1829, defeated a "gigantic specimen of manhood" identified only as Weaver. A witness described Fox as "low of stature" in this David-and-Goliath battle, but what he lacked in size, Fox made up for in manly courage, quickness, and meanness. He was "quiet, inoffensive, when not under stimulants," and always ready

Rowdy young "hell-of-a-fellows" in places like Marion spent their days and nights drinking, swearing, fighting, pranking, and loafing. (Library of Congress, Prints and Photographs Division)

to battle in defense of his honor. A writer observed that boys like Fox engaged in an "intensely competitive status system" that rewarded the "most prodigious drinker or the strongest arm wrestler, the best tale teller, fiddle player, or log roller, the most daring gambler, original liar, skilled hunter, outrageous wearer, or accurate marksman." To fail in these manly pursuits would bring shame and dishonor. Honor, on this destitute frontier, was the only thing of value that these boys possessed.[5]

During the day, when not gathered in Price's tavern, Red Fox and the boys often loitered in the streets of Marion and made mischief on unsuspecting locals. By night, they drank and fought. "It looked to me," one early settler noted, "as if the devil had a clean bill of sale to all this country." These hedonistic men and boys, author W. J. Cash wrote, were known "far and wide" as "hell-of-a-fellows" who stood on their heads in a bar, "tossed down" pints of who-hit-John whiskey, fiddled and danced all night, bit off the nose or gouged "out the eyes of a favorite enemy," and "fought harder and loved harder than the next man." During the withering hot summer months, they slumbered and stored power "under the sun of August" until the energy exploded like a strong thunderstorm in "a violent outburst of emotion."[6]

One afternoon in 1835, Marion's "hell-of-a-fellows" visited a caravan of wild animals in a traveling circus near town before retiring for an evening of reverie at Price's saloon. After gulping down a large amount of whiskey, one of the boys announced that he was "drunk as a badger," which only compelled the others to ask, "Just how drunk can a badger get?" To settle the matter scientifically, Samuel A. Townes reported, they sought out the circus owner ("the varmint man") and a thirsty badger to invite "down to the doggery to be made drunk." When the proprietor refused to cooperate, the boys stormed the circus, overturned wagons, and opened the cages of bears, lions, tigers, elephants, monkeys, and "various other rarities." Once they found the badger, the triumphant boys returned to Price's place and proceeded to make the critter drunk. "The poor animal was completely intoxicated," Townes wrote, "and, to the amazement of his drunken companions, only behaved like themselves or any other drunken beast."[7]

One resident believed that, if the discipline-minded Francis Marion visited his namesake town when "the boys" were up to their mischievous merriment, he would have been less than "flattered by the compliment." With the lax nature of law enforcement in Marion, men had to enforce a code of honor to maintain order. In 1837, attorney and newspaper publisher Samuel A. Townes reacted to two "overgrown mush-head" brothers who confronted him on the streets of Marion armed with a brickbat, a Bowie knife, and three hostile bulldogs. One of the men accused Townes of slander and pronounced his intention to "whip up" on him. As soon as the words were out of his mouth, Townes drew, cocked, and aimed his pistol at the man with the reckless tongue and called him a "convicted damned liar." If you lay a finger on me, Townes said, I will send you to "hell to answer for the falsehood" you propagated. Unlike other incidents that often ended in injury or death, the two panic-stricken men fled from Townes's threat, and he proclaimed a "glorious triumph" for law and order over the evils of frontier living.[8]

In the early years of Marion, the front door of Billy Price's tavern was in the direct line of sight of the judge's stand across the road inside the court building—a rough-hewn cabin that looked more like an oversized smokehouse with windows than a legal edifice. From the vantage point of his bench, a judge might find inspiration for a ruling, a writer noted, from the anticipation of the genuine 100-proof rotgut that awaited his arrival. Dispensing alcohol was more important than administrating law and justice during these years. While Marion remained a small and poor hamlet, justice was dispensed through the extralegal measures inside "Chandler's Coach"—so named for Perry County sheriff David Chandler—a large empty hogshead from Price's saloon that a wayward offender was fastened inside and rolled out of Marion toward the river by a group of volunteers known as "Captain Slick's Company."[9]

When Marion's population grew during the 1830s, "His Honor Judge Lynch" joined "Captain Slick's Company" as extralegal enforcement of community standards took a more brutal turn. A writer for the Marion-based *Alabama Mercury* found much pleasure in welcoming the "able and energetic judicial officer" to town on July 13, 1836. A man simply identified as Mr. Merit was accused of stealing, and then selling, a horse belonging to Joseph Evans. This double-dealing act and Merit's "general character of worthlessness" justified a mob of gentlemen of "high character" to seize the suspect and give him a vicious flogging. "That poor devil deserved all he received," the writer supposed, and the "peculiar circumstances of his guilt rendered the administration of Lynch's law the only proper punishment for his daring offence." In the minds of many, mob violence was justified in Marion when guilt was obvious, the crime atrocious, and the courts too slow or too lenient in administering justice.[10]

Marion's population boomed during these years, growing from 144 citizens in 1826 to over 1,000 during the decade that followed—many more were transients looking to make a quick dollar and move on. A few miles south of town was the prairie soil of the Alabama Black Belt—a fertile crescent of dark earth perfect for growing cotton. As planters learned how to grow cotton on a mass scale in the sticky black dirt, land sales skyrocketed, slavery expanded, and Marion grew wealthy—a peculiar mingling of frontier intemperance and emerging cotton capitalism. For many, like the boys who occupied Price's saloon, the financial boom offered little economic advancement and no incentives to abandon the status quo of loafing, drinking, and fighting. For newcomers, however, rampant speculation of cotton and slaves resulted in significant population growth that, for a short time, not only reinforced Marion's sinful ways, but led the town into a new era of sadistic violence.

When flush economic times arrived in Marion in the 1830s, so too did unsavory cotton and slave speculators. Many of these speculators were also roughneck hedonists who escaped to the frontier or were second or third sons of wealthy families in states back east. All were eager to make a quick dollar. Alabamian Daniel Hundley described them as villainous ill-bred men with poor manners, cross-looking faces, whiskey-tinted noses, tobacco-stained mouths, tattered clothes, and the blackest of hearts. At the time, one pious settler observed that Marion was crowded with people who talked about nothing but land, cotton, and slaves. "Every man we met," he added, "either wanted to buy a slave or take a drink." But as quickly as it began, however, the flush times of cotton and slaves ended with the nationwide economic Panic of 1837. In Alabama, the state bank teetered on insolvency, cotton prices remained low, and money was scarce. By the end of the decade, hard times deepened with another financial crisis, a severe drought that stopped navigation on many of the state's rivers, and the disclosure of a banking scheme that left most bank notes with little value. While most of the unsavory speculators moved farther to the west, especially to Texas, established citizens in Marion seized the opportunity to bring discipline, virtue, and social order to town as the cotton and slave economy slowly recovered in the 1840s.[11]

Leading these reforms were the growing numbers of Baptist, Methodist, and Presbyterian churchgoers in Marion who became part of the town's emerging civic and evangelical elite. Comprised of pastors, educators, lawyers, entrepreneurs, and planters, these leaders looked to eliminate the lingering vestiges of frontier vice and fashion an enlightened society like the settled areas to the east—a place where citizens followed the rule of law and embraced the refining influences of education and religion. Many of the new people were northerners, like James Harvey DeVotie and Samuel Sterling Sherman, who also recognized the sins of the frontier: idleness, worldliness, swearing, drinking, and dancing. These pious evangelicals often clashed with the hedonistic hell-of-a-fellows. "If some Southerners raised hell to dramatic heights," Ted Ownby observed, "others felt a special need to bring heaven down to earth on a very personal level." This emerging evangelical culture clashed with Billy Price's frontier Epicurean notions, leading Price to close Dum Vivimus, Vivamus; and he too was gone to Texas.[12]

The reformers used two ways to bring order to a frontier town like Marion: revivalism and church discipline—both of which grew in importance during the 1830s. The revival fires of camp meetings and protracted church meetings swept through many areas of Alabama, including Perry County, which resulted in conversions of sinners and renewals of believers. At a camp meeting near Marion in Perry County in 1831, one participant observed many "precious souls" found salvation and listened to the praises, prayers, songs, shouts, and the "groans and cries of repenting sinners" which "formed an awful, yet delightful harmony." Characterized by emotional preaching, modified Calvinist theology, and calls to pious living, the revivalist spirit led to an unprecedented growth in church membership, more money in the offering plates, and increased status for preachers and churchgoers. "The different churches were all very successful," one writer noted a few years later, "in their efforts to accomplish good" and bring order and piety to the frontier.[13]

In Marion, Siloam Baptist Church emerged as the largest and most visible religious community. Founded in 1822 by two itinerant Baptist ministers, Siloam took its name from the pools of water near Jerusalem where Jesus healed the blind man—perhaps the founders hoped that their mission would bring sight to the unseeing sinners living in the area. In the early years, large numbers of Baptists from the East moved into the area but, with all the comings and goings of the people in and around Marion, stable growth was slow and discipline, an essential ingredient for community order, was lax. In general, the Alabama Baptist State Convention was critical of the Baptist churches in Perry, Bibb, and Dallas (the territory of the old Cahawba Association) for supporting the "benevolent plans" of the convention in word but not in deed, keeping a safe distance in "fear of injuring the feelings" of those opposed. "We think it is time," the convention urged in 1837, "for our brethren to arouse from their lethargy, for the time is short, and souls are perishing for lack of knowledge."[14]

But with the growing frequency of well-attended camp meetings and church revivals, combined with the arrival of settlers with families throughout the 1830s, Siloam added members and wealth—opening a new $7,000 brick building the same year that the convention issued its critical report. Like other churches in frontier areas, Siloam adopted "Rules of Decorum" that introduced a church-based honor code that regulated behavior of church members and provided an alternative value structure for "the boys" in Marion and other wayward frontiersmen in the area. One writer discovered that churches were less interested in chastising "wanderers" than calling individuals back to "full fellowship within a sacred community" of faith.[15]

The Siloam congregation based their rules on the "Gospel Steps" found in Matthew 18: If a Christian sinned, it was the duty of a fellow believer to meet with them one-on-one and point out their sin. "If they listen to you," Jesus said, "you have won them over." If they refuse to listen, however, go back to them with witnesses. If they still refuse to listen, let the church address the sin. "If they refuse to listen even to the church," he added, "treat them as you would a pagan or a tax collector." This type of church discipline placed a strong emphasis on piety and virtue, historian Robert Elder wrote, and tied individual believers to church authority which safeguarded "communal purity no less than personal holiness." Elder described church discipline as a "public ritual" that targeted four audiences: (1) the individual sinner who was called to repent and restore his or her relationship with God; (2) the religious community whose purity was violated by sin; (3) the outside world who would see a good witness through the ritual; (4) to bring honor and glory to God and reveal his holiness.[16]

Although church discipline and revivalism played significant roles in bringing order to Marion and other southern communities, the introduction of Sabbath Schools at Baptist churches in the frontier areas served as essential tools of "moral reform" and "nurseries of piety" for young people. Baptist leaders believed it was necessary to instruct the rising generations in biblical truths, sound theology, and character education. As Rev. Daniel P. Bestor emphasized in 1835, Sabbath Schools provided "innocent and useful exercise to the idle and wicked, instruction to the ignorant, opportunity for improvement to the busy, and a stream of good into the habitation of poverty, of vice, and of ignorance." Bestor believed that Sabbath Schools also advanced the cause of temperance by dissuading drinkers of hard liquors, drying up the makers of the "fountains of poison," closing the saloons, and preventing a "vice and habit" that led to "poverty, disgrace, crime, disease, and a premature grave." Rev. James H. DeVotie would join Bestor in the crusade for Sabbath Schools.[17]

Bestor envisioned strong moral and theological education for young men and women each Sunday at Sabbath Schools and a public or private school education during the weekdays. A native of Suffield, Connecticut, Rev. Daniel Perrin Bestor moved to Alabama in the 1820s and emerged as one of the early proponents of education in the state. One Alabama Baptist minister described Bestor as a near incarnation of pure intellect, "refined and pious emotion," and a man of "broad culture and elevated and refined sensibility." He established a female academy in the Tennessee Valley, before moving to the Black Belt in the 1830s and serving in the state legislature as an advocate of public education. He played a key role in the development of the Manual Labor Institute in Greensboro—insisting that the school offer students both liberal arts and theological training.[18]

Like Bestor, other education-minded Baptists in Marion and other small towns focused their attention on evangelism both in the Alabama wilderness and around the globe. With the centrality of the gospel message in educating young people, their work was an extension of earlier Baptist missionary efforts in the late eighteenth and early nineteenth centuries which included the overseas work of Adoniram and Ann Hasseltine Judson and their associate Luther Rice. When Rice returned to the United States, he made an extensive nationwide tour to awaken Baptist interest in global missions—it was during this tour he met with the young James H. DeVotie. Although he received enthusiastic support around the country, opposition from anti-mission forces convinced him that ignorance was the archenemy of missions and that the only way to support the cause and move the denomination forward was to establish schools to educate future Baptist leaders. Several years later, the Baptists in Marion embraced the spirit of Rice's admonition and, with a renewed missionary zeal, recognized that education was a way to "go ye therefore, and teach all nations." This group of evangelical reformers—like DeVotie and Samuel Sterling Sherman—also acknowledged that they had a bountiful mission field in Marion, where salvation, virtue, and education would be the essential trilogy to bring a measure of social control over the host of drunkards and unruly boys. It was not without opposition.[19]

To the north of Marion, in Tuscaloosa, students at the University of Alabama during the 1830s rebelled against the strict discipline of President Alva Wood, a Harvard graduate and Baptist minister. Wood's Harvard-inspired rules of rigid discipline clashed with the rowdyism of wild frontier boys and the rebellious sons of plantation owners. On one occasion, the unruly boys threw brickbats and fired pistols at Woods, who jumped out a window and hid from the pursuing mob. The students conducted a lengthy search for Woods, but when they could not find the president's hiding spot, they returned to his office and threw rocks through the windows. This was no isolated incident. Disorder on college campuses occurred throughout the nation during the Early National and Jacksonian periods. Boys along the frontier, both northern and southern, outdid their eastern counterparts in the frequency and intensity of violence and mayhem as ways to express their autonomy and manhood. Woods's successor at the university, Rev. Basil Manly, also faced defiant students during his years as president. Ministers like Woods and Manly failed to curtail student rowdyism. To many parents and church leaders, the only way to calm these calamitous boys was for denominations themselves to establish schools.[20]

* * *

In Marion, as in other remote frontier areas, educational opportunities were limited. A few private schools and academies provided the rudimentary basics of spelling and reading; grammar and basic mathematics were senior-level studies. Schoolhouses were primitive structures. In 1838, a young teacher, Philip Henry Gosse, described a typical Alabama school as a "funny little place" built of rough logs, with uneven split-pine desks attached to the walls for the students: "A neat little desk, at which I write, and a chair on which I sit, are the only exceptions to the primitive rudeness of all our furniture, and the pupils are, mostly as rude as the house—real young hunters, who handle the long rifle with more ease and dexterity than the goosequill, and who are incomparably more at home in 'twisting a rabbit,' or 'treeing a 'possum' than in conjugating a verb."[21] Most teachers in these schools were stern taskmasters who enforced discipline with an oft-used hickory stick. Misspelling a word during recitation or breaking a rule would result in a stinging rebuke. Regularly, students and parents retaliated against a teacher for his strict rules and frequent whippings by carrying him down to a nearby pond or stream for a "ducking." In 1840, patrons of a Marion school seized a teacher and almost drowned him in a deep hole in a creek. "As fast as he crawled out," recalled a witness, "he was thrown in again. This 'fun' was continued until the poor fellow, overcome with exhaustion, sank in a drowning condition and with great difficulty was dragged ashore and revived."[22]

When Alabama Baptists entered the frontier college-building crusade in the 1830s, the manual-labor school movement was popular throughout the country. The concept seemed simple and well-suited for a frontier agricultural economy and a culture based on self-reliance. The denomination would purchase a farm, erect buildings, and provide equipment. In turn, students would provide hard labor: plowing, planting, and harvesting. The gathered crops would feed the students and faculty, and the sale of the surplus would provide salaries for teachers and administrators. In the minds of many, this educational philosophy had other advantages for the young men, including physical labor working in harmony with the liberal arts. As one writer concluded, years of hard farm labor prepared the students for the backbreaking work on the mission field as "hardened soldiers of Christ." With the rich soil in the Black Belt and the cotton boom underway, local enterprise of this nature should be a success.[23]

Beginning in 1832, the Alabama Baptist State Convention began discussing a "Seminary of learning in the State of Alabama, on the Manual Labor Plan, for the education of penniless young men called to the ministry." Marion and nearby Greensboro each offered the convention $3,600 to build the institution in their respective towns, but with the Presbyterians starting the Manual Labor Institute of South Alabama in Marion in 1833, Greensboro was selected. Trustees purchased 355 acres of land for cultivation. In addition, the convention expanded the institution's educational offerings to include a literary department (or broad liberal arts courses)—reflecting some of the competing visions over what type of studies should be offered at the school: manual labor, theological training, or literary studies, or in this case all three. This was true across the country. As one historian concluded, supporters of manual labor institutes often articulated conflicting views as to whether the schools were for students to learn agricultural and mechanical sciences in the classroom and then use that knowledge as they worked in the fields; some believed the schools were a combination of classical learning and field labor; other supporters saw the schools as reinforcing the Jeffersonian ideal and the republican concept of personal liberty; and some Christians believed the manual labor institutes fulfilled the biblical mandate to toil as Adam did after the fall. Of course the irony of offering manual labor training to white boys in a land filled with the enslaved seemed lost on the founders of the institute.[24]

On the third Monday of January 1836, with the buildings completed and the faculty and administrators hired, the Greene County Institute of Literature and Industry opened with high hopes and thirty students. This Baptist school, the first in Alabama, held its first classes without a theological department or a library. Morning instruction began around 8 a.m. and lasted until lunchtime; afternoon sessions ended around 2 p.m., and then the faculty were required to lead students to the farm for two hours of farm labor. As historian Mitchell Bennett Garrett wrote, the backbreaking work was a "hateful task" which brought complaints from students and faculty alike.[25]

Even as the trustees reported to the convention in November 1836 that the institute was in "flourishing condition," farm income fell well short of expectations, which they blamed on the small stature of the students. Adding to the financial woes was the lack of a local market to sell produce, as most residents grew their own food. Although the school opened for a second session at the beginning of the next year, it closed by April. Faculty dissension, student demoralization, mounting debt, and the nationwide financial Panic of 1837 all factored in the institute's demise. By the end of 1837, the convention ordered the property sold and proceeds used to pay debts and provide support for impoverished young ministers. This failure of the institute, wrote one observer, was a "nightmarish disappointment and embarrassment" which diminished Alabama Baptists' desire to establish another school anytime soon. In Marion, the Manual Labor Institute of South Alabama also struggled financially and closed after operating less than a decade—another failed enterprise in boys' education. By the mid-1840s, the manual labor school movement failed across the country, one writer noted, because it "could not withstand its inherit contradictions."[26]

While the Alabama Baptist State Convention considered other ways to support male students, Baptists in Marion turned their attention toward other educational endeavors. Leading these efforts was once again Siloam Baptist. One of Siloam's most generous leaders was General Edwin Davis King—described by one writer as the layman with the most "far reaching influence" among Alabama Baptists during the late antebellum period. Born April 12, 1792, in White Plains, Georgia, E. D. King fought against the Creeks in present-day Alabama in 1813 and served under Andrew Jackson at the Battle of New Orleans. He moved to Alabama in 1816 and was one of the earliest settlers of what would later become Perry County. From humble origins as a poor farmer and tavern keeper, King became a major slaveholder (enslaving 164 persons in 1840) and one of the wealthiest men in Alabama during the cotton boom. Marion resident Samuel Townes believed King had been blessed by divine providence for the "promotion of the cause of learning and piety." He made "noble use of a noble fortune" which stood in contrast to other Perry County men who applied their wealth to "their own selfish gratifications."[27]

General King was involved in numerous religious and educational causes, including the efforts to establish the interdenominational Marion Female Seminary in 1836. The financial arrangement lasted but a short time, before King and the other Baptist benefactors withdrew support after the administrators ignored their repeated requests for a greater voice in the general operation of the school. While serving on the Board of Trustees at the University of Alabama, King became acquainted with Milo P. Jewett at a December 1838 meeting in Tuscaloosa. Jewett, a New England educator, was on a tour of the South, looking for a location to open a college for young women. King quickly recognized the opportunity and invited Jewett and his wife to Marion to meet with members of Siloam Baptist Church.[28]

Wealthy widow Julia Barron funded Baptist enterprises in Marion with money she earned from cotton and slavery. Her son, John Barron, was both the first student and the first graduate of Howard College. (Samford University, Special Collection and University Archives)

The Jewetts were enthusiastically welcomed to the home of Julia Barron, a wealthy patron with a deep interest in education. Born on December 13, 1805, in Abbeville, South Carolina, Julia Ann Tarrant moved to Elyton in Jefferson County with her family around 1820. She married William Barron on April 28, 1828, and relocated to Marion, where her husband owned and operated a successful mercantile business. Contemporaries described Barron as a "well-bred tradesman" of keen wit and possessing "warm and benevolent impulses." He died four years later, leaving Julia a wealthy young widow with a small son, John

Tarrant Barron. Throughout the antebellum period, Julia Barron remained one of the wealthiest individuals in Marion. In 1840, she owned several tracts of land, thirty-five enslaved persons, and a large cotton plantation near town. This provided her with enough money to contribute liberally to benevolent causes throughout Marion.[29]

With the financial generosity of Barron and King, Jewett opened the Judson Female Institute on January 7, 1839, in a small two-story frame building with nine students. One Marion native described it as a grand undertaking for a small community, where "religious affinities" were still being established, and many citizens possessed a "low stage of moral and intellectual development." Nonetheless, the new school was named in honor of Ann Hasseltine Judson, a missionary to Burma who inspired Julia Barron. Milo Jewett served as "principal," and E. D. King was the first president of the Board of Trustees. By December 1839, seventy students were enrolled, and locals were touting the success of the new educational venture. Judson remained a local Baptist enterprise in Marion, apart from the Alabama Baptist State Convention, for several years. As one historian observed, the denomination was in "no humor to assume another undertaking that might go the way of the late Manual Labor School." This also signaled the unlikely prospects of a male counterpart to Judson College by the state convention, but in Marion, Julia Barron had a young son who needed education. And so, the Baptists of Marion turned their attention to new avenues to educate their sons and contain the lingering rowdy elements of "the boys." As one hyperbolic Calvinist later wrote, "It must have been predestinated before the foundation of the world, that here [in Marion], should become, for the Baptists of Alabama, a great educational center."[30]

2

HOWARD ENGLISH AND
CLASSICAL SCHOOL

In 1841, James Harvey DeVotie met with Milo Jewett and Edwin D. King in Judson's new brick building on Early Street. During their conversation, King, who was standing in a front window, called Jewett and DeVotie over to look at Judson's original building, which stood empty some quarter-mile down the road. "There is the very place for a male college," he proclaimed. All three men, having served together on the Alabama Baptist State Convention's committee on education the previous year, were well poised to establish a new male college. "The determination was formed," DeVotie later recalled, "to make an effort to carry that ideal into reality." Jewett was tasked with finding a leader for the new institution while DeVotie became the principal organizer, fundraiser, promoter, and founder. Julia Barron gave $4,000 to the cause and, by November 1841, DeVotie had secured enough money to purchase the vacated Judson property. They agreed to donate the lot and the building to the state convention if, in turn, they would allow Marion's local Baptist community to create the college.[1]

At the annual meeting of the state Baptist convention in Talladega on November 13, DeVotie, chairman of the committee on education, and members Rev. William Carey Crane of Montgomery and Rev. A. W. Chambliss of Wetumpka presented a report which called for the establishment of a new Baptist college or university of the "highest character" in Marion. The proposal touched off a "spirited debate" among the attendees, but in the end, the convention agreed to undertake this "great enterprise" and establish the school. The new endeavor would include a theological institution dedicated to the training of future ministers and missionaries. To avoid a similar debt-ridden fate as the Manual Labor Institute, the convention decreed that the college would not begin

Shaped by revivalism in New York's "Burned Over District," James
Harvey DeVotie was the driving force behind the creation of Howard
College. (DeVotie Baptist Church, Griffin, GA)

operations until a $50,000 permanent endowment was secured, but a classical
school could be opened until the institution achieved monetary stability.[2]

The convention selected thirteen trustees for the new college: James H.
DeVotie, Edwin D. King, Oliver G. Eiland, William N. Wyatt, Ovid C. Eiland,
James Massey, Daniel P. Bestor, William C. Crane, William P. Chilton, Jesse
Hartwell, Edward Baptist, Robert J. Ware, and Henry C. Lea. On Decem-
ber 14, 1841, Lea, an attorney from Marion and a state senator representing
Perry County, introduced a bill in the Alabama Senate to incorporate "Perry

College." Lea, who was working without the minutes of the convention, improvised as he composed the charter document. He selected the name of the new college and expanded the list of trustees from thirteen to fifteen—adding the names of Walter Reynolds, L. Y. Tarrant, and Langston Goree, but eliminating Jesse Hartwell. The Lea Act also gave the trustees, not the convention, the power to select vacancies on the board, although this power was returned to the convention in 1845.[3]

Nonetheless, on December 20, 1841, Lea amended his original bill and substituted the name "Howard College" for Perry College. Most likely the name change followed the meeting of the college's Board of Trustees in which James H. DeVotie proposed naming the new institution in honor of British philanthropist John Howard. Just as the Judson name became synonymous with foreign missions, American evangelicals lionized Howard as a righteous example of Christian self-sacrifice, benevolence, and virtue. "Such were the moral endowments of this extraordinary man," eulogized Rev. Samuel Stennett at Howard's funeral in 1795, "such his fortitude, his humanity, and disinterestedness, and temperance. Such was the character of this excellent man. 'He went about doing good.'" Although John Howard was best known for his work as a prison reformer, naming an upstart college after him was less about what he *did* specifically and more about who he *was*. DeVotie and the other trustees recognized that the name brought lessons in faith, benevolence, and virtue to the wild young men of the Alabama frontier.[4]

Naming the institution after John Howard also revealed the connections between American and British Evangelicals and the influences of the British Enlightenment on American frontier reformers. In Great Britain, Evangelicalism was the ally of the Enlightenment and not the enemy. As author Gertrude Himmelfarb emphasized, the central focus of the Enlightenment in Great Britain was not reason (as it was in France), but the "social virtues" with an emphasis on a "moral sense" and a spirit of "benevolence, compassion, sympathy, fellow-feeling, [and] a natural affection for others." As British statesman and philosopher Edmund Burke proclaimed in the eighteenth century, benevolence to the impoverished was a "direct and obligatory duty" for all Christians. At the time, so many people gave money, time, and effort, philanthropy became a full-time vocation and calling, as for John Howard. In 1780, Burke praised the work of Howard for opening the "eyes and hearts of mankind" through his willingness to plunge into the darkest dungeons, visit the sickest hospitals, examine the "mansions of sorrow and pain," measure "misery, depression, and contempt," remember the forgotten, serve the neglected, visit the forsaken, and "compare and collate the distresses of all men in all countries." John Howard, Burke added, was on a "voyage of discovery" and a "circumnavigation of charity." With the benevolent work of Howard and others the term "philanthropist" became synonymous with evangelicalism in the British Empire.[5]

Although he died in 1790, John Howard's benevolent service and moral prestige only grew over the next half-century. Publications in Great Britain and America carried stories, anecdotes, adages, poems which extolled Howard's "active benevolence" and virtuous character. In 1834, a Boston newspaper printed a dying man's advice to his children to "make it your study to copy the example of my much-esteemed and worthy master, Mr. Howard, especially his diligence and activity in promoting the honor and glory of God, and the real good of all his fellow-creatures. What an example has he left!" The *Alabama Baptist* reprinted an article which described John Howard as an "unselfish martyr of philanthropy" and a pioneer of the widespread reform movements of the nineteenth century. One British writer believed that the name Howard represented the highest honor of English character and must be remembered through "corresponding memorials of . . . veneration and gratitude."[6]

During the first decades of the nineteenth century, these commemorations kept John Howard in the public eye of many Americans. In 1812, citizens in Boston, Massachusetts, inspired by his humanitarian work, founded the first Howard Benevolent Society to serve the sick and poor. Their work proved so successful that reformers in other cities began their own autonomous philanthropic societies in the name of John Howard. Popularly known as Howard Associations, these organizations existed in almost every American city, including those in the South, and focused on poverty, public health, crime, and prison reform. Among the Baptists of Alabama, Howard College was also a memorial to John Howard. On December 29, 1841, Alabama governor Benjamin Fitzpatrick signed the bill (the Lea Act) incorporating Howard College.[7]

In turn, Judson College president Milo Jewett and Siloam pastor James H. DeVotie worked to hire a leader for the fledgling college. They offered the position to Rev. Daniel P. Bestor, but he declined. "I will come," he wrote with sardonic wit, when the $50,000 endowment was ready which should take about a thousand years, "but I hope you will go ahead." Next, DeVotie and Jewett turned to another New England native, twenty-six-year-old Samuel Sterling

Samuel Sterling Sherman, a self-described industrious New
Englander, brought to Alabama an educational philosophy
shaped at Middlebury College and influenced by the curriculum at Yale. (Samford University, Special Collection and University Archives)

Sherman, who at the time was working as a tutor at the University of Alabama.
On December 4, Sherman received a letter from Jewett offering the use of a
building for the "purpose of opening an English Classical School Preparatory to
the College contemplated in Marion." Jewett asked for an immediate response.
Before deciding, Sherman, as he later recalled, sought the counsel of University
of Alabama president Basil Manly. He told the young teacher to reject the offer.
Manly explained that Alabama Baptists would never donate enough money to

endow or sustain a college or university. In general, the irascible Manly opposed the founding of a new college, because he thought it would weaken Baptist influence at the University of Alabama. Although Manly was correct in the short term and perhaps prophetic in the long term, Sherman's youthful optimism trumped the Baptist sage's pessimism.[8]

The next day, Sherman wrote James H. DeVotie to accept the position. Four years earlier, as Sherman considered a move to the South, Middlebury College professor William C. Fowler suggested that he contact Rev. Basil Manly in Charleston, South Carolina. Manly, however, recently moved southwest to serve as president of the University of Alabama. Sherman's letter was forwarded to Tuscaloosa and, in reply, Manly explained to Sherman that a "competent teacher would do well in Tuscaloosa" and invited him to come to the university. Sherman hoped to open a private preparatory school in Alabama's capital city, but Manly persuaded him to accept a position as a Latin and Greek tutor and librarian at the university.[9]

Sherman found Tuscaloosa a restless frontier town with a mixture of law-abiding citizens and a host of "rowdy and lawless characters." When the Alabama legislature was in session, gamblers, swindlers, and other shady sorts descended upon Tuscaloosa and the violence and murder rate soared. At the university, Sherman had a quiet first year, but students in his second year resumed their unruly ways, compelling university officials to close the school and send the students home for a three-week holiday. "I cannot understand why," Sherman wrote decades later, "the students of the University of Alabama should have been so ungovernable." By 1841, Sherman had grown weary of the disorder and the repetitive work as a mere tutor and not a full-fledged faculty member at the university. "I felt that I was capable of more and better work," he remembered.[10]

In Marion, Samuel Sterling Sherman found more work than he had anticipated when he discovered the Baptists had made few "efforts to establish a college or even the nucleus of one." No one had contributed any money. No administration or faculty had been hired. All he found was bold talk, a recently vacated frame building, and an advertisement announcing the opening of Howard University. Perhaps Basil Manly was correct in his assessment of Alabama Baptists and money. "I did not like the outlook," Sherman wrote, "felt discouraged, and feared that I made a mistake." In addition, Sherman must have realized that the Baptists were expecting him to not only establish a school which would prepare students for college, but the college as well.[11]

No doubt James DeVotie, Milo Jewett, and other Marion Baptists assured Sherman that the money for the endowment was soon coming and that he should proceed with the preparatory school—after all, they told him, the denomination was "ripe for the harvest." As Sherman later recalled, he put his "hand to the plow and resolved never to look back." With new determination, he printed a new advertisement and announced that the Howard English and Classical School would open on January 3, 1842.[12]

On this first Monday of the new year, Samuel Sterling Sherman welcomed nine young boys to the old Judson building, an unassuming inverted U-shaped wooden structure with a two-story center, a mere thirty by forty feet, and two one-story wings. He wrote the names of the students in a registration book. They were John T. Barron, Thomas Booth, William Miller, Thomas A. Cravens, William D. King, William Blassingame, Samuel Escridge Goree, Thomas J. Anderson, and Thomas A. J. Oliver. Except for Mr. Anderson of Montgomery, all the students were from Marion. During this first session, twenty-two other students joined the original nine—a few from neighboring counties and at least one from Mississippi. Sherman placed the boys in one of four classifications based on age and ability: nine were in the preparatory class, seven in English-Science, fourteen in English-Classical, and one in Common English. For most of this first term, Sherman served as the only instructor, but he hired the Rev. Solon Lindsley, a Connecticut native and the founding pastor of the First Baptist Church of Selma, to assist him during the term's final weeks. When the academic year ended in June or July 1842, the tuition money received was not enough to cover Sherman's board.[13]

The lack of money, books, equipment, faculty, and students never deterred Sherman, DeVotie, the trustees, or the Baptists of Marion. With the help of a large enslaved man pushing a wheelbarrow, Sherman went house-to-house in Marion and secured donations of at least eight hundred books for the boys to have a library. When the Presbyterians closed the Manual Labor Institute of South Alabama, Sherman purchased several thousand dollars' worth of expensive European scientific equipment for $1,500, which he used to instruct students in chemistry, natural philosophy, and astronomy.[14]

On September 1, 1842, twenty-five students enrolled at the Howard English and Classical School to receive "instruction in every branch of a liberal education." It was a difficult course of study for the young men, lasting ten months and divided into two five-month terms (September to January and February to June). The only extensive break, other than a week at Christmas, occurred during the "sick season" in Alabama—when yellow fever and other infectious diseases occurred with more frequency. English and chemistry provided the most challenging courses of study for students. A writer for the *Alabama Baptist* opined that Howard students would receive as "complete and thorough" education as any other institution in the United States.[15]

In addition, Sherman taught the principles of Christian piety and the classical ideals of virtue. He enforced discipline that was mild but persuasive. "The young men are treated as gentlemen," he wrote, "and are expected to demean themselves at all times in a gentlemanly and courteous manner." If correction was necessary, Sherman administered discipline with the goal of reformation and not retribution. When reform efforts failed, a student would be sent home with as "little publicity as the nature of the case will permit." The Bible, Sherman believed, influenced his discipline, and provided students with moral instruction that freed the earth from vice and left the crumbled altars "moldering in irretrievable ruin." Without regard to "sectarian influence," Sherman required Howard students to attend public worship at least once on the Sabbath at a church the parents or guardians designated.[16]

For parents and guardians, Howard's tuition was modest. Beginning students in preparatory school taking spelling, reading, and writing were charged $12 per term, while those in arithmetic, grammar, and geography paid $16. It cost $25 each term to take advanced courses in English, mathematics, chemistry, ancient languages, and other subjects. Modern languages, mainly French, cost $20. In addition, each month the school charged students $11 for room and board, $2 for washing, and $1 each for fuel and a light. Half of the payment was required at the beginning of the term, with the remainder due at the conclusion.[17]

By the fall of 1842, Sherman had a better understanding of the interests, divisions, and peculiarities of the Baptists of Alabama. Many Baptist ministers, he discovered, were illiterate, and those who could read were bivocational and indifferent to theological training or disciplined learning. The more primitive anti-intellectual hard-shell Baptists rejected both missions and an educated clergy in the strongest terms. In contrast, within both the lay and pastoral denomination leadership, Sherman discovered a wealthy group of Baptists who believed that the most pressing concern for the new school was to provide a better-educated ministry. With this in mind, Sherman devised a shrewd plan to convince the Board of Trustees to raise money for an endowed professor of theology to educate the future generations of preachers. Even so, Sherman understood that a theology professor would be unneeded at Howard for several years, and until then, the person could "render valuable service" in the literary and classical areas of Howard. As Sherman later recalled, this would compel Baptist churches throughout the state to "become interested in the school and, in this way, a better foundation would be laid on which to build in [the] future."[18]

The board embraced the plan with enthusiasm and, for the moment at least, postponed any further action in establishing a four-year college devoted to just theological training. Most board members agreed, however, that a Baptist school for men was necessary to improve the "rising ministry" of a new generation of preachers in the state by filling their minds with a classical education and their hearts with virtue and piety. Now was the time, the board supposed, for immediate and vigorous action to make real the promise of this education. In justifying the need for an endowed professor of theology, the Board of Trustees proclaimed that the war waging between "truth and error," and "holiness and irreligion" demanded an urgent call for an educated clergy. Those called to this sacred duty should be *"thoroughly furnished* unto every good work—prepared, not only to explain the cardinal doctrines of Christianity, but to defend the entire Christian system against the assaults of infidelity and skepticism, and the anti-Christian powers of a fallen world." With this emotional call to action, the board appointed James H. DeVotie as the agent to raise the $20,000 necessary to endow the professorship. The state convention endorsed the decision at its annual meeting on November 12, 1842, and by December, DeVotie began to solicit funds from the Baptists of Alabama.[19]

By the end of the academic year, the Howard students, now numbering seventy-seven, took a series of examinations held on Thursday and Friday, June 22 and 23, 1843. Each day's exams concluded with a series of public declamations held in the sanctuary at Siloam Baptist. Marion citizens gathered to watch the Howard boys draw diagrams and provide recitations on scientific and mathematical problems. The math students, one observer wrote at the time, "sustained themselves well, and proved to their hearers . . . that they comprehended very clearly, the reasoning of every problem which they were called on to solve." Students also entertained the audiences with orations based on famous historical addresses and texts or original compositions. The best speakers were awarded a gold medal by the judges—presumably Samuel Sterling Sherman and Solan Lindsley. Soon after the examinations, a writer in the *Alabama Baptist* encouraged parents, who wanted their sons taught "good morals" and a complete classical liberal arts education, to send them to Marion to study under the watchful eyes of professors Sherman and Lindsley. "They will do them good.'"[20]

During the late summer and early fall of 1843, while Sherman traveled to Vermont to visit his family, James H. DeVotie completed his fundraising campaign—he spent 222 days in the service of the institution, traveled 2,700 miles, and preached seventy sermons. His expenses were $80. Combined with a $1,754.29 donation from board member Daniel Bestor, DeVotie raised $19,403.69 (over $700,000 in 2023 dollars) for the permanent theological fund. Even with these substantial gifts, board members concluded that most Baptists in the state failed to support the school. Howard's mission and goals were "imperfectly understood" by a majority of the denomination who were withholding donations based on "distrust or want of proper information." The board proposed keeping the Howard name before the church and in the public sphere in an ongoing fundraising and publicity campaign. Even as Baptists outside of the western Black Belt viewed Howard as a local enterprise of Marion, the trustees hoped that their effort would increase awareness in the school and make "cheerful supporters" out of the uninterested.[21]

Writers for the local and denominational papers praised the successful campaign and announced that the Howard trustees had appointed Rev. John Leadley Dagg, a prominent theologian and leader of the Baptist girl's school in Tuscaloosa, as the new professor of theology. The announcement was premature. Dagg declined the offer, and the trustees turned to Jesse Hartwell, the pastor of the Baptist church in Carlowville in southern Dallas County and president of the Alabama Baptist State Convention. James H. DeVotie's former professor at Furman, Hartwell accepted the position. He wrote to the board and requested their prayers for God to empower his work to advance ministerial education and the "cause of the Redeemer" throughout the world."[22]

A writer for the *Alabama Baptist* believed that, by hiring Hartwell, the trustees accomplished three important objectives: appointing an educated minister with high literary credentials, hiring a sound theologian, and securing an individual with "true and unquestioned piety." Born in Buckland, Massachusetts, on May 2, 1795, Jesse Boardman Hartwell was baptized by his minister father in 1815 and attended Brown University with plans for becoming a missionary in

India. Graduating in 1819 (along with future education reformer Horace Mann), Hartwell chose instead to preach and teach, but retained a lifelong passion for missions. Plagued by poor health, Hartwell moved to South Carolina in 1822, where he pastored several churches and taught theology at Furman Theological Institution. In December 1836, he moved to Alabama as an itinerant agent for the Home Mission Society and advocated the "great and good cause" of missions to those Alabama Baptists skeptical of such endeavors. His campaign worked, Hartwell wrote, and many Baptists opponents proclaimed their conviction that missions were for God's glory. Eventually, Hartwell accepted a pastorate in Carlowville, where he soon gained prominence within the Alabama Baptist State Convention.[23]

With the hiring of Jesse Hartwell, the trustees changed the school's name to the "Howard Collegiate and Theological Institution"—although it was still functioning as a boy's prep school. Classes for the 1843–44 academic year began on October 3 with Sherman, Hartwell, and Lindsley listed as the faculty, although Hartwell would assume duties in January. The denominational paper suggested that the parents of Baptists could display their denominational principles by sending their daughters to Judson and their sons to Howard. If Baptists supported Howard and Judson as well as other denominations supported their institutions, both schools would overflow with students, the writer supposed. Many Baptists sent their children to "confessedly inferior" schools conducted by another denomination. "They thus weaken the denomination, and also dole out to their children a scanty, broken, shapeless mass of driblets of notions about masters and things in general, which they fancy may be palmed off upon the world as an education!"[24]

In January 1844, Jesse Hartwell arrived at Howard and discovered four older students waiting to begin their theological education. These men were Samuel C. Johnson and Hampton B. Mathis from Alabama and brothers Valentine and Azor Van Hoose from Mississippi. The quartet was so ill-prepared to study theology that Hartwell sent them to Samuel Sterling Sherman and Solon Lindsley to first receive a broad liberal arts education. Several weeks later, three more Alabama boys entered the program, but were also assigned to other classes. A sudden illness took the life of Valentine Van Hoose, whom professors described as "zealously engaged in the prosecution of his studies to the time of his decease." Van Hoose was seen as a young man of great piety, virtue, and self-sacrifice. While younger classmates pursued pleasure, he zealously studied his Bible in the hope that he would one day "proclaim its sacred truths to the destitute, but the master came and called him away." It was a dark start for Hartwell's efforts to train the next generation of Baptist ministers in Alabama, and the future would soon look darker.[25]

At 1 p.m. on Friday May 10, 1844, a fire broke out on the roof or attic of the Howard building. Quick action on the part of the faculty, students, and the citizens of Marion saved the library books, most of the scientific apparatus, and furnishings from offices and recitation rooms. Within an hour, the fire destroyed the wood-frame building. The next day, May 11, the citizens of Marion, and a handful of visitors, gathered at the small brick courthouse on the town square. One observer at the public meeting made note of the eclectic mix of people who were present "without distinction of party, sect, or class." The crowd embraced a suggestion to begin raising funds to rebuild Howard and elected Edwin King to oversee the effort. From there, the meeting took on the tone of a political rally and ecumenical revival. King, a Baptist, spoke first. Next, Circuit Judge John Dennis Phelen, Alabama's former attorney general and an Episcopalian, gave a "calm, deliberate, but lucid and forcible" speech on the importance of education to "the patriot, philanthropist, and the Christian." Alabama's Speaker of the House and future governor, Andrew B. Moore, followed with an exhortation on the virtues of learning. "A kindly feeling, a generous sympathy now pervaded the assembly," the *Alabama Baptist* reported, but the final speech provided an "electric spark" and a call to action. Methodist minister Jesse P. Perham, a popular camp-meeting preacher, left the audience "all on fire" with his rousing sermon, and nearly $4,000 was donated to the cause. "The promptitude, energy, and liberality evinced by our citizens," wrote a reporter, "will confirm favorable impressions already cherished towards this community, and will doubtless secure, as is richly deserved, the generous cooperation of the friends of patrons of learning throughout the state."[26]

Within months, Marion's citizens contributed an additional $4,000 to the building fund, but the appeals for help from Baptists around the state went unheeded. "We were much disappointed," Samuel Sterling Sherman wrote, "for we had prepared the foundations of a large building." Sherman refused to put the college in debt for the building, so he reduced the size of the structure. In turn, the trustees approved the erection of a four-story brick building, 112 feet in length and 44 feet in width, with a chapel, laboratory, preparatory department room; eight rooms for recitations, lectures, and the library; and twenty-four 16-foot-square dormitory rooms. The total cost for the structure would be $14,000—still well above the amount of money donated. Nonetheless, at the insistence of Edwin King, the trustees purchased a lot adjacent to the burned building and directly facing the front of Judson College. "The boys' school must stand face to face with the girls' school, with no obstruction between," King reportedly said. Construction on the new edifice proceeded at a slow pace. When the money ran out, construction stopped until more funds were raised, and then it began again.[27]

For the next two years, Howard held classes at Siloam Baptist Church and in an adjacent house. The students boarded in private homes in Marion. At the end of the 1843–44 academic year, ninety-five students attended classes at Howard—a few freshman-level college classes were offered to "one promising class of young men." Other than the University of Alabama, no other institution in the state offered students such a thorough English and classical education as Howard, Samuel Sterling Sherman boasted. "The course of instruction is elevated and extensive," Sherman added, "and we know from daily observation that it is most thorough and practical." Students studied philosophy, physiology, astronomy, chemistry, geology, history, math, engineering, mental science, moral science, logic, rhetoric, and numerous classical works. At the close of examinations in July 1844, Sherman praised the boys' "propriety and decorum" in their conduct at school and with the community. "We are happy to say," the *Alabama Baptist* reported, "the citizens of Marion are unanimous in pronouncing the tribute thus paid, to be truly deserved." In short, Howard was playing a key role in educating virtuous, pious, intelligent, and benevolent young men and tempering the rowdyism in Marion.[28]

Temperance efforts proved so successful in Marion that only one saloon was still in operation in 1844. Most of the hotels in Marion were run by temperance men, including one operated by Howard student William Hornbuckle, and these establishments no longer served alcohol. "There is but one doggery now in the place," a writer for the *Alabama Baptist* emphasized, "and it is so hoped that this gate of hell will soon be shut."[29]

3

A DILIGENT WATCH
OVER MORALS

For many Baptists in the North, the issues of virtue and benevolence were a paramount concern as the debate over slavery reached a tipping point. As one historian wrote, "Just as evangelicals thought that drunkards would give up drink, that criminals after contemplation of their ways would reform their behavior, and that 'sinners' would turn away from sin . . . so too they hoped that converted slaveholders would instantly reject their involvement in the practice." Slavery, however, was too entrenched in southern politics, culture, and economics to see a mass conversion. Author Bertram Wyatt-Brown later asked, "how could they so glibly reconcile slaveholding with pretensions to virtue?" But they did.[1]

Baptists in the South confronted the issue in 1844, when the executive board of the Home Mission Society rejected a slaveowner's application for missionary service and pronounced that slave ownership disqualified anyone, on moral and theological grounds, to serve on the mission field. With the state's Baptists leading the charge, the denomination's leaders created the separate Southern Baptist Convention—organized by 293 delegates that included several with Howard connections: Jesse Hartwell, E. D. King, Henry Talbird, and James H. DeVotie. Most of the principal founders and leaders of Howard were enslavers, including northerners DeVotie, Samuel Sterling Sherman, Daniel Bestor, and Milo Jewett. Edwin D. King, Julia Barron, Henry Talbird, and most of the original Board of Trustees were also slaveholders. Slaves were valuable property and served as symbols of economic status for owners—their labor drove the southern economy and provided the money necessary for building colleges in the South, like Howard.[2]

After analyzing the content of public orations at Howard College in the 1840s and 1850s, historian Alfred L. Brophy discovered that the school offered limited rhetorical support for slavery. Speakers explored themes of virtue, enterprise, republicanism, and education—all echoing the sentiments of the surrounding culture. In addition, Brophy found key support for "maintaining the union" at Howard that reflected a deep support for the American constitutional system. This contrasted with the University of Alabama, where faculty and administrators, led by slavery's "intellectual defender" Basil Manly, provided important justifications for the slave institution based on theology, politics, science, and economy. At some southern colleges, the rhetoric and the curriculum used Common Sense philosophy and proslavery ideology to support the system. Courses on moral philosophy provided students and presidents an opportunity to explore a variety of defenses of slavery. As historian Eugene Genovese recognized, southern nationalists needed to be "steeped in moral philosophy" to justify their ideology. In comparison, Brophy argued, Howard College was a "place of moderation."[3]

Throughout the antebellum period, most of Howard's students came from slaveholding families. The 1844–45 school year at Howard was one filled with "unprecedented trial and anxiety" with the burning of the building and the inability to raise the additional funds. That year, 114 young men and boys attended the Howard Collegiate and Theological Institution: 47 preparatory students and 7 theological students. S. S. Sherman now offered college-level courses for freshmen and sophomores. Solon Lindsley took a leave of absence to act as the college's agent in raising money but proved so ineffective as a fundraiser that the trustees recalled him after three months and he returned to the classroom. Even with these trials, board members took comfort in acknowledging "the hand of God, in controlling the affairs of the institution committed to their charge." At the conclusion of the following academic year, the trustees lamented that Howard was "destitute of most of the conveniences which are essential to the successful operation of any institution." Students and faculty, however, confronted these discomforts with "cheerfulness and patience," and the board publicly acknowledged the "zeal and faithfulness of the instructors, and the diligence and gentlemanly demeanor of the students." To hasten the construction of the new building, the trustees reluctantly decided to go into debt to finish the project. "Either the house must be left untenable, and therefore useless, or it must be finished and means devised to pay for it." The builders, most likely enslaved laborers, completed the structure in 1846.[4]

In July of that year, the Board of Trustees authorized the faculty to prepare a complete curriculum of "collegiate studies, embracing the usual period of four years." Samuel Sterling Sherman adopted the Yale–Middlebury College curriculum that reflected his commitment to providing Howard students with a college education grounded in the classics and history combined with intensive studies in philosophy, science, and mathematics. Entrance requirements to the rechristened Howard College required students to be over fourteen years of age and to be able to "sustain a credible examination" on Latin and Greek grammar; Caesar, Sallust, or Cicero's Select Orations; Virgil and the Greek Reader, or the equivalent; and the branches of common English. Samuel Sterling Sherman believed that education must provide "adequate development and discipline of the physical, intellectual, and moral powers of man." The best ways to teach students these principles was through a Common Sense liberal arts curriculum rooted in the classics and the Bible.[5]

As historian Mark Noll emphasized, in the late eighteenth and early nineteenth centuries, college presidents were among the most effective in spreading the "principles of commonsense moral reasoning," along with professors, preachers, and editors. At Howard, as at colleges throughout the county, the president of the institution taught a senior capstone course in moral science. The textbook used by Sherman and other college presidents was Francis Wayland's *Elements of Moral Science,* which served as a manual for instruction in scientific approaches to moral philosophy through classification and illustration. Wayland, the Baptist president of Brown University, defined a moral act as the "voluntary action of an intelligent agent, who was capable of distinguishing between right and wrong, or of distinguishing what he ought, from what he ought not to do." Humans were moral agents, Wayland argued, because they had an innate, universal (or common) sense of "knowing better." A sense of right and wrong, he added, was "manifest to everyone" and stemmed from an awareness of the relationships people had with one another and with God; in other words, a "consciousness of moral obligation." The conscience, which originated with God, gave humans a natural "impulse for virtue" and engrained sense to act "according to his or her God-given commonsense nature." As Wayland added, Christianity was designed to "bring us under the dominion of conscience, enlightened by revelation, and deliver us from the slavery of evil propensity." Christian colleges and universities became the place where students learned this intermingling of virtue, morality, and Christianity.[6]

In October 1846, classes began in the new brick building. For students, each school day began and ended with prayer led by the faculty. Five faculty members were engaged in teaching at Howard during the 1846–47 academic year. Sherman taught the natural sciences, and Jesse Hartwell trained students in theology and moral science. Amos Bailey Goodhue taught Greek and mathematics. A native of New Hampshire, Goodhue was a recent graduate of Dartmouth College and previously taught at an academy in Claiborne County, Alabama. William Locke Moseley, a nineteen-year-old Howard student, served as a tutor in Latin and math, and R. S. Lewis taught in the preparatory department.[7]

The Board of Trustees granted Howard College faculty the power to "direct all things pertaining to the instruction and discipline of the college" and to use "higher motives than the fear of punishment" to inspire the students in their studies and conduct. In addition, faculty were required to "diligently watch over the morals" of each student, strive to protect them from the temptations of vice, and to encourage them as they pursued virtue. If students failed to meet expectations, they were given a "friendly admonition and private warning" just so long "as it can be done without injury to the Institution." The students were required to keep the Sabbath day holy by refraining from "their usual studies, exercises and amusements and whatever is unbecoming the sacredness of the day." Sabbath worship was a required "moral duty" for students each week. Sherman granted the students the right to choose the Christian church of their choice.[8]

In what served as the "Rules of Decorum" for Howard College, the faculty identified fourteen "crimes and misdemeanors" that could result in punishment or expulsion:

1. The students shall be required to treat each other at all times with that courtesy and propriety of behavior, which become young gentlemen associated together for the purpose of moral and intellectual improvement and shall maintain towards their instructors due honor and respect.

2. If any student shall be guilty of fighting, quarrelling, abusing a fellow student, intoxication, wearing any disguise or unbecoming apparel, fraud, lying, defamation, or any other similar crime, he shall be punished by admonition, suspension, dismission or expulsion, according to the nature and demerit of the crime.

3. As every student is at liberty to withdraw from the Institution at any time by payment of his bills, with every testimonial of merit to which his scholarship and conduct may entitle him, all opposition to the laws

of the College or combinations for the purpose of resisting them or the authority of the Faculty, are considered altogether inexcusable and are expressly forbidden.

4. Should any student be guilty of any flagrant immorality, or any crime for which an infamous punishment may be inflicted by the laws of this State, he shall be immediately expelled.

5. If a student shall deface, wantonly injure, or unnecessarily meddle with, the property of any citizen of the town of Marion, he shall, on complaint and proof thereof made to the Faculty, make such reparation as the Faculty may deem proper and shall be further punished for disorderly conduct.

6. No student shall play at cards or other unlawful games or suffer such games to be played in his room.

7. No student shall keep in his room any deadly weapon.

8. No student shall furnish any festive entertainment in his room, or being or suffer to be brought there, wine, or any spirituous liquor, or frequent any public house or other place where intoxicating drinks are sold.

9. All cutting, writing on, or any way defacing the walls of the College, or any of its appurtenances is strictly forbidden, and any student convicted thereof shall besides paying for the amount of damage done, be punished at the discretion of the Faculty.

10. No student shall keep company with persons of known bad character, or with an expelled student.

11. Students shall be amenable to the laws of the Institution for all improper conduct during vacation.

12. All loud and boisterous noises, jumping, dancing, playing ball, and the like within the College walls are prohibited.

13. If any student shall be guilty of habitual neglect of College duties, or of a disregard for College laws, or shall not improve his time as diligently as he ought, he shall be privately admonished, and if he does not reform he shall be quietly dismissed, or his parent or guardian informed of his remissness and requested to take him away.

14. As the laws of this College are few and general, it is probable that many offences may occur which are not expressly enumerated, or for which no

specific penalty is provided, in all such cases the Faculty shall proceed according to their discretion and may enact such additional laws as in their judgment are necessary.[9]

Almost six weeks after classes began, on November 16, 1846, the new Howard College building was formally dedicated during the annual meeting of the Alabama Baptist State Convention at Siloam Baptist Church in Marion. Just before 11 a.m., a processional of delegates and trustees was led by the sons of two members of the Board of Trustees: twenty-two-year-old Porter King (son of Edwin D. King) and seven-year-old Robert Goree (son of Langston Goree). The group marched the block and a half to the new building and into the chapel on the first floor and listened to music and speeches. Rev. Edward Baptist, a member of the original Board of Trustees and one of the state's most gifted preachers, delivered a dedication address that focused on the importance of education and the work of Howard College. Baptist also told students to be dedicated to the "unyielding importance" of study and virtue and to let the Bible serve as the only "infallible standard" of their faith. Although the "lightnings of genius" flashed from their eyes, the "thunders of eloquence" rolled from their lips and held the "multitudes charmed and chained" to every word; even if they reasoned with the decisiveness of Newton or Locke, it will all be nothing but "sounding brass or tinkling cymbal" without any moral principle and character to guide what they see, hear, say, and think. A reporter for the *Marion Review* attempted to hear Baptist's speech but found the crowds so great that he was unable to get close enough to hear. "The exercises, barring the jamming, treading on toes, etc., (about which we might speak feelingly), were of an imposing character, and the Howard College is now marshalled into the ranks of those who are striving for the elevation of man, with prospects bright, for a long and successful course, in the field of educational labor."[10]

At the conclusion of the academic year in July 1847, the Board of Trustees appointed Samuel Sterling Sherman as the first president of Howard College. The Alabama Baptist State Convention hailed the appointment of a man "who from the commencement of this Institution has exerted himself with so much energy, ability, and success, in its management." The convention also adopted a resolution that Howard College set a vigorous goal of raising $100,000 in five years (by 1852). The trustees accepted the challenge, but believed it was important to provide benefactors with a return on their investment to secure public support and build deep connections between the donors and the college. The plan the trustees adopted stipulated that any individual who gave $1,000 to the institution would receive a permanent scholarship to Howard College and those giving $500 would be given tuition to the preparatory school and the college. Raising funds, however, proved difficult in the late 1840s as a European economic crisis and a steep decline in cotton prices in 1848 and 1849 sent the southern economy into a downturn. While some cash, and promises of more, trickled into the Howard endowment, the trustees believed it was too little. To encourage increased giving, the board lowered the giving threshold for scholarships to a mere $100 donation to cover "tuition of one particular individual, through the regular collegiate course for four years, or to the tuition of any equivalent number of years in any department of this institution." It was a noble but short-sighted fundraising plan that would come back to haunt the trustees and the college decades later.[11]

While trustees fixated on the endowment, students and faculty pursued ways to expand academic opportunities beyond the classroom. In 1847, Howard students organized the Franklin and the Adelphi literary societies to give them an independent venue for debating, refining, and applying what they learned from the faculty. Literary societies of this type were a key part of college education in the nineteenth century and served as a complement to classical learning. "Grounded in the intellectual traditions representing both reason and persuasion," one writer concluded, the literary societies "flowered within a wider oratorical culture of republican ideology and an accompanying rhetoric of public consensus and civic virtue." Apart from the watchful eyes of their professors, students strengthened their comprehension and retention of classical thought, moral philosophy, Biblical precepts, and benevolent enterprise through writing, speaking, and critical thinking. Specifically, at each meeting of the societies, members gave original speeches or memorized historical discourses; wrote and discussed essays, debated ideas, texts, and issues; developed leadership skills; and practiced parliamentary procedures. In time, each society drew up a constitution, wrote bylaws, and elected officers, including a president, vice president, counsellor, secretary, treasurer, librarian, chaplain, critic, door keeper, and monthly orator.[12]

Each year, the Franklin and Adelphi societies, on the anniversary of their founding, invited a distinguished orator to deliver a provocative talk to both groups. As political tensions rose over slavery in the late 1840s, the Rev. Thomas G.

Keen of Mobile warned the young men, on the societies' third anniversary, that the storm clouds of disunion were gathering. "We are disturbed by the muttering thunder," he said. "We begin to feel the rumblings of the incept earthquake. We are startled by the breaking out from various quarters, of the imprisoned fires." Only the hand of God and the work of intelligent young college men, he supposed, could stop this march to dismemberment and domestic anarchy. Keen, a Philadelphia native, believed that the enlightened and independent thinking of a classically trained college graduate could counter the belligerent and delusional words and deeds of both northern and southern demagogues. The college mind had something these firebrands, especially the lawyers and politicians, lacked—mental discipline, humility, and character. "When will come the time, when the name of . . . John Howard, will be pronounced with other than feelings of reverence and admiration?" Keen asked. "From where did his honor come? From a well-regulated mind coupled with a highly cultivated moral sense, and an underlying benevolence." The nation needed, Keen emphasized, strong, disciplined, moral leadership.[13]

As Howard College graduate William Garrott Brown wrote, "The spoken word, not the printed page," influenced southern society and made history. Never was there a society, he supposed, "in which the orator counted for more than he did in the Cotton Kingdom." Audiences throughout the South listened to orators at political rallies and camp meetings and in courthouses and churches. "The man who wished to lead or to teach," Brown added, "must be able to speak. He could not touch the artistic sense of the people with pictures or statues or verses or plays; he must charm them with voice and gesture. There could be no hiding of the personality, no burying of the man in his art or his mission. The powerful man was above all a person; his power was himself. How such a great man mounted the rostrum, with what demeanor he endured an interruption, with what gesture he silenced a murmur—such things were remembered and talked about when his reasoning was perhaps forgotten."[14]

According to W. J. Cash in *The Mind of the South*, the essential ingredient of leadership for white southerners was excellent oratory skills. Another writer explained that oratory and debate serving as the only extracurricular activities available to college students helped "to explain certain . . . characteristics of southern leadership in years ahead." This was true at Howard College. Along with his classically trained mind, a student's ability to speak persuasively and to demonstrate leadership skills opened opportunities for middle-class careers as

William S. Blassingame was one of the nine young men who attended
Howard on the first day of classes on January 3, 1842, and was the third
person to graduate on July 27, 1848. (Mickey Bright Griffin)

teachers, lawyers, preachers, doctors, merchants, and politicians. Of the seven
in Howard College's first graduating class on July 27, 1848, two became medical
doctors (John T. Barron and Milton Weisenger), two went on to receive master's degrees (William S. Blassingame and Singleton Williams), and one each
worked as an attorney (Henry W. Nate), a teacher (William L. Mosely), and a
merchant (Thomas Booth).[15]

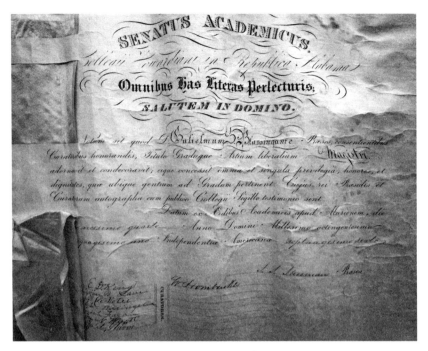

Blassingame received this diploma, written in Latin, for completing the rigorous classical course at Howard College. The document translates in part: "Let there be a vow that the president with the consent of the trustees (caretakers) grant the honor [and] has adorned and decorated William S. Blassingame with the title and degree of 'master of the liberal arts.' He has granted to him all the individual privileges, praises and honors which pertain to this degree everywhere in the world. Let the signatures of the president and trustee members along with the public seal of the college be evidence of this matter." (Mickey Bright Griffin)

Graduates who completed all three major fields of study (classical, English, and scientific) at Howard College received two degrees and two diplomas. Each diploma was signed by Samuel Sterling Sherman and those members of the Board of Trustees that lived in Marion or were visiting town before commencement. The parchment was embossed with the college seal and a blue ribbon. William Blassingame earned a bachelor of science for completing the "full course of English and Scientific Studies" and received a diploma written in English. For completing the more rigorous coursework in the classics, Blassingame received a liberal arts degree and a diploma in Latin.[16]

Also at graduation, professor of theology Jesse Hartwell announced his intention to leave Howard in 1849 to move to the Arkansas frontier. In over a decade
of work in Alabama, Hartwell made a significant impact on the denomination:
For nine years he served as president of the Alabama Baptist State Convention,
participated in the formation of the Southern Baptist Convention, and was
one of the state's leading advocates for missions and education. "No man in
the South," a writer for the *Alabama Baptist* opined, "was more beloved for his
many virtues." In an emotional farewell sermon at Siloam Baptist Church, Hartwell explained that his work called him to a "far distant land" and he doubted
he would ever return to Marion. He encouraged his audience to "Live in peace;
be perfect; be of good comfort; be of one mind. . . . Live near to God. Shun the
appearance of evil. Do not trust in anything but Christ."[17]

The trustees hired as Hartwell's replacement the Rev. Thomas Fenner Curtis,
the embattled pastor of First Baptist Church of Tuscaloosa and another target
of Basil Manly's criticism. While Manly admired Curtis's intellect and morality,
he believed the pastor failed to remind the congregation that the consequences
of sin were eternal hell fire and damnation. "He pinches nobody," Manly added.
"He makes no one feel either afraid or ashamed of sin." His sermons appealed
only to angels and Christian intellectuals and not to lost sinners. "Alas!" Manly
wrote, "What is to become of the souls of his poor hearers?" Born in England
on September 27, 1815, Curtis was the son of a prominent Baptist preacher,
theologian, and scholar who immigrated to the United States during the 1830s
and settled in Bangor, Maine. He graduated in 1839 from Bangor Theological
Seminary and moved south to begin his ministry. While Manly criticized Curtis
during his short time in Tuscaloosa, others found the preacher to be one of "the
freshest, most original and fertile of the preachers of the time." The *Alabama
Baptist* praised Curtis's extensive literary and theological training, his modest
piety, and his orthodox views. Reflecting a classic Scottish Common Sense
perspective on Biblical authority, Curtis believed that some Bible passages
were difficult to understand or explain, but there remained "plain evidences"
of scriptural authority that the "wise man will bind . . . close to his heart."[18]

Like Jesse Hartwell, Curtis recognized the conflicting opinions on ministerial education among Alabama Baptists. One group of anti-missionary and
anti-intellectual Baptists believed that educating ministers created only "manmade preachers" and was not the type of apostolic training conducted in the
Bible. They concluded that theological schools operated apart from scripture,

threatened religious liberty, and fostered persecution and bloodshed. A more moderate and less apocalyptic faction supported some ministerial education if it was focused exclusively on theological training and contained no classical or literary distractions. While Curtis seemed more sympathetic to these views than his predecessor or successor, he still argued that broad intellectual pursuits were essential to the effective communication of the gospel message. The ability to think, speak, and write in correct and plain English was worth "more than all the time and expense bestowed upon an education," Curtis wrote. The goal of a theological education, he added, was to provide future ministers the "discipline of mind that shall enable him to think more clearly, and reason more accurately," and be more useful in spreading the gospel.[19]

In 1850, perhaps coinciding with Curtis's invigoration of theological education that reinforced Howard's commitment to evangelism, a revival broke out among students and resulted in many coverts who, as the denominational newspaper emphasized, "passed from death into life." Young men who professed Christianity, a writer noted at the time, made the best students, and provided the basis for good character and a life of piety. If large numbers were to convert to Christianity, it must come through the influence of "pious young men." Now, most Howard students professed Christianity and participated in prayer meetings to fan the flames of revival fires. "This," wrote E. D. King on behalf of the trustees in 1850, "ought to afford encouragement to the friends of the College, and lead to more active and efficient exertions for its support on the part of the denomination generally." In addition, the number of theological students was increasing, and their education, under Curtis's tutelage, was "beginning to answer more fully the expectations of its founders."[20]

The theological course of study, presumably influenced by James H. DeVotie, Jesse Hartwell, and Thomas F. Curtis, reflected the strong Calvinist influences on Alabama Baptists and appeared harmonious with classes offered in Reformed seminaries. Students took courses on the harmony of the gospels, evidences of revealed religion, intellectual philosophy, systematic theology, the trinity, the purposes of God (election), moral accountability (natural and moral ability), man as a sinner (the fall and depravity), salvation by grace (covenant of redemption, atonement, regeneration, justification by faith, and perseverance of the saints), resurrection (future rewards and punishments), the church (baptism, communion, officers, and discipline), moral science, ecclesiastical history, preparation of plans, criticisms of sermons, philosophy of rhetoric, evidences of Christianity, and pastoral duties. When the editor of the *Alabama Baptist Advocate* eavesdropped on Curtis's systematic theology class, he came away with deep admiration for the professor and his efforts to train the students to go forth as ambassadors of Christ, sound theologians, and "soul stirring Christians."[21]

4

SHALL HOWARD COLLEGE
LIVE OR DIE?

Shall we go further . . . or shall we retrace our steps . . . fold our hands, sit
down in inglorious ease and indolence, and permit that enterprise to fail?
—REV. SAMUEL HENDERSON, 1853

At the 1851 commencement ceremonies held at the town hall in Marion, Washington Wilkes and James S. Abbott became the first two theological graduates of Howard College. The son of a carpenter in Barbour County, Alabama,
Washington Wilkes received his early education at a tiny log schoolhouse and
at the local Louisville Academy—a school one hyperbolic writer described
as the "very acme of literary attainment." Called to the ministry, Wilkes quit
the academy and was licensed to preach by the Salem Baptist Association on
October 5, 1847. The next year, he enrolled at Howard. At graduation on July 23,
1851, Wilkes delivered his oration on the "Diversity of Opinions in Religion" in
a style that one listener described as pleasant, easy, and graceful. In addition,
James S. Abbott spoke on "The Tendencies of Modern Science" and argued that
the "efforts of infidelity and skepticism" failed to align science and religion into
opposing camps and thus embarrassed the "enemies of truth, whether natural
or revealed." In the years following graduation, Washington Wilkes emerged
as one of Alabama's best-respected preachers and poets and James S. Abbott
served as a missionary preacher along the South Texas frontier.[1]

Professor of theology Thomas Curtis also turned his attention to mission
work, resigning from Howard College to take over as head of the Southern Baptist Home Mission Board—a position he held for two years before returning to
teaching at the University of Lewisburg (later Crozer Theological Seminary) in
Pennsylvania. Following Curtis's departure, the board selected Henry Talbird

Henry Talbird, a classically trained Baptist minister from South
Carolina, guided Howard College through the turbulent 1850s. He
served as a Confederate regimental captain at the outset of the Civil
War and spent much of his time in Virginia visiting Howard College
students in other regiments and, as he said, sharing in the evangelistic
"glory of caring" for their souls. (Library of Congress, Prints and
Photographs Division)

as the new chair of theology at Howard. A member of a wealthy slaveholding family from Hilton Head Island, South Carolina, Henry Talbird was born
November 7, 1811. He received both a classical and a theological education at
the Hamilton Literary and Theological Institution in New York (later renamed
Colgate) and earned a bachelor's degree in 1839 and a master's in 1841. Upon
graduation, Talbird moved to Tuscaloosa and succeeded James H. DeVotie as
pastor of the city's First Baptist Church. He stayed just one year, perhaps also
clashing with Basil Manly, before he accepted the call to First Baptist Church,
Montgomery, where he led the congregation for nine years.[2]

Samuel Sterling Sherman believed Henry Talbird lacked vision and enthusiasm, but he still possessed a disciplined and well-balanced intellect. He was
"more philosophical than imaginative" and at times seemed slow, because of
his deliberate and perfectionist nature. "In the pulpit" Sherman added, "he
appealed to the reason rather than to the emotions of his hearers." A writer
once made the contradictory observation that Talbird preached his sermons
extemporaneously but used so many notes that a casual observer might assume
he "spoke entirely from the manuscript," a practice that annoyed some Baptist
laymen who believed that "preachers should leave their sermon manuscripts
in their pockets and preach as men did in the primitive church." Nonetheless,
Talbird's sermons were rigorous, pragmatic, logical, and convincing. He exhibited a "laborious study and research," an observer noted, "and he always secures
the attention of his audience from the beginning to the close of his discourse."[3]

Talbird's hiring coincided with a significant downturn in the southern economy, as cotton prices dropped in 1851 and 1852 and cash grew scarce. For Alabama farmers, drought and excessive heat led to crop failures. "The country is
literally burnt up," one farmer said in 1851. Other crop growers prayed for rain:
"O Lord, send us rain—not a gully-washer; not a root-soaker; but a drizzle,
drizzle." With money in short supply, donors to Howard College were unable,
or unwilling, to honor their promissory notes to the institution, and by the end
of the 1850–51 academic year, interest from the endowment and tuition money
were insufficient to pay faculty salaries. In the July 23, 1851, issue of the *South
Western Baptist*, the board published an appeal to those who pledged financial
support of the college. Without donations, the board would be forced to borrow money to pay faculty salaries which "no friend of the College would will-
ingly subject it to such a loss." Apparently, donors ignored the appeals and the

board most likely borrowed money from the endowment to cover expenses—including some or all the faculty salaries.[4]

The Board of Trustees reported that the following academic year (1851–52) was filled with "mingled feelings of encouragement and depression." A record 148 students enrolled in Howard College, and another revival brought more student converts into the Baptist and Methodist churches. The board praised the work of the theological students in these evangelistic efforts. "These young brethren, while pursuing studies which exclude them from the active duties of the ministry, have exhibited the spirit of their calling, and have been made a blessing to their young associates." Despite the increased enrollment in Howard College (and in God's kingdom), the financial condition of the institution remained stagnant. For a decade, Samuel Sterling Sherman operated the college on a cash basis and paid faculty salaries from tuition dollars and, as he recalled, appropriated "to my own use what might be left." The financial strains took a toll on Sherman and his growing family. Sherman believed that he could accomplish no more at Howard and needed a more reliable source of income since "an increasing family had higher claims upon me." With little doubt, this prompted his surprise resignation from the presidency of Howard. "We hope," opined the *South Western Baptist*, "that discouragement exercised no influence in causing the resignation though the [economic] facts . . . would seem to warrant the surmise." He purchased property near LaGrange, Georgia, and began a new school, naming it "Brownwood."[5]

Although multiple primary sources pointed to financial reasons for Sherman's resignation, other writers had differing views on the reason for the president's departure. In 1894, B. F. Riley concluded that Sherman left Howard so that a minister could be elevated to the presidency, since the institution "was founded more upon the idea" of theological training than classical learning. Without citations, Riley offers no sources for this claim. It was most likely conjecture on his part. Of the twenty-six students who graduated while Sterling Sherman led the institution (1848–52), only three entered full-time ministry (11.5 percent). No doubt this caused some consternation among those Alabama Baptists who saw little value in a classical liberal arts education and believed Howard College existed only as a vocational training institute for ministers. Nonetheless, the number of graduates entering the ministry under Sherman's successor (1853–61) increased with thirteen of the sixty-one students (21.3 percent). Even so, only 18.3 percent of the graduates of Howard College (1848–61) entered the ministry.[6]

In June 1852, the Howard College Board of Trustees reluctantly accepted Sherman's resignation. "Besides the consciousness of duty performed to the best of my ability," Sherman later wrote, "I enjoyed, as the chief reward of ten years of earnest labor, the confidence and esteem of the public, especially of the citizens of Marion." A few weeks later, members of the board and many of Marion's leading citizens met in the town hall and drafted a resolution. For ten years, Sherman led Howard College with talent, energy, and perseverance, the resolution read. The board and the citizens were indebted to Sherman for the "existence and success" of the institution and his "unwavering fidelity" and self-sacrifice in educating students in liberal arts and moral instruction. Through his efforts, he won the respect, admiration, and endearment of the college and its supporters. "And whilst we lament his loss to ourselves and to our community," they continued, we commend "him to the world as a man of great private worth and high literary and scientific attainments, as a gentleman in every way worthy of confidence, and eminently fitted as an instructor of youth." They presented him with a service of plate and "wishes for his prosperity and happiness wherever his future lot in life may be cast."[7]

While Samuel Sterling Sherman and the board "parted with feelings of mutual regret and esteem," the question of hiring a new president proved to be a simple task. Following "mature and prayerful deliberation," the board unanimously invited Henry Talbird to become the second president of Howard College—this united the presidency and the chair of theology. Continued financial concerns "demanded this arrangement," the board reported, and only after "earnest solicitations" did Talbird agree to serve the college in both jobs. One writer noted in the *South Western Baptist* that, although Talbird had both literary and theological training at one of the nation's most prestigious colleges, the fact that he was a "southern man by birth and interest" made him "well qualified to manage and execute the disciplinary duties of the college." In other words, Talbird was both a slaveholder and a defender of the southern way of life.[8]

Some of the money saved from the unified position was used to hire a new professor of natural sciences—the primary area of instruction vacated by Sherman's departure. In turn, the board hired twenty-two-year-old Noah Knowles Davis. Born May 15, 1830, in Philadelphia, Davis was the stepson of prominent Baptist theologian John L. Dagg, who once declined Howard's chair of theology and later served as president of Mercer University in Georgia. Noah K. Davis graduated from Mercer in 1849 and moved to Philadelphia to continue his study of chemistry for the next three years. While there, he also taught, worked in an architect's office, and edited two textbooks, *The Carpenter's New Guide* and *The Model Architect.*[9]

In the fall of 1852, Davis joined a Howard College faculty that consisted of Talbird (theology and moral philosophy), Amos B. Goodhue (mathematics), Leander Brown (languages), Richard A. Montague (tutor), and J. Appleton Melcher (preparatory). In addition to sciences, Noah Davis also taught English, but his standards were so high that his pupils "worked in vain to win his praise," one former student recalled. Nothing short of the quality of English essayist Joseph Addison was worthy of praise to Davis. In a last act of desperation, a student copied an essay word-for-word from Addison's *The Spectator* and handed it to the professor as an original composition. Davis graded the paper severely and commented that the writer was "pompous," "turgid," and "ridiculous." Many years later, Davis (who was then a professor at the University of Virginia) learned of the student's trickery for the first time and said: "Well, I always had a lingering suspicion that I was a fool, and this confirms it."[10]

Members of the Board of Trustees boasted that the Howard faculty was more "completely organized" than at any time in the institution's history. Board president Isham W. Garrott added that the college's teachers were "all worthy of the fullest confidence as men, as gentlemen, and [as] instructors." For the first time, the college offered language instruction in Spanish and French, in addition to the classical languages. Under Noah Davis's tutelage, a student could study natural science, civil engineering, and applied chemistry in an agricultural context—all as part of a broad liberal arts education. "Any young gentleman," the board reported, "who desires to prepare himself to become a complete and thorough farmer may find help in this Institution which can be found in no other College in the South."[11]

With Henry Talbird's classical training at Hamilton, the new president made no substantial modifications to the Howard curriculum, other than adding more Greek texts: Herodotus, Sophocles, Euripides, and Thucydides. In addition, the college maintained a growing array of equipment. In mathematics courses, students were supplied with a theodolite, compass, chain, leveling staves, and other surveying equipment for classroom instruction and field practice. The "philosophical apparatus" (natural science) was used for experiments to supplement the textbook recitations. Instruction in the "geography of the heavens" (astronomy) included the use of a telescope, orrery, globe, circle, and transit. The chemistry apparatus included minerals and geological specimens for conducting a wide range of experiments.[12]

In Talbird's first year as president, enrollment increased to 148 students, and in the second year (1853–54), the number grew to 152 students. Despite the increases, and a general feeling of optimism, the endowment continued to shrink, and the financial situation left the board angry and frustrated at those Alabama Baptists who refused to honor their commitments to the college fund. "The *only* discouraging feature in your educational enterprise," the board reported to the Alabama Baptist State Convention in 1852, "is the utter failure of all the efforts of your Board to increase the fund for the permanent endowment of the College." The prospects were no better the following year. The history of Howard College, wrote one observer in October 1853, showed that "the almost overwhelming difficulties . . . encountered" were all monetary.[13]

At the Alabama Baptist State Convention in December, the Rev. Samuel Henderson, the firebrand pastor of First Baptist Church, Tuskegee, and chair of the convention's education committee, made a dramatic plea on behalf of Howard College. The institution, Henderson believed, was founded by the "necessity of the times." The Baptists of the state held vast wealth, displayed "intellectual piety," and were honor bound to build a college "which would commemorate to posterity their high appreciation of this sacred interest, and vindicate the claims of the Baptist Church to the confidence of an enlightened public." Along the darkened frontier, it was an imperative to provide proper education to young men, and the thought that this educational endeavor would fail "entered not into the calculation of the projectors of this noble enterprise." James DeVotie and the other founders displayed an "unfaltering trust" in God, intellect, and piety as they moved forward with a "noble self-sacrificing spirit" and built Howard College with a substantial edifice, a sensible faculty, and a "most flattering number" of students. An unbridled spirit of optimism indwelled in everyone associated with the college.[14]

"But alas!" Henderson proclaimed. This changed and now the "whole enterprise" was paralyzed, and the faith, even of the strongest, "staggers under the refluent tide." The truth was sobering. With inaction, Howard College was doomed and would only serve as a malignant memorial to the "folly and imbecility" of the founders and the denomination. Those in the future would look at the college's decaying building and bellow: "Fifty thousand Baptists in Alabama began to build but were not able to finish." It was a picture of fear, Henderson supposed, that would entomb the institution without any hope of resurrection. The pain of failure would be so great that Baptists would hang their heads in shame and "banish all recollection" that Howard College ever stood. Henderson hoped to spare the state this pain and woe, but the question remained: "SHALL HOWARD COLLEGE LIVE OR DIE?" Shall we "preserve and protect" the institution or go backwards, sacrifice the work of the last dozen years, "fold our hands, sit down in inglorious ease and indolence, and permit that enterprise to fail?" He hoped that, for generations, Howard would send forth "enlightened, educated, and efficient" graduates and that the college would stand as a "substantial and enduring monument" of our Christian benevolence. "Shall we be frightened into imbecility by the first storm that impends over the work of our hands?" Henderson asked. Shall this institution "languish and die" from want? The answer should be "No! no! no!" The time was ripe, he believed, to make one last attempt to save Howard College from "utter and hopeless ruin" and the denomination from "merited disgrace." The time was now to summon new energy and pray to God "whose sacred cause we have consecrated the enterprise."[15]

The success of Howard College—through educational training for both ministers and the rising generation in general—would determine the future of the Southern Baptists in Alabama. Henderson believed that the state's Baptists practiced the Christian "faith in its purity, as it was once delivered to the saints." This faith, he emphasized, was destined to spread throughout the world by benevolent men of character, virtue, and intellect—the type of men being educated at Howard College. The impact of Howard boys was being seen throughout the state. In the summer of 1853, Henderson said, the labors of these students led to the conversion of more than three hundred souls. "Such a seal of the divine approbation upon the enterprise, we trust will not appeal to our Churches in vain," he concluded.[16]

Following this appeal, the convention unanimously appointed Samuel Henderson as agent of Howard College and tasked him with collecting funds at a salary of $1,600 per year. Henderson was met with a "liberality as great as could have been expected" as he canvassed the state and collected over $10,000 in subscriptions. "All the circumstances considered," the Board of Trustees reported in 1854, "probably no agent was at any previous period more successful." The large sum revealed a strong desire on the part of Alabama Baptists to support and sustain the college, the trustees supposed. This called for the appointment of a full-time agent who would stay in the field until he raised enough money to fully endow Howard College. "Giver of all good," president of the board Isham W. Garrott prayed, "that the Howard College shall no longer have a doubtful and precarious existence." Only through tragedy, however, did the college's finances improve.[17]

Each day at 9 p.m., Henry Talbird checked the third and fourth floors of the Howard College building to make certain each student was in his room. On Sunday, October 15, Talbird paid his routine visit and, seeing nothing out of the ordinary, retired for the evening. Near 11 p.m., a physician strolled by the building and noticed a light shining through a window on a lower floor. He gave no other thought to the sight and continued walking, unaware that a small fire was burning at the bottom of the stairway. The flames moved quickly up the dry resinous pine stairs. Several minutes later, theological student James C. Wright, who lived on the third floor in room 13, was awakened, "not by friendly hands," he recalled, "but by suffocation." Wright jumped from his bed and opened the door to see the stairway—the only way out of the building—engulfed in a firestorm. The flames burned away most of his hair as he pushed the door shut and awakened his roommate. Nearby, a few students began to stir, but others still slept.[18]

Also asleep in the building was the college's custodian, Harry, a twenty-three-year-old enslaved by Henry Talbird. Harry, who lived in a small room adjacent to the president's office, dashed up the burning stairs and ran through the hallways, shouting and banging on the doors to the dormitory rooms. When told to flee for his life, Harry reportedly said, "Not till I wake up the boys." When Harry finished warning the boys, he found himself trapped at the end of the hallway on the top floor with no way out. Badly burned, he jumped from a window and tumbled to the ground, critically wounded. Witnesses reported that Harry was delirious in the moments before his death, saying over and over: "I can get out, but I must wake up the boys."[19]

By midnight, the ringing of the college's bells and the cries of fire roused the slumbering residents of Marion. John Blandin, a member of the Judson faculty, recalled that people around town "seemed to take the alarm calmly" and assumed that the Howard students had time to evacuate the building, "but such was not the fact." The only means of escape was by a perilous leap from the high windows. Out they went; one-by-one; falling to the ground far below. One student reportedly jumped from a third-floor window, hit the ground unhurt, hopped up, and proclaimed that he would "whip the scoundrel that set the . . . fire." Others sustained broken bones in their frightful leaps and crawled away from the burning building, while students with the most serious injuries were dragged away by citizens who gathered at the scene. When Blandin arrived, he found burned students "mangled and bruised and broken" who were "crawling or hobbling, and uttering . . . frenzied cries." The scene, he wrote a few hours later, "was far more horrible than anything I have before witnessed."[20]

Richard Montague, a tutor and an 1852 graduate of Howard, rescued three boys with a ladder borrowed from a neighbor, but Montague's lungs were so damaged by the smoke, he would suffer from severe breathing problems until his untimely death a few years later. In room 13, James Wright lowered his panic-stricken roommate out the window and onto a long wooden plank leaning against the building. He slid to safety, but Wright remained trapped in the burning room. In desperation, he threw two beds to the ground and leaped from the window. He sprained his ankle upon landing. "Such was my escape," he wrote a few days later. "I thank God for his mercy and saving power." Nearby, Anderson Talbert in room 14 was not so fortunate. Overcome by the dense smoke and intense heat, Talbert was unconscious on the floor of his room. Professor Noah Davis led a desperate effort to reach the student in time. According to a second-hand account written by Rev. A. C. Dayton in November 1854, Davis used a ladder to climb to Talbert's room, but when he entered, the window shut behind him. "A fearful thrill of horror froze the hearts of those who from below witnessed the good deed," Dayton wrote. "Few doubted but that they were lost. Some wrung their hands in silent anguish. Some groaned and shrieked aloud. Some stood and gazed with big tears streaming down their faces, unable for an instant to turn away their eyes from that window which held them like a spell." But Davis kicked out the window and lowered Talbert to safety.[21]

The *Marion Commonwealth* reported that twenty-two of the twenty-five students living in the building were injured, including three with severe burns, six with mangled legs or arms, and those with a variety of bumps and bruises. In addition, Professor Leander Brown was badly injured, as was Richard Montague. The enslaved Harry died on October 16, just a few hours after warning the boys of the deadly fire. Following a funeral service at Siloam Baptist Church (where Harry attended), he was buried on the far edge of the white cemetery—a few years later, a prominent marble memorial was placed on top of his grave. Following a full investigation, a committee led by faculty member Amos B. Goodhue believed that the fire began in the stairwell in the basement or the first floor, "but from what cause the committee was unable . . . to come to any conclusion." Others agreed that the fire's origin was a mystery. James Walker, writing in the *South Western Baptist,* argued that the fire was a spontaneous combustion of several kegs of oil-based paint stored in a closet under the stairs. "There was no doubt," he added, "that this was the origin of the fire." Writing in the *Tennessee Baptist,* Rev. Amos Cooper Dayton agreed that the fire began due to spontaneous combustion, not from the paint cans but from rags saturated with paint and linseed oil left in a heap on the floor of the closet—a phenomenon well known by scientists and the public at the time. The *Montgomery Journal* reported that, following a thorough investigation, the "act of an incendiary" was ruled out. "The innocence of some persons who were suspected of having fired the building," the paper concluded, "was fully established."[22]

Nonetheless, a self-described eyewitness to the blaze claimed that a disgruntled student set fire to the Howard building. According to this anonymous writer, school was only in session for a week or so when students threatened to beat sophomore Judson Mercer Archer for stealing money. Soon afterwards, while the fire burned that midnight, a student (identified only as one of the Johnson brothers) recognized Archer, who was still dressed in his Sunday clothes, hiding behind a tree, and watching the gruesome scene. When this news reached the trustees, several board members traveled to Archer's house and confronted him with the accusation. At first, he denied starting the blaze, but when they brought up stealing the money, Archer supposedly confessed. The vengeful young man set fire to paper in the closet under the stairs in hopes that the "boys couldn't get out" and that "they would all die." The trustees decided against prosecuting Archer, however, because of his age, but demanded that he leave town. If he ever returned to Marion, they promised to see him hanged.[23]

Whatever the cause of the fire, the building, the scientific equipment, the "cabinets of curiosities," the libraries of the two literary societies and the president, and the students' personal possessions were all lost. The injured boys were invited into the homes of citizens throughout Marion to recuperate, but Anderson Talbert's injuries, especially the damage to his lungs from smoke inhalation, were too severe, and he died on November 9, 1854.[24]

Within a few weeks of the fire, the people of Marion (and other donors from the vicinity) pledged almost $20,000 to rebuild the college. Howard, the Board of Trustees reported, was more than just a brick-and-mortar building, or the curriculum, or the books and equipment, but was "altogether independent of its edifice, and dependent for its existence on the generous, warm hearts of its benefactors." John T. Barron, from the first graduating class, donated a large piece of land a few blocks south of the burned-out ruins of the old building. Professor Noah K. Davis, with his architectural background, drew up the plans for the new campus, which would feature three buildings. Recognizing the deadly design flaw in the old building, Davis designed nondescript dormitories, two stories high, 122 feet long and 50 feet wide; both would flank an administration building which would include a chapel, a library, a president's office, literary society rooms, and classrooms. A writer for the *South Western Baptist* praised the "beautiful specimen of architecture" that he believed would one day become some of the preeminent college buildings in the South. The board hired Larkin Y. Tarrant as the general contractor to build the first two buildings: a dormitory and the administration building. Tarrant relied on enslaved labor (he held sixty slaves in 1855) to prepare the site, to make bricks from local clay, and to construct each of the buildings.[25]

The Board of Trustees lacked the money to construct the second dormitory, however, and the overall financial condition of Howard College continued to worsen. Board members pleaded with the convention to help the institution to achieve the long-suffering goal of a permanent endowment of at least $100,000. They hoped that, with the work of a new agent and the help of God, Howard could establish an enduring foundation. "It shall be what the denomination, if united and determined, can make it," board chairman Isham W. Garrott wrote, "an ornament to the State, a monument to Baptist zeal and liberality in the cause of education, and, with the approving smiles of the Great Redeemer, an instrumentality in aiding to effect the regeneration of mankind."[26]

With the college in ruins both physically and financially, the Board of Trustees and the convention entered a period of reflection on the past and future of Howard College. They discussed three options: to close the school immediately, making note that the people of Marion were too optimistic about Howard's future; allow the institution to limp along for a few more years until the money ran out and then shut the doors; or allow the college to sink into insignificance as a local high school. Rev. H. E. Taliaferro, chairman of the convention's education committee, believed that the "heart and purse" of Alabama Baptists were not with the college. While some, like Basil Manly, attributed Howard's financial difficulties to "downright stinginess" among the state's Baptists, Taliaferro believed that the source of the college's difficulties was owed to the evil work of the "down pulling demon" of "sectional prejudice" and the insulated attitude of individual churches within the convention—something natural to congregationally governed churches. The sectional divisions within Alabama impacted the state's independent-minded Baptist congregations, especially in the northern third of the state, where residents were often alienated from the southern Black Belt counties by geography, class, ideology, culture, and economics. Taliaferro thought these churches abused the independent congregational form of church government. "This infernal spirit," he wrote, sneaked into Baptist communities, however small, and magnified "their territory into the dignity and importance of an empire." These island communities depended upon the "ill-success or downfall of every other interest unpromotive of their own," he supposed, and they needed to hear the trumpet call of truth and turn from their transgressions. "We would go further," the minister proclaimed, "and become exorcist," for if the Holy Messiah would not assist us "against a demon so loathsome and filthy," we would, if Satan would for once, depart from his usual policy, form an alliance with him, and it should be proclaimed to an astonished world that "Satan had cast out Satan."[27]

Taliaferro listed all the "specimens of ranting" (excuses) that he heard from Baptists who refused to support Howard College. Some believed the school had no impact on their communities because it was in Marion; "let them sustain and endow it; they wish it done; it will never do us any good; they can't Marionize me"; Marionites were too self-absorbed, and the town was too "proud, vain, and expensive" to allow outside support. Others wanted to build their own private schools in their own imagined communities or develop public schools for local education. "As long as this feeling exists," Taliaferro believed, "and a tongue given to it, just so long will the College [Howard] remain in a crippled condition and unendowed."[28]

In one last desperate attempt to increase the endowment and save the college, the trustees asked the Rev. James H. DeVotie to serve as financial secretary and agent for the school. The ever-vigilant DeVotie was already raising funds for the school on behalf of the Cahaba Baptist Association. On the Monday morning after the fire, October 16, 1854, DeVotie addressed the pastors at the association meeting at the Pilgrim's Rest Baptist Church in Perry County and announced the "unfortunate and painful" destruction of Howard College, and the injuries received by many of the students. The ministers immediately suspended all business and raised $2,231 in cash and subscriptions to rebuild the college. They also appointed DeVotie as agent to solicit contributions within the counties of the Cahaba Baptist Association, which included Bibb, Perry, Dallas, Green, and Tuscaloosa. Soon afterward, the Howard College Board of Trustees broadened DeVotie's fundraising territory to include the entire state. For fourteen months in late 1854 and throughout 1855, DeVotie rode five thousand miles on horseback to complete what he called the "arduous task" of soliciting funds on behalf of Howard College. He raised almost $40,000, at a time when money was tight and the prospects for the season's harvest looked bleak. This made the year, DeVotie reported to the board, "peculiarly unpropitious for rebuilding [the school] and the endowment of the College, yet the success has been as great as the most sanguine could reasonably have anticipated." After fifteen years of "toiling and begging," one friend of the college announced, Howard had an endowment of almost $80,000.[29]

Perhaps one reason DeVotie found such success along the fundraising trails was due to the resignation of his old critic, Basil Manly, from the presidency of the University of Alabama in 1855. Manly, as one writer observed at the time, was a "mighty magnet" who attracted Baptist boys to Tuscaloosa. "Providence has now hedged up the University and opened the Howard and points our brethren to her consecrated halls with an unerring finger." Manly's departure brought the end of Baptist influence at the University of Alabama—his successor reportedly refused to hire Baptists, leaving the "Methodist and Pedobaptists" to dominate the faculty and administration. This "strange treatment" showed little respect, opined the *South Western Baptist,* to the "large and influential denomination like the Baptists in Alabama from whom nearly one half of the patronage of that College was derived." Those Baptists who previously opposed or ignored Howard College were now willing to provide money.[30]

At the end of 1855, James H. DeVotie resigned his position with the college and later accepted the pastorate at the First Baptist Church of Columbus, Georgia. He left a significant legacy of institution building in Alabama, including Howard College. For the next few years, President Henry Talbird, and alumni, including Washington Wilkes, Z. G. Henderson, John C. Foster, and ministers, like William S. Barton, continued to raise funds for Howard College. In 1856,

Wilkes wrote that he was encouraged by the success of his fundraising. "The Howard is gaining ground," he added, pointing to a much-needed "general interest waking up among the Baptists. This is the very thing needed." Wilkes prayed that one day the college would have 10,000 patrons and a $150,000 endowment. The prophetic young minister was partially correct. Within four years, the "reliable endowment" stood at $209,999.80. This included $161,099.80 for the literary endowment, $45,400 for the theological endowment, and $3,500 of railroad stock.[31]

Nonetheless, the 1855–56 academic year began on an optimistic note for Marion's patrons of Howard College. "The last year was dark, unpropitious, and fatal to the hopes and happiness of friends and patrons," a writer explained in the South Western Baptist. "[T]he present promises fair to turn the darkness into light." The enslaved workers completed construction of the new South Dormitory, and the students moved into their rooms at some point in October or November 1855. The building had twenty-two eighteen-square-feet rooms for students on either side of a ten-foot-wide hallway that ran the length of the building—each with a fireplace and two windows. The dormitory also had recitation rooms that were most likely used for instruction until the "main college edifice" was finished the following year. Once completed, the design of the main building was simple: four columns on a front portico entrance, a clock and bell tower, and large windows with commanding views of the front drive and surrounding fields. The central feature of the inside was a large multistory chapel with a U-shaped balcony capable of seating several hundred people. Also in the main building was the library, containing new books donated by the women's societies in Montgomery and Mobile, a gift of $500 from Colonel Edmund King of Montevallo, Alabama, and $10,000 from Baptists around the state. Professor Noah K. Davis secured a new chemical cabinet and the latest in scientific equipment, including an expensive refractor telescope purchased with money donated by the Ladies' Benevolent Society of Marion.[32]

Although the college reached a measure of financial stability in the late 1850s, enrollment failed to reach pre-fire figures for another decade. On average seventy-seven students enrolled in Howard College each academic year between 1855 and 1860, but the trustees pressed forward on building the North Dormitory, which opened in 1858. With extra space available in dorms, Talbird worked tirelessly to attract more ministerial students, which was met with some success following an offer from wealthy Alabama planter and slaveholder Jeremiah H.

Brown to provide scholarship funds for at least fifty students in theological training at Howard. "I thought this [was] a very generous proposition," wrote one
student in 1858, of "Christian liberality." Upon the recommendation of President
Talbird, a student would receive $250 a year for theological training that covered
all expenses: tuition, books, room, board, and incidentals. A few years later
Brown gave Howard College $25,000 for a second chair of theology to develop
the next generation of ministers. "Much is expected from you," advised one
Alabama Baptist pastor to a Howard College student. "Remember your responsibility. . . . Think, be thorough. Apply yourself diligently." Preach at every opportunity, "but never read a sermon to a congregation." Rely on the Holy Spirit
and be prayerful, decided, firm, and persevere, he added. Seek advice from
"older brethren" and have someone trustworthy critique each sermon. "Our
desire is," the pastor emphasized, "that you and the young brethren of Howard
College may all be more useful in our master's cause, than we have been."[33]

With such a small number of theological students enrolled at Howard, Talbird often took students to small Alabama churches and, as one observer noted,
put them up in the pulpit to preach a sermon. "The only way to learn how to
preach," Talbird believed, "was to preach." One of those students was James
Boardman Hawthorne. A native of Wilcox County, Alabama, the six-foot-four-
inch Hawthorne, with his powerful oratorical skills, offered a commanding presence before a congregation. As Hawthorne became more comfortable in the
pulpit, he partnered with fellow student J. Alexander Chambliss for a "preaching tour" of South Alabama. The tenderfoot evangelists each prepared a dozen
or so sermons and set off on horseback to stir the revival spirit among Baptists
in the region. When the duo exhausted their supply of sermons, they ended
their protracted meetings no matter how high the revival fires were burning.
"They would close it," B. F. Riley later wrote, "and go elsewhere"; no amount
of "persuasion or inducement" could convince them to tarry longer. But at one
church, a pastor's unexpected illness forced Hawthorne, despite his protests, to
stay behind and preach beyond his usual number of prepared talks. "He threw
himself on God," one minister later wrote, and when Hawthorne completed his
additional sermons, at least eighty people professed faith in Christ. Hawthorne
graduated from Howard College in June 1859, and three months later, on September 22, 1859, Hawthorne received his ordination at Friendship Church in
Pine Apple, Alabama, and entered full-time ministry.[34]

5

OUR PECULIAR PROPERTY

A sense of normalcy returned to campus, but the lingering tragedy of the fire re-mained in the memories of everyone. In 1857, the students, with funds provided by the Alabama Baptist State Convention, erected a prominent marble grave marker to commemorate Harry's "noble act" of saving the lives of the students at the cost of his own. It was a great irony that an enslaved man provided a clear model of virtue, benevolence, and faith to the liberty-minded students at How-ard College. Harry's paternalistic enslaver, Henry Talbird, held the dedication on Sunday, so large numbers of the enslaved could attend on the one day of the week that they did not work. The monument was a gleaming white marble obelisk, ten feet high, placed at a perpendicular angle from the tombstones in the rest of the cemetery. The inscription read:

[Front]
Servant of H. Talbird, D.D., President of Howard College, who lost his life from injuries received while rousing the students at the burning of the Col-lege building on the night of Oct. 15th, 1854. Aged 23 years.

[Side]
He was employed as waiter in the College, and when alarmed by the flames at midnight, and warned to escape for his life, replied, "I must wake the boys first," and thus saved their lives at the cost of his own.

[Side]
A consistent member of the Baptist Church he illustrated the character of the Christian servant, faithful unto death.

Funded by Alabama Baptists, this monument was erected by Howard College students to memorialize the enslaved young man named Harry who sacrificed his life in saving white students from a deadly fire in 1854. (Samford University, Special Collection and University Archives)

[Rear]

As a grateful tribute to his fidelity, and to commemorate a noble act, this monument has been erected by the students of Howard College and the Alabama Baptist Convention.

In keeping with the paternalistic nature of some southern white slaveholders, the monument's inscription described Harry as a servant and not a person enslaved by Henry Talbird—the word "servant" suggested that Harry had some freedom of choice about his condition. He did not. He was born into slavery in 1830 or 1831 and lived his entire life as a slave—never knowing any type of freedom. The historical record of Harry remains sparse. In 1850, while Talbird was living in Montgomery, he held seven slaves: a sixty-year-old female, a thirty-year-old male, a twenty-year-old male (probably Harry), a twelve-year-old male, a seven-year-old female, a four-year-old male, and a one-year-old female. It was unknown whether Talbird purchased these slaves or if they were previously owned by his wife, Mary Griffin Talbird. The phrase "employed as waiter" suggested that Harry was a hired laborer who was paid for his service to the college. He was not. Harry was considered to be human property, forced by his slaveholder to serve the needs of the white Howard College boys. In addition, Harry most likely had no choice but to be a "consistent member" of Siloam Baptist Church—most slaves worshiped at white churches under the careful supervision of their masters and white ministers.[1]

One observer suggested that the monument to Harry was intentionally designed to encourage loyalty among the enslaved during a time of heightened unrest and to highlight the paternalistic image of kindly slaveholders (Talbird) in contrast to the tyrannical image of Simon Legree in Harriet Beecher Stowe's *Uncle Tom's Cabin*. A few days after Harry's monument was erected, the *Marion American* newspaper praised the slave for exhibiting "high humanity and courage which does honor, not only to his humble race, but to human nature itself." His devotion, self-sacrifice, and fidelity illuminate the "reciprocal affection between master and servant." Likewise, the *South Western Baptist* applauded Harry's "heroic virtue" of "such noble daring" who deserved to be "chronicled, commemorated, and cherished in everlasting remembrance." More honored than Napoleon or Caesar, his grave, the writer added, was where the good and faithful servant slept as he awaited for the trumpet to sound and arise with the "dignity of a king and priest unto God forever!"[2]

Articles of this type appeared in the proslavery newspapers throughout the South, but other publications pointed out the hypocrisy of the monument to a slave. "This slave, had he escaped with his life" one journalist wrote, "would not have deserved the proprietorship of himself, according to the young men who erect this monument." Ironically, the dedication of the monument came a month following the U.S. Supreme Court's Dred Scott decision in which Chief Justice Roger B. Taney proclaimed that slaves of African descent were "beings of an inferior order and altogether unfit to associate" with whites. "They had no rights which the white man was bound to respect," he wrote, and blacks were simply an "ordinary article of merchandise" and held in slavery "for their own benefit." This irony was not lost on many newspapers in the North. "When one thinks that the noble fellow who sacrificed his life," a writer for the *Pittsburgh Gazette* observed, he had no rights whites should respect and was nothing more than a piece of merchandise like leather, hay, or codfish. "What price was that article of merchandise worth?" the journalist added. "What would it have brought at auction, an hour before it sacrificed itself to save its owner and pupils?"[3]

Just a few weeks after the monument's dedication, and with the new campus nearly complete, Henry Talbird thought, perhaps, that his efforts to rebuild Howard College were complete and tendered his resignation. The Board of Trustees, however, believed that if he left, the result would be "disastrous to the interests" of the college. They requested that he withdraw his resignation. The trustees expressed complete confidence in Talbird's devotion and ability to lead the institution with "zeal and a self-sacrificing spirit." Within a few weeks, Talbird withdrew his resignation and would only resign when he thought it was in the best interest of the institution. Talbird, however, apparently continued to seek a way out of the presidency—so much so that he offered the job to Basil Manly in 1858.[4]

Nonetheless, Henry Talbird returned to Howard College as president and disciplinarian. The "noble old Roman," as he was described, was a tall, stately, and dignified southern man of "magnificent presence" who "commanded all most [sic] universal respect from those who came in contact with him." A writer (perhaps a student) in the *Marion Commonwealth* believed that Talbird was "dearly loved" by almost all of the young men at the college and had "our temporal and eternal interests at heart." Unlike other colleges across the South, Howard College had few reported incidents of misconduct, which brought praise for the students' morality and virtue from the Board of Trustees, faculty, and local newspapers. In fact, the faculty kept the students so busy with classes, studies, recitations—from dawn to dusk—that they had little time for mischief. Out of a mixture of fear and respect, few students dared to challenge the authority of Talbird, and those that did violate the rules were met with severe punishment.[5]

In 1858, one Howard student, Thomas Espy, wrote that the college's rules were "very strict" and that an offender was "never detained, but immediately dismissed" for the "slightest deviation" of the college's rules. He reported to his father that Talbird sent home "several fellows" for violating their pledge (code of honor) or for getting drunk. One of the students dismissed had gone to Selma to a barbecue, most likely a political rally during the 1858 Alabama gubernatorial campaign, and got drunk. "Somehow it reached the ears of the faculty," he wrote, "and the president announced publicly that he was no longer a student of the college. . . . I think it is exactly right, otherwise it would be impossible to have any discipline." As a temperance leader, Talbird had a clear rule on alcohol: "Touch not, taste not, handle not." At some point, apparently, Perry County convened a grand jury to investigate who was selling whiskey to the students at Howard College. Henry Talbird hand delivered the grand jury's subpoenas to a handful of Howard students. "That a very few of our number sometimes buy liquor (and perhaps clandestinely)," one student wrote, "we do not deny," but "we pronounce as false" anyone who suggested that Howard was filled with many "habitual drinkers."[6]

Most Howard College students, however, spent most of their hours outside of the classroom participating in one of the two college literary societies, Franklin and Adelphi. For several years, the two societies published the *Howard College Magazine,* which served as a creative blend of artistic expression, moral inquiry, and intellectual pursuits. The students wrote poetry, philosophical essays, short stories, historical papers, contemporary treatises, and humorous anecdotes. Frequently, the magazine published orations from various meetings of the societies, including one by John T. Caine of the Franklin Society entitled "The Honest Gentleman" that revealed his thoughts on the distinctive character traits of a southern gentleman. Most of the southern elite looked to English author Lord Chesterfield and his popular *Letters to His Son* as a guide for a young man's social refinement and conduct. For their sons, as one historian argued, the wealthy southern planter class "valued a reputation of social refinement over all other attributes." John T. Caine, however, argued that gentlemen were principled, dignified, and polite, but he was "no Chesterfield." He was "urbane and affable," but he was "no fawning sycophant."[7]

Caine listed six character traits of a gentleman—each reflecting one of the principles of faith, virtue, benevolence, and intellect: (1) *Virtuous principles and honorable (benevolent) sentiment;* "The true gentleman is honest from an innate love of virtue," he wrote, "and an earnest desire for the welfare of society." (2) *Complete devotion to the truth;* Caine described the truth as the "crowning virtue" of a gentleman and his "chief glory to bear along with him, this talismanic virtue, this proud emblem of Divinity." (3) *A stable character;* he believed that character was the foundation of virtue—where a person with principles of justice and honor "expanded by the generous precepts of wisdom and justice, of honor and religion," of intellect and aspirations, would stand at the "pinnacle of virtue" as a moral hero." (4) *High bearing and benevolence;* Caine saw this as the true honor to live by and not the false standard of honor which was "fanciful and grotesque." This false honor, he added, was formed by an illogical pattern, dictated by "false conceits and incongruous whims," and aroused by a "storm of passion about some imaginary slur or trivial jest; staking his reputation upon a sickly thought, or a petty innuendo; standing up, in short, to be shot at for a supposed injury or insult." This was the stylish man of honor, but low character—a duelist who lived by his guns and not his intellect. He was yet to learn that the "contest" of the nineteenth century was an "intellectual one."[8]

In contrast, a true gentleman of honor, Caine argued, was honest, frank, generous, courageous, bold, studious, moderate, forgiving, wise, and judicious. He exhibits (5) *a delicate regard for the feelings and character of others;* the honest gentleman was polite, gentle hearted, selfless and modest. And he (6) *cultivates a genuine devotion to his friends and to his country;* Caine wrote that sacred friendships were seldom seen any longer (Ruth and Naomi, Jonathan and David, Nisus and Euryalus, Damon and Pathos), and equally rare was the "self-sacrificing devotion" which prompted "men to give themselves up, soul and body to the cause of their country." From ancient Greece (Aristides and Phocion) to Rome (Cato and Camillus) to England (Hampden and Sydney) to America (Washington) was a line of gentlemen who put country before selfish ambition. "Have we any such spirits among us? Are the days of generous patriotism departed?" Caine asked on the eve of the Civil War. Political prospects were barren, but a "noble sentiment" still burned in the hearts of citizens which may yet burst into a "magnificent blaze of patriotic devotion."[9]

Caine's optimism, however, was soon dashed as the long-simmering issue of slavery reached a climax during the presidential campaign of 1860. A few weeks after the publication of Caine's oration, the Democratic Convention met in Charleston, South Carolina, on April 23, 1860, where the Alabama delegation led the other Deep South states out of the convention over the issue of the federal protection of slave property in territories. The deeply divided Democratic Party split into factions over the issue and nominated two candidates, Stephen A. Douglas and John C. Breckinridge; a compromise former Whig Party candidate, John Bell, ran on the Constitutional Union ticket; and the Republican Party, which wanted to prohibit slavery in the territories, nominated Abraham Lincoln.[10]

The 1860–61 academic year began with sixty-two students and seven faculty members: Henry Talbird (moral science, pastoral theology, and ecclesiastical history), Amos B. Goodhue (mathematics and natural philosophy), David G. Sherman (Latin), William A. Parker (Greek), Thomas W. Tobey (intellectual philosophy and systematic theology), Edward Quin Thornton (chemistry and natural history), and William C. Ward (mathematics and ancient languages). Campus facilities were complete, and a women's group in Marion raised $1,400 to enclose the campus with a fence and beautify the grounds. The board reported an endowment of $278,900. The number of ministerial students grew to record numbers, and Rev. Thomas Tobey, a Rhodes Island native and former missionary to China, joined the faculty. But then, as Benjamin F. Riley wrote a few years later, "the time for strife had come."[11]

When Lincoln won the November 1860 election, southern states moved toward secession. Meeting less than a week later, the Alabama Baptist State Convention, led by President Henry Talbird, unanimously approved a resolution written by Basil Manly. They spoke not for individual churches, but as men, citizens, and Christians who loved their country and recognized that the union of states had failed. The federal government was no longer protecting "our peculiar property [slaves] recognized by the Constitution—we can no longer hope for justice . . . or safety." Although Alabama had not yet declared secession, the ministers affirmed their willingness to submit "to the call of proper authority in defence of the sovereignty and independence of the State of Alabama, and of her right, as a sovereignty to withdraw from this Union" and make a new covenant to secure the rights of slaveholders.[12]

In state politics, Alabama governor Andrew B. Moore of Marion called a secession convention in Montgomery on December 24. Two days later, at Howard College, students passed a resolution that, if the Union dissolved through secession of slaveholding states, they would be ready to "obey the call of *our section of the country,* or to aid in repelling any assaults made upon" the South by an invading force. On January 11, 1861, the convention voted in favor of secession. Following the vote, secessionists celebrated the formation of the independent republic of Alabama, with hopes of forming a new confederacy of slaveholding states. As revelers lowered the American flag over the Alabama capitol and hoisted the new Alabama flag, one opponent of secession wept as he watched and later warned of the impending storms and that he could "not see how we are to pass through them."[13]

With the firing on Fort Sumter in South Carolina on April 12, 1861, the war began. That same day, John B. Mynatt, a junior classical and theological student from Talladega, sat down and composed an article for the *Baptist Correspondent* newspaper, published on April 27. Mynatt argued that the "fruits of sin" that could be seen in the actions of men revealed the reality of a nation falling apart. For Christians, prosperity, religious zeal, brotherly love, and peace have been replaced by disruptions, divisions, strife, and envy, he added. Quoting the prophet Jeremiah, Mynatt proclaimed that the "people have forgotten the Lord" during these days of strife. This was the sad reality of the present crisis. "Whence is the cause and what is it?" he asked. "It is the effect of error to the hearts and minds of the people" who allowed Satan to work "evil in the midst of the people professing God's name." Mynatt's remedy to the problem was to engage the "hearts and minds" of the next generation as a reminder to the leaders of the day that, if they were filled with God love, "how soon would the present public disturbance be quelled and we as a nation, enjoy again the sweets of harmony and peace."[14]

War, not peace, was on the mind of most of Mynatt's fellow students, and the administration found it "impossible to restrain them" from volunteering for military service. By the end of the term, forty-two out of sixty-two students and three faculty members (William A. Parker, William C. Ward, and Edward Quin Thornton) joined the army of the South. Earlier in the second term, the Board of Trustees proposed the creation of a military department at Howard College to teach students the disciplines of military life and tactics—although some board members questioned whether military and ministry training were compatible. Regardless, the board believed military training was important because, following the South's "emancipation from Northern oppression," it would be Howard College's "duty to contribute our part in fitting our young men for this responsible work."[15]

Throughout 1861, students from all across the country left colleges and academies to fight in one army or another. Several Howard College students enlisted on April 24, 1861, as members of Marion Light Infantry, also known as the Marion Dragoons, under the command of Edwin D. King's son, Porter. On May 2, they were officially organized as Company G of the Fourth Alabama Infantry Regiment; by June they were in Virginia, marching through the streets of Harpers Ferry, displaying the new hand-painted company flag hand-delivered from Marion—nicknamed the "cotton flag" for its display of a cotton bale and bloom. War was hard on schools, one writer noted in the *South Western Baptist* of May 16, 1861, "but they have educated us a noble generation, serviceable for the times. Don't be discouraged, good friends; your faculties and school-rooms will all be wanted soon. A better day is coming." That day never came. During the summer of 1861, the Dragoons fought with the regiment at the first battle of Manassas (Bull Run)—a southern victory that foretold the large bloody battles to come.[16]

At Howard College, the professors continued to hold classes for fewer and fewer students. In early June 1861, just weeks before graduation, Henry Talbird turned the leadership of the college over to Amos B. Goodhue and joined the Confederate Army as captain of Company K, Eleventh Alabama Infantry Regiment. Talbird marched off to war with a Bible, a sword, and an umbrella. His regiment traveled to Virginia, joined the Army of the Shenandoah, and spent the summer training near Manassas, but they never participated in the battle. While his troops were training in Virginia, Rev. Talbird visited Howard College students in other regiments and, as he said, shared in the evangelistic "glory of caring" for their souls. Revivals broke out so frequently among southern troops that one soldier observed that they felt like they were at a camp meeting rather than "in the army expecting to meet an enemy." As the children of revivalism, these Confederate soldiers were deeply influenced by the impulses of reform, evangelism, and piety. Talbird described their regiments as "schools of morality and virtue" and seminaries of a growing revivalist spirit. His own Company K, Talbird added, was filled with gentlemen who engaged in orderly conduct. "I speak literally in the truth," he wrote his men during the summer of 1861, "when I say that no case has occurred in which I had to punish one of your members for any improper conduct or breach of discipline."[17]

In August, the fifty-year-old Talbird resigned his command because he had "not enjoyed one day of good health" since he arrived in Virginia and because the Board of Trustees of Howard College refused to release him from his obligations as president. "Allow me, gentlemen," he wrote the men of Company K, "to assure you of the regret I feel in being compelled to leave you. I ask you to believe me when I say that I feel impelled by a solemn sense of duty in pursuing the course which I have."[18]

When the academic year opened in October 1861, Henry Talbird was back at Howard College, where he taught moral philosophy, theology, and military tactics. By the spring of 1862, however, he organized another group of volunteers from Perry County, who joined with other men from West Alabama, and formed the Forty-First Alabama Infantry Regiment. Now with a higher rank in the Confederate Army, "Colonel Talbird's Regiment" was in Tennessee by June 1862. The regiment participated in a few minor skirmishes in Middle Tennessee before participating in the bloody battles in Murfreesboro, where Talbird's men sustained heavy casualties. By January 1863, the colonel was back in Marion recovering from a severe bout of gastroenteritis. "The labor of the last summer and winter campaigns," the *South Western Baptist* reported, "had told sadly upon his constitution." No man in the state of Alabama, the writer supposed, sacrificed more than when he "cheerfully relinquished" his position at Howard College, "bade adieu to his happy home," and joined the service. "Many a pious heart has followed him in his perilous career, beseeching the father of mercy to preserve his valuable life, and to restore him to the institution over which he presided so long and ably."[19]

Henry Talbird, however, stayed away so long from his regiment that officials charged the minister with being absent without leave (AWOL) and ordered him to appear before a board to testify as to his fitness and competence to serve in the army. Records suggest that Talbird left Marion in April 1863 to return to his regiment in Tennessee, but instead found himself admitted to Newsom Hospital in Chattanooga. From the hospital he pleaded his case against the charges. "It is simply ridiculous to charge me," Talbird wrote General Samuel Cooper. "I respectfully tender my resignation unconditional and immediate on the ground of disease alone."[20]

While Talbird waited for a reply, the poor conditions in the hospital only prolonged his illness as the months of suffering caused his weight to drop from 210 to 165 pounds. There were no changes of clothes for the hundreds of sick and wounded at the hospital, except those periodically sewn by the nurses. The diet consisted of toasted bread, a little butter, and beef tea. "One of our greatest trials," one Newsom nurse wrote at the time, "is want of proper diet for sick men. We do the best we can with what we have." When the board of examination evaluated Henry Talbird, they accepted his resignation and declared him unfit for field service due to his age and health. When he was well enough to travel, he would return to Marion.[21]

As Talbird remained hospitalized in Tennessee, Confederate officials looked for new hospital facilities in western Alabama—far away from the fierce fighting in and around Vicksburg, Mississippi. In May 1863, they selected Marion and the campus of Judson College for the site of the new hospital. With Judson still holding regular classes for over two hundred young women, President Noah K. Davis objected to the plan and pointed to Howard College, his old school down the long dirt road, as a better location. With the two dormitories mostly empty, the trustees agreed to rent the buildings to the Confederate government for use as Breckinridge Hospital, presumably named for Confederate General John C. Breckinridge—a former vice president of the United States and a presidential candidate in 1860. It was later simply called "General Hospital."[22]

On campus, Howard faculty members Amos B. Goodhue, who served as de facto president, and David Sherman were nearing completion of the 1862–63 academic year with some fifty-six students, the majority from Marion. As the institution began its transition from college to hospital, the trustees suspended classes for a time, but two students still graduated in the class of 1863: Henry Harrell and David P. Goodhue—they would be the last to graduate Howard until 1866. Nonetheless, the latter's father, Amos B. Goodhue, was retained by the trustees as the sole faculty member to "take charge of the main building, with its contents, library, apparatus, cabinet, furniture, etc., to protect them from injury, and also to afford instruction to such students as might apply for it." Twenty-seven boys received instruction from Goodhue during the 1863–64 academic year.[23]

When the wounded and dying soldiers filled the two Howard dormitories, the hospital expanded into the main building; when that filled, they pitched tents on the college campus. "I found the Hospital to be like all the rest," one wounded soldier wrote, "a most disagreeable place to be." Men in the hospital were treated for wounds and a host of diseases: diarrhea, asthma, mumps, pneumonia, scabies, fever, typhoid, syphilis, gonorrhea, cholera, hemorrhoids, rubella, gangrene, ulcers, and others. Medicines included Hope's Mixture, muscadine tea, boneset tea, morphine, opium, and whiskey—the latter was the most prescribed medicine in the hospital, which accounted for the large consumption of hard liquor on the Baptist campus.[24]

While these wounded Confederate soldiers received adequate care in Marion, others were less fortunate, especially prisoners of war held in makeshift camps in the northern states. Former Howard College student John Moore was confined to Johnson's Island Prison on Lake Erie in northern Ohio in 1864 in what he described as a "land of strangers." Moore attended Howard College in the 1840s, later graduated from the University of Alabama, and practiced law in Marion before the war with Howard trustee Isham W. Garrott. When captured by Union troops at Big Shanty, Georgia, Moore was serving as a lieutenant in the Fortieth Alabama Infantry. In Ohio, he found the prison conditions bleak, and, in desperation, he wrote to the northerner who taught him the importance of benevolence, Samuel Sterling Sherman. Following Sherman's departure from Howard College in 1852, he ran his own academy in Georgia for three years, before returning to Marion in 1855 to serve as president of Judson College. With the coming of the war, Sherman resigned in 1859, sold his slaves, and moved north, "far from the seat of trouble possible," where he lived quietly and raised his children. In 1864, Sherman was living in Milwaukee, Wisconsin, when the first letter arrived from John Moore. "I trust," Moore wrote on July 6, 1864, "that the Kindly relations & friendship existing between us during your long residence in Marion will be a sufficient excuse for me calling on you *in this time of need* for assistance."[25]

For the next three months, John Moore wrote Samuel Sterling Sherman a series of letters asking the former Howard College president to send money, food, clothes, and newspapers. Without question, Sherman fulfilled Moore's every request. When the weather grew cold, Moore asked Sherman to send him winter clothes: common heavy wool gray pants, a button-up-to-the-throat gray vest, a pair of lace-up heavy-soled shoes, and a carpet bag. He also requested that "Mrs. S." send along a can of fruit preserves and other small delicacies. As the packages came to the prison, Moore opened each one with the excitement and pleasure of a child opening a present on Christmas morn. Moore praised Sherman's willingness to alleviate the suffering of those affected by the cruel war. "Such Kindness can never be forgotten," he added. John Moore was not alone in receiving the generosity of Samuel Sterling Sherman, who apparently

Between 1842 and 1887, pastors of Siloam Baptist Church (seen here in 1861) served the spiritual needs of Howard College students and faculty. These ministers included James H. DeVotie, William H. McIntosh, Edwin T. Winkler, and Augustus C. Davidson. (Samford University, Special Collection and University Archives)

assisted other Howard College prisoners at Johnson's Island and at Camp Douglas near Chicago.[26]

In his letter, Sherman asked Moore to share the latest about Marion: Noah K. Davis was resigning as president of Judson; Isham Garrott and E. D. King were dead; Rev. William McIntosh, who succeeded James H. DeVotie as pastor of Siloam Baptist Church, married for the fifth time; Julia Barron looked "as well as ever," and her son, John, was practicing medicine; Henry Talbird was there, discharged from the hospital, and "broken down in health from exposure" while in the army; and Amos Goodhue was doing well running Howard College and maintaining "his high position in the public estimation." Moore believed that, if Sherman visited Marion, he would "scarcely recognize the place" with all the changes in population and social dislocation during the war years. Most of the older citizens had retired and withdrawn from public life, and the town was filled with strangers—mostly refugees from Mississippi and North Alabama.[27]

By October 1864, Moore gained his freedom through a prisoner exchange and returned to his family in Marion—pledging never to take up arms against the United States again. In Marion, the mood of the town was dark. Most young men were gone; many would never return. "There is scarcely a family which has not lost one or more of its numbers," Moore wrote. Every Sunday, the congregation at Siloam Baptist was made up of women and "old gray-headed men . . . all clad in the habiliments of grief." This was the "sad and melancholy" effect of war.[28]

At Howard College, the trustees decided against holding regular classes during the 1864–65 academic year and instead charged Amos B. Goodhue with teaching the sick, wounded, and disabled Confederate soldiers who were "desirous of educating themselves for future usefulness." One trustee visited the "College Hospital" in March 1865 and "saw nearly a hundred students on the grounds, representing every state in the Confederacy." Goodhue, with the help of his son David, taught 125 students during the five months Howard served as a wounded soldier school.[29]

As the war neared an end in April 1865, Confederates evacuated many of the injured men from the Howard College buildings and officially abandoned the facility—although some wounded and crippled soldiers remained. The college's Board of Trustees complained that the southern armies simply gave the buildings to the conquering northern forces, specifically several companies of soldiers of the Ninth Minnesota Infantry under the command of Colonel Josiah Marsh and Lieutenant Colonel William Markham. Markham was a hard-living New

York native who served previously on a whaling ship, participated in the California gold rush, fought in the Mexican War, and battled Native Americans on the Minnesota frontier. During the Civil War, he gained a reputation as a fearless fighter and an impudent and hard-drinking soldier who knew how to command men. He was working as a bricklayer in Rochester, Minnesota, when the Civil War began, and he organized one of the first companies of volunteers to fight from the state. In 1863, he was kicked out of the Union Army for excessive drunkenness but was reinstated by Secretary of War Edwin Stanton.[30]

The Minnesota Ninth reached Marion on Saturday May 20—almost six weeks after General Robert E. Lee surrendered the Army of Northern Virginia to Union General Ulysses S. Grant. Just before entering the town, one soldier remarked, "Oh what a beautiful country this would be if not disgraced by slavery." Although skirmishes occurred across central Alabama after Lee's surrender, these Minnesotans were the first Union troops to reach Marion. "It was a very pretty little place," a soldier wrote, but "the people were not gratified at our arrival."[31]

Some white residents met the blue coats with what Lieutenant Colonel Markham described as a cold bitter reception. Marion's white citizens were "just as rebellious at heart to-day as they were four years ago. It does me good to see them pass under the stars and stripes." Marion, he believed, was "one of the most bitter [towns], if not the very most, in the entire South." On Sunday morning May 21, several of the Union soldiers and officers attended a local church service, much to the embarrassment and chagrin of the congregation. "There was not too many Hallelujahs at that meeting," one soldier quipped. That afternoon, freed slaves flocked to Marion with "hearts . . . overflowing with joy" to embrace their Union liberators. The freedmen were "ready to die for a Yankee, the whole of them," William Markham believed. "They bring us all kinds of fruits, vegetables, chickens and everything else that they have any idea we can make any use of." Soon, however, necessity forced the freedmen to look to the Union troops to feed, clothe, and house them.[32]

Several members of the Ninth bivouacked on the campus of Howard College and set up a commissary to feed both Union soldiers and hungry former slaves. While troops lived in tents or makeshift huts on the college grounds, the freedmen that gathered nearby were allowed to sleep in Howard's main building and a dormitory. The other residence hall continued to serve as a hospital and provided care for the remaining "large number of maimed" Confederate soldiers and the sick and wounded Union troops. Following years of marching and fighting, the men of the Ninth found the occupation of Marion a nice change of pace. "Our duty here consisted of taking it easy," wrote one soldier, "and enjoying the fruits of a well-earned rest. Aside from seizing all the cotton that could be found and shipped by rail, the regiment had no particular duty to perform." Cotton remained a valuable commodity and could bring high prices at market or among thieves and black marketers. The Ninth's commanding officer, Colonel Josiah Marsh, gained an "infamous reputation" for the illegal sale of cotton and profited enough to purchase two nearby plantations. Following his discharge, Marsh returned to live in Marion for a time, before selling his land and returning to the Midwest. The presence of the wounded soldiers in late May suggests that the hospital continued to operate after Confederate officials left the facility and may explain the statement of an elderly Black woman who claimed that John T. Barron served as the head of the hospital for a time.[33]

By late July 1865, Marsh and the men of the Ninth marched out of Marion to begin their long journey to their homes in Minnesota. The town's new occupying force, the Eleventh Missouri, under the command of Colonel Eli Bowyer, arrived in Marion to find the summer sun unmerciful and the land parched from a worsening drought. The regiment's doctor, Thomas S. Hawley, wrote that all of Marion was consumed by a dust cloud as "fine as flour; flowing into everybody's eyes, ears, nose & mouth; penetrating into the most secluded nooks & cranny of these abodes." Tempers and tensions were also hot among the gruff, unruly, and disgruntled soldiers of the Eleventh. The men were anxious to return home. "I almost fear," the doctor added, that "sometimes they will rebel and go anyhow." Some did. The desertion rate for the regiment was high, and those that remained in Alabama were insubordinate and, at times, violent.[34]

The Freedmen's Bureau (the government agency charged with providing relief to the former slaves and impoverished whites) reported that Union soldiers in Marion were beating and robbing local freedmen, including one incident where a Black man was shot for refusing to sell a soldier liquor. The town's residents, both Black and white, feared the soldiers from Missouri and saw no benefit to their presence. At the time, Dr. Thomas S. Hawley agreed that the presence of the Eleventh Missouri in this "distracted land" made little difference in the restoration of a civil law in Marion. "Every man fears his next neighbor," he wrote. "Law and order has given place to chance and anarchy. Thieves mature their plans at daytime and carry them into effect at night. I never saw or heard of such a state of things."[35]

In September, the mutilated body of a Union soldier from the Eleventh was found near the Cahaba River—suspicion for the crime fell on a man identified as just "Williams." When arrested and brought to the Perry County jail in Marion, Williams was carrying the soldier's watch, pipe, and wallet. The prisoner asked to remain in the custody of the Union soldiers and was sent to the "College Hospital" for safekeeping. During the night, persons unknown attacked the guard and seized Williams, who was taken behind the main college building, beaten, and then hanged from the limb of a tree near the soldier's graveyard.[36]

Inside the main college building, as many as three hundred former slaves lived until most were hired out for work; by September only around forty or fifty remained. The Howard College Board of Trustees protested the use of the property for freedmen. "As was foreseen," the trustees reported, "this resulted in serious damage to the building, and has added to our loss the cost of repairs." The board failed to mention, however, that the buildings and campus property also received extensive damage from their various uses as a hospital, commissary, detention facility, and a soldiers' burial ground. In response to the complaints, the commanders of Union forces in Marion removed the last of the former slaves and returned the Howard College property to the trustees, but the U.S. district marshal threatened to confiscate the property. Ultimately, the marshal's office abandoned the effort, but the college still faced an uncertain future. So too did the rest of Alabama.[37]

6

A WILD AND STORMY SEA
OF DISORDER

"No pen," wrote one Baptist historian, "can properly describe the wild chaos which prevailed in Alabama just after the close of the war." The economy collapsed, and money was in short supply. Slavery was gone. In 1865, the crops failed from lack of seed or drought. Union soldiers confiscated and burned or sold stored cotton across the state. Many poor whites and Blacks struggled to find enough food to eat. Widows and orphans faced an uncertain future. Schools remained closed, and churches locked their doors. Social dislocation stretched across the state as people wandered about, looking for shelter or work. "Reconstruction," historian Robert Weibe wrote, "had guaranteed confusion, disappointment, and recrimination." In Marion, businesses refused to open for fear of looting. At Howard College, a bewildered Board of Trustees pondered anew whether to abandon the institution or begin the long road to revitalization. A writer for the *Religious Herald* wrote that Howard College "probably suffered more than any of our [Baptist] institutions from the war." The endowment was gone. Former students were unable to return. Leaders and benefactors were dead or destitute. The facilities were in disrepair. It was as if the town, the college, the state, and the region had once again returned to frontier days.[1]

But unlike the years of optimism and enthusiasm on the old southern frontier, this new frontier emerged from defeat and despair. During the 1820s and 1830s, settlers and slaves provided order to the Alabama wilderness, but now their sons and daughters, in the 1860s and 1870s, were called upon to reinvent civilization, refashion institutions, and reinstitute law and order. A reconstructed and restored Alabama, one observer wrote, would not be built upon a solid foundation but "upon a wild and stormy sea of disorder." The victorious northerners dictated the terms of this Reconstruction to the defeated southerners during years of military occupation, uncertain peace, and partisan politics.[2]

From Washington, DC, President Andrew Johnson, a Tennessean, believed it was his executive prerogative to set the federal policy for the South's readmission to the Union. He appointed provisional governors throughout the South in hopes of restoring state governments. In addition, Johnson embraced Abraham Lincoln's notions of leniency and forgiveness by offering a pardon to most Confederates who took an oath to "faithfully support, protect, and defend" the Constitution and the Union of states; and to support all laws regarding the abolition of slavery. In Marion, Alabama, as in other areas of the South, occupying Union troops administered the oath to the average men and women who supported the Confederate cause. Johnson stipulated, however, that wealthy southerners (as of 1860) and those who participated in the Confederate government were ineligible to take this simple oath. For these privileged sons and daughters of the South, their only recourse was to apply to President Johnson for a presidential pardon on a case-by-case basis.[3]

Some Alabamians applied for presidential pardons through the state's provisional governor, Lewis Parsons, while others appealed directly to President Andrew Johnson. At times, the process was slow. Longtime Howard College board member William P. Chilton, the law partner of wild-eyed secessionist William Lowndes Yancey, worked through Parsons to secure his amnesty and restoration of his full rights as a citizen. In a July 26, 1865, letter forwarded to Johnson by Parsons, Chilton proclaimed that he was a "peaceable, loyal, useful citizen" who now disavowed his words and deeds during the "late misfortunate struggle." In September, Chilton submitted another request with supporting letters from Georgia governor James Johnson and former Alabama governor Benjamin Fitzpatrick—the latter described Chilton as a man of the "highest moral character and sterling integrity." On October 19, Johnson granted Chilton's request.[4]

Five days later, on October 24, 1865, the president pardoned another prominent Alabama Baptist, Jabez Lamar Monroe Curry, a pugnacious southern patriot, former slaveholder, and member of the Confederate Congress. For Curry, the immediate postwar period was difficult. In April 1865, his wife died, and the war was lost. The following month, Union troops occupied his hometown of Talladega and he was arrested by Union general Morgan H. Chrysler for allegedly supporting the mistreatment of northern prisoners of war and the murder of President Lincoln. Curry rejected the "cock and bull story," and Chrysler released him on "personal parole." In September, Curry learned of a complaint filed in federal court aimed at confiscating his property due to his participation in the war. He later recalled that the complaint left him at the "mercy of as despicable and unprincipled set of adventurers and robbers" that ever "plundered a helpless people." He hired William Chilton to defend his interests against the charges and settled with the ravenous officials for $250. By October, Curry traveled to Washington, DC, and received his pardon from President Andrew Johnson.[5]

Soon after returning to Talladega, Curry journeyed across the state to attend the Alabama Baptist State Convention in Marion, where he listened to the grim reports on the condition of the denomination's churches and institutions. The news from Howard College was especially bleak. Board president W. H. McIntosh reported that Henry Talbird declined to resume his work as the college's president, preferring instead to return to the pulpit. While de facto president Amos Goodhue opened the 1865–66 academic year on October 3 with twenty-four students, federal officials threatened to confiscate the property and close the school. Ultimately, the U.S. government abandoned the effort, but Howard's long-term survival was questionable. Echoing the financial despair of the early years, McIntosh saw three possibilities for the future: (1) abandon the college; (2) let Howard "eke out a weary existence and die by inches"; (3) make a spirited effort to revive and restore. The board president favored the latter strategy. "Is it not easier in the days of our calamity to call an earnest faith to the rescues and lay our plans for the future in reliance upon Him," McIntosh proclaimed, "than to abandon our enterprises, as if the conviction was fixed in our minds that God either will not or cannot deliver us from dangers?" Would the denomination yield to hopelessness and misfortune or display a "noble, Christian manhood" and choose "to suffer and be strong" by rising superior to the depressing tendency of the times?"[6]

Reacting to McIntosh's sobering words, Howard College alumnus Samuel Freeman encouraged the ministers and laypeople at the convention to persevere and "rejoice that misfortune's ruthless hand" would never destroy their desire to further the "noble cause" of education. Through the "fiery ordeal of war" that destroyed the South physically and economically, the southern mind remained steadfast and undeterred along the "path of light and knowledge." Howard College needed a "vigorous and resolute effort" from a bold new leader. "Let us

A firebrand southern nationalist in antebellum Alabama, Jabez Lamar Monroe Curry assumed the presidency of Howard College during Reconstruction and emerged as one of the South's leading proponents of the myth of the Lost Cause. (Library of Congress, Prints and Photographs Division)

select from our brethren," Freeman proclaimed, "a man highly endowed by nature and cultivation for the office of president." The convention would send him forth to dwell among Alabama Baptists as a circuit-riding ambassador of the college who might reconstruct the endowment, restore faith in the institution, and remind them of the value of denominational education. The convention needed no lamp of Diogenes to find this man. "He is already among us," Freeman said. "Let us lay violent hands upon him" and say: "Here, our brother, is the task we commit to your hands. We lay upon you the onus and honor of rescuing this important instrumentality of usefulness to man and glory to God from the dust." Freeman added, "In the name of our God and our cause, we call you to this trust, and we pledge ourselves to sustain you."[7]

In Samuel Freeman's mind, the only hope for the future of the college was Jabez L. M. Curry. Having earlier elected Curry as president of the convention for 1865–66, the delegates agreed to entrust Howard College to the care of the forty-year-old attorney, planter, politician, and Baptist lay member. From his years in public life, Curry developed excellent oratorical skills and political instincts, which he used frequently at Alabama Baptist conventions for over eighteen years. He was well-liked by the state's Baptist leaders and well-known as a spirited reformer who advocated for more educational opportunities for whites and Blacks. Leaders in the denomination, one historian later wrote, considered Curry "a blazing meteor in the dark theological sky of Reconstruction." After several weeks of deliberation, he accepted the position with a salary of $5,000 in greenback currency or $3,000 in gold—a large sum of money for a penniless school located in a region stripped of everything of value. But as a Curry biographer later wrote, these Alabama Baptists clung to the hope that the "resuscitation of their impoverished and prostrate country" rested in the hope of education.[8]

From an early age, Curry recognized the importance of education and developed a love of politics. Born in Lincoln County, Georgia, on June 5, 1825, Curry moved to Talladega, Alabama, with his well-to-do planter family in the 1830s. Following private tutoring in a classical education, the young Curry graduated from Franklin College (now the University of Georgia) in 1843 and moved to Massachusetts to study law at Harvard. While there, Curry listened to speeches from the great orators of the age, including former president John Quincy Adams, education reformer Horace Mann, and "noisy and fanatical" abolitionists Frederick Douglass and William Lloyd Garrison. Upon graduation in 1845, Curry returned to Alabama to read law with Samuel F. Rice, a local attorney in Talladega, and write articles for the *Democratic Watchtower*. The following year, Curry, overwhelmed by feelings of patriotism and a self-described "fool-hearty spirit," traveled to Texas on a romantic crusade to fight in the Mexican-American War. Sickness, however, compelled Curry to return to Alabama, where he settled near Talladega, married Ann Bowie, continued his work with Rice, and gained admission to the Alabama Bar.[9]

Throughout much of the antebellum period, Curry's greatest passion was politics. He embraced the political philosophies of John C. Calhoun—the southern sectionalist and defender of slavery—who Curry once described as a statesman on a par with Aristotle, Edmund Burke, Otto Von Bismarck, and

William Ewart Gladstone. While Curry embraced the centrality of character and virtue in public life, he had no set religious convictions and only attended church services as a social outlet. Curry struggled with his faith, and at times felt the "physical excitements" of the call to Christianity, but he remained an anxious skeptic—a viewpoint that frightened him so much that he once burned a copy of Thomas Paine's *Age of Reason*. Following years of church attendance and having neither a "conviction of sin or a desire for salvation," Curry embraced Christianity in 1846 after witnessing his father's baptism at a revival meeting. The younger Curry brought a fire-eating intensity to his faith and began conducting prayer meetings, delivering exhortations, and teaching Sunday school. He soon emerged as a lay leader in the Coosa River Baptist Association and an education advocate at the state Baptist convention. Curry believed that "evangelical influence" on the intellect, virtue, piety, and character of young people was an essential element of a quality education. Religion, he added, served to chastise, refine, and sanctify education. "Cultivated intellect, unsanctified," he wrote, "is a blind Samson, using its powers for its own destruction." Education should produce more than just scholars, but enlightened Christian men and women.[10]

Susie Curry, J. L. M.'s daughter, was receiving such an education at Judson College in Marion when her father accepted the job at Howard. A widower, the new president along with his son Manly joined Susie in Marion during December 1865, although he would not assume the duties of president of the college until January 1866. During the final weeks of 1865, Curry assisted in ongoing revival meetings at Siloam Baptist Church, where forty souls accepted the gospel message. A newspaper reporter at the meeting observed that Curry worked and preached "with the energy and purpose of Paul"—high praise for a man who gave his first sermon a few months before. After much badgering from other Alabama Baptist leaders, Curry was "over-persuaded" to accept ordination at Siloam on January 28, 1866—a decision he later called a "great mistake and error" because he never received God's calling to be a pastor. Nonetheless, the ministerial ordination provided more opportunities for Curry to speak to audiences about Howard College.[11]

As prescribed by the convention and the Board of Trustees, Curry spent most of his time focused on finances and fundraising—traveling throughout the state, preaching sermons (119 in his first year), addressing prayer meetings, talking to Sunday-school classes, and speaking at revival services, association meetings, and other functions. He touted the virtues of education and the importance of Howard College to Alabama Baptists. He asked for donations and encouraged his listeners to send their sons to the denominational school. At times, Curry preached simple but eloquent sermons in Sunday morning church and made persuasive appeals on behalf of the college in evening services, but often Curry's sermons devolved into political orations on the South.[12]

During these years, J. L. M. Curry became one of the most articulate spokesmen for the myth of the Lost Cause. A phrase coined by journalist Edward A. Pollard in 1866, "the Lost Cause" was an interpretive framework that allowed southerners to deal with military defeat and occupation, and to present a more favorable history of the Old South, the Confederacy, and the Civil War. Historians identified six major tenets of those articulating "the Lost Cause": (1) Secession led to the Civil War, not slavery; (2) enslaved persons were happy and loyal, guided by benevolent masters, and ill-prepared for freedom; (3) the North's industrial advantage led to the South's defeat; (4) Confederate soldiers were examples of virtuous, heroic, and godly men; (5) Robert E. Lee was the greatest example of a saintly hero; (6) the South's women were virtuous, loyal, and "sanctified by the sacrifice of their loved ones." Curry believed that the "purity of our women" was a key ingredient of the "virtue of southern civilization."[13]

For Curry, and other whites of his generation, the Lost Cause provided justification to restore and perpetuate white supremacy. As J. L. M. Curry assumed the leadership of Howard College, he also emerged as an outspoken, yet paternalistic, supporter of educating the formerly enslaved. In 1865 and 1866, the influx of northern educators into the state motivated Curry to encourage white southerners to quickly take control of Black education "on a large scale." As one historian observed, Curry's advocacy would assure that the former slaves would receive a "so-called proper southern education, meaning religious schooling romanticizing race relations during slavery." This would prevent, Curry supposed, Blacks being exposed to the "quarrelsome Northern" educators who could cause the freedmen to "relapse to barbarism, perhaps cannibalism." In Marion, however, Blacks would largely work independently and with northerners to realize their educational goals apart from southern whites. On the one hand, Curry was a strong advocate for educating former slaves, but on the other hand he thought whites should control what was being taught to Blacks.[14]

While Curry promoted Howard College and education in general, he also advocated for honoring the memory of the Confederacy, preserving a distinct southern identity, and rigidly maintaining white supremacy. In one speech, he encouraged his audience to both "preserve the record of the gallant dead" and "train their offspring" in southern values that reinforced traditional concepts of virtue. As historian Charles Reagan Wilson wrote, Curry, and others of his generation, recognized that education in virtue for young southern men and women was the "best protection of southern liberty" during Reconstruction and in the years beyond. Most denominational schools in the South, like Howard College, became "Lost Cause institutions" that reinforced the ideals of the Old South through virtue-oriented instruction. The presidents of these institutions used the same Lost Cause rhetoric that ministers in the region did, "to warn southerners of their decline from past virtue, to promote moral reform, to encourage conversion to Christianity, and to educate the young in Southern traditions." Although he spent little time on campus in Marion, Curry articulated the ideals of the Lost Cause that future Howard College presidents would put into practice.[15]

But in 1865 and 1866, Curry faced the cold reality of another losing cause, Howard College. Across the state, Curry discovered that Alabama Baptists had little or no money to contribute to the college; other needs were more pressing. During Curry's talk at a church in the East Alabama hamlet of Opelika, he discovered the congregation had no Sunday school because they lacked a stove to keep the building warm. Curry immediately shifted his appeal for money from the college to the church, grabbed the nearest hat, and walked among the brethren to collect donations. After presenting the church with twenty-five dollars for a stove, he returned to the podium and proceeded with his talk on Howard College.[16]

On campus, the buildings and grounds remained in poor condition, but the venerable Amos Goodhue, with the assistance of his son and returning veteran Edward Quin Thornton, held classes for forty-two students during the 1865–66 academic year. As one observer noted, Howard College opened that fall with "every vestige of furniture gone." Nonetheless, an editorial writer in the *Christian Index & South-Western Baptist* emphasized that Howard was functioning as a "proper college" under the guidance of the elder Goodhue. "There is not a more laborious, painstaking, conscientious, and capable teacher in any institution in the country," the paper added. Modest and unassuming, Goodhue accomplished work "which would ordinarily be burdensome to two men." While theological and ministerial training was no longer an option for students, Goodhue added vocal music for the young men. "It is more than an accomplishment," one observer noted. "It is a source of both mental and moral improvement." Singing also lifted the spirits of the students and faculty during the darkness and uncertainty of Reconstruction.[17]

Perhaps the only joyful memory during these cold wistful days in Marion was a public dinner honoring Samuel Sterling Sherman for his leadership at Howard and Judson, as well as the "beneficence and Christian charity" he showed to the "suffering sons and brothers" held in northern prisons during the war. For white Marion citizens, it was also a time to escape the present and return to a more idyllic time before the war—a romanticized sentiment that many white southerners would cling to during the subsequent decades. On Friday, January 26, 1866, with the entire town "decked out in gala garb," Sherman arrived with much fanfare and delight. A great banquet was prepared in his honor, which included an extensive menu of soups; pork, mutton, beef, turkey, chicken, duck (either smoked, roasted, or baked); fruits and vegetables. In addition, since the banquet was a town event, not just a Baptist affair, the hosts justified the use of vinous beverages (claret, sherry, and champagne). When Sherman asked how the impoverished people of Marion could afford such "wines and delicacies," a resident seemed to suggest that the fare might have been intended for the Union troops who left a few weeks earlier. While Sherman was delighted with the celebration, the atmosphere, at times, seemed more like a repentant political gathering with apologetic speeches that were neither bitter nor vengeful. The irony of the scene, however, was not lost upon Sherman, who recognized that seated with him at the head table were three of Alabama's most rabid secessionists: attorney William McLin Brooks, former governor Andrew B. Moore, and Howard College president J. L. M. Curry. At some point, one young man, perhaps John Moore, showed up wearing the suit of clothes Sherman bought him while he was imprisoned on Johnson Island. He told Sherman that they were still the best clothes he owned.[18]

While Sherman returned to his more prosperous life in Milwaukee, Curry continued his statewide campaign, but by the early summer, the state's economic, political, and social conditions worsened. Across Alabama, crops failed early in the season and thus ended the possibility of Curry finding more money and students for Howard College; nonetheless, he continued his journey to "prepare the way" for the future when prosperous times returned. "Although the financial condition of the college was embarrassed," board president William McIntosh proclaimed, "it was not hopeless." An abundance of hope was all anyone had to give to Howard College.[19]

An unrepentant Henry Talbird blamed these financial woes on the cruel war "ruthlessly waged against us," that only ended with the "downfall of our country." Most all the endowment that Howard College possessed when Talbird marched off to war was consumed in the same whirlwind which devoured everyone's "worldly possessions, except honor." The time was now, the former president exhorted the state convention in 1866, to begin anew the enterprise of Howard College. Although resources were few, expenses great, and the labor hard, rescuing the college would be a "glorious undertaking" which would bring rich blessings to their sons and grandsons. God called each man at the convention, the minister emphasized, to oversee the next generation. "You cannot escape the responsibility," he thundered. "Nor should you wish to escape." If they failed in this endeavor, they would receive a "withering rebuke" for neglecting to provide for their own households. "If you fail here," Talbird continued, "you deny the faith and are worse than infidels." If Howard College was devoured by the whirlwind and the professors scattered from the storm, "ignorance and barbarism" would reign throughout the denomination. "You see, then, dear brethren, that your college must be sustained. Education is a sacred interest."[20]

Yet, even with Henry Talbird's prophetic warnings, neither the money nor the students came. Evangelist Washington Bryan Crumpton recalled that Howard was "little known" around the state and "indifference to general education was rife, everywhere." Even lowering tuition and eliminating entrance requirements attracted no one new. This left Howard with enrollments so low and donations so few that the trustees were unable to pay the salaries of the faculty and president. The board simply issued promissory notes. "Unless the convention shall devise some better plan," the board reported, "we see no alternative but to suspend operations as a college." By the end of the 1867–68 academic year, the board held $10,983.32 of notes due the faculty and president—with the largest amount, $4,330.06, owed Amos B. Goodhue. In turn, the trustees borrowed almost $2,000 to help pay small fractions of each of the salaries.[21]

Adding to the financial uncertainty was the continued political chaos of Reconstruction in the southern states and in Washington, DC. President Andrew Johnson's Reconstruction plan allowed white secessionists to return to power, failed to protect the civil and voting rights of the freed slaves, extended pardons to former Confederates, and provided generous terms for the rebellious states to rejoin the Union. The shortcomings of this presidential plan, combined with the unchanged southern temperament, led to a backlash from congressional

Republicans, former slaves, and southern unionists. "The attitudinal defeat of the Confederacy," observed Alabama historians William Ward Rogers and Robert David Ward, "if ever real at all, lasted for the briefest of times."[22]

During the midterm elections of 1866, northern voters overwhelmingly rejected Johnson's plan by sending veto-proof majorities of Republicans into both the House of Representatives and the Senate. Once in power, they seized control of the Reconstruction process, divided the southern states into military districts, rejected their readmission to the Union without new state constitutions, and attempted to secure civil and voting rights for the freedmen. Years later, Curry expressed a view common to white southerners of his generation that the horrific age of Congressional or Radical Reconstruction was filled with: "duplicity, ignorance, superstition, pauperism, fraud, robbery, and venality." Nonetheless, he encouraged his son, and others, to let go of bitterness, passion, and "cherished hatred" of the North. "To go about shaking our fist and grinding our teeth at the conquerors," he wrote, "dragging as a heavy weight the dead, dead corpse of the Confederacy, is stupid and daily suicidal." The South must leave the "dead past to take care of itself" and live in the present.[23]

Throughout 1867 and early 1868, Curry grew disheartened with the political situation and uninterested in the floundering Howard College. His attitude seemed to be the prevailing mood for Baptists around the state, leading one observer to write that little of "practical value" was accomplished by the denomination during these years. Following a failed attempt to get funding from the Peabody Education Fund for the college, most of Curry's speaking engagements were out of state, where he espoused the importance of education in the South— for Blacks and whites. He spent increasing amounts of time in and around Richmond, Virginia, where he courted and married a woman; the couple left on an extensive honeymoon in Europe before commencement exercises in 1867 and returned over a month after the new semester had begun. With no interest in administering the day-to-day operations of the college in Marion, he continued to articulate the virtues of the Lost Cause, to preach in churches around Alabama, and to find time to publicly oppose the ratification of a new state constitution based on Congressional Reconstruction measures. Although the statewide vote failed to provide the necessary majority for ratification, Congress still enforced the Constitution of 1868 and readmitted Alabama to the Union.[24]

This convinced J. L. M. Curry, as his biographers later noted, to "get away from the ocean of political degradation and misrule" that surrounded him in

Alabama. In 1901, Curry recalled his "deep reluctance" to leave Alabama, but he refused to allow his family to live under "radical misrule" and live in a state "where a generation or more would be needed to recover from the disastrous consequences of the War and hostile legislation." On April 21, 1868, two months before the end of the academic year, he resigned as president of Howard College. "The country was too bankrupt," Curry wrote, "and the political outlook too discouraging to make a continuance of efforts" to raise funds for Howard College. While some of Howard's supporters grumbled that Curry gave too much time to his own personal interests and too little to the college, one alumnus believed that their discontent was due more to their frustrations with Reconstruction, and less about the president's inability to restore the institution. Historian Mitchell Garrett believed that Curry failed to help Howard College for the simple reason that little could be done. "Neither J. L. M. Curry," he added, "or any other southern man could have resuscitated Howard College" during those difficult years.[25]

Although Curry held the title of Howard's president, his duties were that of a general field agent, much like the fundraising work James DeVotie and others had done in the antebellum period. During the 1840s and 1850s, Presidents Sherman and Talbird's duties included teaching, mentoring, disciplining, directing finances, maintaining campus, overseeing faculty, and other unnoticed day-to-day activities. During the war years, Henry Talbird held the title of president but was absent from campus fighting in the army or convalescing at home. For almost seven full academic years (1861–68), Amos B. Goodhue took on the traditional duties of the president during the absentee years of Talbird and Curry. With little support, infrequent pay, and no fancy title, Goodhue sustained the college's intellectual life and kept the institution active during some of its darkest years.[26]

With Curry's abrupt departure, it seemed likely that the Board of Trustees would *formally* hire Amos Goodhue as the next president of Howard College. They turned, however, to another faculty member. History fails to record whether they offered the position to Goodhue. Perhaps he rejected their overtures because of the thousands of dollars in back pay that they owed him and the poor prospects of any future compensation. Regardless, Goodhue soon left Howard, with more than twenty years of service, and joined the faculty at the more financially stable Judson College. Whatever the reason, in July 1868, the trustees offered the presidency to Edward Quin Thornton, the professor of chemistry, natural history, and modern languages. Born on May 12, 1832, in Georgia, Thornton spent his formative years in Eufaula, Alabama, before moving to Tuscaloosa to attend the University of Alabama. A student of geology and natural history, Thornton studied with Professor Michael Tuomey and served as his research assistant on the first geological survey of the state—a significant study which revealed the abundance of Alabama's mineral resources. Following graduation in 1853, Thornton served as the state's assistant geologist and completed a master's degree at Alabama in 1857. He studied geology in German universities and joined the faculty at Howard College in 1860.[27]

With Thornton's selection as president in 1868, the board had no additional means to pay the salaries of the other faculty members and concluded that hiring anyone else was pointless. In turn, the board washed their hands of the matter and turned over Howard's facilities to Thornton "free of rent" on the condition that he make the college self-sustaining and hire and, presumably, pay the faculty. Thornton recognized that, to make the plan work, he needed a minimum of one hundred students to obtain self-sufficiency and cover the salaries—a number not seen on campus in years. Thornton negotiated the number of students down to sixty students, and the trustees agreed to make up the difference and pay full salaries—although it was unclear how those extra funds would be obtained.[28]

The easiest way to attract more students, at least in theory, was to continue the open admission policy. Thornton, however, chose to reinstate rigorous entrance requirements. Students must pass examinations in English language, Latin and Greek grammar, Caesar, Virgil, Sallust's Histories or Cicero's Orations, the Greek reader, and elementary algebra. The postwar classical curriculum differed little from Sherman's instruction a quarter-century earlier. Freshmen read the Odes, Epistles, and Satires of Horace; three books of Xenophon's Anabasis; Herodotus and Thucydides; Mitchell's *Ancient Geography*, Arnold's *Latin Prose Composition*, and other Greek texts; they also studied algebra, geometry, and English composition and declamation. Sophomores read Tacitus, Terence, Homer's Iliad, Zenophon's Cyropaedia, Demosthenes, Bojesen's *Grecian and Roman Antiquities*, Knapp's *French Grammar*, and De Fiva's *Classic French Reader;* they also studied trigonometry, surveying and navigation, analytical geometry, calculus, and English composition and declamation. Juniors read Sophocles and Euripides, Juvenal, Cicero's *De Officio*, natural philosophy, hydrostatics, pneumatics, acoustics, optics, heat, electricity and magnetism, and meteorology; Whatley's *Rhetoric and Logic*. They also studied general chemistry, agricultural chemistry, English composition and declamation. Seniors took courses in zoology, mineralogy, geology, botany, political economy, moral science, intellectual philosophy, and philosophy or rhetoric. In English, all declamations were required to be original.[29]

President Thornton also emphasized discipline and the "strict economy of time." When the bell rang at dawn, students were expected to rise, dress, and recite or study for one hour before breakfast. For the remainder of the day, the faculty regulated all classes, recitations, and recreation. Each month, Thornton sent a report to each student's parent or guardian, showing class standings and numbers of absences from "prayers, recitations, and rooms during study hours." Thornton, the faculty, and the trustees were pleased to see 116 students enrolled at Howard College during the 1868–69 academic year—just enough to provide the other faculty members with modest salaries.[30]

Despite this slight upturn in optimism, Edward Quin Thornton resigned the presidency in the summer of 1869 to return to the classroom, which was "more suited to his tastes." When he announced his intention, Thornton reportedly informed the board, "All I want to do is to teach." The trustees accepted his notice—with regret—and commended him for his efforts. In turn, they promptly offered the position to Rev. Samuel Freeman, whom board president William McIntosh praised as a "gentleman distinguished" for his tact, clear judgement, common-sense wisdom, solid scholarship, and sound theology. "In the vigor of his physical and intellectual powers," McIntosh added, "he brings . . . experience of ripened years, and the discipline of a well-balanced mind."[31]

Born July 5, 1825, in McMinn County, Tennessee, Samuel R. Freeman grew up in a poor, isolated farming community in East Tennessee. The son of a devout Presbyterian mother, Freeman converted to Christianity at a young age and felt the call to the ministry, but he lacked the money to acquire the education needed to become a pastor in the denomination. As a young man, Freeman found work as a hog drover in Tennessee, Alabama, and Mississippi and settled into the unseemly lifestyle of a nomadic herder or "pig boy." His quest for education, however, remained. Freeman recalled driving hogs near the campus of the University of Alabama and longing to be part of "that favored throng" of students. Southerners frequently sang songs and told tales about the legendary hog drovers and pig boys (as opposed to the later cowboys) who herded thousands of piggies to market all over the region. One song's lyrics went, "Hog drivers, hog drivers, hog drivers are we; a courting your daughter so fair and so free." But apparently fathers did not much care for those grunting, stinky, hard-living pig boys. This was not the life for Freeman. In the late 1840s, he moved to eastern Mississippi, joined the Ebenezer Baptist Church near Heidelberg, and accepted ordination in the denomination to gratify "his heart's desire to acquire an education" and to preach. In the fall of 1850, Freeman gathered his meager belongings and rode horseback to Marion to enter Howard College.[32]

A most "unpromising looking specimen" arrived to meet with President Samuel Sterling Sherman. Over six feet tall, muscular, erect, and ruddy faced, Freeman, as one observer noted, had an "indifference to toilet [hygiene]" due to habits formed from his "humble birth, childhood training," and hog droving. The uneducated Freeman had little hope of passing Howard's strict entrance requirements, so Sherman assigned the twenty-five-year-old student to the sub-freshman class with the youngest boys—provided he could pay the twenty-five-dollar tuition. Freeman sold his horse—his sole possession of value—to pay the cost. He took room and board at the Marion home of widow Maria Cody, whom he later married.[33]

Although Freeman possessed the work ethic to succeed at Howard, a severe infection left one eyeball sightless and bulging in a peculiar manner; his other eye suffered severe damage. Pain from the affliction plagued him the rest of his life, and he wore dark glasses to protect his "well eye" and to give him a less frightening appearance. "His experience was hard," wrote Rev. William H. McIntosh, "but as is always the case with the strong, it developed a manliness of character that a life of ease might never have obtained." Freeman overcame his misfortune and excelled as a student at Howard College; to pay for his expenses, he preached at the affluent Hopewell Baptist Church near Marion. His self-described "Holy Ghost power" preaching, combined with a "deep, rich, sonorous, and well-managed" voice that sounded like the triumphant "blast of a bugle," proved more important to the congregation than his untidy look. He soon gained a reputation as one of the most powerful preachers in the state, and his photographic memory was legendary. "With the masses," McIntosh believed, "he was, I think, the most popular preacher I ever knew." Another long-time Alabama Baptist minister added that Freeman "hardly had a superior in the South," and everyone seemed to glory in the "admitted superiority of 'Freeman,' as they familiarly called him."[34]

In the fall of 1869, Samuel Freeman began his tenure as president and professor of theology and moral and mental philosophy with high hopes. For the first time since before the war, students could receive theological training, and for the second year in a row, enrollment increased, but the income was insufficient to meet expenses. William McIntosh once again used the word "embarrassing" to describe the financial condition of Howard College. Only through God's faithfulness and "kind providence," he added, did the institution survive the severe economic trials. And only with God's continued protection would those blessings continue to be "perpetuated to the end of time."[35]

McIntosh, along with other Howard College leaders, blamed the financial problems on the lack of support from white Baptists throughout Alabama—a long-standing criticism leveled since the institution's founding. At the least, he supposed, Alabama Baptists should send their sons to Howard and support their denominational school located in their home state. Why send a young man away for education at a greater cost with "no higher, and rarely equal advantages?" This was a "strange hallucination," he added, but even stranger was the trend toward sending children to Roman Catholic schools. Although he knew of no Baptists in the Black Belt region who were guilty of this "criminal folly," other sections of the state participated in this "evil" enterprise and these parents would soon reap what they sowed. "I am sorry for the children," McIntosh continued. "Such parents deserve the reward which many of them will receive, in the apostasy of their children from the faith of the gospel."[36]

Despite the financial difficulties and the finger pointing, Samuel Freeman and the Howard College faculty stayed focused on educating 184 young men enrolled at the institution. President Freeman implemented a more rigorous daily schedule that included sunrise chapel services, six hours of classroom instruction, six and a half hours of study time, and two hours of recitation—six days a week. The busy fourteen-hours-a-day schedule kept most students away from mischief-making, but when they transgressed, the president administered strict discipline. Seventeen-year-old Joseph T. Crenshaw of Hamburg, Alabama, was charged with disturbing a quiet building, carrying a firearm, drawing a pistol on another student, and using profane language. Freemen expelled the young man for disregarding the Howard College laws and rules of decorum. On another occasion, two students caught fighting, Zachary Taylor Weaver and B. Richardson, were brought before the president and privately admonished. "Since the collision appeared to be not premeditated by either," a faculty member reported, "and since these gentlemen pledged themselves to avoid the recurrence of such an event," only Freeman's rebuke was necessary. Overall, students saw Freeman as a "benevolent father" whom they affectionately called "Uncle Sam."[37]

Also in the fall of 1869, another new professor arrived on campus, Thomas John Dill, the professor of Latin and Greek. The son of a wealthy South Carolina planter, Dill graduated from the state university in Columbia and began his career as a teacher near his home. In 1849, he moved to Carlowville in Dallas County to open a boys' academy and gained a reputation as a teacher who had "vigorous muscle" for using the "educating power of the hickory switch." At Howard College, Dill inspired students to discover their own passion for studying Latin and Greek. "With a genius for philology and the fine points of syntax," wrote one of his students, "he made the dry bones to live and the dead roots to bring forth life." Professor Dill taught Howard students for the next thirty-one years.[38]

The most dramatic change for Howard College students was the opening of a mess hall on campus, which reduced the price of boarding to the "actual cost of living." The student members of the "mess club" ran the dining hall as a members-only society and charged on average $7.38 per month in dues to cover expenses. "The fare," wrote student treasurer John R. Bell, "has been such as to give general satisfaction." Most students, however, continued to pay private families for board, which cost between $12.50 and $15.00 per month.[39]

Despite the continued financial despair and the lingering upheaval of Reconstruction, Freeman, Dill, Thornton, and the other faculty members brought a renewed spirit of optimism to campus in 1869 and 1870. "Brother Freeman took hold of Howard College when its friends had almost given up hope," a writer noted in the *Christian Index and South-Western Baptist,* and although his prospects were gloomy, efforts were crowned with a dramatically increased enrollment. Freeman, the writer supposed, had "proven himself to be the man for the place." The institution no longer suffered from a protracted "dead spell" and the threat of an "early ending" but was now in a "flourishing condition." A former student agreed that Freeman brought Howard College to a prosperity equal to, or surpassing, the antebellum years. "Let us keep it before the people," he added, "and the minds of the brethren that Howard College . . . is a live institution."[40]

The reality, however, failed to match the hopeful, yet hollow, rhetoric. No matter the quality of teaching and facilities, Howard College teetered on financial ruin. In the fall of 1870, enrollment dropped to 108 and William McIntosh again announced that tuition was insufficient to cover the cost of salaries. Howard must receive voluntary donations to pay the faculty or, McIntosh said, "we must abandon the thought of having the college." He asked the Alabama State Baptist Convention in 1870 whether the work inherited from "our fathers" to provide young men the ability to receive the best mental and cultural training should end? The answer was unclear. A writer in one newspaper believed Alabama Baptists had the money necessary to support Howard, but "intended to keep it" and let a "noble and energetic" president take care of it for them. Samuel Freeman, however, was not an endowment unto himself. "His pockets are not so full of rocks," the author noted, "as his head is of hard sense." The only solution was a large sum of money to endow a "first-class" college.[41]

At Howard, Zachary Taylor Weaver was the only graduate of the class of 1871 and received his diploma at commencement on Thursday, June 29. Samuel Freeman also announced his resignation from the presidency of the college but offered to continue in his role as professor of theology and assume new responsibilities as Alabama's "State Evangelist." At the end of the fall term, however, Freeman accepted a call to the pulpit at a Baptist church in Jefferson, Texas. After only a few months of ministering to his small congregation, he died following a brief illness on November 19, 1872. Just a few days before his death, he told his wife not to grieve for him. "My life is in God's hand," he said. "If it is His will to restore me; He will do it; if it is His purpose to take me, it is right and best. Remember that what God does is always right."[42]

For the third time in as many years, Howard College was without a president. A measure of change, however, was coming. The arrival and expansion of the Selma, Marion and Memphis Railroad in the late 1860s and early 1870s helped end Marion's postwar isolation and provided more mobility, improved communication, and encouraged a new interest in accumulating knowledge. Howard College's promotional literature boasted that the school was now accessible by railroads from throughout Alabama and bordering states. With the breakdown in isolation and a growing interconnectivity of communities throughout the state, Howard's boosters looked to benefit from increased mobility, but at the same time they hoped to preserve the school's commitment to the traditional values of virtue, faith, benevolence, and intellect. "It is evident," Howard's leaders boasted, "that Marion affords the wholesome restraint of a moral and intelligent community, without presenting those extraordinary temptations to young men incident to great centres of trade." In many ways, this was in keeping with the views of other Alabamians. The state was not in the "process of ending the old and starting the new," wrote one historian. "Instead, the old ways were kept and the new was added." Traditional social norms, community values, religious convictions, and moral principles would endure alongside modern technology. "Dreams of the past and hopes for the future were inextricably entangled." And Howard College needed a new leader who would embrace tradition and lead the institution into the future.[43]

7

COLONEL MURFEE'S SCHOOL

Following the Civil War, educational institutions throughout the South, including Howard College, struggled to exist. Many antebellum schools never reopened after the war; others opened for a short time but soon closed due to the lack of money and students. Sixty miles north of Marion in Tuscaloosa, Union troops burned most of the educational and dormitory buildings at the University of Alabama in 1865, and the institution remained closed until 1868. The Alabama trustees tasked the former commander of the core of cadets at the university, James T. Murfee, to rebuild the school. A tall man of military bearing, Murfee provided unimaginative building plans that borrowed heavily from the Spartan gothic architecture at Virginia Military Institute (VMI), his alma mater. The new edifice, he supposed, was a "masculine expression of neatness, simplicity, and strength." Far exceeding his architectural duties, Murfee provided the trustees with a "new scheme" on how to reorganize the university as a classical military school. The partisan upheaval in Reconstruction-era Montgomery and the politicization of the university's leadership, however, left Murfee with little hope that his plan would be implemented. With the completion of his building in 1868, he resigned from the university. With an interest in scientific agriculture, J. T. Murfee spent the next three years working as the Alabama general agent (salesman) for the Southern Fertilizer Company of Richmond, Virginia. A Tuscaloosa newspaper hailed Murfee as "one of the most successful and scientific agriculturalists in Alabama."[1]

With hopes for reconstructing and growing Howard College, the Board of Trustees offered Murfee the presidency in July 1871, and he accepted the position. Born September 13, 1833, in Southampton County, Virginia, James Thomas Murfee was the son of wealthy slaveholding parents James W. and Ann Parker Murfee. The young James Thomas received education from private tutors and

The earliest known photograph of the Howard College campus (circa 1870) following ren-
ovations to the building and grounds after the campus was used as a Confederate hospital,
Union troop headquarters, and housing for the formerly enslaved. (Samford University,
Special Collection and University Archives)

at the nearby Stone Mount Academy before entering the Virginia Military Institute in August 1849. Murfee thrived under the watchful eye of Superintendent
Francis H. Smith and the rigid military discipline at VMI. Smith described
James T. Murfee as a talented man of "indomitable energy" and solid virtue.
"His chief defect," Smith wrote, was a "too high estimate of his own ability
which leads him into extravagancies. But he is, I think, a reliable man." Murfee
graduated first in his class in 1853 with first honors in mathematics, French,
drawing, chemistry, natural philosophy, engineering, English, geology and agricultural chemistry, tactics, and artillery tactics.[2]

Although Murfee possessed a keen intellect and strong military bearing, a
career in the U.S. Army held little interest for him. "I resolve to make myself a
scientific man," he wrote. "I am determined not to spare any labor to accomplish
my design." In the fall of 1854, Murfee began his academic career as a professor
of math and natural sciences at Madison College in Uniontown, Pennsylvania—
a Methodist Protestant school deeply divided over the issue of slavery. "Such
has become the state of things," Murfee wrote in May 1855, that northerners
refused to support the college because all the professors were southerners
and the South withheld funding because the institution was in the North. The

strife culminated at the end of the academic year when President Samuel Cox, James T. Murfee, and the rest of the southern faculty resigned and moved to Lynchburg, Virginia, to start a new school.[3]

Lynchburg College began with great fanfare and high expectations, but tensions soon emerged. In 1856, Murfee joined the First Baptist Church and was baptized by Rev. Henry Harstein Wyer (the son of Henry O. Wyer, who immersed James H. DeVotie decades before). Most likely, the Methodist Protestant Church leaders that governed Lynchburg were displeased with Murfee's decision to make fellowship with the Baptists in a church led by a Princeton-trained, Calvinist minister. At the college, Murfee drew up the architectural designs for the new campus and introduced military instruction to the students to instill "manly carriage," precision, order, morality, and discipline. Methodist officials were unhappy and opposed Murfee's militarization of the Christian college and declared that they had "no sympathy with war or war training." Many in the denomination withdrew patronage and financial support; this, combined with the economic crisis of 1857, left the college devastated and the faculty disillusioned—leading to Murfee's resignation at the end of the 1856–57 academic year. The following fall, Murfee served as a principal at Westwood School, a classical, mathematical, and military academy near Lynchburg. In 1858, newspapers reported that Murfee purchased a 250-acre farm in northern Virginia with plans to build a military institute on an "extensive scale." The venture was most likely unsuccessful and, in February 1860, the *Montgomery Mail* reported that Murfee was in Alabama's capital city with a proposal to establish a state-sponsored military school. Montevallo was the proposed site, where students would benefit from "pure air, cheap living, good society, and opportunity to become acquainted with the great mineral treasures of Alabama."[4]

In Tuscaloosa, University of Alabama president Landon C. Garland had long hoped to introduce the military system at the university to quell the perpetual student unrest on campus. For years, the state legislature and the Board of Trustees resisted Garland's efforts but, following the shooting death of a student in 1858, a decline in financial and moral support from around the state, and the inevitability of war, the trustees approved the military system in 1860. In turn, Garland hired James T. Murfee to serve as assistant commandant. During the Civil War, Murfee declined an appointment as a lieutenant colonel in Henry Talbird's Forty-First Alabama Infantry Regiment and remained at the University of Alabama to serve as the new commandant—a position he held throughout the war. On April 4, 1865, Murfee's cadets prepared to defend the university against invading Union forces, but when the situation looked hopeless, President Garland ordered the boys to retreat to Marion.[5]

Six years later, Colonel James Thomas Murfee returned to Marion as the new president of Howard College. William H. McIntosh described Murfee as a "remarkable organizer" who was "eminently practical, prompt, and energetic"; he was also a chivalrous southern gentleman, a reliable Christian, and a Baptist. One former student remembered that Murfee's tall stature, probing eyes, and penetrating voice commanded the respect of all who knew him. He was direct, disciplined, courteous, and a "cultivated scholar." The students recognized his leadership inside and outside the classroom and "waited for the expression of his will" that revealed his "keen and massive mind and his vigorous moral manhood." As the malaise of Reconstruction continued, Murfee brought energy and urgency to Howard College, leading the *Marion Commonwealth* to describe the colonel as "emphatically a live man."[6]

Murfee was just one of scores of former Confederate officers who took leadership or faculty positions in higher education throughout the South—a path emblazoned by General Robert E. Lee in 1865 when he accepted the presidency of Washington College (later renamed Washington and Lee University). "I think it the duty of every citizen in the present condition of the Country," Lee wrote at the time, "to do all in his power to aid in the restoration of peace and harmony." These men also discovered that they could once again command young men and instill disciple and honor to a new generation of southerners. Many of the superlatives used to describe Lee, courage, character, manly, noble, virtuous, were also used to describe Murfee. In the defeated South of the Reconstruction era, former Confederate military leaders like Murfee discovered that leadership in higher education provided one of the few opportunities for a professional position that brought prestige, deference, respect, and command—and in many ways hero worship. Their presence on a college campus would also attract students and, perhaps, generous benefactors.[7]

Murfee and Lee were examples of Confederate veterans who brought their wartime experiences to campus and a set of ideals shaped by defeat on a much more personal level than their young students. As one historian wrote, men like Murfee possessed specific ideas on "how to build . . . a progressive New South" that could reconcile contradictory notions of southern progress with the myth of the Lost Cause. Confederate academics, like the "progressivist" Murfee, accepted southern defeat without guilt because of their evangelical adherence to God's providential plan. "Their faith in Providence," one writer observed, "allowed them to develop the idea that national progress had necessitated Confederate defeat so that the United States could resolve the problems of slavery and secession and fulfill its national destiny of achieving a perpetual republic."[8]

A self-described "professor and disciplinarian," J. T. Murfee brought a utilitarian educational philosophy to Howard and an academic plan to reorganize Howard based on his blueprints for the "new scheme" at the University of Alabama and modeled after the elective curriculum of Washington and Lee University in Virginia. He hoped to provide an education of the "greatest value" for the greatest number of students by developing and strengthening their minds and preparing them for the "special business of life." Murfee's plan was to combine the best of the classical curriculum with the practical innovations of scientific methodology and the "barrack discipline" of the military system. "Select from each what is valuable," he wrote, "and reject that which is not good."[9]

Although Murfee embraced classical education as "essential to the learned world," he disliked the traditional use of large classes and limited recitations. This led to a poor work ethic and a lack of discipline. Instead, Murfee envisioned a necessary arrangement of small classes, expanded recitations, and mental discipline—based on the hope of reward, fear of punishment, and the pride of emulation—all virtues of the military system of West Point, VMI, and other schools. This was, he added, the most "powerful means of inducing labor," both mental and physical. What the military institutions lacked, however, was a grounding in classical education and a mastery of the English language, which compelled the colonel to expand the requirements in grammar, composition, and literature.[10]

Professors at Howard College, Murfee believed, must be engaged in "energetic and practical methods of teaching" and give each student an extraordinary amount of personal attention. "Impracticable and slothful plans of teaching," he wrote, would never lead the students to become "efficient and practical men." The colonel was particularly critical of the monotonous hours students spent memorizing and reciting from textbooks. This was the laziest method of teaching, which required no laborious effort on the part of the professor and encouraged no discipline from the student. Murfee asked, "Is such instruction really worth anything to a young man whose success in life depends not upon saying lessons and hearing lectures but depends upon his ability to *think* and to *act?*"[11]

Beginning in the fall of 1871, Howard students responded to this teaching by increasing their intellectual power through application, example, precept, ambition, and discipline. Beyond the ideas and philosophies of authors, Murfee expected students to gain a "practical application" of every subject. The "mode of instruction," Murfee wrote, made each student self-reliant and gave him the "power to master and appropriate the facts and philosophy of books, and to make original investigations in any subject of thought." In the sciences, students, not the professor, lectured, experimented, and illustrated. In mathematics, students worked out "original problems" and applied every test possible to "prove the thorough comprehension of the subject." In the humanities, Murfee required more history classes and a stronger emphasis on modern languages, including French and German. Nonetheless, Latin and Greek remained the preferred languages for students.[12]

"With laborious professors and industrious students," Murfee explained, "the most efficient of methods of instruction can be adopted." Murfee believed that the best way to learn was: (1) to imitate the words and deeds of a skilled operator; (2) to reason and analyze the operation performed; (3) to read and learn what books have been written on the subject; (4) to write a composition based on your thoughts and analysis that were obtained from your own reflection, from your teacher, and from your books. When a student applied these methods to any academic discipline or practical work, Murfee argued, then the pupil became an "expert operator, a logical thinker, and a good writer and speaker." He was "thoroughly and practically educated." No one would deny, he added, the "superiority of an education" which was "engrained by *doing,* by *thinking,* and by *writing.*"[13]

In 1871, a writer for the *Marion Commonwealth* praised this new emphasis; English was the "foundation of all education in this country" and took on new and "untold importance" due to the "necessitous circumstances" of Reconstruction that so limited the opportunities for southern young people. Murfee required each student to compose numerous essays and submit them to the "searching criticism" of both classmates and professors. Daily composition and the careful reading of literature, philosophy, and history provided students with a "command of the language," quickened "all the energies of the mind," and cultivated analysis, intellect, and discipline. This also forced students to understand the "idea and reasoning" of the authors of the great Western texts and to methodically and instantly "arrange" them "in his own mind."[14]

Murfee divided Howard College's course of study into separate "schools" (closely resembling today's departments): Latin; Greek; Modern Languages; English; Moral Science and Theology; Mathematics; Chemistry, Geology, and Mineralogy; Natural Philosophy and Applied Mathematics; Civil Engineering; and Business. Recitations increased to at least fifteen a week—compelling most students to take a variety of classes in at least six of the schools. This reorganization provided students with some options within the restrictive system because Murfee believed that an open system of electives would permit students to "select any subject his ignorance or laziness may suggest." The "common pursuit" of core classes in the classical Western traditions remained at the heart of this system because without them, Murfee added, students never gained a strong and disciplined mind. Overall, Colonel Murfee's plan was no radical departure for the Howard students, but a reordering of priorities with an emphasis on "individual responsibility."[15]

Murfee believed, as did his predecessors before him, that the "highest aim" of the faculty at Howard College was to provide students with an education within a moral culture that instilled virtue and character. "While the young man is becoming wise in books and the affairs of the world," Murfee wrote, the virtues must be instilled, the "lower passions" repressed, and the "better qualities" of the young men encouraged. Years before, the people of Marion overcame frontier hedonism and established a "moral culture" in the town that compelled citizens to maintain watch over the "conduct and habits" of the students attending Howard. "Never before," Murfee emphasized, "have I known a community to render so much service to the cause of education; nor to look so carefully to the moral and social welfare of students sent unto their midst." Often, colleges maintained a hostile relationship with local colleges. Citizens complained about the disorder and debauchery of students who found pleasure in sinful and immoral activities. "How different here!" Murfee added. "The trustees and people hold themselves in relation to the students as parents, and no more allow any impropriety in the college family than in their own."[16]

During his first year at Howard College, one local newspaper writer described J. T. Murfee as "genial, scholarly and irrepressibly active," a man with as many hands and heads as Aegaeon of Greek mythology—a god of sea storms with a hundred hands and fifty heads. In contrast to the seldom-seen J. L. M. Curry, James Thomas Murfee seemed ever present as he energetically built up, refitted, and beautified the Howard campus with a flurry of building, painting, roofing, and landscaping. "All the while," a reporter for the *Marion Commonwealth* noticed, the colonel never relaxed his strict rules or rigorous discipline, but was "everywhere . . . guiding, directing, encouraging, and pushing ahead."[17]

For the Howard College students, Murfee's most obvious innovation was the introduction of military uniforms. The heavy wool uniforms were a brilliant royal blue (an interesting contrast to Confederate gray uniforms so prevalent at other southern schools) with lines of brass buttons that a Marion observer described as a "most beautiful and suitable devise" cast with a "cross and crown irradiating a halo of light and glory" with the words "Howard College" in bold letters. "The whole costume is in elegant taste and adds wonderfully to the appearance of the young gentlemen." The coat, gray pants, and cap cost the student twenty-nine dollars. The uniforms gave the students the appearance of military cadets, but Murfee provided no military training for the Howard boys for several more years.[18]

It took little time for J. T. Murfee to become inseparable from Howard College, and locals began referring to the institution as "Colonel Murfee's school." One alumnus believed Murfee's "personality permeated the campus," and his rules of decorum were known by all the students. At his frequent chapel talks, Murfee "discussed moral and religious questions, brought out the difference between moral courage and brute force, and had a way of making his talks stick." Because of the college's emphasis on virtue, discipline, and morality, most "idle and vicious" young men chose not to attend Howard. When Murfee learned that underclassmen were hazing the new students by dragging them from their rooms and "plundering their trunks and furniture," he called the entire student body to the chapel. He told the students that for centuries common law held that a "man's home was his castle." In England, royalty could not "enter the lowliest hut" without an invitation. Likewise, Murfee explained, your dormitory room was your home while at Howard College. "He who dares enter there unheralded and uninvited to molest your privacy or to maraud," he added, as "true American boys, you will throw him from the window even at the sacrifice of breaking his neck." After Murfee's speech, hazing at Howard ended. The students respected and feared Murfee, which kept moral conduct at a high level, but the Howard boys were still willing, at times, to challenge the colonel when they believed he was acting in a tyrannical manner.[19]

When Professor Joseph Harrell reported student P. P. Parham for insubordination during an English class, Murfee ordered the accused under arrest, but Parham refused to abide by the colonel's command. In response, Murfee announced the student's expulsion at an assembly, leading Parham to proclaim in a "most insubordinate and defiant" tone that Murfee was treating him in a most "ungentlemanly manner." Fifty-one of Parham's fellow Howard College students appealed to the Board of Trustees to investigate the matter, charging that Murfee refused to meet with Parham and, in response, the student being "conscious of his innocence and feeling himself aquiver," refused arrest. The trustees investigated the "state of discipline" at Howard and found no reason to overturn Murfee's expulsion of Parham and affirmed all of "Murfee's laws" to instill discipline and morality to the young men of Howard College. In addition, the board emphasized that, in the future, only the student aggrieved could apply for an investigation from the trustees—giving the president more power to enforce disciplinary cases. The board wanted no more student petitions, uprisings, or protests. Board president William W. Wilkerson described Murfee's disciplinary rules as "mild and not irksome" but sufficient to keep students under control and "stimulate the latent ambition of the most careless."[20]

Throughout the summer and early fall of 1872, J. T. Murfee crisscrossed Alabama and Mississippi, recruiting students and proclaiming the virtues of Howard College. "If anyone can build up a college," a writer noted in the *Montgomery Advertiser,* "and if anyone deserves success, the Colonel certainly does. He is a gentleman of the most pleasing address and captivating manners." He explained to prospective students and their parents that, at Howard, good habits and "fine morals" came first, followed by the development of an intellect based on reason, observation, and good judgment. This intellect, Murfee emphasized, "shall have the power to acquire knowledge, to work with skill, to think profoundly, and to give language and eloquence to any cause that it may advocate." Then the "thoughtful boy" would become the "studious young man." Beyond morality and intellect, the colonel also expected Howard students to develop a "fixedness of purpose" and physical strength (the "outer man") to maintain energy and "mental vigor."[21]

With the uncertainty, chaos, and disarray of the Reconstruction Era, Howard's young men embraced Murfee's rigid discipline. All that was required to succeed at the college, one student wrote in 1872, was a work ethic. No slothful students attended Howard, and if "any find their way into our midst, they would either be forced to abandon their habits of idleness or leave in disgrace."

Echoing Colonel Murfee's way of thinking, the student added, "We know no such word as fail but on the contrary lay hold to the business in hand with an earnestness and zeal that ensures success."[22]

As the school year opened in the fall of 1872, five faculty greeted 136 students to campus. Colonel Murfee instructed the Howard boys in mental science, architecture, and engineering; E.Q. Thornton taught chemistry, natural history, and romance languages; Thomas J. Dill trained students in Greek and Latin; George D. Bancroft focused on mathematics; and James Harrell was a professor of English. At the end of the academic year in June 1873, students were given oral and written exams. In each discipline, the topics for students to discuss were selected randomly from boxes. Whatever the subject, one observer noted, the students gave intelligent responses and "beautiful lectures" in chemistry, astronomy, physical geography, rhetoric, laws of euphony, and in reading and analyzing the ancient and modern texts and languages. The skill on display proved that "the scholastic year had been one of unremitting toil and application both to the students and the faculty. . . . For certainly these young men have not been spending any time in the wild dissipations so often engendered by college life."[23]

In chemistry, Colonel Murfee's pragmatic educational philosophy was on display as the professor "threw the *whole* burden" upon the student scholar. In the presence of Professor E. Q. Thornton, members of the Board of Trustees, and a host of visitors, a student selected his subject from the box, delivered a lecture, performed an experiment—handling the apparatus, chemicals, and tests—to demonstrate the subject, answered every question asked, and discussed the errors of other students. "This class excited great interest," an observer later wrote, and attracted one of the largest audiences for any public examination. Every student was "unsparingly subjected" to this "catechizing ordeal" with no mercy from the audience or the instructor. "Like the fencing master, the Professor put each boy on the defensive, with the cry *gardez* ringing in his ears as a warning to watch all points." As in the art of fencing, the student assessed his opponent, then attacked the "weakest or least guarded" area. "Like skilled swordsmen," he added, "the students were ready to meet the thrusts and cuts and strokes wherever aimed and however adroitly and scientifically made." These examinations, one newspaper wrote, "made Howard a school of discipline and mental culture second to none in the South."[24]

8

HOW LIFELESS OUR
COUNTRY LOOKS

One Howard College student participating in the examinations in June 1873 was David Gordon Lyon. Born May 25, 1852, in Benton, Lowndes County, Alabama, Lyon was the son of Dr. Isaac Lyon, a native of the English port city of Kingston upon Hull, who renounced his Orthodox Jewish upbringing and converted to Christianity while in medical school in London. Alienated from his family, he immigrated to the United States, settled in Alabama, and became a Baptist minister—while continuing to practice medicine. He died in 1860, when his son was seven years old. But David Gordon was a passionate learner from a young age and came to Howard College in the fall of 1872. Following the end of the academic year in June 1873, D. G. Lyon traveled to New York and boarded the steamship *Samaria* and began a transatlantic voyage to Kingston upon Hull— becoming perhaps the first student to study and travel abroad while enrolled at Howard College. Lyon looked forward to visiting "that historic land and tread the soil that gave my father birth."[1]

For the twenty-one-year-old Howard College student, his visit to Hull and London was a transformative experience that he captured in his personal diary and in other writings. Like students today, he explored the cities and visited churches, museums, government buildings, gardens, cemeteries, and memorials. Accustomed to the racial mores of the South, Lyon was surprised to see Blacks and whites socializing with one another. "Negro equality seemed to suit the English mind very well," he wrote. When he saw a Black man and a white woman engaged in a pleasant conversation, Lyon commented: "This was a novel scene to an Alabamian."[2]

While visiting London, Lyon attended church services at the Metropolitan Tabernacle, where he heard Charles Hadden Spurgeon preach a sermon on

Matthew 9:37–38. Lyon believed attending a service led by the internationally acclaimed Baptist pastor was among the most important destinations for any visitor to London. When Spurgeon stepped to the pulpit to nearly six thousand people in attendance, the brash young Lyon was unimpressed. "I have seen more men of far more intelligent appearance," he wrote; "indeed there was nothing in the physiognomy of the man to lead one to suppose that he is the wonder of his hearers." Likewise, Lyon found Spurgeon's fifty-minute sermon on the harvest and the laborers uninspired. The Baptist minister was a conversationalist and not a sermonizer, he wrote. "He stands before his congregation and talks to them. Indeed, his power over the heart of the people is said to lie in the fact that they feel that he is one of them." This style was key to Spurgeon's mass appeal. When a newspaper writer described his sermons as being of "bad taste, vulgar, and theatrical," the pastor responded, "I am perhaps vulgar, but it is not intentional, save that I must and will make the people listen." It was his belief that England was filled with too many "polite preachers," and that required a change. "God has owned me among the most degraded and off-casts. Let others serve their class; these are mine, and to them I must keep."[3]

Following Spurgeon's sermon and the benediction, a friend asked D. G. Lyon how he liked the preacher. "Very well," he responded, "but I've heard better." Lyon explained that, if what he experienced was a "fair specimen" of a Spurgeon sermon, then he would prefer to be under the ministerial guidance of someone he knew. "It would be the height of presumption for one as ignorant as I," he added, "to pass sentence on one whom the world admires but each one has his standard of excellence [and] . . . I think Spurgeon lacks." Lyon considered Rev. Edwin T. Winkler, the pastor at Siloam Baptist and a member of the Howard College Board of Trustees, a much "superior" preacher. But the student admitted that Spurgeon was a phenomenon who "won the admiration of the world" but required numerous hearings to appreciate him.[4]

As he explored the streets of Hull, Lyon wandered into the Jewish areas where his father and grandparents lived and worked. With his father being ostracized from his family and dying when D.G. was so young, the Howard College student had little or no connection to the faith of his ancestors. On Robinson Row, he saw that the doors were open at the synagogue of the Hull Hebrew Congregation. Outside the synagogue, he asked a man if he could enter the building. He said yes. Lyon watched as everyone washed their hands in a tiny stream of water that dripped near the door so they would not "profane the house of God." It was Saturday morning, August 2, 1873, and the Orthodox Jewish congregation was about to begin their Shabbat service.[5]

Lyon entered the synagogue with the other men and stepped into a small room with pews on three sides and an elevated platform in the middle. He noticed that everyone wore small hats and had a "cloth of coarse texture" draped across their shoulders that was "colored slightly brown, having around the edges some stripes of a darker color." Lyon stood in the rear of the synagogue and watched with wonder as the service began. A man stood on the platform and began reading words in Hebrew. "Yet it was not reading," Lyon observed. "He was singing; yet it was not singing." The man's voice changed in tone—"sometimes low, sometimes loud, sometimes slow, sometimes fast, sometimes soft, sometimes harsh." In intervals, the congregation "burst forth in rapid exclamations" in the same language. "It appeared to me but confused jargon," Lyon later wrote.[6]

Next, an older man stood, walked across the room, and unlocked a door. The reader then went to the door and uttered words. "He then opened the door," Lyon observed, "and brought forth, closely embraced in *his* arms, an object about 2½ feet in length and wrapped in costly cloth." The reader stood with the object (the Torah) in his arms, cried out, and began to walk to the platform. As he passed the worshippers, they reached out, touched the covering, and then kissed their hands." Within the covering, the Howard College student saw a roll that he presumed to be the law. "It resembled pictures of ancient scrolls," he wrote, "being rolled up on both ends." Soon the reading began again, and he watched the congregation's response. "Much of the service," he said, "seems to be passed in chanting and . . . continual bowing and straightening." He left the service feeling enriched from the experience.[7]

When Lyon returned to Alabama in late September 1873, he traveled across a state still mired in economic hardship and Reconstruction. "How lifeless our country looks," he wrote. "The veins of prosperity have certainly ceased to flow. . . . Alabama is a dying carcass." But to make matters worse, Lyon learned that the bank (Jay Cooke & Company) that held his money (presumably inheritance from his father) failed and set off a series of bank failures leading to the financial Panic of 1873. Lyon lost all of his educational funds, and his return to Howard College looked doubtful. "In a moment," he wrote, "I am aroused to the solid reality of extreme poverty. How shall I bear the blow?" He prayed for God to help him see this as part of his plan. "An education I must or will have," he proclaimed. "If health remains, I will have it. I cannot do without it. By teaching, preaching and studying it will come."[8]

As the financial panic deepened into a severe depression, other banks failed, railroads went bankrupt, and foreclosures were widespread. A writer observed that many Americans viewed an economic downturn as a "moral judgement, precise punishment for the country's sins." This was in the minds of many Baptist proponents of the Lost Cause throughout the South. In Alabama, cotton and corn crops fell shortest in at least three decades and kept many students from returning to Howard College. Only 82 students began in 1873–74, including David Gordon Lyon, a significant drop from 136 enrolled the previous academic year. The president of the Board of Trustees, William W. Wilkerson, hoped that more students would enroll once cotton prices rebounded, but for the year, only 95 students enrolled, leaving the school short of cash and a mounting debt of over $12,000—including $1,285.78 still owed former president J. L. M. Curry. Much of the debt came from renovating and refurnishing the dormitories with new bedding and furniture and the building of an "Italian Cottage" dining hall on campus.[9]

The School of Moral Science and Theology was being funded solely by the Board of Trustees and the faculty at an annual expense of $1,500. Howard College was still seen as an enterprise of the Baptists of Marion, and the Alabama Baptist State Convention invested little money into the institution. At a special fundraising event for Howard, the convention contributed $27; in contrast, Siloam Baptist gave $500. Faculty salaries were paid exclusively from the tuition dollars generated by the students. It cost $123 per academic term to attend Howard College: $95 for tuition and board; $22 for room, fuel, and servant; and $6 for washing. The lone graduate at the end of the 1873–74 academic year was Joseph Mason Dill, the son of Howard College professor Thomas J. Dill. The younger Dill followed his father's path into education, teaching in Tuscaloosa and at Howard College before deafness forced him from the classroom. He became the first president of Troy Normal School (now Troy University in Alabama) and later the superintendent of Bessemer city schools.[10]

During the 1874–75 academic year, the financial depression continued and left the state of Alabama on the verge of bankruptcy. This enabled the Democrats, in November 1874, to regain the governorship and recapture control of both houses of the state legislature. The following year, they rewrote the state constitution and ended Radical Reconstruction in Alabama. The changes, however, brought little relief for the state's dire economic conditions. At Howard College, ninety-eight students enrolled, but many could not pay for tuition, forcing the school to accept promissory notes and drafts instead of the cash that the institution desperately needed. Nonetheless, Colonel Murfee and the trustees were able to use what money they received to reduce the debt and pay the five faculty members (including Murfee) during the academic year.[11]

At the close of the school year in June 1875, three young men graduated, including valedictorian David Gordon Lyon, who delivered his valedictory address entitled "How Large Is the World?" Following graduation, Lyon worked for a year at the *Alabama Baptist* before entering Southern Baptist Theological Seminary in Louisville, Kentucky, where he gained a reputation as the "finest scholar at the seminary." In Louisville, he fell under the influence of controversial Hebrew scholar Crawford Toy. When Toy resigned over criticism of his historical-critical method of interpreting scripture, he urged Lyon to quit the seminary and begin studies under the German Assyriologist Friedrich Delitzsch at the University of Leipzig. Lyon left Louisville without completing his degree and moved to Germany. When Lyon completed his PhD in 1882 under Delitzsch, Crawford Toy, the recently named Hancock Professor of Hebrew at Harvard Divinity School, advocated for his thirty-year-old protégé to receive the oldest endowed chair at Harvard, the Hollis Professor of Divinity. Once offered, Lyon enthusiastically accepted the position and became the first professor of Assyriology in the United States—a professorship that Lyon held until 1910, when he replaced Toy as the Hancock Professor. When David Gordon Lyon died in 1935, one of his colleagues wrote that the Howard College graduate was a "devoted helper, a dignified and courtly gentleman, in whom the old traditions of the South still lived, one who made himself the companion of his pupils and their life-long friend, and a scholar whose standards were so exacting that he published little, lest there should be some imperfection in his work." David Gordon Lyon was just the type of man that James T. Murfee wanted to see graduate from Howard College.[12]

But for Colonel Murfee to continue shaping virtuous, benevolent, Christian, intellectual young men at Howard College, he needed money. "Brethren," members of the denomination's education committee reported, "neither the Board of Trustees, Dr. Murfee, and his co-laborers, nor anyone can build up a denominational institution of this character without students and without money." Most Alabama Baptists had little interest or incentive to keep Howard College solvent.[13]

In 1871, the trustees approved a scheme to endow the college from a percentage of premiums from insurance policies sold by Baptist ministers working for the National Life Insurance Company. Newspapers reported at the time that the Howard endowment would reach $1.5 million through the arrangement. A writer for the *Marion Commonwealth* praised the plan and encouraged people, regardless of their denominational preference, to invest in Howard College. When institutions like Howard prosper, the writer added, "wealth will return to us and we may confidently look for our land to be filled with a happy, independent, moral and religious people." Despite the enthusiasm, it was an odd scheme to have Baptist ministers throughout the state to sell life insurance to support a so-called denominational institution of higher education that was struggling to stay alive as a local enterprise of Marion, Alabama.[14]

One of the Baptist ministers selling insurance and Howard College was Azor Van Hoose, who also served as the college's financial secretary and field agent. Ordained a Baptist minister in 1842, Van Hoose entered Howard College as a student in 1844, but he lacked the funds to continue his studies and dropped out. For years to come, the minister moved from place to place, preaching and working at several additional jobs because of the financial difficulties suffered by his family. During the early 1870s, he traveled throughout the state, preaching the gospel, proclaiming the virtues of Howard College, peddling insurance, and begging for money. In April 1872, Van Hoose was in the southeastern Alabama hamlet of Troy. "We cannot too highly commend this excellent gentleman," the *Troy Messenger* reported, "and his noble work to the favorable notice of the people . . . who are in sympathy with the Baptist denomination." But within a few months, Van Hoose quit. "I have given up the work, severing all connections with Howard College," he wrote. Perhaps if the cotton crops had not failed or the political troubles had not deepened, he might have succeeded. But the dark "gloom over Alabama" prevented any possibility of raising funds. "I cannot endow Howard College," he concluded, "and hence I have given up the work." By 1873, the insurance scheme was never again mentioned in the newspapers or the records of Howard College.[15]

In 1874, the Alabama Baptist State Convention recommended that Howard College raise a $100,000 endowment to provide stability for the institution. Even raising funds for Howard during flush times was a daunting task, but it proved nigh impossible during the ongoing economic depression of the 1870s. Predictably, by 1875, no money had been raised. What many Alabama Baptist leaders failed to understand was the provincial views of many of their congregations. Many churchgoers, especially in North Alabama, viewed Howard as a school of the planter-dominated Black Belt or simply Marion's college and not a denominational school for all Alabama Baptists. As historian Robert Weibe observed, nineteenth-century America was a land of isolated "island communities" unto themselves. "The heart of American democracy," he added, "was local autonomy" and not statewide or national interests. By the 1870s, these island communities were losing their independence, but many local leaders "continued to assume that they could harness the forces of the world to the destiny of their community." Of the 112 students enrolled at Howard College in 1876, 100 were from the Black Belt region or bordering counties; 48 of the 100 students from the Black Belt were from Marion or Perry County; 7 students were from out of state, 4 from North Alabama, and 1 from South Alabama. Of the 29 members of the Board of Trustees, 25 were from the Black Belt region or bordering counties: 3 from North Alabama and 1 from South Alabama.[16]

Nonetheless, denominational leaders once again decided to embark upon their most ambitious fundraising plan yet. In 1876, the Alabama Baptist State Convention announced a populist campaign to encourage every white Southern Baptist in Alabama to contribute one dollar for Howard College in honor of the centennial of American Independence. With around 100,000 Baptists in the state, the hope was that the common people would rally around Howard and donate enough money to provide the school with a well-funded endowment. The Centennial Campaign was simple—perhaps too simple—as denominational leaders were so confident of the plan's success that they gave little thought to the possibility of failure. As historian B. F. Riley later wrote, "Many a well-constructed plan has fallen to pieces by reason of the omission of a single minor consideration." Riley added a quote from the apocryphal *Ecclesiasticus:* "He that despiseth little things shall fall little by little."[17]

The convention appointed a Central Centennial Committee which would work with various pastors and local associations around the state. Members of the committee believed that they maintained a solemn duty, as the heirs of the patriotic American Christians of the Revolutionary Era, to permanently immortalize their triumphs as a "perpetual reminder of their mighty deeds" of the past and as an avenue to further the noble goals of church and state. "In all objects which appeal to our benevolent concern," they supposed, "we can think of none so worthy of a grand centenary offering as the endowment of Howard College, whether viewed in the light of patriotic or Christian service."[18]

Historian Benjamin F. Riley later noted that the Alabama Baptists "set aside every other interest in the state for 1876." To lead the populist and patriotic fundraising crusade, they selected Rev. John Jefferson DeYampert Renfroe. Born in Montgomery County on August 30, 1830, J. J. D. Renfroe was the son of a profane father who attempted to keep his son insulated from Christian influences as he grew up among the hedonistic people of frontier Alabama. Nonetheless, the young Renfroe converted in 1848, felt the call to preach, was ordained, and emerged as one of Alabama's best-known preachers—pastoring the First Baptist Church of Talladega for many years. Following the Civil War, he was a strong advocate of the "Lost Cause," a promoter of New South economic development, and a leader in rebuilding the various institutions controlled by the Alabama Baptists—especially Howard College. As the logical choice to lead the Centennial Campaign, Howard bestowed upon him an honorary doctorate of divinity in 1875. "No minister in Alabama," William Cathcart wrote soon afterward, "occupies a larger and more tender place in the affections of his brethren, no man has more of the confidence and respect of the denomination of which he belongs."[19]

J. J. D. Renfroe started his campaign for Howard College on horseback. He crisscrossed the state and "threw his soul into the work" for the endowment. At one Baptist church, he preached a rousing sermon that stirred the hearts of patriots and aroused Baptist fervor for religious liberty. "My, how our hearts swelled within us!" an observer noted. As he concluded his sermon, Renfroe turned to the centennial appeal and asked each member to give one dollar to the Howard College endowment. The pastor of the church, Washington Bryan Crumpton, believed that his congregation "would all give and give until it hurt . . . under the inspiration of this great address." Crumpton expected that one of the richest men in his church would respond with much more money than a dollar. After Renfroe's sermon, the man stood, praised the speaker, proclaimed his pride in being an American and a Baptist, hailed the centennial movement, and spoke of the worthiness of the endowment. "Brother Pastor," he added. "I have a wife and seven children and three grandchildren. . . . I am going to give one dollar for each of them just the same; put me down for twelve dollars." The wealthy man's meager offer shocked Renfroe and Crumpton. "We were whipped," Crumpton later wrote. "We were almost speechless."[20]

Renfroe and Crumpton quickly realized that the centennial campaign was a "foolish undertaking" ruined by a narrow focus. "A pair of lunatics in any asylum, ought to have known better," Crumpton added. Baptist leaders were dazzled by the prospects of raising so much money but, as a historian noted, it was "reckless presumption" that every Baptist in the state would respond to the appeal with cash during an economic depression with limited circulation of money. One Howard College alum called the fundraising effort, the "inglorious failure of '76." In the end, J. J. D. Renfroe raised barely enough money to cover his expenses and provide a small salary for his efforts. When the campaign closed at the end of 1876, Renfroe was physically exhausted and "laid into silence" for eight months. When he did return to the pulpit, he later recalled, his preaching was of "little force" and to survive his family relied on the "charity of my faithful and much loved church." Although his eighteen months of work for Howard College brought him nothing but heartaches, he still supported the efforts of the school to raise an endowment.[21]

President of the Howard College Board of Trustees William W. Wilkerson believed that the only way the institution would survive without an endowment was through merit. "So, what your centennial effort has failed to do through a munificent endowment," he wrote, "must be accomplished by a character of work that will make our young men the peers of any." All that Howard College now asked of the Baptists of Alabama was to send their sons to receive an education.[22]

Colonel J. T. Murfee agreed with Wilkerson's assessment and decided that one way to demonstrate Howard's merit was to transform the school into a regimented military academy. Just as Samuel Sterling Sherman drew from his experiences at Middlebury College to craft the classical curriculum at Howard, James Thomas Murfee brought VMI's tradition of southern military training to the college. Like other former Confederate officers in higher education, Murfee saw the military component as a way to build character, discipline, and respect. Drills kept the young men so busy that they were less likely to engage in mischief, leading to an increase in virtue and morality on campus. Perhaps the most potent motivating factor, however, was the obvious imitation of what historian Rod Andrew described as the "image of the knightly, valorous, virtuous, and pious Confederate soldier." This was the legend of the Lost Cause in action on college campuses across the South that legitimized the "southern cultural notion that martial and moral virtues were inseparable."[23]

As part of the nation's centennial celebration in 1876, Howard College became a full military institution under the leadership of President James Thomas Murfee, a former Confederate officer and graduate of the Virginia Military Institute. (Samford University, Special Collection and University Archives)

Colonel J. T. Murfee would serve as superintendent of the Howard College Cadet Corps and head of the new Military School of Art and Science. In addition to their classical training, the cadets would receive "theoretical and practical" instruction in military tactics, strategy, artillery, fortifications, and other areas taught by Murfee and a new commander of cadets. The young men would be organized into more than one company, and Murfee would select company leaders based on who was most "soldier like" in their performance. The Howard boys were required to wear their uniforms at drill and all public or formal occasions. Various newspaper accounts revealed that the uniforms were now Confederate gray in keeping with other southern military schools and in furthering the myth of the Lost Cause. For the Howard cadets, military drills would be held on the grounds in front of the main building and would be limited to one hour a day and not interfere with their academics.[24]

In addition, the cadets would receive daily room inspections and be subject to military discipline for a variety of offenses. The Officer of the Day (O.D.) inspected the rooms and the cadets—noting all violations of the Howard College Law. Every infraction, no matter how minor, had to be reported regardless of "persons or circumstances." Failure to do so resulted in the O.D. violating not only duty and pledge, but also losing the good faith of Colonel Murfee, the faculty, and those students who followed the code of conduct. "Honor," wrote one student, "is no longer his." One Howard cadet described his experiences in verse:

Who doth rise at half past five,
And with the dust and bed quilts strive,
And sweeps up room at double-quick,
Before the O.D. taps at six?
Who doth stand behind the bed,
Frightened till he's almost dead,
Trying to hide his feet so fair,
While the O.D. think his shoes are there?
A Howard Boy.

Who goes to bed before release
And gets caught up with—slick as grease,
And gets demerits for the same,
But then Saturday says he's lame?
Who hath long lessons, who hath woe,
Who to his mamma wants to go,
And when he writes the same to her
Gets an emphatic, "No, no, Sir?"
A Howard Boy.

Who doth on Monday early go
To the Colonel with his woe
And tries that day to get excused,
But in lieu of that gets abused?
Who then resolves next to get
The Monday lessons on Friday set?
Who doth then to the class rooms go
"Busts" all day long and gets zero?
A Howard Boy.

Who doth visit his neighbor so free
And with him doth talk so gaily and free,
Till, "O.D." is coming," by someone said,
Then mingles with dust under the bed?
Who scratcheth his head as he pours over "Math,"
Thinking that his is an uneven path
And as he marches his Saturday tour,
Of that one thing he's certain and sure?
A Howard Boy.

But who after all is noble and true
And does with his might what his hand find to do,
Who, through full of fun and mischief, he
The ruler of state and country shall be?
Who takes "duty" as a watchword and guide
And follows it closely with manhood and pride?
Who shall an honor, an ornament be
To himself, his family, his country so free?
THE Howard Boy.[25]

Overall, the Howard boys embraced the military component as a way to elevate the college's distinction and to honor, in their minds, the virtues of the Lost Cause. "Military is all the go among us now," wrote one student. "Some of the cadets love it so much that they practice marching up and down the principal walks of the campus for an hour or two on Saturdays." The cadets marching on Saturdays, the sarcastic student writer explained, were actually being punished for some violation of Colonel Murfee's strict rules. A writer for the *Alabama Baptist* visited campus during the weekday drills held in the afternoon following classes. He witnessed the cadets engaged in field duty, marching, carrying shelter tents, setting up and striking encampments; the week before, the students engaged in an efficient display of a "sham battle" on campus. "This department," the writer added, "is unusually thorough."[26]

Across town, female students at Judson supported the "diligent and daily" military activities of the male cadets. The young women raised money and purchased material to create a flag/banner for use by the Howard Corps of Cadets in parades and drills. At a formal presentation on the grounds of Judson, the cadets marched from the Howard campus, wearing their gray uniforms and gleaming polished shoes and carrying shiny fixed bayonets. One witness commented that the boys "presented a most soldierly and commanding appearance." The cadets' procession stopped in front of the Judson chapel, and immediately the doors opened and the female students filed out in columns of two. Loulie Gwaltney stepped forward and delivered the presentation address, illustrating the mythology of the Lost Cause and intentionally drawing parallels between the Howard banner and the Confederate flag sewed by women in Marion in 1861. "The banner we present today does not call you to field," she proclaimed. "It guides that discipline of attitude, movement and exercise by which your physical frames will be developed with manlier proportions." Gwaltney believed that the Howard banner symbolized honor, order, obedience, and discipline; echoed the virtues of a warrior, and signaled the triumph over vice, sin, and ignorance. Adjutant Lieutenant Thomas Ware Raymond stepped forward on behalf of the cadets and accepted the banner in "his usual graceful manner." The banner was made of silk with a field of blue on one side and white on the other. In gold lettering at the top was the word "Howard," at the bottom "Cadet Corps," and in between a large cross and crown—then the coat of arms of Howard College. Raymond handed the banner to the color bearer, P. T. Hale, who unfurled the flag, and the cadets gave the Judson women three cheers. "Wheeling into line," a writer for the *Marion Commonwealth* reported, "they marched on the lawn, proud of the banner which floated above them, and thankful to the young ladies for their considerate and surely highly appreciated kindness."[27]

Colonel Murfee's regimented military drills—combined with VMI's barracks discipline, Christian virtue, and classical liberal arts training—educated the mind, body, and soul of the Howard students. From James T. Murfee and the faculty, Howard College graduate P. C. Drew learned the "Obedience to laws, subordination to authority, due deference to superiors, promptness and fidelity to duty, correctness in dealing, and neatness of person and work." These were, he added, "charming virtues" that deserved "to be taught and acquired as ornaments for the character as much as any attainment of knowledge for the mind."[28]

At commencement in 1878, the merit of the new military training was on display as the colonel, members of the Board of Trustees, and the Howard Corps of Cadets marched into the chapel. The students stacked their arms in front of the elevated stage as the spectators revered "their manly bearing which reflects great credit upon our college." It was precisely the effect that James T. Murfee had hoped to achieve. Thomas Ware Raymond received a master of arts degree for "attainments higher and more extended" than other students seeking a bachelor's degree. Raymond received certificates of distinguished proficiency in seven of the schools at Howard and proficiency in Latin, Greek, English, mental and moral philosophy, history, mathematics, chemistry, mineralogy, geology, natural history, natural philosophy, two modern languages (most likely French and German), literature, and applied mathematics. He passed exams in all of the subjects. Three years later, in 1881, Raymond completed coursework and received ordination at Union Theological Seminary (then part of Hampton-Sydney College in Virginia) and began his career as a Presbyterian minister and educator. That same year, he also found time to marry Loulie Gwaltney, the Judson student who presented T. W. Raymond the cadet banner.[29]

9

TO THE HIGHEST BIDDER

With the college's financial embarrassment in the post–Civil War era and the depressed economic condition of the South in general, the Howard board realized that the college would be unable to honor the "Certificate of Permanent Scholarships" issued before the war. Many of the Howard College donors who held the scholarships "cheerfully relinquished them," the trustees reported in 1866. "It is to be hoped that all will." As one historian later observed, the trustees anticipated that the public statement would dissuade any other certificate holders from sending students to the college because "finances could not sustain the scholarships at that time." But one surly certificate holder demanded the college honor its pledge.[1]

A resident of Talladega County, Matthew Turner was one of the state's wealthiest plantation owners in the years before the Civil War, with real estate and personal property valued at $200,000 in 1860 (including seventy slaves) and an estimated value of "not less than $100,000" in 1870. In 1855, Turner met with Howard College agent James H. DeVotie and signed five $100 promissory notes toward the college's endowment. On January 23, 1863, he paid the last of his notes ($300) in Confederate currency and the college issued the "Certificate of Permanent Scholarship." At some point following the trustee's statement on the scholarships, most likely in 1867, Howard College president J. L. M. Curry dispatched the pastor of the First Baptist Church of Talladega, J. J. D. Renfroe, to petition Turner to relinquish the scholarship. He refused.[2]

That same year, the sixty-four-year-old Matthew Turner was embroiled in a nefarious scheme to divorce his young wife, Ann Macon Turner (thirty years his junior), and prevent her from receiving any of his assets in a settlement. During the fall of 1867, Turner transferred most of his real estate to his children from a previous marriage (and to his son-in-law Thomas W. Curry, J.L.M.'s

By the 1870s, Marion, like the rest of Alabama's Black Belt, struggled through the new cultural realities and economic uncertainties of the Reconstruction and "Redemption" eras. (Samford University, Special Collection and University Archives)

brother). As part of his scheme, Turner invited his wife to travel with him. She accepted but only if her husband promised not to abandon her or continue to treat her harshly. He refused to answer her requests and, in turn, left the state and filed for divorce in Indiana on the grounds that she had abandoned him. In response, Ann filed for divorce in Alabama on the grounds of "adultery, cruelty, and abandonment." Following a protracted legal battle, the Alabama Supreme Court concluded in 1870 that there was "no possible doubt" of Ann Macon Turner's charges against her husband. The courts found that Matthew Turner beat, choked, and humiliated his wife—especially after she discovered her husband's sexual relationship with one of his slaves. For years, she suffered as a "patient martyr of his tyranny and brutality," and in his final act of cruelty, Turner stripped her rights as a citizen by transferring his wealth and denying her any share in his estate. The court voided Turner's real estate transfers to his children and son-in-law and ordered him to provide Ann Macon Turner a large alimony settlement. On October 3, 1870, Turner's land was sold on the courthouse steps in Talladega to satisfy the court order.[3]

Four years later, in October 1874, Matthew Turner's grandson, William T. Curry, enrolled at Howard College. When Curry's father attended the Alabama

Baptist State Convention in November of that year in Marion, he brought with him Turner's "Certificate of Permanent Scholarship" and presented it to an official at Howard College. Curry was informed that Howard College "could not receive pupils on these scholarships, that they were not able to do it, and that they were refusing all of them at that time." Curry paid his son's $113 tuition bill and returned to Talladega with Turner's unredeemed certificate. The younger Curry only attended Howard College during the 1874–75 academic year and never returned.[4]

Almost two years later, following the embarrassing failure of the centennial endowment campaign, Howard's Board of Trustees reiterated that the college would not honor the scholarships purchased before the Civil War. In the minds of members of the board, their position was clear. Since the scholarships were given to establish an endowment, and since an endowment did not exist, Howard had the right to disavow the scholarships. Matthew Turner rejected this argument and hired Selma lawyer and future Alabama U.S. senator Edmund Pettus to commence legal action against the school. On August 22, 1876, Pettus filed a lawsuit against Howard College for a breach of contract—with the cash-strapped Turner seeking damages from the financially desolate institution.[5]

In 1878, during the spring term of the Fourth Judicial Circuit of Alabama, the case was first presented in the courtroom of Judge George Henry Craig. A native of Dallas County, Craig was a student cadet at the University of Alabama in 1865, serving as an infantry lieutenant under the command of James T. Murfee. Following the war, he read for the bar under attorneys in Selma and began his legal and political career as a Republican. In 1874, when Alabama voters ended Republican rule, Craig bucked the statewide trend and defeated Democrat John Moore for a six-year term as the judge of the Fourth Judicial Circuit, which included Marion. Although many whites in the district looked askance at Republican Craig, he gained a reputation as an "affable gentleman" who was "intent upon a faithful and impartial administration of justice."[6]

In Judge Craig's courtroom that spring, Edmund Pettus represented Turner, while John Foster Vary argued on behalf of Howard College. The sixty-seven-year-old Vary was a native of Oneida, New York (a contemporary of James H. DeVotie), who initially came to the South as an educator but read for the bar in Demopolis, Alabama, and began practicing law in 1850. Vary rejected Turner's claim because he paid three of the promissory notes ($300) with Confederate currency and not with U.S. currency. The treasurer of the Board of Trustees had no authority to accept Confederate money from Turner in 1863; therefore the issuing of the scholarship was illegal, and the claim was nonenforced. "If the agent's action were legal," Vary added, "the value of the Confederate money was very little compared to the value contemplated when the contract was initially made." The jury, however, sided with Turner and awarded him $331.20.[7]

For unclear reasons, the court granted Howard College a new trial, but the case was continued nine times until September 1882. During the intervening years, vocal opposition to the "radical" Judge George Henry Craig became more pronounced from white, Black Belt Democrats. Apparently, several attorneys practicing in the Fourth Circuit nominated Craig for federal patronage positions around the state. "We 'vastly preferred' having him collector in Mobile to having him judge in our circuit," they wrote. With Craig out of the way, they supposed, Democratic governor George S. Houston would appoint a more acceptable judge. When Craig's appointments failed to occur, white Democrats throughout the district focused on supporting former Howard College student John Moore in his election bid to unseat Judge Craig in 1880. "We should regard his defeat a calamity," they wrote, "his election a blessing, to our people." Moore won the election and would preside over the retrial of *Matthew Turner v. Howard College*.[8]

At this 1882 trial, Howard was represented by attorneys William B. Modawell of Perry County and William McLin Brooks of Selma—the latter one of the state's most acclaimed lawyers and a former law partner of the deceased head of the Howard Board of Trustees, I. W. Garrott. Once both sides presented their cases, Judge John Moore instructed the jury that, if they found evidence that Turner was entitled to recover damages, they should do so from the moment that Howard College refused the certificate of scholarship presented by William Curry. The jury should also consider the value of tuition from 1874 to 1882. Nonetheless, on September 21, 1882, another Perry County jury found in favor of Matthew Turner's claim and almost doubled the damages, awarding him $640.[9]

Five days later, on September 26, the executive committee of Howard's Board of Trustees met at the Marion Savings Bank to review the college's finances and to craft a response to the jury's decision. The committee agreed with the advice of attorneys Modawell and Brooks and filed a $1,660 appeal bond to the Alabama Supreme Court. Trustees W. W. Wilkerson and J. B. Lovelace acted as sureties on behalf of the college.[10]

On July 16, 1883, the state's highest court published its decision in the *Trustees of Howard College v. Turner* and ruled in favor of Matthew Turner without dissent. In writing the opinion of the Alabama Supreme Court, Associate Justice Henderson Middleton Somerville rejected the arguments of Howard's attorneys that the college representative had no authority to receive payment of Turner's promissory notes in Confederate money. When Howard accepted the Confederate currency, then the only currency in circulation, they validated the contract and Mathew Turner fulfilled the requirements by paying $500. "This obligation," Somerville wrote, "he has, in the eye of the law, fully discharged." The certificate of scholarship gave Turner the right "to send any fit person within his option to the college, as a pupil, to be educated . . . free of tuition." By denying Matthew Turner the right to send a student to Howard, free of tuition, the school failed to "recognize the binding obligation of the contract." Howard College, the justice concluded, had a legal duty to fulfill the terms of the con-tract, but the school failed to do so, which compelled the plaintiff's legal action and justified the damages. The circuit court based the amount of damages on the annual value of tuition in 1874 (when Curry presented Turner's certificate) to the opening of the trial in 1882. "We discover no error in the rulings of the court," Somerville concluded and affirmed the lower court's ruling.[11]

On July 23, a week following the published decision, members of the Board of Trustees met to discuss the ruling. On August 1, the board met again and lis-tened to attorney John Foster Vary explain the execution of the verdict rendered by the court, which was in the hands of Perry County Sheriff J. B. Cocke. The sheriff would sell the Howard College campus—land, buildings, furnishings, equipment, library—from the steps of the Perry County Courthouse. Also, in order to pay eight years' worth of attorney's fees and court costs, the trustees authorized board secretary J. L. Wyatt to mortgage the president's home and land and all personal property belonging to the college and deliver the mortgage to trustees J. B. Lovelace and W. W. Wilkerson to "indemnify, protect, and save them from harm on account of any and all money which they have advanced and for which they have become liable for the use and benefit or on account of the College."

Throughout March 1884, the following advertisement ran in the Marion newspapers:

By virtue of an execution issued by L. S. Jones, Clerk of the Circuit Court of Perry County, State of Alabama against the Trustees of Howard College and others and in favor of Matthew Turner. And one in favor of said Turner and against some parties from the Supreme Court of Alabama, which said expectations have been placed in my hands for collection, I will sell to the highest bidder for cash at public outcry in front of the Court House in said County of Perry, on the FIRST MONDAY IN APRIL, A.D., 1884, the following described real estate levied on by virtue of said executions as the property of said defendants, to-wit: A lot of land situated in the town of Marion in said County, and bounded on the North by an Alley, on the East by Parish street, on the South by a lot formerly owned by William Stewart, and on the West by Polk street, said described property will be sold to satisfy the above named executions. J. B. Cocke, Sheriff, Marion, Ala., March 4, 1884.[12]

On Monday, April 7, at noon, Sheriff J. B. Cocke stood on the steps of the Greek Revival courthouse, built in 1856. He opened the public auction and asked

On April 7, 1884, Sheriff J. B. Cocke stood on the steps of the Perry County Courthouse and auctioned to the highest bidder the land, building, furnishings, equipment, and library of Howard College. (Library of Congress, Prints and Photographs Division)

for bids. He received just one. W. W. Wilkerson and J. B. Lovelace of the Board of Trustees bid $1,080—the exact amount needed to meet the obligation to Matthew Turner and additional court costs. Ironically, Matthew Turner never saw any of the money from the sale of the property, having died a little over a week before the auction on the courthouse steps. A Talladega newspaper reported that Turner "quietly left the scene of his long and busy life and sank to rest."[13]

At the next meeting of the Howard College Board of Trustees, Attorney John Foster Vary explained that Wilkerson and Lovelace were now the sole owners of the campus and could dispose of the property as they saw fit. "I know it to be a bonafide purchase," Vary said, and the two men used their own personal funds to execute the acquisition. "No money belonging to the college was used in the payment of the purchase." Wilkerson and Lovelace then explained that they purchased the campus for the sole purpose of saving it for the state convention and intended to transfer the property to the convention as soon as possible. On July 13, 1886, Wilkerson and Lovelace conveyed the property to the state convention for $1.00. The deed specified that the campus must be used "as a college and as schools connected therewith and for no other purposes and be forever under" the Alabama Baptist State Convention. "Apparently by shifting ownership to the convention," one historian observed, "the college could continue to operate as a Baptist entity, but the campus would be shielded from future levies arising from the scholarships." Nonetheless, even with the lingering burden of the scholarships lifted from the college, Howard continued to teeter on the edge of financial ruin, and relationships with the state convention deteriorated.[14]

While the conflict over the Matthew Turner lawsuit kept the Board of Trustees well occupied, the business of educating the cadets continued. Between 1868 and 1887, Howard College graduated 117 young men, and almost all entered middle-class professions. Ministers and educators led the way with 21 graduates each; lawyers and judges were next with 20 graduates, followed by merchants at 17 and medical doctors at nine. Surprisingly, even with Murfee's strong emphasis on practical and scientific training, only a handful of graduates entered engineering fields (3) or banking (3).[15]

Much to the chagrin of many leaders in the Alabama Baptist State Convention, Howard was still producing only a small percentage of graduates for the ministry. The pastor of Siloam Baptist Church, Edwin Theodore Winkler, often mentored the Howard College students entering the ministry. Arriving at Siloam in 1872, Winkler possessed degrees from Brown University and Newton Theological Seminary and pastored several prominent Baptist churches, including the First Baptist Church of Charleston, South Carolina. A Confederate stalwart, Winkler served as chaplain under General P. G. T. Beauregard and maintained a warm friendship with General Robert E. Lee. Following the war, he was a leading orator of the Lost Cause and no doubt infused many in his congregation—including many Howard College students—with these notions. Just before moving to Marion in 1872, Winkler suggested that the state of affairs in South Carolina was so corrupt and shameless that it justified citizens forming "vigilance committees" (like the Ku Klux Klan) to bring order and justice to society. "In a state of society where there is no law, and where men must form temporary organizations for the redress of intolerable grievances and the maintenance of social order, justice itself is perverted by an attack upon these organizations." In declining health and frustrated by the situation in South Carolina, Winkler moved to Alabama and served at Siloam until his death in 1883.[16]

In 1881, the Howard students preparing for ministerial careers praised Rev. E. T. Winkler's efforts in providing invaluable comprehensive notes on biblical doctrines with detailed references to proof texts and parallel passages. These notes furthered Winkler's outstanding reputation both as a scholar and an orthodox theologian. "We are prompted to give this expression from sincere appreciation of the advantages we have enjoyed and we do it the more heartily," the students wrote in the *Alabama Baptist,* because neither Winkler nor Murfee had any obligation to provide the ministerial students with such mentoring and instruction. "We believe they have been incited by the interest they feel for our common cause and from a desire to extend the Redeemer's Kingdom," they added. For all young men called to the ministry "who desire to qualify themselves more thoroughly for the work they have undertaken," the students "commend Howard College."[17]

Even with Winkler's mentoring efforts, many Baptist leaders believed that only vocational training, not liberal arts education, would produce an educated clergy. Colonel Murfee, and the handful of Howard College students called to the ministry, disagreed. They believed in educating the whole person through a classical curriculum combined with physical and mental discipline. "Howard College does not call men to preach the gospel," student P. C. Drew wrote in

1883; "neither does it give spiritual endowments, nor in many cases does it execute discipline to correct the moral conduct of theological students, but on account of natural laxity peculiar to all undisciplined men, and for their good and the good of the institution, Col. Murfee tightens the screws on all alike and the best men come out regulated, shaped, and largely benefited." Through experience and observation, Murfee's military discipline contributed to the success of ministerial students who learned a "system of principles" and "tone of character" which sustained them as they contended with difficulties and struggled with entanglements.[18]

Colonel Murfee worked closely with the ministerial students each Saturday evening with an "exercise in sermonizing." Murfee chose a text and assigned students to prepare each part of the sermon. One student gave the introduction; others presented the argument, the subject, and the applications—with one student focusing on an application for Christians and another offering an application to nonbelievers. Following the sermon, Howard College student J. R. Sampey recalled, Murfee offered criticism to each of the speakers. "While no credit toward a degree was given," Sampey added, "this exercise was exceedingly helpful to beginners in the art of preaching. Aid of this kind could be found only in a Christian college."[19]

For James T. Murfee, John Richard Sampey represented the type of young, disciplined minister that Howard College could produce. Born September 27, 1863, in Fort Deposit, Alabama, Sampey was the son of a circuit-riding Methodist preacher who, after a heated discussion with some "aggressive Baptists," forewent his sprinkling ways, embraced immersion, and henceforward preached in Baptist churches. In addition to his ministry, the elder Sampey also labored as a sheep farmer, which provided enough money for his son to attend Howard College. "I never think of the manner in which my parents toiled and skimped that I might have an education," J. R. Sampey wrote, "without unspeakable appreciation of their sacrifices on my behalf." At fifteen, Sampey felt the call to the ministry and received a license to preach from the Ramer Baptist Church. Some years later, as his father lay dying, he told his son: "I am about done for and cannot hope to preach any more: Preach the best you know how, and then think of your old father and preach a little better for my sake."[20]

Just before his sixteenth birthday, in the fall of 1879, Sampey traveled across the state to Marion and enrolled in Howard College. "There was no hesitation,"

Sampey wrote, "as to the school to which I should go for my college education." Over the years, Colonel Murfee made several visits to the Sampey home and often peppered the young J. R. Sampey with questions to measure his intellectual prowess. Murfee: "How much are six apples and seven peaches?" Sampey: "Thirteen, sir," Murfee: "Thirteen what?" Sampey: "Thirteen pieces of fruit, sir." Murfee: "Ah, you got out of the difficulty pretty well." The colonel reminded Sampey that only matching things could be added.[21]

At Howard, Sampey and the rest of the freshmen during the 1879–80 academic year took classes in algebra, geometry, English, elocution, parliamentary law, declamation, rhetoric, and laws of thought; the students also read Cicero, Virgil, and Horace. In addition, Sampey thrived under the military system at Howard and found great inspiration from the stern disciplinary spirit of Colonel Murfee. During his freshman year, a revival swept across campus. Sampey and other Christian students fanned the revival fires by choosing a friend to lift in prayer and invite them to accept Christ as Savior. In the quiet of his room, Sampey prayed for fellow student J. T. Hayes, whom he later described as an "attractive fellow" from a Methodist family. Following his prayer, Sampey walked to Hayes's room and asked him to give his heart to Jesus. "I had never before asked anyone to accept my Saviour," he recalled, "and my heart was in my throat." The next day, Hayes said, "Sampey, I just invited you in to thank you for the good words you spoke to me. I have given my heart to Christ, and yesterday I united with the Methodist Church." Hayes's decision affirmed Sampey's calling into the ministry.[22]

Before classes began in the fall of 1880, Sampey preached his first sermon on "Eternity" with the text focusing on Psalm 90:2: "Before the mountains were brought forth, or ever thou hadst formed the earth and the world, even from everlasting to everlasting, thou art God." The young preacher believed he spoke "rapidly and earnestly, touching on almost every phase of the gospel message."[23]

As with other Howard students, Sampey sharpened his oratorical and debating skills by participating in the college's Franklin and Philomathic literary societies; the latter replaced the Adelphi society following the Civil War and was a Greek word for a scholar or a lover of learning. As one student later recalled, these literary societies "reached the heyday of their activity" under Colonel James T. Murfee. Each society maintained rooms (or "halls," for example, "Franklin Hall") dedicated for their use on the second floor of the main building where they met every Saturday evening under the guidance of the elected officers: president, vice president, counselor, secretary, treasurer, librarian, chaplain, critic, monthly orator, and door keeper.[24]

The meetings followed strict parliamentary procedures, and the vice president made note of any member who violated the society's rules of conduct, resulting in some form of punitive action:

- Anyone who applauded "with his feet" was fined 10 cents.
- Anyone who spit on the floor was fined 10 cents.
- Anyone who turned his back on the society's president was fined 10 cents.
- Anyone who used obscene language was fined 25 cents.
- Anyone who disrespected any officer of the society was fined 50 cents.
- Anyone who disrespected the president of the society was reported to Colonel Murfee.

During the Saturday evening gatherings, the society's president called the meeting to order, the chaplain offered a prayer, and the secretary called roll and read the minutes of the last meeting. The next "order of business" was often a member offering another student's name as a "Proposition of Membership," which brought thunderous applause from the audience. The proposed member was escorted from the hall by his sponsor, and the society voted on his membership. "The action being favorable, as was always the case," one student later recalled, "the applicant was readmitted to the hall and escorted to the rostrum amidst applause, where the president administered" a simple pledge of membership. The new society brother was required to pay a two-dollar membership fee.[25]

Every January and February of each academic year, the Franklin and Philomathic societies held separate public meetings to celebrate the anniversaries of each organization. The program provided an opportunity for students to display their maturing rhetorical skills and included a "declaimer" who delivered a passage from a well-known piece of poetry or prose. An "extempore orator" was selected by the president just before the start of the meeting. "This unhappy individual," Mitchell Garrett later wrote, "might retire from the hall for a few minutes, if he so desired, to prepare his oration; but at the time designated . . . he must be ready with his offering sans notes, sans manuscript, sans everything." This was followed by debates on contemporary or historical questions. One year, the students debated the question, "Ought a state to adopt a system of

compulsory education?" The judges commended the students' arguments, logical skills, and delivery styles as filled with "facile grace and manly dignity." The
audience, Rev. E. T. Winkler wrote, believed that the young men who debated
the question were "destined for eminence" in their future endeavors. "We felt
that we were listening to men, not boys," Winkler added, those men who were
"dexterous and powerful in argument, poetry, and oratory."[26]

During the 1880–81 academic year, J. R. Sampey and the Philomathic Society debated the question, "Would a peaceable separation of the United States
into a North and a South Republic, be beneficial to the South?" Sampey spoke
against separation and based his argument to preserve the union on the notion
of "united we stand, divided we fall." In addition, he believed, the tax burden
on the southern people would be too great to maintain a viable republic. On
the other side of the question, Sampey's chief opponent was the "fire eating"
Sidney J. Catts, who would later become the reckless, demagogue governor of
Florida in the early twentieth century. Catts blasted the South's total economic
dependence upon the "energetic" North. He concluded that "this deplorable
state of affairs, being the result of oppression, could be obviated by a separation." It was no surprise when the judges, all former Confederates, including
Reverend Winkler, "gracefully rendered" a decision in favor of Mr. Catts and
the affirmative group. "The debate," one observer later wrote, "though in a mea-
suring lacking in vigorous prosecution and spicy repartee, exhibited germs of
argumentative talent which, if cultivated, will bring forth a rich harvest."[27]

The following year at the Philomathic anniversary, on February 24, 1882,
members debated the question: "Was the banishment of Napoleon Bonaparte
to St. Helena justifiable?" Those on the negative side of the issue convinced the
judges that Napoleon's exile was unjustified. J. R. Sampey gave an oration entitled "Stonewall Jackson: The Military Genius of the South." No doubt Sampey's
discourse venerated Jackson and the myth of the Lost Cause, leading a writer
for the Marion paper to praise his oration as "very touching, and carried us back
to the scenes which he pictured so vividly and in which we were actors." A few
months later, John R. Sampey graduated as the valedictorian of the graduating
class of 1882 and entered the Southern Baptist Theological Seminary in Louisville, Kentucky, where he graduated in 1885. Sampey was invited to stay on and
teach—emerging as one the seminary's most thoughtful intellectuals and Old
Testament theologians. In 1887, Sampey encouraged young men entering the

ministry to recognize the wisdom of older Christian leaders (like J. T. Murfee) and draw upon the "resources of older heads" to provide congregations with "strong food" for the heart and mind. "It may not be pleasing to our vanity in this age," he emphasized, "to recognize our dependence upon the men who have grown gray in the service of the Lord."[28]

10

AWAKE, ARISE, OR BE
FOREVER FALLEN

By the fall of 1882, seventeen years had passed since the end of the Civil War, and as one writer noted, the South "still sat crushed, wretched, busy displaying and bemoaning their wounds." Throughout Alabama—and the rest of the South—conflict was at every turn: politically, socially, and economically. Land held no value; both planters and industrialists struggled with labor issues; prohibition reemerged as a moral issue with the growth of new urban areas; and then there was the long-term struggle between Black Belt aristocrats and hill country commoners; in addition, urban boosters clashed with rural standpatters; farmers felt the agrarian ideal slipping away and fought with the railroads and other middlemen; the Greenback-Labor Party challenged the hegemony of the redeemed white Bourbon Democrats; and racial violence and unrest continued unabated. Another economic depression between 1882 and 1885 fueled more dissatisfaction. And riding the waves of this discontent were Howard College and the Alabama Baptists.[1]

Several prominent Alabama Baptists continued to complain about the lack of ministerial preparation at Howard College, especially as Rev. E. T. Winkler's health declined, leading to his untimely death in 1883. The conflict was as old as the institution—between those who favored broad liberal arts education versus those who favored vocational training. During the 1882–83 academic year, 118 students enrolled in Howard College, but only 10 of these young men were preparing for ministerial careers. Rev. Washington Bryan Crumpton grumbled that the central task (or "prime idea") of the men who founded Howard College was to provide an inexpensive education for students entering the ministry. "The question is," Crumpton asked, "is Howard College doing the work for which it was founded?" The answer, he believed, was no. "Our college is not fulfilling the mission designed by its founders." The congregants of the white Baptist churches of Alabama were demanding minsters with "cultivated brains and piously concentrated hearts" to fill their pulpits. That Howard had such a low number of ministerial students, Crumpton believed, shamed the entire denomination. "The trustees and faculty must understand that if the college was knit to the heart of the denomination, it must be educating ministers." Crumpton and his protégées were more interested in the quantity, not the quality, of young men entering the ministry.[2]

James T. Murfee, however, refuted Crumpton's conclusions. In his annual report to the Board of Trustees, Murfee noted that, in its first twenty-four years of existence, Howard College graduated seventeen theology students, but during the twelve years of his presidency (1871–83), Howard graduated fourteen theology students. "Does this look like a decline in ministerial education at Howard College?" Murfee asked. "Instead of decline, the increase has been wonderful; and the change in the agencies by which the work has been done is quite remarkable." The colonel praised the efforts of the faculty to prepare the ministry students more thoroughly than a narrow vocational approach. In general, he added, most colleges failed to give ministerial students training in rigorous liberal arts subjects, but also preparation in parliamentary law, practical logic, rhetoric, and elocution—all subjects of vital importance to young men entering the ministry.[3]

When Crumpton complained that the cost of Howard College was too high "for a poor boy to pay," Murfee pointed out that the ministerial students paid no tuition, and the college carried the "theologies" with no "appreciable help from the denomination." The Alabama Baptist State Convention should provide more financial support for educating young ministers, Murfee argued. "It would be a small matter for the 80,000 Baptists of Alabama to educate a few theologues, but it was a very heavy burden for the faculty of one College to bear." Several years earlier, the convention had promised more financial aid for theological education, but the scant funds were only a tiny fraction of the costs associated with the ministerial students' education. "But the professors have gone on," Murfee added, "and have given encouragement to every worthy brother who felt inclined to enter the ministry." In addition, the college furnished "direct and practical instruction in theology and sermonizing," something other Baptists schools were no longer doing in deference to the Southern Baptist Theological Seminary in Louisville.[4]

Many Alabama Baptists were more interested in funding the out-of-state theological seminary than the in-state Howard College. In 1883, the convention collected $1,294.47 for Southern Baptist Theological Seminary and $95.54 for Howard College. Some withheld support until the college established a theological chair—a position last held by Henry Talbird, revived briefly by Samuel R. Freeman between 1869 and 1871, but abandoned due to the institution's deep financial difficulties. A tree was known by its fruit, wrote one Alabama Baptist and, without a vigorous theological chair, Howard was "simply a college dispossessed of its crowning grace and beauty." Another observer argued that Baptists throughout the state had a "heap of faith" in preachers and wanted to send their sons to a college with a trusted pastor as a faculty member. "I don't suppose," he added, "there is a Baptist college in the world without a preacher connected with it but Howard."[5]

To address these ongoing issues, the college's Board of Trustees recommended that the convention create a board of ministerial education to raise funds and contribute aid toward the education of "indigent young men who are seeking to prepare themselves for the ministry" and to make certain that the number of students who received free tuition "shall not at any time be so large as to endanger the support of the faculty." The convention agreed that the demand for an "intelligent ministry" led by "godly, cultivated men" was in high demand throughout the state. "There are scores of young men in our State who, in answer to the prayers of God's people for more laborers to be sent into the harvest, are ready to say: 'Here am I, send me.' Are we doing our duty to these young men? We fear not." The board accomplished little during their first year of existence.[6]

But the next year, as Howard College spiraled toward insolvency, the convention appointed a new board of ministerial education led by Rev. David Ingram Purser of First Baptist Church of Birmingham. Over the next few years, Purser would emerge as one of Howard College's most vocal critics and most ardent supporters. Born in Mississippi on December 27, 1843, Purser was ordained in 1870 and began his career as a circuit-riding minister serving seven churches over a distance of seventy-five miles. Mississippi Baptist leaders took note of Purser's "marvelous energy, great earnestness, and striking ability" and appointed him an itinerant evangelist covering territory throughout the South. In 1883, Alabama Baptists hired Purser to serve as the state evangelist, which led him to Birmingham and ultimately the full-time pastorate of First Baptist Church.[7]

This board, based in Birmingham, took a much more aggressive approach, as the high-spirited and outspoken Purser decided that the board should take over supervision of the ministerial students at Howard. He traveled to Marion to convince Murfee to give the ministerial students more autonomy and exempt them from activities required of other students—namely participation in the military aspects of the college. In addition, Purser believed that these "theologues" should receive room and board in an off-campus house rented by the board. This way, the indigent students could avoid the additional expenses of uniforms and the higher costs of room and board in the on-campus dormitories. It also provided the board with much greater control over the students' daily lives and training. Colonel Murfee rejected the idea. "Let the young brethren stay here in the dormitories," he told Purser. "Just as they have been doing, and they will be treated exactly right; but they must do the things that are to do."[8]

Most of Howard's board supported Murfee, but the outspoken Porter King (a local judge and the son of E. D. King) embraced D. I. Purser's proposal. As one observer wrote, this usurpation of both Murfee's and the Board of Trustees' authority stirred up "considerable feeling," but the trustees' minutes remain strangely silent on the continuous debate—instead focusing on the aftermath of the bankruptcy and selling of the property. Perhaps it was no coincidence that Purser and the board of ministerial education chose this vulnerable moment in the history of the institution (and following the death of Rev. E. T. Winkler of Siloam) to make their dramatic takeover of Howard College's ministerial training. Nonetheless, Purser and other members of his board, including Rev. W. C. Cleveland, moved forward with raising money, renting a spacious house in Marion, and hiring a young couple to oversee the property and run the "mess hall" for the students. Just before classes started in the fall of 1884, Cleveland wrote: "Christian men and women, we see good, great good, and nothing but good in the mission upon which you have sent us."[9]

The state's most "venerable and venerated minister," Samuel Henderson, supported the actions of Purser, Cleveland, and the board to open more opportunities for theological training. "They mean business," Henderson wrote in the *Alabama Baptist*, and any young man with the "right grit" should come study at Howard College. But he still believed that the ministerial students should receive a full liberal arts education and depend upon their own "well-trained minds to grapple with theology." The critical thinking and life skills developed through liberal arts and applied to theology enabled "an earnest man to make fair proficiency in that study without any instructor except a good supply of theological works." Howard College played the vital role, Henderson believed, in educating "young ministers in Alabama for Alabama."[10]

For the following two academic years, the board directed the training of Howard's ministerial students apart from the college's oversight. Guest lectures were delivered by some of the state's most prominent Baptist ministers. J. J. D. Renfroe spoke on "Hold Fast to the Old Symbols of the Baptist Faith"; Samuel Henderson lectured on "The Relation between Doctrine and Duty"; and W. B. Crumpton talked about "Practical Suggestions to Young Preachers." The latter believed the most important advice he gave to young ministers was to make the most of their first years in the ministry by spending them pastoring a country church. "If you will be content," Crumpton said, "to give these years devotedly to your work, laying well the foundation and gathering material, you may have no fears for the future if everything else is right."[11]

The new pastor at Siloam, A. C. Davidson, took on the mentoring role left vacant by the death of his predecessor, E. T. Winkler. He too saw value in the students receiving a broad liberal arts training as foundation for studying theology. A preacher must have books, he once said. "They are not merely a luxury; they are a necessity." Davidson impacted many Howard College students. "To me he was a man sent from God to touch my life at its most important period," student L. O. Dawson later wrote. "In everything he was my ideal. As a pastor and as a man, I have never seen any greater than he. He loved the boys with a genuine shepherd heart, and in return they lavished on him their extravagant affection and youthful enthusiasm. In all those years his influence has been felt in my life, and whatever good I have done, his hand was in it all."[12]

Despite these positive results, tensions within the Alabama Baptist State Convention and between the board of ministerial education and Howard College continued to fester. "All this," one alumnus wrote, "seemed to many to be an uncalled-for interference with the internal administration of the college and a usurpation of authority which properly belonged to the Board of Trustees." For months, the two sides continued this tug of war. It was obvious, an observer later noted, that the trustees "lacked full control" over the management of the college. In July 1886, the entire board of ministerial education resigned, and a new board was appointed with narrowly defined responsibilities to raise funds, examine and recommend ministerial candidates, and "arrange with the authorities of Howard College for them to secure the benefits of ministerial education."

In turn, the house in Marion was closed, the furniture sold, and the students moved back to the college dormitories.[13]

Colonel J. T. Murfee and the Howard College Board of Trustees prevailed in the battle with the convention, but in the process, they alienated many of the state's most powerful Baptist ministers. This led to continued conflicts among Alabama Baptists over not only the mission of Howard College but whether the institution should continue educating students in the economically stagnant Alabama Black Belt of the 1880s.

"Perhaps," Samuel Henderson wrote in August 1885, "the most perplexing question that now agitates the Baptists of our state is, what can be done for Howard College?" The ever-present Henderson understood the long-term financial struggles of Howard better than most Alabama Baptists. In his forty-six years ministering in the state, he missed but three state conventions. In 1841, he was at the convention that gave charge to the creation of the Baptist school for young men. Twelve years later, Henderson rose before the same body and asked the brethren, shall the underfunded Howard College "live or die?" Whether as a writer, editor, preacher, or trustee, he was the institution's most articulate, impassioned, and colorful advocate of placing the college on sound financial footing. "He was not at all handsome," one fellow clergyman recalled, "but he was an entertaining speaker [and] no one wielded a more graceful pen than Sam Henderson." Now in his fifth decade of advocacy, Henderson still found Howard a troubling matter. He asked, shall we set the college adrift and let it try to survive without an endowment? "Or shall we abandon the present location and seek one where we can hope to build it up under happier auspices?"[14]

Samuel Henderson's writing in the *Alabama Baptist* was perhaps the first public musing on relocating Howard College. In 1885, however, few of the state's Baptists, including Henderson, advocated for the removal of the college, but instead favored another attempt at creating an endowment—something not tried since the failed campaign a decade earlier. In the fiscal year from July 1884 to July 1885, the convention received six dollars in contributions to Howard's endowment. In response, Henderson wrote a series of public lamentations on Howard College that appeared in several issues of the *Alabama Baptist* throughout the fall of 1885. Assuming the voice of an Old Testament prophet, the southern minister used honor and shame to urge the state's white Baptists to arise and endow the college. Not being able to build an endowment for Howard was a humiliation that should flush everyone's cheeks with shame. Henderson pointed out that the state's secular colleges (University of Alabama), as well as Methodist (Southern University) were building large endowments. But of particular emphasis for Henderson's rhetoric were the "rapid strides" that Alabama's Black Baptists were making toward endowing Selma University. "If our self-respect, our moral sensibilities, have not fallen so low that no appeal can reach them," Henderson wrote, "let the self-sacrificing spirit of our colored brethren provoke us to something worthy of our past history, our present abilities, and the crushing responsibilities of the near future." In other words, remind whites of their racial unity and superiority, while highlighting that the inferior "colored" folks were outpacing them.[15]

Before the Civil War, Henderson emphasized, white Alabama Baptists made liberal contributions to Howard and established an endowment, but now they "scarcely maintained a respectable mediocrity . . . in the matter of benevolence." Howard was abandoned—left alone to struggle on "bare subsistence." Henderson had no plan to bring an endowment to Howard, but he knew something, anything, must be done to "break this twenty years monotony of mutually condoling each other's poverty." Henderson grieved: "How long shall we suffer? O, for some Moses to smite the flint rock of our selfishness and cause the waters to flow to fertilize all the waste places of our languishing Zion! O, for some Nehemiah whose courage is equal to the task of rebuilding the walls of our fallen Jerusalem, and thus restoring to our people the full benefits of a heritage our fathers left us, a heritage despoiled by the vandal spirit of war." Other ministers around the state joined Henderson's crusade and, by the end of the 1885–86 academic year, many of the state's white Baptists were heeding the call for an endowment.[16]

Colonel James T. Murfee agreed that the time was ripe for securing a solid financial foundation for Howard College. He told the Board of Trustees in 1886 that under his leadership Howard was now free from debt for the first time since the Civil War. Through his steady leadership, Howard persevered through every stormy wind that blew. Potential donors could now see the value of the college's indispensable educational work and its solid stewardship of money and resources. Howard competed successfully with other well-funded schools because of the college's unique mission in helping a student develop noble and Christ-like character, acute and powerful intellect, and rigorous discipline. The fruits of this labor could be seen throughout Alabama as churches and "society circles" were filling with "choice specimens of manhood and Christian worth."[17]

The graduating class of 1886: (*standing left to right*) John William McCollum, Joel Herron
Rainer, Lemuel Orah Dawson, William M. Webb, Charles Alston Thigpen, James McIntosh McIver, William Garrott Brown, David Jackson McWilliams; (*seated left to right*)
Robert Lee Goodwin, James Beecher Adams, William L. Pruett, William Walter Ransom,
and John Gamble Jr. (Samford University, Special Collection and University Archives)

And in the future, Murfee emphasized, when the college was rich and stable, let it not be forgotten that the "chief excellency" of the college was due to
the character of the professors and the attention they gave to the students. An
institution's greatness should never be measured by the number of professors,
he added, but upon the amount of brilliance they displayed in the classroom,
and the attention that they gave to the students. The professors assisted and
supervised students before breakfast each morning; they spent the next five or
six hours in classrooms teaching subjects and listening to recitations; at night,
professors worked with the students during study hours in the dormitories.
Murfee asked, "Where is there such a system of discipline—so favoring study
and promulgating good habits? In what other college is it that a student is not
allowed to neglect with impunity a single recitation? And is it not reasonable

to suppose, as the scholarship and conduct of our students show, that these labors, these motives, and this discipline have led to the adoption, discovery, and application of advantageous methods of instruction?" Now was the time, Murfee supposed, to establish an endowment to continue the good work of the faculty in impacting the character, intellect, and faith of young men. "Let the work continue as it has been."[18]

The proof of Howard's success, Murfee argued, was in the type of young man that graduated from the institution. He looked no further than the valedictorian of the graduating class of 1886, William Garrott Brown. A Marion native, Brown's oldest brother, Charles Gayle Brown, was the lone Howard College graduate in 1866 and went on to serve as attorney general of Alabama. The younger Brown entered Howard as a fifteen-year-old freshman in October 1883 and quickly established himself as one of the college's brilliant young thinkers, orators, and writers. Near the conclusion of his junior year, in March 1885, he helped establish *The Philomathian*—a publication of the literary society in which he belonged. Brown proposed that the newspaper would present literary, intellectual, and philosophical musings by members of the society that were both original and inspired; that would delight minds, elevate tastes, and be to readers a "perfect and indestructible source of mental felicity, providing an impenetrable armor against the darts and javelins of the worlds of displeasure [and] accomplish a complete revolution in the sphere of creative literature."[19]

The editors of the paper would also provide analytical discourses to bring light and warmth to readers "chilled by the freezing winds of earthly ingratitude." W. G. Brown believed that readers would find a "profound and inscrutable" inquiry into the nature of man (and woman) that was beyond the "childish conjectures of such philosophical triflers" as Plato, Aristotle, Seneca, Kant, Locke, Darwin, and Hegel. In turn, neither atheists nor deists would find any shelter from the writers' "artillery of orthodox belief." If these hyperbolic endeavors failed, Brown supposed, then the subscribers would "go to the devil" and proclaim that the editors and the members of the literary society were nothing more than "imposters and cheats" that from that moment forward: "shall cause them to be distrusted and scorned in all nations of the world and all periods of future time, and shall forthwith cast them without favor or mercy, into the Pandemonium of disappointed literary cranks . . . through endless ages of misery and darkness, to give vent to wails of agony, yells of rage and disappointment, and smothered cries of despair."[20]

When he graduated with first honors from Howard in June 1886, William Garrott Brown was just a few weeks beyond his eighteenth birthday. A writer for the *Marion Standard* praised Brown as the "smartest young man of his age in Alabama," having recorded a 99.4 grade on his final exams—the highest grades ever made at the college. "Hurrah for Marion's 18-year-old prodigy!"[21]

Brown delivered a powerful oratory that June in which he invited those of the older generation to remember that neither the minerals in the hills nor the crops growing on the plains but the "moral and intellectual elevation of her people" were what made Alabama great. Echoing the influences of James T. Murfee, Brown asked his audience to embrace scientific progress, serve as defenders of enlightenment and knowledge, and never hinder the redemption of the uneducated common people of Alabama. In stark contrast to the prevailing political climate of the age, W. G. Brown encouraged his southern white listeners to reject the "bonds of prejudice and sectionalism" and learn to imitate the broadminded activity of northerners, while carefully avoiding their selfish pursuits. "And above all, as you would value your manhood itself, crush not, in obedience to the behests of political or social demagogues, aught that is tender and beautiful; profane not aught that is sacred, oppose not, for your own or your party's interest, aught that is just and true. . . . Already a broader thought and a purer morality has breathed its 'peace be still,' upon the boisterous passions that have caused so much unhappiness and error in the past. Be it yours to bid the scattered energies of our higher nature now lying in worse than archangelic ruin, 'Awake, arise, or be forever fallen.'"[22]

After graduation Brown stayed in Marion, engaged in independent study, and taught at a local school. In the fall of 1889, Brown and fellow Howard College graduate Francis Gordon Caffey left Marion, traveled to Cambridge, Massachusetts, and entered Harvard University as juniors to study with American historian Edward P. Channing. In one of Channing's seminars, Brown explored the origins of the southern Confederacy. Brown later visited Marion and delivered lectures on the topic with several old Confederate soldiers in the audience. Fortunately, he wrote at the time, "I escaped with no bones broken." Brown and Caffey both graduated with bachelor's degrees in 1891. When Brown earned his degree with summa cum laude distinction, his brother, Charles, in Alabama told a newspaper reporter that William's achievements at Harvard demonstrated the "success of the methods adopted at Howard College." The following year, Brown and Caffey earned master's degrees. At that point, the Howard duo's career paths diverged. Caffey attended law school at Harvard, graduating in 1894, and had a long and distinguished career as a lawyer, U.S. attorney, and judge on the U.S. District Court of the Southern District of New York. William Garrott Brown, however, remained at Harvard—first working as an archivist in the university library and later as a lecturer in history.[23]

A career as a writer and teacher of history was Brown's great hope, but deafness forced him from the classroom and into a period of introspection. "To be baffled in the course for which he had fitted himself," journalist Edward S. Martin wrote, "distressed and depressed him, and for a time threw him out of his stride." While he pondered over his future, Brown was diagnosed with tuberculosis. He determined to make the most of his final years and emerged as a nationally known writer and the first historian of the American South. "It always exasperates me that another man should have such a power of language and statement!" One of his contemporaries wrote. "Everywhere I hear the same story—that W. G. Brown is one of the few men in the country who can actually write history." He rejected the "dry as dust" scientific methodology popular among historians at the time, in favor of writing imaginative narratives which focused on painting pictures of the human elements in history. As one observer later noted, Brown's writing success flowed from his "lucid, unlabored style, pliantly responsive to the exact pressure of the thought he sought to convey." A gifted storyteller and lyrical writer, Brown was hailed for his "plain and human narrative, as from the pen of Herodotus, of a man who knew and could talk. His is the task to tell a simple tale."[24]

Brown filled his days with a pen in hand—lying in bed, propped up by several pillows—and writing page after page of lyrical prose. In just a few short years, he published a well-received history of Alabama; a collection of essays; a novel entitled *A Gentleman of the South;* and biographies of Andrew Jackson, Stephen Douglas, and Oliver Ellsworth. His completed manuscripts on Ulysses S. Grant and a history of the United States perished in a fire while he was convalescing in Asheville, North Carolina. He also contributed scores of articles to *Atlantic Monthly, Harper's Weekly,* and the *New York Evening Post.* After reading one of Brown's articles in the *Post,* President Theodore Roosevelt asked, "Who is William Garrott Brown?" and went on to describe the article as a "scandalous perversion of the truth."[25]

Brown's most important work was *The Lower South in American History*—a collection of thought-provoking essays that established the new academic field of southern history. "If he had written nothing else," one contemporary wrote, "that alone should perpetuate his memory." Brown's experiences in Marion, Alabama, and Howard College colored his perspectives on southern history as he came of age in a place and time that still struggled with the impact of the Civil War, Reconstruction, race, and economic decay. "I am heir," he wrote in the book's preface, "to all the sorrow and all the tortured pride" of the South—a sense that C. Vann Woodward later called the "burden of southern history" and Robert Penn Warren personified in his fictional character Jack Burden. "For this," Brown proclaimed, "like every other great and tragic human thing, passes forever into the mind and character and life of whosoever touches it, though he touch it never so lightly." A person born in the South inherited all the region's past. It stained his experiences forever. It "darkened his doubt into bewilderment." It insisted upon a portion of his accomplishments. It echoed his "failures and surrenders."

> Such his days and nights must be, and firm his will must be, his mind at peace, his silence undistracted, who would enter into the body of this civilization which I have tried to intimate with outlines, and make it live again through these and other of its times and seasons, he also living in it, and dying in it, and rising in it again. For that, and nothing less is the demand it makes of its historian. . . . I have come out of it and stood apart, and it drew me back with a most potent charm. Through and through it I have plunged from end to end of it in physical dimension. Emerging on the other side of it."[26]

W. G. Brown's thoughts on both the historical South and the contemporary South of his day influenced generations of southern historians and journalists. But the self-deprecating Brown wrote his fellow Harvard alumni that he had accomplished little in his career: "No foreign travel, no adventures more distinguished than getting slightly smashed between two trolley cars, no public office, no marriages or divorces—in fact surprising little of anything." In the months before he died, William Garrott Brown complained that his illness forced him into solitary exile. He loathed existing on the sidelines while his friends stayed in the game. "But that doesn't mean that one loses interest in the game or loyalty to the team. You fellows who are allowed to play mustn't forget that we who are banished to the side lines are with you all the same."[27]

Following Brown's death at age forty-five in 1913, the widespread accolades

showed that few intellectuals and politicians of his day disremembered the re-
clusive writer. President Woodrow Wilson wrote, "It is really an irreparable
loss to the scholarship and thought of the country." Literary critic Bliss Perry
recalled that those who knew Brown struggled to explain his "indescribable
charm of speech and behavior" and decided that the best word to describe him
was: "thoroughbred." Author Charles Eliot Norton described him as a modest
man of "refined nature," a high moral character, and a "strong and cultivated"
intellect—the type of Howard College man that Colonel J. T. Murfee hoped to
send into the world.[28]

By many measures, Colonel James T. Murfee's leadership of Howard College was a success. He guided the institution through the uncertainty of Reconstruction and the turmoil of the 1880s. Under his watch, Howard survived
bankruptcy and was free of debt by 1885. He hired a well-trained faculty and
used military discipline, moral education, scientific progress, and classical liberal arts, as one observer noted, to transform young men and lift "their thoughts
to higher things and nobler aspirations." But, after almost fifteen years as the
president, Howard maintained little support apart from Black Belt Baptists
and had no endowment. Student enrollment was declining steadily throughout the decade: 118 in 1882–83, 115 in 1883–84, 111 in 1884–85, and 108 in 1885–86.
Criticism of Murfee, the Board of Trustees, and the rural institution emerged
from this combustive mixture of cultural discontent in Alabama and was led
by two urban ministers from Birmingham (and former members of the board
of ministerial education), D. I. Purser and W. C. Cleveland. At the heart of this
conflict, Mitchell Garrett later concluded, was the "dissatisfaction of the new
industrial South with the manners and methods of the old agricultural South."
The economic "center of power and influence" was beginning to shift from the
Black Belt to the mineral-rich regions in the northern part of the state.[29]

11

RACE, REBELLION, AND
RELOCATION

Colonel Murfee and the Howard College Board of Trustees took their new bid
to raise an endowment before the Alabama Baptist State Convention meeting
in Birmingham during the summer of 1886. At the gathering, president of the
board William W. Wilkerson and fellow board member Jesse B. Lovelace (and
their respective wives) presented the state convention the deed to Howard College for $1. (Wilkerson and Lovelace paid $1,080 for the property at auction.)
In the deed they specified that the campus must be used for education and "for
no other purposes and be forever under the Convention." As with most worthwhile ideas considered by Baptists, the convention appointed a committee to
study the idea and report back, which they did. First, the committee formally
accepted the gift of deed from the Wilkersons and Lovelaces. Second, since the
institution was now "unencumbered," debt free, and owned by the convention,
the committee concluded that the time was ripe to secure a new endowment.
They authorized the Board of Trustees to begin the work immediately, and
several ministers rose before the assembly to praise Howard College. Rev. B. H.
Crumpton argued that one of the main reasons Howard should be endowed was
because "stagnation was the death of everything." The denomination's leadership was responsible for the future of Howard, another minister added. "It has
been entrusted to you, and you cannot get rid of it unless you" unleash an
"incendiary" device. "We ought to endow this college to allow it to fulfill the
purposes for which it is intended."[1]

And so it went, speaker after speaker espousing the need to properly fund
Howard College. During the enthusiasm, over $6,000 was pledged to the in-
stitution. But then Rev. Eldred Burder Teague stood and offered his thoughts.
Teague loved to talk. He was once described as "gifted beyond measure in con-

versation," filled with inexhaustible anecdotes, and one of the "most companionable" of men. Since the Civil War, the denomination tried in vain to endow Howard College, he said, and now was the time to try something different: move the college to Birmingham and start over. "You must bring the Howard to Birmingham," he proclaimed. "You cannot endow it where it is." Teague's proposition caused quite a stir. He later offered a resolution to appoint a committee to confer with land companies and citizens in and around Birmingham or any other area of the state that might want to submit a bid, a gift, or a grant for relocating the college to their town. Teague believed that his proposal was a way to simply gather information on the possibility of relocating Howard College. "What harm in getting up the facts?" he later wrote. Teague favored Birmingham because it was a "live, stirring city." The new Howard College that he envisioned would include new academic buildings but no dormitories—he favored quartering students in private homes under the influence of families. If the students became unruly, he argued, then he would "turn the police loose on them."[2]

What Teague turned loose, however, was a whirlwind at the Birmingham meeting, and, after much discussion and many speeches for and against, the convention tabled the resolution by the slim vote of twenty-six to twenty-five. Teague's proposal, however, generated such a hullabaloo, Rev. Benjamin Franklin Riley of Livingston wrote, that "It swept the city over within twelve hours. It became the reigning topic of conversation in all circles." A day later, Riley moved to bring the resolution back to the floor because the question remained unsettled and would cause friction among Baptists throughout the state. He suggested the convention form a committee to report back at the annual meeting in 1887. "Let the matter be determined," Riley said at the time; "otherwise the question would remain unsettled and be agitated from year to year at the detriment of the college." The motion carried and, as Riley later recalled, a "rattling, excited debate ensued."[3]

It was no coincidence that these forces supporting the relocation of Howard College jumped into the fray as soon as the Alabama Baptist State Convention received sole ownership of the institution. Unwittingly, the benevolent gift of the Wilkersons and Lovelaces allowed the convention to seize control of the future of Howard—even against the wishes of the Board of Trustees or J. T. Murfee. The board and the colonel opposed the change of location—preferring the agrarian Black Belt and what they saw as the superior moral environment in Marion. Those that supported relocation believed that a large city was better

Lieutenant Colonel James Thomas Murfee served as president of Howard College from 1871 to 1887. When Howard College moved from Marion to Birmingham in 1887, Murfee chose to remain in the agrarian Black Belt and start a military school on the old Howard campus. (Samford University, Special Collection and University Archives)

for Howard College. B. F. Riley wrote that several wealthy residents guaranteed that local industries would give $25,000 if Howard would move from Marion to Birmingham. "Now that shows what we are willing to do," one local Baptist leader proclaimed. "That's the way we do things here. We never do them by halves." It was hyperbolic New South boosterism at its finest. Throughout the city, white residents dreamed of the new college with impressive buildings and a fat endowment. In 1886, Birmingham was just fifteen years old and still a frontier town filled with violence and rowdy men. But just like Marion on the Alabama rural frontier over a half century before, a growing town needed an institution of higher education to demonstrate the town's civilizing features.[4]

An editor in one Birmingham paper proclaimed that "Birmingham wants Howard College and Howard needs Birmingham." This was a new industrial age, and Birmingham was on the cutting edge of "new thought in the South." The college was in a small rural village in the Black Belt, still clinging to an isolated, agrarian mindset that had faded long ago. Howard was a college for the present, not the past, and Birmingham was a city of today. "The two seem to be made for each other." If Howard moved, the sleepy rural college would become a vibrant local enterprise and "assume the dimensions and dignity of a great university." Birmingham, the overstated writer supposed, had it all: expanding railroads, booming industry, healthy climate, and a cosmopolitan citizenry. Here was where Howard students would associate with the energetic promoters of the New South: men who were "doing something," men "with whom they would spend their future lives."[5]

A newspaper writer in Marion, however, looked at the news much differently. "This was all bosh," he wrote. There was no danger of Howard College ever moving from Marion. "This is the place for it," he added, "and it is here to stay. Build up as many colleges as you please, but do not be so selfish as to try to pull down Marion." The writer argued that Alabama had no more "moral and refined community" than the small Black Belt village and Baptists had "too much good sense" to let Howard move away from this paradise. Unlike Birmingham, there were few temptations for the boys. "With all due respect," the writer added, "we do not think [Birmingham] is a fit place for a college." W. E. W. Yerby, the editor of the nearby *Greensboro Watchman,* agreed that a great educational institution must be located in a quiet town away from a blustery, raucous metropolis. In Marion, the incentives to study were greater and the enticements to vice were less. If student could not benefit from such a climate, he concluded, then that "pupil must certainly be incorrigible." Yerby predicted that, if the Baptists were foolish enough to move Howard from Marion, then the denomination would have nothing more than a weak and destitute male college with no future. "Better let Howard remain where she is," he added, and concentrate efforts on strengthening the college at its traditional home.[6]

The debate over moving Howard from Marion that began at the July 1886 convention would be discussed in Baptist churches and in communities throughout the state for the next year. Meanwhile, both sides, pro- and anti-relocation, proceeded. The convention charged a committee of five men—Joseph E. Chambliss (Furman), Porter King (Marion), H. S. D. Mallory (Selma), R. H. Sterrett (Birmingham, chair), and E. B. Teague (Birmingham)—to begin soliciting proposals for the removal of Howard College from Marion and to report back to the convention the following year. The committee consisted of three Baptist laymen, all lawyers: King, Mallory, and Sterrett; and two pastors, Chambliss and Teague. Those attending the 1887 Alabama Baptist State Convention, Rev. E. B. Teague predicted, would weigh the facts—both moral and material—in making a decision on relocation. If Birmingham, or another city, provided "pecuniary inducements of a high order" and promised a high moral and religious culture, then "it will be worthwhile in our impecuniosity, to give the fact due consideration." On the other hand, Teague supposed, if Marion offered a "phenomenally superior" moral and religious environment, then "it will be a great, not to say overwhelming, reason" for leaving the college in the Black Belt. But the minister warned his colleagues that the question of relocation of Howard College was so important and so momentous that no one should rely on "sentimentalism" in making a decision.[7]

Nonetheless, Colonel J. T. Murfee and the Board of Trustees held unyielding romantic notions of the Old South and the Lost Cause that, in their minds, kept Howard College anchored to Marion. They were so confident that Howard would remain in their small town that they moved forward with the endowment and with little thought of relocation. It was an opportune time to look to the future, they supposed. The college was debt free and its legal status clear. "Now that all the difficulties have been removed," W. W. Wilkerson said, "the time has come for us to enter upon this important enterprise." The board unanimously elected Rev. Gustavus Alonzo Nunnally of the First Baptist Church of Eufaula as a field agent to collect an endowment, to increase patronage, and to "arouse the Baptists of Alabama to the importance of denominational education." His pay was seventy-five dollars per month. A graduate of the University of Georgia, Nunnally spent much of his early career as an educator and part-time preacher before entering the ministry full-time in 1876. Described as a serious scholar with "fine literary tastes," Nunnally traveled thousands of miles, attended district association meetings, wrote hundreds of letters, and published regular columns in the *Alabama Baptist*—all on behalf of Howard College. He hoped that the Baptist men of Alabama would embrace the "zeal and passionate determination" of Cato—the great Roman statesman—who ended all of his speeches (no matter the subject) with the demand that "Carthage must be destroyed." Centuries later in Alabama, Nunnally wanted every "pastor, deacon, professor, trustee, and friend" to begin all orations or conversations with the command: "Howard must be endowed." Women would also play an important role (although Nunnally never mentions women giving any speeches). "They will give the men no peace," he believed, "nor take any rest for themselves until an adequate endowment has been realized."[8]

Nunnally's appeals were vivid, emotional, and often hyperbolic. "Divide and defeat is our doom," he proclaimed, but "combine and conquest shall bring us a crown. Let everybody pay or pray or go off behind the hills and cry for shame." Nunnally believed that a pastor who passed the offering plate and received a solid collection would "feel happy"; a pastor who collected a fair donation would "feel good"; but the pastor who made no effort to support Howard College would "feel meagerly mean and moderately miserable." Nunnally found silence about Howard was the greatest barrier to raising an endowment. "We want every tongue unloosed," he said, "every purse unclasped, and every hand out-stretched." The choice was to pay the debt or go into bankruptcy. Which shall we do? he asked. Shall we "rise in our might" and endow the college or tell God that he demanded too much of us? Are you willing to have this as your epitaph: "Here lies the man who refused to give and thus prevented the endowment of Howard College?"[9]

Nunnally compared the Howard College faculty to the enslaved children of Israel who were forced to make bricks without straw. "Do you hear the laborers' cry of distress in the pit?" he asked. "Even so, the tired teachers in weariness, in self-sacrifice, in honest services, suffer as they labor under so many disadvantages to produce for this state, for the world, and for Christ polished and perfected stones for the social and civil and spiritual structures of time and eternity." Howard College was a miracle in higher education, he believed, and "let us rise in the might which God's grace supplies and wipe out the shame and share the glory." But as Nunnally crisscrossed the state, he discovered that the minds of Alabama Baptists were so troubled by the question of relocation that fundraising proved to be a more arduous task than usual. Nunnally also encountered the age-old conflict between northern and southern regions of Alabama, which hindered the development of any consensus behind the Howard College endowment. "The rivalry . . . became intense," Rev. Benjamin F. Riley noted, and the newspapers throughout each section heightened the tensions with "strong statements of local pride flying between them like bullets in battle."[10]

As Nunnally persisted in his work and the Baptists continued to debate the issue of relocation throughout the summer and into the fall of 1886, classes began as usual at Howard College in October. One new student arriving that fall was John Evan Barnes. Born on March 18, 1869, in the Black Belt town of Pleasant Hill in Dallas County, Barnes was part of a yeoman-class family of farmers. In the early 1880s, Barnes and his older brother worked their family's farm and also sharecropped a five-acre tract of land owned by his father—cultivating, harvesting, selling, and settling at the end of each year. He only attended school during the winter months—when the crops were out of season—paying for his tuition with firewood for the teachers. He described his educational foundation as "imperfect" and simple "fragments of time," but when he felt a calling to the ministry, he knew he needed more schooling. On the way home from a Sunday-evening service, Barnes recalled a conversation with former Howard College student Sidney J. Catts.[11]

When Barnes explained to his friend how much he loved helping others and working in the church, Catts turned to him and proclaimed, "God wants you to preach." Barnes objected: "I have no education and how will I get it?" Catts told him that he would write Colonel James T. Murfee at Howard. In short order, Catts arranged for Barnes to enter Howard College. "It certainly seemed," Barnes said, "that the Lord was leaning in all of this." His father supported his decision but explained that he was unable to help him with even "a single dollar." He released the young Barnes from his "home duties" and recommended that "you may make it with HIS help."[12]

After he finished helping his father take in the harvest in the fall of 1886, J. E. Barnes hitched a mule to a small wagon and rode to the Pleasant Hill Railroad Station, where he climbed aboard a train running on the Cincinnati, Selma, and Mobile Railroad. This was Barnes's first train ride, which took him from Pleasant Hill to Selma and then on to Marion. Along the way, he pondered his first journey away from home. He possessed little education and even less self-reliance. He had no real understanding of what college was all about. "I had never seen one," he recalled, "and did not know what it was, but felt that it would help me get the training I needed."[13]

When he arrived at the depot in Marion on a dust-dry fall day, three friends (brothers Francis and William Caffey and Claude Hardy)—all Howard cadets—greeted Barnes and escorted him to campus. According to Barnes, a large group of students were awaiting his arrival and as soon as they saw him they shouted, "A new rat, boys! Another new rat!" The Howard cadets, just like those at Colonel Murfee's alma mater, VMI, referred to each other as "rats." Barnes seemed unimpressed. "The introduction to campus was rather trying," he recalled, and "not very helpful."[14]

After suffering from a severe bout of homesickness ("It seemed that I would die"), Barnes settled into life at Howard, but his poor preparation placed him into classes with the little fellows in the preparatory department. He excelled in Latin and Greek, but he floundered in mathematics. "I just did not know anything about them." Nonetheless, he joined the Philomathic Literary Society and gained confidence in his speaking and debating skills.[15]

John Evan Barnes arrived at Howard just as the college entered the most critical period in its history. The possibility of a fresh start in the booming industrial New South of Birmingham began pulling Howard College away from the decaying agrarian society of the Old South in Marion. At the Alabama Baptist State Convention in July, longtime Howard trustee Porter King disagreed and argued that the healthy moral climate in Marion negated any possibility of relocating the college. But the agrarian Black Belt never recovered from the Civil War and Reconstruction, and some disillusioned Marion residents slipped back into frontier hedonism and violence. Taverns reopened, like the White Hall Saloon, where young men could find trouble playing billiards and drinking "choice" liquors—Old McBrayer, Old Gum Spring, xxxx Rye, or Old N.Y. Exchange Rye—served by handsome bartenders and well-mannered waiters. White Hall's specialty was providing "jug trade" for those thirsty souls living in prohibition districts in Perry and surrounding counties. Bring an empty jug, the owners proclaimed, and "call on us when you come to Marion."[16]

Contributing to Marion's decline was the loss of almost 25 percent of the town's population between 1870 and 1887. In addition, the perceived moral decay was due to an upturn in violence and a decline in race relations during the 1880s. As historian Bertis English argued, between 1865 and 1874 Perry County was an "anomaly in the Black Belt" as Blacks and whites maintained relatively harmonious race relations. English discovered that racial unrest and violence were less common in Perry County while biracial cooperation was more common than in surrounding counties. He attributed this "anomaly" to the county's cultural, religious, and educational institutions, affluence, and political power. "Whites and blacks developed relationships and institutions that helped African Americans realize citizenship," English emphasized. "Such biracial cooperation and mutual uplift were different from the prevalent patterns."[17]

By the 1880s, relations between Blacks and whites declined with increased societal tensions. In 1881, in a saloon in nearby Uniontown, an intoxicated young Black man from Marion was shot and killed by town marshal Benjamin A. King. Apparently, there were serious questions about whether King was justified in killing the man (who was simply identified as "Jewett"), and a special grand jury was empaneled to consider the matter. When the grand jury failed to indict King, an outraged Black community in Marion held a public meeting to "censure" the jury for perjury and racial bias. Many of Marion's white residents believed that these meetings were "incendiary in the highest degree," promoted racial discord and violence, and "evoked from the worst passions of the human race: a blood mania . . . and propensity for personal vengeance." A few weeks later, King was murdered by a shotgun blast to the head. In turn, another Perry County grand jury found no evidence linking anyone to the crime.[18]

The most visible decline in race relations in Marion was the increase in tensions between white Howard College cadets and Black students from the Lincoln School. According to local legend, the Lincoln School had its origins at the end of the Civil War when an injured Union soldier began teaching the children of freed slaves. In reality, the school began when representatives of the American Missionary Association (AMA) worked with the Black community in Marion to establish an educational institution for the freedmen in the late 1860s. The community raised funds, purchased land, built a modern facility, and hired a faculty which provided students with a classical education—not unlike the curriculum at nearby Howard College. By the 1870s, the AMA deeded the school to the state and its name was changed to the State Normal School for Colored Students, but local residents still referred to the institution as the Lincoln School. While many white Marion residents supported the school, others resented their state tax dollars going to a Black school.[19]

Conflict was inevitable between Howard cadets who were embracing the racial mores of the Lost Cause and the Lincoln students who were experiencing their first measures of freedom. The two schools maintained a distant relationship, even though the campuses were just a short walk from each other. The uneasy rapport between Blacks and whites during and after Reconstruction developed into a set of customs (and later Jim Crow laws) that governed every type of interracial contact. One of the most contentious public spaces for this type of interaction was on the sidewalks of most every southern city, including Marion. As a historian later observed, sidewalks "became a battleground over what freedom would mean" as both sides struggled over the uncertainty of racial expectations. In general, whites believed that Blacks should show deference and give the right of way. The conflict over sidewalk space seemed to provoke more racial animus between Black and white college-age boys.[20]

In 1874, the *Marion Commonwealth* reported that a Howard student and a young Black man scuffled over space on a local sidewalk following Sunday-evening church services. E. A. Heidt, the paper's editor, wrote that a "small frying size negro tried to elbow" the white boy from the sidewalk. The Howard student "ditched the youngster and put him in a condition to use about 25 cents worth of sticking plaster on his head." The next morning, the duo appeared before Marion's mayor, Jesse B. Shivers, an 1859 Howard College graduate, who fined the Black man ten dollars for his role in the incident. Ironically, both the young men were Baptists, but neither one, as a writer later quipped, learned much about the golden rule at their respective Sunday-evening church services.[21]

No doubt other points of conflict existed between the Howard and Lincoln students, but an 1886 incident was the most dramatic and long-lasting. On Saturday evening, December 11, 1886, a group of Howard cadets was returning to campus from viewing a fire. What happened next on the sidewalks and streets of Marion would be debated and discussed for years to come as each side described two vastly differing accounts of the incident. According to the Howard boys, they were confronted by a "large party" of Lincoln School students who pulled knives and challenged them to a fight. The small group of cadets was outnumbered, carried no weapons, and refused to fight. The Lincoln students, however, continued to curse and threaten the boys, until one of them, later identified as a Lincoln School senior, charged the white cadets, slashing his knife left and right. Two Howard students, John Motley Keitt of Birmingham and Richard Pickering Prowell of Marengo County, both received knife cuts. "He escaped," wrote one white resident, because of "the simple fact that the boys had no weapons."[22]

When Colonel Murfee learned of the incident, he rushed to the scene and ordered the cadets back to campus. A journalist later asked Murfee how he "kept the boys down" following the "unprovoked" attack. "They are taught to obey orders without questioning why," the colonel said. He gave the cadets the command for them to return to their barracks and back they went, although "indignation burned in every bone." At the scene, Murfee was reported to have said esoterically: "If the Howard College boys wanted to do any shooting, it was a game that two could play at." Nonetheless, three of the Howard students, along with the Perry County sheriff Lewis C. Litesey and two deputies, went to the Lincoln School to identify the alleged assailant, but the young man was being hidden or lived "somewhere on the other side of the Cahaba River."[23]

According to one account, the Lincoln students armed themselves and expected an attack by the Howard cadets. "The latter were justly incensed at the injuries received by their fellow students," a writer in Marion pointed out two days after the incident, but the "excellent discipline of the college prevailed over their desire for reparation." The *Alabama Baptist* reported that the boys' "coolness and self-possession" during the incident brought forth widespread admiration from "men and women all over the state" of Alabama. Not long after the incident, a writer for a Marion newspaper complained that Howard College students were not alone in having trouble with Lincoln students knocking children and girls off the sidewalks in town. The writer asked which was best, to have Howard and Judson "ruined" or have Lincoln School moved to another location. Throughout December 1886, newspapers around the country carried stories about the "race war among students" in Marion, Alabama, and how the town was divided—Black versus white—and more "unpleasant incidents were probable." No other incidents, however, were reported in the newspapers.[24]

In contrast, Marion's Black community viewed the December 11 incident in a much different light. According to these accounts, there was but one Lincoln student in uptown Marion that evening—a student described in one account as quiet, studious, inoffensive, and young. As he walked down the sidewalk, he encountered a group of Howard College cadets (between twenty and fifty) who surrounded him when he refused to "get off the sidewalk to let them pass." According to some accounts, the Howard boys pulled knives and threatened to kill him, while others said that the cadets "clubbed him." He begged the white boys to let him be, but to no avail. Fearing for his life, he rushed the crowd, trying to fight his way out with his fists. This only infuriated the cadets, who rushed the Lincoln student with open knives. In turn, his only recourse was to pull out his "old Jack knife" and begin thrashing his way through the mob—

cutting two Howard students, one in the throat, and the other in the wrist. But for his "agility and bravery," wrote Lincoln president William B. Paterson, they would have killed him. "He defended himself heroically and no one knowing the truth can blame him." The Black student fled the scene in a panic with a "howling mob" of whites giving chase and "ready to cut him into mincemeat."[25]

At some point during the chase, the Lincoln student cut through the property of Henrietta H. Curtis. She was the mixed-race twenty-two-year-old daughter of former slave Alexander H. Curtis, one of the founders of the Lincoln School and a state senator and representative during Reconstruction. According to this account, she confronted the Howard cadets in her front yard and told them to stop chasing the Black student. When the white boys continued to advance, she pulled out a revolver and explained that, if they stepped any closer, she would "blow their brains out." The Howard students made a hasty retreat from Curtis's premises and the Lincoln student was saved. "Would that every colored woman whose dignity is insulted," a writer emphasized at the time, "would imitate her example."[26]

The Black community hid the Lincoln student and confronted another white mob later in the evening—hell bent on burning the Lincoln School to the ground. "Only the certainty that all our colored people were ready for them," one witness wrote, "kept us from a general fight and conflagration." William Paterson later wrote that "we were prepared to repel an attack by Howard boys." Most sources identify the assailant/victim as simply "Brown" or W. Daniel Brown, but evidence suggests that the young man's name was Daniel Webster Brown. In 1870, Brown was nine years old and living in Jones Bluff in Sumter County with his parents (Lemon and Ann Brown) and five siblings. In 1880, Daniel W. Brown was a student living in Marion and attending the Lincoln School. Following the incident a few years later, members of the Black community gave the fugitive Lincoln student provisions and sent him away one dark night. He made his way to some distant train station and traveled to safety in the North—presumably to Chicago, where Paterson arranged for him to stay. "I dare not tell even now where," one witness wrote, "only that he is safe now. He would be killed instantly if he were ever to come back to this part of the country." Although Brown's whereabouts for the next three decades were unclear, he returned to Alabama by 1920 and the census of that year revealed he was living in Sumter County with his sister's family. When he died from pellagra in 1923 at the psychiatric hospital in Mount Vernon, Alabama, Daniel Webster

Brown's death report noted that he had never married and his occupation was school teacher.[27]

Whatever took place between Brown and the Howard cadets thirty-seven years earlier will never be known with certainty, but at the time the reaction to the incident from the white community was incendiary. Six days after the violent encounter, the Howard College Board of Trustees met to discuss a "remedy" to the December 11 "serious cutting of two of the cadets by students at Lincoln." Of the twenty-four members of the board, only seven were present at the meeting: W. W. Wilkerson, J. B. Lovelace, J. W. Crenshaw, Porter King, J. H. Lee, J. L. Wyatt, and W. B. Crumpton. Following a lengthy discussion, the board adopted a resolution which pointed out the "frequent altercations" between Lincoln and Howard students the last few years that culminated in the knife cutting of the two white students. The board expected these types of violent encounters would only grow more frequent and would result in fatal consequences. These clashes damaged the peace and harmony within the local community and distracted students at both institutions from their educational endeavors. "For the good of both races," the resolution concluded, Lincoln School must "be removed from this place." The board would select a representative to travel to Montgomery to lobby the state legislature to pass a bill to remove Lincoln School "from our midst as early a day as practical."[28]

The *Marion Standard* and other newspapers in the Black Belt supported the removal of the Lincoln School. "As a plain matter of fact," one writer suggested, "a white college and a colored college cannot exist side by side" in a small town like Marion. It was a zero-sum game. Either Howard or Lincoln must be "removed or perish," and the white school had the "best and first" right to stay in Marion.[29]

In February 1887, several white Marion residents made the journey to the capital to plead their case to the state's politicians. "The very life of Howard College," one newspaper reported at the time, "depends on this measure." In contrast, Black citizens of Marion vocally opposed the legislation. Whites were determined to move or abolish Lincoln School, one observer wrote, "and unless God interposes, it will be done." No doubt many of Marion's white citizens believed that removing Lincoln School would prevent Howard College from relocating. A writer for a newspaper in nearby Greensboro pointed out that, once the racial incident had occurred, the white Baptists of Marion, who favored Howard College remaining, "set to work immediately to remove Lincoln." They hoped that, by moving or abolishing the Black school, those favoring Howard's relocation "would not have that as an argument" at the Alabama Baptist State Convention in July 1887. During these weeks, while the state legislature debated the removal of Lincoln School, the *Alabama Baptist* withheld an opinion article that supported Howard's relocation because of the racial unrest in Marion. If the article were published, the *Alabama Baptist* editor argued, members of the legislature might "refuse to vote for the removal" of the Black college, "and thus fasten on a long-established white school community an institution [Lincoln] that was a positive menace to virtuous womanhood and helpless children."[30]

Within days of the Marion delegation's visit to Montgomery, the bill to remove the Black school was introduced and passed by the legislature. Alabama governor Thomas Seay signed the bill into law and the Black normal school in Marion was abolished and a new one (the Normal School for Colored Students) established in Montgomery with classes beginning in October 1887. One writer noted at the time that the white Baptists of Marion "accomplished their aim—Lincoln School was destroyed." The legislature also stipulated that no one could establish another normal school on the Lincoln campus. Nonetheless, as a writer emphasized in a Black newspaper in March 1887, the Black community determined to maintain an independent school on the Lincoln Campus. "They [the legislature] abolished the Lincoln Normal School . . . to satisfy a narrow-minded denomination whim." Although the teacher's college was removed from Marion, a public Lincoln School continued at the site until integration forced its closure in 1970.[31]

The violent encounter between the Howard and Lincoln students had a dramatic effect on both institutions. For Howard, the racial clash undercut one of the central arguments for leaving the college in Marion, and many Baptists around the state questioned the "moral climate" in the small Black Belt town. Some parents became reluctant to send their sons to a place where racial violence would occur and where Blacks outnumbered whites by large margins. To make matters worse, enrollment in 1886–87 saw another decline—down to 103 students—the lowest levels in six years. By the end of the academic year, the trustees reported a deficit in the operating expenses. "There was a growing sense of disappointment," Rev. B. F. Riley wrote, that the college was declining in influence and enrollment and the "one fact [that] was manifest—the denomination was not sustaining the college." Since before the Civil War, many men eulogized the plight of poor Howard before each year's Alabama Baptist convention. "Again, and again hopes had been excited," Riley continued, "that the college would soon be placed beyond the necessity of these repeated presentations of its claims." Some of Howard's backers raised the expectation that the college would someday become the leading institution in Alabama, but those days never came and, by 1886, Baptists from outside the Black Belt stopped listening. All plans for "kindling hope" or even "arousing interest" were nothing more than "well-beaten straw" to Riley. In the end, he believed that all efforts to raise an endowment would fail because of Howard's poor state in 1886 and 1887. Raising an endowment, he supposed, was a foolish endeavor.[32]

Rev. Gustavus Alonzo Nunnally's fundraising efforts fell well short of the goal. For months of energetic work, the agent received $2,172.97 in cash, but almost half of that total went for Nunnally's salary and expenses. While he received around $14,000 in promissory notes, he had little hope of collecting these pledges with the "total crop failure" of 1886, which resulted in little money circulating in many areas of the state. In addition, Nunnally added, "the financial results would have been much longer had not certain perplexing and diverting questions arisen concerning the removal of the College." Many Alabama Baptists of "wealth and liberality" promised to come forward with sizeable donations to the endowment, once the question of Howard College's location was settled. By 1887, the donations and pledges dwindled to a scant few as the debate over relocation intensified and in the wake of the violence between Howard students and Lincoln School students. By the late spring of 1887, Nunnally suspended all fundraising efforts, but the agent remained encouraged that Howard College maintained a "warmer place in the hearts of Alabama Baptists than was generally thought." He believed that the Baptist brethren held a "strong and growing conviction" and a "fixed determination" to build an endowment that was "essential."[33]

A host of factors converged to convince many Alabama Baptist leaders that Howard College needed a new beginning away from the declining Black Belt. The promise of the New South and a dissatisfied Alabama Baptist State Convention pulled Howard away from its traditional home, while moral decay and worsening race relations pushed the college out of the Black Belt. "No more eventful period has occurred in the history of the denomination in Alabama," Riley wrote. "It was the result of a combination of causes. One of these was the general restlessness of our people, the peculiar circumstances investing certain leaders of the denomination, and the gradual decline of Howard College in its original location."[34]

12

THEY OUT FIGURED US

In May 1886, Colonel James T. Murfee attended the annual meeting of the Southern Baptist Convention held at the First Baptist Church in Montgomery, Alabama. At the gathering, Murfee met seventy-five-year-old Samuel Sterling Sherman, who was returning from a trip to Florida and stopped in Montgomery during the convention. The colonel was delighted. During their brief visit, Murfee urged Sherman to sit for a formal portrait for display at Howard College. Six months later, in early November, as the debate over the future of Howard continued, a large crate arrived at Murfee's office. It was Sherman's portrait, painted by one of Chicago's best artists. Enclosed was a letter from Sherman: "I have fulfilled the promise I made you when we met in Montgomery," he wrote, but he "felt some delicacy" in having a portrait that would make him "so conspicuous" on campus, especially as most of the people that Sherman either taught or worked with were dead. "But it is gratifying to me to know," he added, "that I am still remembered in connection with the institution to which I gave many, and, I can truly add, the happiest years of my life."[1]

Although Samuel Sterling Sherman expressed no clear opinion on the possibility of relocating Howard College, he still hoped that denominational leaders would not "undervalue Marion" in their ongoing deliberations. Marion, Sherman added, was a quiet, "charming," and healthy town filled with "cultured homes," a "fine moral atmosphere," and an "open-handed liberality that . . . characterized her people." From his northern home in Chicago, Sherman still maintained the same romantic notions of a bygone agrarian ideal, not unlike Colonel Murfee or others of their generation. But those days were gone. Throughout the 1880s, as historian Ed Ayers observed, many agrarian areas in the South were "in a declining or decaying state, with agriculture on the wane and the social order disturbed." Throughout the Alabama Black Belt, once-thriving churches and communities were dying a slow death. Many churches disbanded, and those buildings, one writer observed, where "the Holy Word has been expounded by eloquent men to cultural and wealthy congregations, are now the homes of goats and hogs and bats." Nothing so dramatic was occurring in Marion, but people were abandoning the countryside and moving to cities—like Birmingham—where they found "more life and activity, more society, and especially more security."[2]

Regardless, those hoping to provide Howard College with a fresh start in a jaunty New South booster town were disappointed. On March 29, 1887, members of the relocation committee met in Birmingham and announced that "no definite proposal had been received' to move Howard College. The committee also discussed the possibility of starting a new Baptist college and leaving Howard in Marion. One minister in attendance said that he "doubted that liberal bids would be made for a new Baptist college with the Howard still in the field." The lack of bids for a viable alternative to Marion led three of Birmingham's most outspoken Baptist pastors, David I. Purser, J. J. D. Renfroe, and E. B. Teague (Teague was the only member of the relocation committee), to begin "stirring the subject . . . in a lively way." As Purser jumped into the fray and spearheaded these efforts, he was already a divisive figure who clashed with Colonel J. T. Murfee over ministerial education. As one pastor later recalled, "When Birmingham cast her covetous eyes on Howard College at Marion, Purser became the leader." Rather than waiting for bids to come in, the forty-three-year-old Purser contacted and interviewed the "heads of the great land companies," and each "manifested a deep interest" in submitting proposals. He wrote down the names of each "subscriber" and the "amounts pledged on loose sheets of paper, old envelopes, and anything else that happened to be convenient." By May 1887, Purser brought his brother, John Frederick, from his church in Troy, Alabama, to fill the pulpit at Birmingham's First Baptist Church, which allowed David Ingram Purser time to devote his energies exclusively to the Howard cause. Ironically, Purser's canvassing in Birmingham to support relocation of Howard occurred simultaneously with Gustav Nunnally's efforts to raise money for the school to remain in Marion—leading one Alabama Baptist leader to point out the "two contesting movements being undertaken at the same time."[3]

Purser was unrelenting in his evangelistic zeal to bring Howard College to Birmingham. When he arrived in the Magic City a few years earlier, he took over a First Baptist congregation with 278 members, and by 1887 that number

Eng⁴ by E G Williams & Bro New York

The pastor of the First Baptist Church of Birmingham, Reverend David Ingram Purser was an enthusiastic advocate of the New South and Birmingham. An aggressive booster, Purser led the effort to relocate Howard to Birmingham in 1887. (Samford University, Special Collection and University Archives)

had grown to over 500. When First Baptist moved into their impressive new house of worship, a newspaper writer noted that the congregation felt "in their hearts devout thankfulness to the Master for having sent them David Ingram Purser." Although Purser received limited formal education, an observer noted that his memory was "so tenacious and his mind so well stored with valuable and varied information," most people thought that he was a learned preacher. Purser possessed the "highest degree" of the characteristics that made up the "loftiest type of manhood: tall, erect, superb physique," boundless vigor, and "marvelous mental power.[4]

Rev. W. B. Crumpton recalled that, when Purser moved to Birmingham, he immediately "mixed up" with all the business and "progressive affairs" in the booming Magic City. Crumpton described him as "a booster, a promoter, [and] a plunger." By 1887, a newspaper writer pointed out that Purser's judgment was "so valuable in secular matters" that he was more than just the pastor of First Baptist but his congregation's "most trusted business advisor," who conferred regularly with banking representatives, railroad officials, and industrial leaders. He received large sums of money from his congregation (and presumably other Baptists), with the "simple request" to invest the funds in the Birmingham economic boom. "His sagacity and foresight in managing investments for himself and his friends," the writer continued, "made him a rich man, and materially increased their prosperity.[5]

Purser emerged as an important orator for the New South, and Birmingham was the heart of this emerging industrial region. Gone were the old rural values built upon cotton agriculture, plantation paternalism, and slave labor; these were replaced with industrialization, urbanization, and individualism. Like other capitalists throughout the country, Birmingham's leaders saw no refrain in the "thunderous cannonade" of economic power and unsurpassed prosperity. All day and all night, the roaring inharmonious symphony of heavy industry was the song of iron, steel, and achievement. As a Birmingham poet declared, this was the "song for titans, gods, and lion-hearted men."[6]

D. I. Purser and a few other lion-hearted Alabama Baptist ministers (namely B. F. Riley) emerged as evangelists for both the gospel of Jesus Christ and the "Creed" of the New South. Purser and other ministers saw their work in creating the New South as "preparing the way for religious advancement itself" by transforming the region into the "Canaan of the New World." As one historian noted, "religious faith and language appeared everywhere in the New South," and Purser was Birmingham's most potent force in both church and business growth in the city. "In every direction he has shown himself to be a man of force and power," a writer emphasized in the *New South* journal; "aggressive in disposition and unwavering purpose," Purser went "straight to the accomplishment of his object, with a courage and strength which overcomes all obstacles, and halts not until success crowns his efforts." It was "safe to say that no man in Alabama," the journalist continued, had "done so much for the Baptist church, so much for Birmingham, so much for himself, and so much for his friends as has David Ingram Purser."[7]

Purser also hoped one of his crowning achievements would see Howard College located in Birmingham. He and his pro-Birmingham colleagues, E. B. Teague and J. J. D. Renfroe, visited several locations around the city and adjacent areas in their quest for a perfect location for Howard. Once Purser and the others toured the sites and received the bids from the land companies, newspapers reported that they planned to hold a "grand public meeting" at Birmingham's O'Brien's Opera House to discuss additional "financial assistance" from the community. History does not record whether this meeting occurred, but one Birmingham resident suggested that bringing the college to the Magic City was understood to be the inevitable outcome of these activities. "There was a general feeling with leading spirits here," the *Weekly Advertiser* reported, "that a college or colleges must be planted within the city or in its beautiful villages; and they are willing to give liberally to that interest. It is believed that our community will submit advantages which cannot be set aside or overcome."[8]

The notion of several colleges coming to the Magic City was a clear reference to the leadership of Birmingham's efforts to not only bring Howard to the city, but also Lincoln Normal School. Ironically, the future of Howard College seemed intrinsically bound to the destiny of the Lincoln School. In May 1887, Birmingham mayor Alexander Oscar Lane traveled to Montgomery to urge Alabama governor Thomas Seay to consider the Magic City as the home of the Black school. The *Birmingham Age* reported that members of Birmingham's Black community held a "mass meeting" and announced that they "would do all in their power to secure the school." Through Lane's lobbying, Governor Seay favored Birmingham as the "best place," because Blacks would make a "better showing" in a "cosmopolitan" city. Blacks from other areas of the state questioned the character of the "colored population" in Birmingham as "being too rough and unsettled with too large an admixture of the criminal class" to relocate Lincoln to the industrial city.[9]

But just as the white Baptists of Marion emerged as the most vocal proponents of moving Lincoln and keeping Howard in the same location, the white Baptists of Birmingham became the most outspoken opponents of Lincoln moving to the city, in fear that the move would keep Howard from relocating to the Magic City. The *Montgomery Advertiser* reported that Howard College leaders successfully pushed Lincoln from Marion, and that same group "would never stultify itself and follow the brother-in-black up to Birmingham." In turn, many in Marion's white Baptist community pushed for Lincoln to relocate to

Birmingham as a "scheme to checkmate the removal of Howard College to the same place." In the end, Birmingham submitted a bid of $3,000 and six acres of land, while Montgomery offered $5,000 and three acres of land to lure Lincoln. At the meeting of Lincoln's Board of Trustees to discuss the proposals, H. H. Brown of Birmingham appeared as the representative of the "Baptists of the Magic City" and submitted a lengthy petition of names opposed to Lincoln's relocation because it would "prejudice their contest" in securing Howard College. Nonetheless, the board accepted Montgomery's proposal, and the reconstituted State University for Colored People opened in the state's capital in the fall of 1887.[10]

As the end of the academic year approached in May and June of 1887, several Howard College alumni and supporters began speaking out against the move to Birmingham. One graduate offered a prayer for God to grant mercy to Howard and "leave her not to the mercies of the money-cyclone" that might sever her connection to Marion—the place that transformed the "sons of our land" into servants of God who displayed "finished, rounded manhood." Rev. Boardman Hartwell Crumpton argued in the *Alabama Baptist* that Howard must not move and abandon its "twin sister" in Judson College. "What terrible crying and heartbreaking," Crumpton wrote, when sister Judson looked into the face of brother Howard and said: "Our parents died and left us orphans and willed me to you for protection, and you are going off and . . . leave your poor lone sister to battle with this heartless age and die in the contest. Brother, will you treat me so?" Crumpton encouraged brother Howard to honor the familial bonds (and southern womanhood) and explain: "No sister, you can't go and I will abide with you and if doomed one of us may be, we will die together."[11]

As passions continued to rise and financial difficulties deepened, Howard finished the year with just 103 students—far fewer than were expected. This left a deficit of $1,632 that the trustees made up by borrowing against the president's home. On June 14, 1887, graduation exercises began with prayers from Rev. Luther Rice Gwaltney (former president of Judson College) and ended with a baccalaureate sermon from former Howard student Rev. J. B. Hawthorne and a valedictory oration by nineteen-year-old William Henry McKleroy. At the alumni banquet that evening, Gwaltney described the efforts to relocate Howard as "nothing better than treason." Gwaltney's choice of the word "treason" resulted in a firestorm of controversy that exposed the underlying tensions in the debate over relocating Howard College and threatened to split Alabama

Baptists into warring factions. A few days later, J. J. D. Renfroe responded that traitors were needed to "perpetuate treason" and it would be a "dreary day in Alabama when the brethren who favor moving the college have imputation affixed to their conduct." Renfroe, however, hoped that, in discussing Howard's possible relocation, the Baptist brethren would "reason together without censure or passion, and act on the logic of facts and not on the appeals of sentiment." Many of those favoring the college's move to Birmingham, he added, were "overwhelmed with anxiety" and "distressed at the thought" of being branded traitors to the interests of Alabama Baptists.[12]

In response to Renfroe and other critics, L. R. Gwaltney argued that his use of the word "treason" suggested "moral obliquity" and the destruction of "some high and sacred cause," and not personal sedition, dishonor, or betrayal. To remove Howard from Marion, he added, would ignore or destroy the college's honor, reputation, "sacred associations," and "holiest influences." This effort would "pull down what may not be so well constructed again" and be destructive to the institution's "highest and best aims." Trying to calm the uproar, *Alabama Baptist* editor John Gideon Harris argued that the phrase "nothing better than treason" was used by Gwaltney as a "pleasantry" and not as an indictment of those who preferred relocation. Harris hoped none of the brethren would "indulge in any unkind word" with each other and believed that everyone was "actuated by pure motives." It was "foreign to us," he added, "to imply any unworthy motive to any brother whatever may be his position on the question."[13]

Contributing to the rising tensions was the lack of information on relocation proposals from the land companies in and around Birmingham and surrounding towns. According to J. J. D. Renfroe, "those brethren who were favorable" to removal "remained silent" until G. A. Nunnally finished his fundraising campaign for Howard's endowment. Even in the days leading up to the Alabama Baptist State Convention in Union Springs, few specifics on the proposals were known outside the committee and a handful of other Alabama Baptists. Before the convention, Rev. W. B. Crumpton received a letter from Benjamin F. Riley explaining that Birmingham Baptists were traveling *en masse* to Union Springs and solicited supporters from around the state to come to the convention and support the removal projects. Crumpton met with James T. Murfee and members of the Board of Trustees and decided that the Howard College–Marion assemblage would travel to the state convention "just as we always had done, without doing anything at all—just let the thing go and depend upon the justice of our cause to win." Perhaps this group of Marion supporters never considered removal as a serious threat as newspapers in July and August continued to run advertisements for the opening of Howard College's academic year in Marion in October 1887.[14]

The 1887 Alabama Baptist State Convention opened on a sweltering, bone-dry day in Union Springs; the mid-July temperatures hovered around 100 degrees throughout the meeting. A high number of "accredited delegates," some 288, arrived at the convention representing twenty-six state associations and sixty-four churches—the delegation from Birmingham was "unusually large." The discussion on Howard College's relocation was scheduled for the third day of the meeting, on Saturday. The day before the discussion, a reporter for the *Union Springs Herald* interviewed several convention attendees on the "vexed question" of the removal of Howard College. Some delegates discussed moving Howard to Birmingham and adding a law school, an engineering program, and a medical school. "In my opinion," one minister said, this was the time "to let the child of Marion, develop into the full-grown man of Birmingham, merging our literary school, into a grand university." Another proposal was to keep Howard College in Marion and allow Birmingham to form its own Baptist college. "Well, it simply means rupture, disunion," another preacher argued; "the very thing we have been seeking to avoid for the past dozen years."[15]

Rev. Josiah Alexis Howard, an 1876 graduate of Howard College and the pastor of the First Baptist Church, Columbia (in southeast Alabama), said that he favored removal to "some point" in northern Alabama—near the center of Baptist population. "That field," he said, was "totally neglected educationally by Baptists." Many alumni, like Howard, were fearful that, should the institution "go down" and shutter its doors, the graduates would then "hold diplomas from a dead college." Rev. Zephaniah Durham Roby of First Baptist Church, Opelika, believed that the Baptists in East Alabama viewed the removal of Howard as a necessity for its "continued existence." Most of the state wanted nothing to do with building an endowment or providing any patronage while the school remained in Marion. "From the mountains and hills," Zoby added, "boys will not be sent to Marion." Another Baptist minister believed that the brethren in South Alabama who remained "warmly attached to the old locality" were willing to sacrifice their personal feelings and support removal if it guaranteed a sustained endowment. Rev. J. C. Hudson of Florence in North Alabama supported Howard's removal "with the old name, its grand record, and precious memories," because it was necessary to create an endowment. The "much agi-tated question" of removal, Hudson believed, was secondary to the question of the endowment. The entire "brotherhood" of Alabama Baptists must speak with one voice, one mind, and one heart in order to make "one purse to perpetuate Howard College, both as a precious memory and a present power."[16]

Rev. John Frederick Purser of Troy felt saddened for the supporters of the college in Marion. To them, Howard was like one of their own children. The Baptists of Marion were a "grand people" who stood with Howard through "storm and calm"; they prayed for Howard, wept during its failures, and rejoiced in its successes. "They can but feel," Purser added, "and feel deeply." The min-ister sympathized with their increasing sense of loss and confessed that, when he looked at the situation, it was "hard to see how it can be right to move." But when he looked to the future and the great potential for Howard in Birming-ham, he concluded "that we would not be true to ourselves, our God, and our race, were we to neglect this present opportunity." Purser proclaimed that he had "not a shadow of doubt" in his mind about the removal of Howard College from Marion.[17]

While the pro-Marion forces stayed silent and relied upon the justice of their cause, the pro-Birmingham forces were outspoken and provided a few more specifics on the proposals. J. F. Purser, who spoke with his brother about the bids from various land companies, favored moving Howard College to the newly created town of East Lake, Alabama—a few miles from downtown Bir-mingham. "I never take a position of which I am ashamed," Purser said. "I do not like to sit on the fence, and certainly do not admire a weathercock." Rev. William Andrew Hobson of First Baptist Church, Avondale (also just outside Birmingham), predicted that Howard College would move to East Lake—a "high and healthy" town populated with "moral and refined" residents who were "strongly Baptist." Hobson thought that the land company would provide Howard with $200,000 in money and land.[18]

Other Alabama Baptists were skeptical about these high dollar amounts. Baptist layman George G. Miles believed that the question of relocation should be decided by "merit, based only on facts," in the denomination's best interest, and not upon "sentiment [or] prejudice." Howard College, he believed, was one of the convention's "chief auxiliaries in sustaining the cause of Christ." Rev. Benjamin F. Riley of First Baptist Church, Livingston, said that he needed more information and refused to believe these monetary and land proposals without thorough investigations. "These were numbers provided by Birmingham," the skeptical Riley said, and needed independent verification.[19]

Although the question of Howard College's location was the talk of the convention, formal discussion of the matter did not occur until the third day, Saturday July 16. During the previous afternoon, William W. Wilkerson reported from the Board of Trustees that the financial results of the 1886–87 academic year were "not satisfactory" and that the college's income was insufficient to cover expenses. "The agitation of the removal question," Wilkerson supposed, had "shaken the confidence of many in the perpetuity of the college" so badly that many parents were "unwilling to enter their sons" while this question was pending. "The superior character of training and mental culture imparted at Howard College," he added, was the "equal of any institution" of higher learning. To retain and build upon this distinction, "the question of removal must be at once definitely settled," the endowment "pushed forward," and patronage expanded. Following Wilkerson's report, Rev. G. A. Nunnally informed the convention that, after expenses, the Howard College endowment fundraising effort brought in $1,349.55 in cash, following months of work and traveling over five thousand miles to sell the idea of Howard College to white Baptists throughout Alabama. Nunnally added that a "grand endowment" awaited "Howard at no great distance in the future." When Wilkerson and Nunnally were both finished, "no discussion followed."[20]

On Saturday, July 16, the morning session opened with a devotional led by Howard alum L. O. Dawson. Before the discussion on Howard commenced, Rev. J. S. Dill offered a resolution "that whatever shall be the issue of the question relating to the future settlement of the College, the members of this Convention pledge their unbroken allegiance to its support." Dill's statement provoked an antagonistic response, and the resolution was tabled. The convention carried on other business until 11 a.m., when it was announced that the discussion of "the removal of Howard College had arrived." Moderating most of the sessions was Alabama Baptist State Convention president Jonathan Haralson, who was in his fourteenth consecutive year as convention president—a position he held until 1892. In 1889, he became the first layman elected president of the Southern Baptist Convention and was reelected for ten consecutive terms. A judge in the Selma city court, the fifty-six-year-old Haralson was a graduate of the University of Louisiana Law School (now Tulane) and would later serve on the Alabama Supreme Court. Quiet, exacting, fair, and firm, the judge, B. F. Riley observed, was a "model of genuine manliness" and "cautious of the feelings of others." When Haralson presided over at the convention, W. B. Crumpton recalled, and gave his gavel a "sharp rap" and called the meeting to order in a resounding voice, the delegates fell into a "perfect quiet and everybody knew" that the "king of parliamentarians was on the throne" and a "master hand was directing affairs." Rev. John Marion Frost also believed that Haralson had no superior when directing an assembly. "He was equally great," Frost added, during a "mighty storm" at a convention or "under the influence of a great surging wave of spiritual influence."[21]

Jonathan Haralson's steady hand was needed to guide the debate over Howard College's possible relocation and to avoid the convention being torn asunder. The judge moderating the session opened with Rev. I. T. Tichenor's prayer of guidance. Expectations were high, Benjamin F. Riley wrote, and most delegates believed that "Birmingham was chafing to pour out its wealth in the interest of imposing buildings for Howard College, and a munificent endowment with which to begin." Nonetheless, the first order of business at the session was the committee's report, read by chair R. H. Sterrett. In it, he outlined each proposal from land companies located in the areas just outside the city limits of Birmingham:

1. The Bessemer Land and Improvement Company led by the "quintessential New South industrialist," Henry Fairchild DeBardeleben, offered a "choice block of ground" on the Alabama Great Southern Railroad line in Bessemer. Founded just a few months earlier in 1887, Bessemer was located about twelve miles west of Birmingham. The proposed value of the land was estimated at $10,000 and included a cash donation of $10,000.

2. The North Birmingham Land Company led by the president of the Georgia Pacific Railroad, John W. Johnston, offered twelve acres of land near the railroad line valued at $4,000 per acre. "If buildings were erected, and the character of the school established be such as was set forth in the said resolutions," then the company would donate the land to the convention. To this offer, the Lakeside Land Company led by Samuel Ullman, a Jewish businessman and philanthropist, offered twenty acres of land valued at $500 per acre and $20,000 in cash

donations from the citizens of Birmingham "to establish . . . a Baptist university of high order." The combined value of the offer was $78,000. Ullman was keenly interested in education and played an important role in Birmingham's development for over forty years. He was often remembered for a widely read poem about youth: "Youth is not a time of life; it is a state of mind; it is not a matter of rosy cheeks, red lips and supple knees; it is a matter of the will, a quality of the imagination, a vigor of the emotions; it is the freshness of the deep springs of life."

3. The East Lake Land Company led by entrepreneur and real estate developer Robert Jemison, donated sixty acres of land in the recently developed town of East Lake—six miles east of Birmingham. The gift to the convention stipulated that the Baptists of Alabama "open a school by October 1st, next, and that the sum of $50,000 be expended on buildings, within eighteen months from date of acceptance." The property was valued at $85,000. To enhance the East Lake offer even more, they offered several additions. These included donations of land and money from the citizens of nearby Woodlawn (valued at $10,000) and subscriptions from the citizens of Birmingham (valued at $20,000) if Howard located to the East Lake area; the citizens of East Lake offered additional land donations valued at $30,075; the Walker Land Company led by attorney William A. Walker Jr. donated fifteen acres to the Alabama Baptists with the provision that the college be located on lands of the East Lake Land Company or the adjoining lands of the Walker Land Company. The property was valued at $15,000; and Ullman's Lakeside Land Company also offered twenty acres of land valued at $500 an acre. The total value of the East Lake proposal was estimated to be $170,075.[22]

Following Sterrett's report, a long, heated debate ensued but, as the *Alabama Baptist* reported, the "brethren on both sides of the issue" displayed "most excellent Christian temper"—no doubt a tribute to Haralson's calming guidance. As W. B. Crumpton later recalled, the Birmingham delegates looked like "princes" with their "rented stove-pipe hats" and long "shad bellied" cutaway coats which southerners referred to as "Jim swingers." They spoke with "prophetic hues" that were rife with New South boosterism. They dazzled the convention with promises that Howard would receive hundreds of thousands of dollars in donations and a magnificent endowment. The college no longer needed to suffer from every financial storm that brewed. "Why should it longer do so," one observer noted, "when a royal welcome awaited it at Birmingham?" All the buildings on campus would be magnificent and cost at least tens of thousands of dollars. "Those poor Baptists who had been bearing the burdens of Howard for years," W. B. Crumpton wrote, "had never heard of such things." Rev. Boardman H. Crumpton, who attended Howard College in the 1850s, offered a "gallant fight for Marion" but would go along with relocation if it was the will of the convention. Porter King gave a tender speech on behalf of Marion, that one listener described as a "father pleading that his child be not torn from his arms."[23]

And the debate continued back and forth until Rev. Morton Bryan Wharton, pastor of First Baptist Church, Montgomery, stood and called the question. Wharton was once described as a "patriot, author, poet, and a Christian gentleman whom the South loved to honor." Another true believer in the Lost Cause, he once rewrote the words to the southern anthem, "Dixie," to include the verse: "The fight we lost, but won a glory; Which still will last when time is hoary." But Wharton's task at the Alabama Baptist State Convention that July afternoon was not to lose another fight but to "cut off debate" and offer a resolution—in what a delegate described as a prearranged move by the Birmingham forces and one that embarrassed Wharton afterward. "*Resolved*," Wharton read, "that we gratefully accept" the proposal of the East Lake Land Company and other incentives totaling $170,075 in land and money for the "removal, establishment, and endowment" of Howard College—an institution "owned, controlled, and fostered" by the Alabama Baptist State Convention. The acceptance was contingent on an investigation to see if the offer was "what it was represented to be" in the committee's report.[24]

To investigate the offer from the East Lake Land Company, Wharton asked the convention to appoint a "Prudential Committee" composed of Jonathan Haralson, Samuel Henderson, Benjamin F. Riley, Zephaniah D. Roby, Gustavus A. Nunnally, Josiah A. Howard, James M. Frost, General Levi W. Lawler, G. A. Loftin, William C. Cleveland, John P. Shaffer, Thomas G. Bush, and Morton B. Wharton. The committee would go forth with the "full power" of the convention to approve or reject the offer—and if they approved the East Lake proposal, they would arrange for Howard College to start the academic year on October 1 with the faculty from Marion teaching the classes. Thomas G. Bush ber and former acting president, Amos Goodhue. Subsequently, Ward practiced law in Selma for several years before moving to Birmingham in 1885 to become general counsel to the Elyton Land Company.[23]

With new leadership in place, the trustees formally appointed Smith, Macon, and Giles to the faculty and granted an honorary degree to the former head of Ruhama Academy, Robert Judson Waldrop, and hired him to the faculty. Professor Thomas J. Dill was appointed as dean of the faculty pro tem—essentially serving as interim president of Howard College through the transition. Born on Edisto Island, South Carolina, on November 8, 1825, Dill received his education at South Carolina College (now University) and taught school in his hometown. In 1849, he moved to Alabama as part of a colony of South Carolinians who migrated to the town of Carlowville in Dallas County. T. J. Dill opened a private academy and led the school for the next twenty years, until his appointment to the faculty at Howard College in 1869. One contemporary described Dill as a "learned scholar, fine instructor, and a Christian gentleman who was admired and respected by all who knew him." After eighteen years with Howard, the trustees called upon Professor Dill to oversee vacating the old campus, constructing the new campus, and recruiting new students to Howard—all to be accomplished in less than eight weeks. "We regret exceedingly to lose Professor Dill," the *Marion Standard* lamented in August 1887, "but since he . . . decided to go, we do not think Howard College could do better than to elect him permanent president."[24]

Howard's Board of Trustees, however, hoped to hire an experienced president during the 1887–88 academic year. In August, the trustees offered the job to former Confederate general Stephen Dill Lee, who was president of the Agricultural and Mechanical College of the State of Mississippi (now Mississippi State), but he declined the position. A few weeks later, Robert Frazer, the former president of Judson College, turned down an offer to become Howard's leader, but Rev. David I. Purser was unrelenting: "I think when I see him, I can convince him that it was his duty to accept," he said. It worked and Frazer accepted the position. "Thank you for your kind favor," he wrote, planning to arrive in Birmingham "ready to do my best to serve the college." Newspapers across the state announced Frazer's acceptance of the presidency, but when he traveled to Birmingham and saw the frontier state of the East Lake campus, he quickly backed away from his commitment and returned to his retirement in Virginia.[25]

* * *

offered an amendment to the resolution that, if East Lake Land Company's offer was "sufficient to justify the removal of Howard College," then the committee should be authorized to consider, and act upon, other proposals offering "equal inducements and advantages."[25]

Bush's amendment opened the opportunity for a rumored "eleventh hour bid" of land and money from Anniston—a town some sixty miles east of Birmingham and labeled the "Model City of the New South" by Henry Grady. Some delegates grumbled that the bid was a result of an effort by forces from Anniston and Marion to block Howard College from moving to Birmingham. William A. Davis of Anniston denied the accusation and recounted that, as soon as the Birmingham bids were presented to the convention, the details were wired to land interests in the East Alabama city, and a counterproposal was conceived. Davis argued that there was no "bad faith or sharp practice" on the part of Anniston's delegates, and a communication from Rev. Elijah T. Smyth of Anniston (dated July 13, 1887) was read to the convention. Smyth wrote that he was authorized to make an offer from Anniston—presumably from the Woodstock Iron Company that developed the city—of twenty acres of land within the city limits, one hundred acres of land within three miles of the city, and $15,000 in cash. "This was to be," Smyth wrote, "a gift to the convention." Smyth argued that, if the college was to be moved, Anniston provided "more advantages and fewer objections" for Howard than "anywhere else in the state." Or as G. A. Nunnally quipped, Anniston had the dynamics of Birmingham cast into the mold of Marion.[26]

Wharton's proposal and Bush's proviso provoked another sharp discussion as several Baptist ministers and laymen held the "large and intelligent" gathering "spellbound." The speeches pro and con continued into the afternoon, but as a reporter for the *Union Springs Herald* observed, Judge John P. Hubbard made a "shrewd piece of parliamentary strategy" and moved that all words in Wharton's original resolutions be struck after the first word, "Resolved." Hubbard, an 1859 graduate of Howard College, instead proposed inserting the sentence: "That it is inexpedient to remove Howard College from its present location." In turn, R. H. Sterrett "checkmated" Hubbard's strategy by making a motion to adjourn—for the hour was long and the stomachs were empty. A "flattering majority" agreed, and the convention dismissed until the afternoon session at 3 p.m.[27]

When they resumed the discussion, the "old Howard boy" B. H. Crumpton offered a "gallant fight" on behalf of Marion. "He thought for many reasons," the *Alabama Baptist* reported, that the college should remain in Marion, but as a "true Baptist," he would accept the "will of the brethren." Industrialist and politician Caswell C. Huckabee defended the character of the teaching at Howard in Marion. "The verdict of an old man," he said, "was that every boy who came from that college was a gentleman." General Levi Lawler told the story of the founding of Howard College and the money donated by Julia Barron that enabled the school to open its doors. "If husbands would turn over their purses to their wives," he added, "there would be more money given for benevolent purposes." Following several more hours of debate and speeches, the convention adjourned until the 8 p.m. session. "Many of us feared hot words," one keen witness wrote, "but the meeting was that of brethren concerned for the safety of the ark."[28]

At the evening session the debate continued, although by agreement, speeches were limited to ten minutes. The *Montgomery Advertiser* reported that the "big guns fired their heaviest charges" over the next two and a half hours—with most of the firepower in favor of removal from Marion. Rev. Benjamin F. Riley recalled that the Birmingham delegation used a host of arguments against leaving Howard in Marion: The college was not thriving; the town was old, and the "best and wealthiest citizens" had moved to larger cities; students from northern Alabama had no desire to receive education in the southern part of the state; the Black Belt had an "immense population" of Blacks; the moral climate was poor, and all efforts to "expel the drinking saloons" in Marion failed. On the later point, though, Porter King retorted that grass grew on the doorsill of the saloon in Marion. An onlooker noted at the time that the Birmingham "brethren displayed no ugly spirit" in their presentations. "They came down like strong men filled with convictions and . . . with the same zeal and belief."[29]

George A. Lofton believed that the prospect of relocation to Birmingham was a "providential opening, not suggested by real estate men." It was preordained, he supposed, that God allowed Howard College to go through this trial to emerge stronger on the other side. After all, another observer emphasized, Rev. D. I. Purser was in Birmingham and along with his "trained soldiers of the Magic City" would "take Birmingham for Christ and the Baptists, if they will continue as they have labored for the college." This back and forth continued until around 10:30 p.m. when M. B. Wharton once again stood to champion the cause of relocation to Birmingham and made many "telling blows" against any other town being a fit location for Howard. Wharton again called the question on his original resolution from hours before, and Jonathan Haralson called for a test vote on whether to sustain Wharton's call. The vote was 115 ayes and 58 nays. As the *Union Springs Herald* reported, when Haralson put forward Wharton's resolutions as amended by T. G. Bush, the convention adopted the measure "by what appeared to be a larger vote" than the test vote. History does not record the actual vote total, but when the convention reconvened on Monday, C. C. Huckabee made a motion (on behalf of the minority) to make the vote to remove Howard College unanimous. Several newspapers reported that Huckabee's motion was "carried amidst great enthusiasm and good feeling," but the *Marion Standard* described the vote as a "Waterloo defeat."[30]

On the other hand, those unchecked emotions blinded the convention to the *realpolitik* of the proposals from the land companies. Most everyone was swept up in the whirlwind vision of a grand Howard College with large, majestic buildings situated on a beautiful campus and boasting a fat endowment. "The convention failed to weigh with deliberation the offers made," B. F. Riley later wrote, "and listened to the rosy suggestions and hints which came thick and fast." Based on the proposals, most everyone at the convention assumed that the land companies or the citizens in and around Birmingham would construct the buildings on the new Howard campus. In addition, D. I. Purser and J. J. D. Renfroe predicted that even more money than promised would flow into the college's endowment and operating budget. During the convention, Purser proclaimed that the limitations on the committee's work prevented him from raising at least $500,000 and not just the $170,000 in the East Lake proposal. The only word of caution at the convention came from Andrew B. Johnston of Birmingham, who warned "against precipitate action" and insisted that land values and cash promises from the land companies were all "fictitious." Johnston's ominous warning, however, was ignored by the delegates at the Alabama Baptist State Convention in July 1887.[31]

13

ALL NATIONS WERE GATHERING
IN BIRMINGHAM

On Monday evening, July 18, 1887, Judge Jonathan Haralson, with a rap of his gavel, adjourned the boisterous sixty-fourth annual meeting of the Alabama Baptist State Convention. The question of relocating Howard College was settled; the school would be removed from Marion. Its destination, however, was yet to be determined. The convention's thirteen-member Prudential Committee (Jonathan Haralson, Samuel Henderson, Benjamin F. Riley, Zephaniah D. Roby, Gustavus A. Nunnally, Josiah A. Howard, James M. Frost, General Levi W. Lawler, George A. Lofton, William C. Cleveland, John P. Shaffer, Thomas G. Bush, and Morton B. Wharton) would answer the question of Howard's new location. Reverend Wharton was selected chair of the committee. The convention tasked the committee with reviewing bids, visiting proposed sites (East Lake and Anniston), and evaluating morals and values of surrounding communities. The committee possessed the authority to render a final decision on behalf of the convention—all before the end of July.[1]

Many Alabama Baptists who supported relocation set forth high expectations of the committee. A writer for the *Tuskegee News* believed that the group was "composed of true, noble, Christian men" who were selected by the convention to serve God and their fellow Baptists. Their task was to locate Howard College in a place "where its future would be most prosperous, and nothing but a firm conviction of right could influence their decision." A new Howard had the opportunity to join the revolutionary changes of the New South and the new industrial Alabama. "The Baptists have met the occasion and have arisen to the demands of the hour," another observer emphasized. "They have grasped with firm hand the grand opportunity held out to them by the God of Alabama and now we will have a grand Baptist University with endowment sufficient to perpetuate its life throughout the circles of time, and the youth of Alabama will still be trained in the classic halls of Howard and go out to impress the world that the God of the Bible is the God of science." It appeared in the minds of many Alabama Baptists, that the thirteen men would be described more aptly as a *Providential* Committee and not just prudential.[2]

The Prudential Committee reconvened in Birmingham on Tuesday, July 26, at the Wilson House at Second Avenue North and Twenty-First Street—just a short walk from Union Depot—which catered to the needs and "comfort of commercial men." The proprietors, Emanuel Solomon and Emil H. Levi, offered members of the committee sleeping accommodations and a parlor for their meetings at $2.50 per day. Perhaps their temperance-minded Baptist guests were unaware that Solomon and Levi owned a thriving nearby saloon and were two of Birmingham's largest distributors of wine, whiskey, and cigars.[3]

The next morning, on Wednesday, July 27, the thirteen men boarded a steam-engine railway motor car for the six-mile excursion to the East Lake development. When they arrived, members of the nearby Ruhama Baptist Church and officials with the Canaan Baptist Association were there to offer horse-and-buggy transportation to the proposed site for Howard College. Once there, Robert Jemison Sr., the president of the East Lake Land Company, offered a warm greeting to the committee and led them on a tour. A New South capitalist with a wide range of interests, Robert Jemison was born in Tuscaloosa on September 12, 1853, and graduated with a law degree from the University of Alabama in 1874. Rather than practice law, he joined a successful grocery brokerage, earned enough money to move to Birmingham in 1884, and speculated in banking, insurance, and real estate. Like many other southern white business leaders of his generation, Jemison worked hard to gain money and prestige in a world removed from the "sadness and defeat" of their fathers' generation. To build their wealth and status, as historian Edward Ayers observed, men like Jemison obtained land surrounding a booming New South city, founded a company to develop the land, sold stock to produce "lavish brochures" to advertise the "burgeoning enterprise," and sent out "excursion trains" to bring potential investors, builders, buyers, and businesses. "Deprived of a chance to make a name for themselves on the battlefield," Ayers added, "they focused their energies on the marketplace" and an "ideology of boosterism" which served as "a gospel, an article of faith, a banisher of doubt." Jemison and other New South advocates repeated this ideology like a high-church litany.[4]

Birmingham in the early 1890s was a curious blend of New South hype and frontier hedonism, which led to its conflicting images as both the "Magic City" and the "Murder Capital of the World." Howard College students could only visit Birmingham one morning a week for a few hours. (Samford University, Special Collection and University Archives)

In addition, thirty-three-year-old Robert Jemison was adept at using the unpretentious language of evangelical Christianity and southern moralism to sell his development to thirteen Baptists looking for a new home for Howard College. The new campus would be built on a "quiet spot" on a hillside that "refreshed the eyes" by overlooking fields of green grass, majestic oak trees, and sparkling spring water. East Lake was where "original country charms" were preserved and "physical and moral purity" were emphasized. Most importantly, the town was free from the evils of intoxicating spirits—the company's charter stated that liquor could only be sold beyond a three-mile limit of the development—and isolated from the immoral influences of "Bad Birmingham." To emphasize the point, the land company would refuse "all persons and practices that did not commend themselves to the moral and religious element of

A train bound for East Lake. New South promoter Robert Jemison sold his new village
of East Lake as a resort community far from Birmingham's vice and violence. The large
manmade lake was a popular tourist and entertainment destination for Birmingham residents seeking to escape the smoke and soot of the industrial city. (Samford University,
Special Collection and University Archives)

society." After all, company officials emphasized, Howard was an institution
honored by time and tried by storms. One of the college's "chief glories" was
the development of Christian morality and manhood from all who studied the
liberal arts within the classrooms. Howard was a "great factory, so to speak, of
high moral influences, and its effect was as powerful, its returns as certain, as
those of the largest industrial establishment."[5]

And so it went, throughout the morning, as the committee wandered about
the property, Jemison engaged in what one writer called the "art of commercial
hyperbole" as he sold the virtues of East Lake. The two-thousand-acre development, Jemison believed, was an oasis far removed from the thick smoke of
heavy industry that obscured the sun, choked the air, and covered Birmingham
in a veil of dinginess. The Magic City was an ideal place to work, but a less
than desirable place to live. Jemison described East Lake as a "country retreat"
surrounded by rolling hills and boarded by a beautiful artificial lake that the
high-minded developers named "Lake Como" after the renowned resort in Italy.

In Alabama, Birmingham was growing in wealth and importance and needed "some favored vicinity" where the best class of people (the "professional men") lived apart from the "poor people huddled together in tenement housing and where the air was heavy and fetid from the overcrowding and uncleanliness." According to Jemison, East Lake was just such a place.[6]

Beyond Jemison's hyperbolic appeals, a strong incentive for relocating Howard College to eastern Jefferson County was the longtime presence of Ruhama Baptist Church. Throughout the 1880s, several strong supporters of Howard College filled the pulpit at Ruhama, including Samuel Henderson, W. C. Cleveland, and the pastor in 1887, E. B. Teague. Founded in 1819, the frontier church took its name from the Old Testament prophet Hosea's daughter, Ruhamah, whose name means "having obtained mercy." Why these early churchgoers chose to name the church, and the community that grew up around it, Ruhama was unclear. Perhaps the church founders chose the name to honor the first pastor, Rev. Hosea Holcombe, or maybe it was a way to ask God for an extra measure of grace and mercy to endure the harshness of frontier life. In 1858, the church began worshipping in a new building with twelve windows and four doors—two at the front, one on the side, and one in the rear for the handful of slaves who lived in the area. The fifty by sixty auditorium was heated by a large stove near the pulpit and the dedication sermon was delivered by Rev. J. J. D. Renfroe.[7]

In the years before the Civil War, the Ruhama community emerged as the education center for eastern Jefferson County. According to the *Birmingham Iron Age*, Evan E. Moor founded the Ruhama Academy in 1855, but his successor, Jacob A. Baker, became synonymous with the school, and it was often referred to as Baker's Academy. Even decades later, the mention of his name, one writer recalled, caused "many a heart all over this section [to] beat in unison with every word of praise that can be written of this great and good man. He was indeed the pioneer educator of this part of Alabama." Ironically, before Baker landed in Ruhama, his educational ventures in Tuscaloosa, Jonesboro, and Elyton all ended in bankruptcy. Nonetheless, in Ruhama, Baker expanded the academy in the late 1850s and built a new fifty-by-one-hundred-foot frame lecture hall with a partition separating males and females. Some sources suggested that Baker was teaching over two hundred students at the academy on the eve of the Civil War. The school survived Baker's death and emerged following Civil War and Reconstruction under the leadership of Robert Judson Waldrop, the son of Ruhama Baptist's long-time pastor, Rev. Andrew Jackson Waldrop.

By the 1880s, local observers noted that the academy produced students with "intelligence and high moral character." In 1887, if Howard accepted the offer from the East Lake Land Company, the meager Ruhama Academy buildings would be turned over to the college as classroom space and the academy would find a new location to operate.[8]

Following the tour of the property, Jemison, the Prudential Committee, East Lake Land Company officials, and residents held a public meeting—most likely in the sanctuary at Ruhama Baptist. The gathering took on the atmosphere of a New South revival for Howard College as speakers testified to all the virtues of East Lake and affirmed all the promises of money, land, and buildings. Howard was preordained, someone said, to have glorious new structures and to extend its educational "scope and efficiency so that it will easily rank among the chief institutions of its kind in the South." Billy Vann, who was once described as a "whole-souled, big-bodied Baptist," stood and spoke in "stentorian tones" and offered $53,000 out of his "plethoric pocket" to purchase additional land and secure the endowment. As one observer noted at the time, Howard College's endowment was secured at the "first jump." Other "perspicacious and public-spirited land-owners" also stood and offered more land and money which totaled at least $500,000 for the endowment. As a witness emphasized, the Prudential Committee would not "hesitate long to accept such advantageous terms."[9]

But all was not as it seemed. The committee discovered that the East Lake Land Company had no authority to offer the Ruhama Academy building as part of the proposal. Due to "some misunderstanding," Rev. B. F. Riley recalled, the proposal included the land the structure sat upon but not the building itself. It would have to be purchased. In addition, the land company reserved all the frontal lots facing the main road and did not include them in their original bid. This left the rest of the property cut off and road access to the proposed campus near impossible. "The best that could be done," B. F. Riley later wrote, "was to ask options on the lots, which were informally granted." Perhaps the committee should have questioned whether the offer from the East Lake Land Company was too good to be true, but nothing seemed to dampen the enthusiasm of the thirteen men.[10]

When the meeting adjourned around noon, the committee, and others in attendance, walked to a nearby grove of oak trees for dinner on the grounds prepared by the women in the church. An enormous makeshift table was filled with a "magnificent profusion" of every type of food that, a writer noted, would have "satisfied the cravings" of a starving Confederate brigade near the end of the Civil War. "How many just such jolly and hospitable occasions as this *fête champêtre* could not this hallowed ground boast of!" From the beginning, the Ruhama settlement was noted, above other communities in the area, for its "open-handed entertainments." If not for progress, he added, it was almost "a pity and a desecration" to see the "ancient landmarks removed" in favor of a "new army of occupation by reason of wealth and numbers, overwhelming the Ruhamaites." Throughout the dinner, Baptists from around Birmingham arrived to enjoy the food and encourage the committee to locate Howard College in East Lake. One attendee, part of a "hungry party of four Baptists in good standing," left Birmingham at 11:30 a.m. on a steam motorcar named "Runaway" in route to East Lake. They arrived an hour late because of a cow grazing on the track that "positively declined to move her mowing," even as the train's motorman blew the shrill steam whistle. The bovine only moved after frustrated Baptists pelted the animal with chunks of coal, allowing the group to arrive at Ruhama to participate in the "bounteous repast." As the dinner concluded, a summer rain shower arrived and drove "even the very Baptist elect under shelter: for, though they do not mind being soused under, they assert their common mortality in a heavenly sprinkle." After a couple of hours of waiting out the rain in the Ruhama sanctuary, all the "clergy, laymen, and worldlings" crowded onto two motor coaches for the ride back to Birmingham.[11]

A couple of days later, the Prudential Committee arrived in Anniston to review that city's bid for Howard College's relocation. Representatives from the "Model City" and local Baptists "royally entertained" the committee, B. F. Riley wrote. They spent the day touring the "beautiful mountain town," which gave Riley and other committee members "ample time to reflect upon the merits of each place."[12]

On Friday, July 29, the committee met and listened as the formal proposals from Anniston and East Lake were read aloud. Other Baptists from Birmingham, like J. J. D. Renfroe, attended the meeting. "I went to Anniston with others to look after our interests," Renfroe said at the time, "and to answer any questions that might be asked us." Throughout the day and into the evening they debated the pros and cons of both proposals and the virtues and vices of both towns. The general sentiment among most of the committee participants from the Black Belt, and a few other areas of South Alabama, was in favor of Anniston because of the "large immoral element" in Birmingham. B. F. Riley suggested that both offers were "simply splendid," but Anniston eclipsed Birmingham in the "unanimity of the entire town" in support of Howard College. The committee members from outside of the Black Belt favored East Lake. What impressed them was how the East Lake–Birmingham offer had increased substantially since the initial bid—with so much money in the area, they could offer $200,000 to $500,000 to build and endow the college, as one committee member noted, "without strain." The discussions continued into the early morning hours of July 30, when they finally took a vote: East Lake easily won the ballot by ten to three. "Nothing was left to conjecture," Samuel Henderson said, 'but everything that could enter into the question was exhaustively investigated" by the committee of thirteen "true, noble, Christian men."[13]

Members of the Prudential Committee composed a press release announcing the decision in favor of East Lake and sent it to the *Alabama Baptist* and other newspapers around the state. "Impressed with the gravity of their obligation," they wrote, "and conscious that a work so fraught with moment should not be precipitately disposed of," the committee prayerfully considered the "merits of the respective bids." The proposals from East Lake and Anniston were generous offers which enhanced the serious nature of the committee's work. Following a thorough examination, the East Lake proposal was accepted by the committee. East Lake was six miles east of Birmingham and far "removed from the contaminating influence" of vice and corruption, but still close enough to enjoy the advantages of a growing urban area. The East Lake community was long "pervaded with a wholesome Baptist influence" through the influential Ruhama Baptist Church and the "thrifty institution of learning," Ruhama Academy. The new home of Howard College was free from diseases, filled with pure air and water, and elevated on a hill above the surrounding countryside. But what convinced the committee of the superiority of East Lake was the large amount of money and property, the prospect of a continued increase in land values, and guaranteed generous contributions from additional sources around Birmingham. This, they supposed, would place the educational efforts of Alabama Baptists on a "high plane of prosperity," lead to the "most propitious era in their eventful history," and provide the denomination with "one of the most splendidly equipped institutions of learning in the country." Anticipating a healthy round of criticism to follow, Rev. Benjamin F. Riley emphasized that East Lake was not Birmingham. "Not by a great deal," he said on August 3, 1887. "As soon as those interested shall learn of the merits of the place. All objections will vanish." Riley, however, was wrong.[14]

The reaction to the committee's announcement did little to ease geographic tensions among Alabama Baptists. Many in Birmingham were ecstatic with the news that Howard College was coming to East Lake. For one journalist, this was another "well-considered and public acknowledgement" of the Magic City's prominence as it was set to become the "great education center of the state, as it is its geographical one." Another writer argued that Howard gave a "very becoming . . . air of substantialness" to Birmingham. "Birminghamites have more git-up-and-git [sic] about them than any class of people I have seen," he added. On the other hand, for many in the Black Belt and several other areas of southern Alabama, the news was embittering. "The removal of Howard College from Marion to Birmingham does not meet with the approval of a large majority of its patrons or admirers in this section of the State," one writer opined. Howard College and Marion were so intertwined that the removal of the college would "destroy the prestige and influence of the institution." Birmingham was an immoral place for a college founded on the principles of virtue and faith. Parents, in selecting colleges for their sons, preferred schools with "healthy and refining surroundings." Birmingham had neither. Marion's influences, however, were "pure and elevating" for college-age boys. "Howard College may go to Birmingham," the writer added, "but the glory of its past will still hover around Marion."[15]

One Marion Baptist believed that the removal forces "would have located the college in hell if money enough was offered," while another local resident complained that the plans to relocate Howard College reeked of the "smell of boodle in them." The *Marion Standard* reported that the Prudential Committee had committed a "great act of injustice" against the Baptist brethren of Marion—against those longsuffering supporters of Howard who faithfully sustained the school when the Baptist brothers of North Alabama "were doing nothing." The town, the writer predicted, would see no ill effects by the removal. "Instead of being a calamity as some seem to regard it," the move "will prove a blessing in disguise," and the committee's words and deeds "overshot" their mark and "aroused a bitter feeling" that would not easily be removed. A Montgomery writer believed the relocation engendered "ill feelings . . . among friends." Howard College no longer had the "earnest and cordial" support from those who "labored most zealously and unceasingly, in season and out of season." The move to East Lake clouded the future of Howard. It was sad, the writer continued, to see a great school, or any other institution, "sold to the highest bidder . . . no matter how conscientiously conducted." Money should have been subordinate to the moral and physical well-being of the location and how it might benefit the students and faculty.[16]

In Anniston, the news in favor of East Lake left many residents enraged—resulting in unjust "rash assertions" against the integrity of the committee. "It was a matter of regret," Samuel Henderson said, that in Anniston's disappointment, several "friends" were "so unkind and unchristian" to accuse committee members of "corrupt motives" in selecting East Lake. A rumor circulated that members of the committee purchased options on lots in East Lake and would financially benefit by locating Howard College near those lots. The story was false. The only lots discussed by the committee were the frontal property not included in the original proposal from the land company. "No member of the committee took any option on a lot or contemplated such a thing," General L. W. Lawler explained to a newspaper reporter.[17]

Fanning the flames of discontent in Anniston was James Ryder Randall, editor of the city's newspaper, the *Hot Blast!* It was predictable, Randall wrote, that these Baptist men succumbed to the "magnetic attraction that was judiciously supplemented by a big pile of cash in sight." The editor hoped that Howard College would not "live to regret" the decision. "One might sentimentally suppose," he added, that a committee of thirteen Baptist men would have considered the "ethical, hygienic, and moral considerations" before choosing East Lake. "The 'old Adam' was strong in all of us," Randall continued, "even in clergymen and pious laymen." Perhaps they should not be blamed for choosing the most lucrative offer, but he asked the committee to reconsider the decision. After all, Birmingham had poor drinking water, free-flowing whiskey, and Sunday baseball games. Randall refused to believe that parents would send their young Baptist sons to a town "whose water was bad, whose morals were worse, and where the sound of the umpire interrupted the man of God as he reads the Holy Book to his listening congregation."[18]

Despite James R. Randall's pleas, the committee of thirteen's decision was final. Following their vote, but before adjourning their meeting that early Saturday morning, the gathering appointed a subcommittee charged with beginning the "inauguration of plans" to oversee the removal of the items from the Marion campus, obtain property deeds in East Lake, collect the promised cash donations, acquire promissory notes on those willing to pay later, and erect temporary buildings on the new campus. They would also plan for Howard College to open its doors to students by October. On August 1, the subcommittee

(Samuel Henderson, Benjamin F. Riley, Zephaniah D. Roby, Josiah A. Howard, John P. Shaffer, and Morton B. Wharton) met in East Lake and announced that the priority for the campus was constructing two temporary buildings: a mess hall and dormitory. The latter would accommodate one hundred students and provide recitation rooms. The old Ruhama Academy building would be used for "odds and ends." Within days, trees on the property were felled and work began on the makeshift wood-frame buildings. When Professor A. D. Smith first visited campus that summer, he said of the New South boosters, "They have out figured us."[19]

With construction underway on the new campus, the question of the old campus and the faculty needed a clear answer. There was much confusion. In Marion, Colonel Murfee continued to run Howard College advertisements throughout July as part of his student-recruiting efforts: "Celebrated for Morality of its Students—for the industrious and economical habits they acquire—for moderate cost of preparation for business and professional life—for superior skills of Professors—and for extraordinary attention and assistance given to the students. For Catalogues and further information, address: J. T. Murfee, President." Adding to the chaos, the Marion and Anniston papers reported that all the Howard faculty refused to move to East Lake; the situation, however, was almost the opposite. All the faculty, with one notable exception, agreed to follow the college to the new campus: Thomas John Dill (Latin and Greek), Albert Durant Smith (mathematics and modern languages), George Washington Macon (chemistry and natural history), and Benjamin Franklin Giles (English).[20]

The lone holdout in Marion was Colonel James T. Murfee. A scientific-agrarian, Murfee could not envision leaving Alabama's Black Belt for the urban, industrial New South. Soon after the Prudential Committee selected East Lake as Howard's new home, the colonel announced his resignation as president of the college. "This brought additional trouble," Rev. B. F. Riley observed. The college had no buildings and no president. Murfee, however, had a contingency plan to stay in Marion and continue to provide leadership to an educational institution. A few weeks before, at the Alabama Baptist State Convention, a group of delegates surrendered the deed to Howard's Marion campus back to William W. Wilkerson and Jesse B. Lovelace, who in 1886 gave the property to the convention. In turn, Wilkerson and Lovelace leased the campus and its buildings to Murfee, and the colonel announced that his new school, Marion Military Institute (MMI), would open for classes on October 1—fulfilling the colonel's original vision to open a military school when he moved to Alabama almost thirty years earlier. MMI would be modeled upon Murfee's alma mater, Virginia Military Institute, and seek to make the "strongest possible man— physically, morally, and intellectually—thoroughly prepared for social and business life." The colonel would serve as MMI's superintendent and continue to exalt the myth of the Lost Cause for another two decades. In the chapel, the portrait of Samuel Sterling Sherman was replaced by a "fine painting" of General Robert E. Lee.[21]

On August 5, 1887, Murfee sent out a public letter to his "old student friends" announcing that, in "these halls so dear to us," his new school would continue the same "discipline and methods of instruction" that he introduced to Howard College in 1871. Murfee was counting on his former college students to support him personally over loyalty to the old institution. Simply put, he hoped these alums would see themselves as graduates of Colonel Murfee's school and not of Howard College. "I shall aim to train other young men as you were trained, and to make them like you in character, popularity and usefulness." All Howard graduates needed to visit their "old college home," Murfee wrote. "I shall rejoice . . . in extending your influence and promoting your welfare." Howard College graduates William Garrott Brown and William Caffey responded to Murfee's call to aid and joined the faculty before both moving on to graduate studies at Harvard. "Marion was not at all dependent on Howard College," the local paper proclaimed, and its place was now filled by a "school equally as good. And more than that, nothing but death . . . can take away from Marion the refinement, culture, and morality for which it is noted." Colonel Murfee's new school, Marion Military Institute, opened in October 1887 with a sizable number of cadets and an enthusiastic group of local supporters.[22]

Following Murfee's departure, board chairman W. W. Wilkerson also resigned, leaving Howard College without leadership at a critical point in the institution's history. On August 10, Howard's trustees met at the First Baptist Church of Birmingham and selected attorney William Columbus Ward as the new head of the board. Ward had a long history with Howard, having served as a tutor in mathematics and ancient languages with the college from 1858 to 1861. During the latter year, he joined the Confederate Army with two other Howard faculty members and most of the students. Wounded at the Battle of Gettysburg and taken prisoner of war, Ward returned to Marion after the war and married Alice Goodhue, the daughter of Howard's long-time faculty mem-

While the trustees struggled to find a permanent president, Thomas J. Dill was in Marion throughout September, packing the college's furnishings, apparatus, and records for shipment to East Lake. Advertisements for Howard College appeared in newspapers across the state—often alongside those from Marion Military Institute. Expenses at Howard for the 1887–88 academic year were: $50 for tuition per term, $12 per month for board and lodging, and $5 for incidental expenses. Within a few weeks, the Board of Trustees reduced the total rate (tuition, board, lodging, incidentals) to $175 for the entire academic year. Howard would continue as a military school, with cadet uniforms costing $23.60 or $27.40, and daily drills for one hour. This daily physical education was an essential part of the Howard experience to produce young men who were "erect, graceful, and manly"; maintained "vigorous and healthy constitution"; cultivated "politeness, moral courage, respect for self"; showed "deference, frankness, perseverance, industry and self-reliance"; and provided the mind with the "power of close and continued attention."[26]

When Dill and his family arrived in East Lake the last week of September, he discovered a college campus ill prepared to greet students on Monday, October 3. The main thoroughfare in front of campus (Underwood Avenue) was still being constructed, and large tree stumps crisscrossed the dirt street; the old Huntsville Road, which for decades served the people of the Ruhama Community before being abandoned with the East Lake development, entered the college's property from the west, meandered up the hill near recently cut loblolly pines and the first of the hastily constructed buildings—a small two-story frame structure with a few recitation rooms on the upper floor and the chapel and president's office on the first. "This was called euphemistically," alumnus Mitchell Garrett quipped, "the administrative building." Just beyond was the dilapidated Ruhama Academy structure, and further up the old road to the northwest, through a grove of pines and tangled vines of underbrush, and beyond an enormous oak tree, stood the larger two-story building which contained thirty-seven rooms for use as dormitory space and a mess hall. With no fence to contain the makeshift campus, hogs rooted and cows grazed about the property. Just beyond, a keen observer noted, the new community of East Lake was "hardly visible on the surface of the countryside."[27]

When the crates of materials from the Marion campus arrived, the furniture and bedding—all old and needing replacement—were sent to the new buildings. In the frantic pace to unpack before the students arrived, assorted mate-

rials and equipment were scattered about any empty space. Unassembled scientific apparatus, including the college's prized telescope from the 1850s, went
unused and were later discarded as garbage. Library books, many of those that
Samuel Sterling Sherman collected from the citizens of Marion, were stored
inside the old outhouse of Ruhama Academy. Many of Howard's photographs
and memorabilia remained in Marion, presumably in the possession of Colonel
Murfee. The portrait of Sherman made the journey, as did the old matriculation
book where he recorded the names of all the students beginning in January
1842—and was still being used in the fall of 1887. Most of Howard College's
historical records went missing. None of the minutes of the Board of Trustees or
the literary societies survived the move; neither did correspondence or written
records of the daily operations of Howard College in Marion. "In the general
mix-up," Mitchell Garrett later wrote, "they were probably one day swept into
the junk heap."[28]

On October 3, the first day of the 1887–88 academic year, eighty-five students enrolled in the college, including several returning cadets who attended
classes in Marion. Students were able to enroll at any point during the school
year, and the numbers continued to grow as the total enrollment increased by
50 percent over the previous year. Most of the new enrollees were from the Birmingham area and other parts of North Alabama. The previous year, 1886–87,
only 4 of the 103 students attending Howard College were from the Birmingham
area. The first year on the East Lake campus, enrollment numbers boomed as 79
of the 157 students enrolled from areas in and around the Magic City. This was
the second largest class size in Howard's history and the most students in attendance since Samuel Freeman's tenure as president in 1869–70 and 1870–71.[29]

As the students arrived on campus, members of the faculty received and
assigned them to either college or preparatory courses. What they found in East
Lake was a wilderness school on the frontier of the New South with makeshift,
unpainted buildings, and old, meager accommodations. Fortunately, as Mitchell Garrett noted, most of the Howard students grew up in rural areas without
modern, urban conveniences, and found the frontier experience agreeable. "The
absence of electric light, lavatories, bathtubs, and furnace heating was not noticed," he added, "for these things were absent from their houses." A small pipe
brought water from the natural spring at the top of the hill to water spigots close
to the buildings, where students filled their buckets for a drink of water or a
spit bath. Kerosene lamps illuminated recital rooms, the chapel, and sleeping

spaces. "To most of the students," Garrett wrote, "greater conveniences would have been strange, bizarre, even embarrassing."[30]

James Edward McClurkin was one of those rural Howard students. A native of the tiny hamlet of Caledonia in Wilcox County, McClurkin attended classes in Marion the previous academic year. When he arrived in Birmingham in late September 1887, he was amazed to see so many people. "I believe the world was *nigh to an end*," McClurkin wrote to his cousin a few days later, "and that all nations were gathering in Birmingham." An urban area crammed with people from across the globe must be a sign of the end times, the country boy supposed. This apocalyptic opinion was only affirmed when he came across a Chinese immigrant. "I saw my first Chinaman on the first day I landed here," he wrote, "and I think that I shall back out of going to China [as a missionary]." After a few days in Birmingham, he arrived at Howard College in early October and found the campus situated in a lovely setting surrounded by mountains with a large stream flowing from the top of the tallest one. He was happier at the campus in Marion but imagined that life would improve once he got "more acquainted" with the area. East Lake was booming, McClurkin explained, and every day he listened to the ringing of "hundreds of hammers" as dozens of houses were being built. "The positive truth," he added, the "business of the world" was being "carried on" in Birmingham—an opinion that would delight the boosters of the New South—but he also recognized the dark side of the Magic City. Everyone had to stay indoors after sunset for fear of being murdered, across the city burglars preyed on people, and the Sabbath day was "hardly known."[31]

McClurkin most likely attended the opening chapel service with other students and the faculty. Chapel focused on the question from Psalm 119:9, "Wherewithal shall a young man cleanse his way? By taking heed thereto according to thy word." Professor B. F. Giles offered the invocation, and acting president Thomas J. Dill encouraged the young men to remember that Howard College's future depended in "large measure upon their noble bearing and devotion to duty." A reporter for the *Birmingham Age* hailed October 3 as the most successful opening day the college had ever experienced. The campus, however, was a "little crowded for room," but soon construction would start on Howard's grand new buildings. "The successful opening," the *Age* writer added, "was very gratifying to the many friends of the college, who worked so hard for its location at East Lake."[32]

On October 4, the Prudential Committee and the Board of Trustees met

in the small makeshift chapel on campus. The committee submitted its final report to the board and reviewed the work they had accomplished since the state
convention in July. The total cost of relocating Howard College, which included
moving expenses, purchasing some furniture, and erecting temporary buildings,
was $8,000. And, the committee noted, there was insufficient room for all the
new students. "It beats anything I ever heard of," one member said. "No college
ever opened with so many students and with such a favorable outlook the first
session after removal." In time, they expected increased enrollment, but they
never anticipated such success on the opening day.[33]

The hopeful rhetoric failed to match the reality of the situation. When a
few members of the committee urged the board to begin construction on permanent buildings, the appeal was met with a cold reaction from some local
pastors and laymen. Those that spoke loudest for removal in July, Rev. Benjamin F. Riley observed, were now "lapsed into a strange and suggestive silence"
in October. "Now that the college was removed," he added, "the visions of gran-
deur had vanished." Some believed that the college could make do with the
temporary buildings for years to come, and one pastor proclaimed that it was
much better to put "money into brains than into bricks." Upon those assembled
in the chapel, the reality of the situation was clear: The great promises from
July were empty. Now Andrew B. Johnston's warning at the convention should
have been heeded; the land values and cash promises were all "fictitious" and
nothing more than New South hype. "Well, if I had known that we were not
to have buildings," Rev. John P. Shaffer proclaimed, "I should never have voted
for removal."[34]

Howard College had the misfortune of leaving a Black Belt region in steady
economic decline and arriving in Birmingham just as the real estate bubble
burst and heavy industry fell into recession. For some, the status of the school
was a matter of opinion. In mid-October 1887, one Howard visitor from Bibb
County was enthusiastic about what he witnessed on campus. "To tell its [How-
ard's] worth seems to me too great a task even for this year," he wrote. The
college was invaluable to the Baptists of Alabama and, all around the state,
people recognized the "great benefit it will do for the denomination we love and
cherish." In contrast, visitors in November described the deplorable conditions
on campus: For students, bedding and food were "miserably poor; water was
unfit to drink; and many of the cadets were suffering from chills and fever. "If
the college had to be removed at all," they wrote, "it seems to us that, before

doing so, comfortable quarters in the new location should have been provided." It was obvious, they concluded, that Howard should have stayed in Marion until a fitting campus was available to receive the college. Rev. Benjamin F. Riley agreed and wrote that the 1887–88 academic year was just the beginning of a new series of hardships at Howard College. The "spirit of the dreams" of Birmingham and the New South awakened to the harsh reality that the economic bubble had burst just as Howard arrived in the Magic City. "The hubbub which reigned for many months," Riley concluded, "was lapsing into the quiet of the graveyard. A strange stillness filled the land."[35]

14

AN EMBARRASSING PILE
OF BUILDINGS

"Discouragement," wrote Rev. Benjamin F. Riley, "began at the start" for Howard College in Birmingham. The money promised the college never material-
ized, and confidence in the future of the school reached a new low. "It now
became manifest," Riley wrote, that the supporters of relocation presumed
too much from Birmingham's promises and took for granted too "many things
which had not even been promised." The problem, one observer emphasized,
was that the trustees never documented these promises "in the shape of iron
clad notes with approved security." So, when Howard officials went to collect the
money, Birmingham "failed to ante up." Adding to the woes was the failure of
every effort to raise money for permanent buildings. Before relocating, Howard
struggled to raise money because most Baptists saw the school as a local enterprise of Marion and not the state of Alabama. Following the move, citizens in
and around the Magic City saw Howard as a local enterprise of the East Lake
Land Company and not Birmingham. The rival land companies in the area
cared little about the college's success and considered it "an element of speculation" in the fierce economic competition of the New South. "Worse still,"
Riley added, "the college was in the midst of friendless surroundings."[1]

When student Paul Lee Abernethy left Howard College near the end of the
first term in January 1888, he cited ill health as the reason for his departure. The
future prospects of the college were "gloomy," he explained, because East Lake
was "unhealthy" and Birmingham was unwilling to provide the money the city
promised. When Abernethy's comments were published in the *Marion Standard*,
the newspaper criticized their "Baptist friends" for listening to the "prejudices
and whims" of a bunch of preachers with "no business tact or experience" and
making the titanic blunder of moving the college to East Lake. Howard needed

to hire a businessman to lead the college or send their students to Marion Military Institute, "where they will be healthy, thoroughly trained, and well educated." The paper later proclaimed that Howard's removal and the advent of MMI "was one of the most fortunate things that ever happened to Marion."[2]

In 1888, as Howard College's woes grew deeper, Black Belt papers—especially the *Marion Standard* and the *Montgomery Advertiser*—flaunted the news in a told-you-so campaign to taunt those who advocated for relocation to Birmingham. When board president W. C. Ward called the *Advertiser*'s coverage of Howard "presumptuous," the paper's editor, William Wallace Screws, embraced the indictment and offered a clear explanation of the Black Belt's raging resentment over the college's removal. With the rise of Birmingham and the mineral district, he wrote, the Black Belt faced an uncertain future. The "institutions of learning" bequeathed by the region's forefathers served as a bulwark against the waves of ignorant citizens who "dashed themselves in vain against our civilization."[3]

But now, Birmingham was drawing young men from the fertile agrarian area—men the people of the "brave old Black Belt" hoped would lead it from the economic "wilderness." Whites throughout the region silently watched the young men leave, but stealing schools elicited a visceral response. "It was uprooting . . . our civilization itself," Screws wrote, "like eating out the heart to be restored no more forever." The worst part of the ordeal was seeing the "grand old institution" of Howard College snatched from the Black Belt by the "glittering and false" promises of New South. Marion's citizens were blindsided because they never believed removal would happen until they awoke one summer morning and discovered the deed was done. "We shall not be caught napping again," Screws added. "No more of the bulwarks of the civilization of the Black Belt will be uprooted if our feeble voice can hold one brick upon another, and we will cross denominational lines or any other lines to be true to these white people struggling here amid the wide ignorance of the cotton plantation." Many whites throughout the region, the writer supposed, hoped that Howard would return and the "awful blunder of believing in promises that were never made and values that never existed could be wiped out with the loss of only a year." As another Black Belt resident observed at the time, Birmingham misled the public over how much support it was willing to provide Howard College. "Baptist friends," he added, "will have to seek another place to pitch their educational tent."[4]

Moving Howard College from East Lake and returning it to Marion or to another location was discussed throughout the state in 1888. Even the usually sanguine David I. Purser predicted that the convention would support the "removal of the college to some other point, and that if the promised money was not raised it would be moved at once." With high hopes of settling the issues of removal and funding, the Board of Trustees hired Rev. John Pilgrim Shaffer to serve as financial agent for the school beginning in January 1888. The forty-seven-year-old Shaffer was the pastor of the First Baptist Church of Roanoke, Alabama, and the founder and former president of the Roanoke Male & Female Institute in East Alabama. One nearby observer described education-minded Shaffer's position as a "grave responsibility" and his job duties as "onerous." The *Birmingham Herald* announced that Shaffer was now "master of the situation" at Howard and was expected to solicit funds from the "wealthy and liberal" residents of Birmingham to develop a handsome landscaped campus with "permanent and substantial" buildings. Shaffer, however, discovered that the pledged donations (subscriptions) were made mostly by people who only hoped to lure Howard College to Birmingham and nothing more. When Shaffer showed up to collect the money, the subscribers were uninterested in providing any financial support.[5]

With an overall economic downturn, a host of counterfeit donors, and no cash available to construct buildings, Shaffer called on Baptists throughout Alabama to pray for the future of Howard College. "If we pray to God for the success of our college," he proclaimed, "we cannot fail; no barrier can stop us." Howard needed at least $750,000 to build a campus, equip the classrooms, and endow the college. Perhaps God would answer the prayer, he hoped, and compel donors to provide the full amount. To make matters more difficult, the donors' outstanding "notes" (written pledges) to the college collected interest each year the debt was outstanding. "No one has sent me a cent of interest," Shaffer complained in the *Alabama Baptist*. These pledges were useless to Howard College and would remain so "until brethren conclude that they should treat these notes as they do other indebtedness."[6]

During the spring of 1888, Shaffer issued a call to all Birmingham Baptists to "show their true colors" and support Howard College at a "great rally" at Rev. David I. Purser's First Baptist Church. On May 27, Shaffer offered the gathering a grave assessment of Howard's condition and future. "Unless the help of Birmingham was given," he said, "the college was lost to them and lost to everybody else." The Baptists of Alabama owed permanent buildings to the students at Howard College and should not leave them forever in "temporary quarters" and expect them to remain loyal "to us who ourselves are not loyal."[7]

For decades, John Jefferson DeYampert Renfroe was perhaps Howard's most faithful advocate. B. F. Riley described Renfroe as "chivalric in disposition," possessing a "soul of honor," and held in preeminent esteem by the Baptists of Alabama. As an unfailing supporter of the college's relocation to the Magic City, Renfroe was confused by the empty promise of this New South city. A few minutes into his talk at First Baptist, emotions overwhelmed the minister and his voice faded. Those closest to Renfroe helped him to a chair for a moment's rest. While seated, he spoke with an increasingly passionate voice on the many decades of economic woe in Howard College's history and how, through this suffering, the school grew to fill the "hearts of the Baptists of Alabama." But those hearts were now broken by failed promises—not only from Birmingham but from the men, like Renfroe, who supported the move from Marion. Behind the college, Renfroe proclaimed, was a great denomination, and Howard was a memorial to all Alabama Baptists. "It is my opinion," he concluded in a feeble voice, "that unless something is done speedily to fulfill our promises this great denomination will turn in disgust from us" and remove the college from East Lake. The fifty-seven-year-old Renfroe was helped from the platform and taken to his daughter's home, where he died just a few days later. "His last public utterance," B. F. Riley wrote, "was made in behalf of the institution which he had loved, and cordially supported even unto death."[8]

At the conclusion of the service, J. P. Shaffer called for donations from the gathering. "The time consumed in calling for money," the *Alabama Baptist* reported, "was most painful" for those present. Like a hopeful auctioneer, Shaffer requested five people step forward with $1,000 each for Howard College. A representative of the East Lake Land Company was the only response. Shaffer then asked for $500. He received no response; neither did his call for $250 or $50, $25, or $10. In the end, Shaffer fell far short of his goal of raising at least $30,000 at the rally for Howard, and a "dark cloud" hovered over the gathering. The mark of disappointment, one observer said, was on "many brows," and "many hearts were sad." Yet, even in failure, there was "no evidence" that Howard College would die.[9]

One Howard supporter, Rev. Samuel Perrin Lindsey, proclaimed that the college "cannot, will not, die" with so many Christian men and women in Alabama offering "deep heartfelt earnest prayers" for the institution's success. Ala-

bama Baptists must continue to rally and support the college. "Send your boys
to the Howard," Lindsey said, "and they will become true men fully equipped
for the warfare of life." Even so, the festering resentment of many whites in the
Black Belt only deepened the foreboding sense that Howard College's imminent
failure would lead to an irreconcilable and permanent split in the state convention. "For a while," Rev. Washington Bryan Crumpton said, "it looked like South
Alabama was going to secede." But John Pilgrim Shaffer believed that prayer was
the answer. "Prayer will settle all the jealousy that troubles any of us," he said,
"in any section of the State, and nothing else will. Prayer will heal all the wounds
that any of us have received in the removal conflict, and nothing else will."[10]

In East Lake, graduation week (June 10–13, 1888) brought a sense of relief
and accomplishment for the students and the faculty. Rev. J. A. Howard delivered the baccalaureate sermon, and Rev. D. I. Purser gave the baccalaureate
address on June 10. The most noteworthy address was delivered on June 12 to
the literary societies by one of Alabama's most gifted orators, Tennent Lomax
Jr. Described as the greatest prosecutor in the state during his long service as
the circuit solicitor from Montgomery County, Lomax warned his audience of
the dangers of socialism, anarchy, despotism, and infidelity lying along the path
of an industrialized New South. "Will our moral and intellectual growth as a
people keep pace with our material development?" Lomax asked. Will people
become so focused on digging holes in search of mineral riches, on bridling
the commercial "winged thunderbolts of heaven," on garnering treasures "left
by the mighty dead in the storehouses of the past" that they forget and destroy
their love of "the good, the beautiful, and the noble?" Will the pursuit of wealth
and success replace the "cultivation of the mind and the propagation of moral
and religious truth?" Unless something can be found to "curb these tendencies,"
he continued, then the sun will set upon this "marvel of the world, this final
refuge of free men, this last hope of man's regeneration, this grand Republic of
the West will take its place eventually in the charnel house of dead Republics
and free government will depart from earth to return no more forever."[11]

Howard College, located in the "great throbbing heart" of Alabama industry,
was the answer to those questions, Lomax emphasized; it was a place devoted to
learning, morality, and Christianity. The college was now a New South school
where the "growth of mental and moral powers will march shoulder to shoulder with the development of industrial and material greatness." One day in the
future, he prophesized, Birmingham would stand as the greatest city of the

industrial world—where the bright light of blast furnaces would be a "pillar of fire" to illuminate the path of industry; the heavy smoke of iron and steel plants would serve as a "pillar of cloud" to guide the way for the "children of toil" (workers) from the "Egypt of poverty to the promised land of happiness and contentment." And when that day came, the "purest, noblest, most potent ray of light in the bright sun of her destiny" would shine from the halls of Howard College and radiate the light of knowledge, power, and truth. The college possessed a storehouse of "immortal freightage" that flowed from the lecture halls as a "product of intellectual courage and moral progress." The sweet sound of music from the college chapel was a "symphony of morality and virtue struck by a master's hand upon the delicate chords" of benevolence and love. "For thine, dear Howard," Lomax proclaimed, "thy bright deeds enweave immortal truths that guide to Heaven and God."[12]

On Wednesday, June 13, 1888, Howard College held its graduation ceremony at the ornate pavilion overlooking the waters of East Lake. (Promoters had abandoned the name "Lake Como.") A large crowd gathered to watch the cadets march into the pavilion in their uniforms and carrying the old Civil War–era muskets that Colonel James T. Murfee obtained years before. Seven young men—Walter J. Bell, John H. Blanks, Claude Hardy, Tyler M. Hurt, William W. Lavender, John M. Reeves, and Eugene R. Rushton—fulfilled all their academic requirements, paid their graduation fees of five dollars each, and received their diplomas. "More than ever," the *Birmingham Herald* wrote after the ceremony, "Howard College impressed the Birmingham public with the importance of that institution, and the great value it was to the city." In time, and with permanent buildings, the college will "rank with the leading institutions of learning in the South. Another enthusiastic response came from Howard board member W. B. Wharton, who believed the first commencement ceremony in East Lake was one of the best he had ever attended. The graduation orations "elicited the warmest commendations" and "delighted" the large audience.[13]

The ever-optimistic Wharton said that the 1887–88 academic year was a tremendous success with decorum, order, and discipline among the 157 students in attendance. Howard College was a "quiet Christian community," he added, with strict prohibition laws enforced throughout the area. For Wharton, the architectural drawings of the permanent buildings for the college that he showed to parents, students, and visitors were the most exciting news of commencement week. Designed by architects L. B. Wheeler of New York and John

Sutcliffe, the buildings would reflect the American Renaissance architectural style. Popular in the United States from 1876 to the early twentieth century, the style embraced the boldness of industrial might with a clear homage to classical and Renaissance architecture—an appropriate choice for Howard College and its continued emphasis on classical education.[14]

The impressive architectural drawings for the "pile of buildings" included an imposing main edifice, dormitory, dining hall, and science building. The trustees, meeting during commencement week, approved the plans and hired the firm Allen & Taylor of Birmingham to construct the foundation for the main building. The "handsome" structure would be "massively built," three stories tall, "conveniently arranged," and cost $50,000 while the entire "pile of buildings" was estimated to cost $125,000. Standing on the site of the future main academic building, Wharton declared that, upon this hallowed spot, which God predestined "before the foundation of the world," was the "final seat of Howard College." With hyperbolic boosterism that was more fantasy than reality, Reverend Wharton claimed that the money was available, "with no hindrance," to construct the main structure. Following the failed meeting a few weeks earlier, he claimed, East Lake's "capitalists" endeavored to calm the panic among Howard's supporters and pledged a large amount of cash. "The buildings," one of the wealthy non-Baptist financiers told Wharton, "will go up on a much grander scale than contemplated." Howard College's success was assured, Wharton added, and Birmingham's monetary pledges were "made good." The "noble and united" Baptists of Alabama will offer thunderous applause for the "glory of the old institution."[15]

Another reason for Wharton's optimism was the announcement that the trustees hired Professor John Lipscomb Johnson of the University of Mississippi as president of the college. In his rush of enthusiasm, Wharton telegraphed newspapers around the state with the announcement. Newspapers hailed Johnson as a "man of ripe experience" as an educator and an accomplished scholar. "The college was to be congratulated," the *Birmingham Herald* noted, "on securing such a man . . . [in] which this city may well be proud." An 1859 graduate of the University of Virginia, Johnson was ordained in 1860 alongside future Harvard professor Crawford Toy. That same year, the Southern Baptist Convention's Foreign Mission Board appointed both men to missionary service in Japan, but Johnson's poor health and the impending crisis of Civil War disrupted those plans and sent both men on divergent paths theologically and professionally. Following his marriage to Toy's sister, Julia Anna, Johnson accepted a teaching position in English literature at Hollins Institute in Virginia and filled the pulpit at local churches.[16]

Following the Civil War, Johnson continued his scholarly pursuits—teaching and writing—while serving as pastor at several churches. During the 1871–72 academic year, he was coprincipal of Roanoke Female College in Danville, Virginia, and introduced the study of Anglo-Saxon as an essential avenue to understand the English language. In the fall of 1872, he then accepted a position as a professor of English at the University of Mississippi, moved to Oxford, and quickly became a leader in the Mississippi Baptist Convention. Upon receiving word of his selection as Howard College's next president, Johnson sent word to the Board of Trustees that he was "useful and happy" at Ole Miss but was "subject to the call of duty." After sixteen years in Oxford, Johnson received the job offer from the trustees of Howard College. Board president W. C. Ward believed Johnson was an "accomplished Christian gentleman" who embodied the qualities (faith, benevolence, intellect, and virtue) needed to lead a "great moral and religious institution of learning."[17]

Apparently, J. L. Johnson delayed making a final decision on the job offer from Howard until he attended the Alabama Baptist State Convention in July 1888. Whether or not Johnson accepted the presidency, W. C. Ward announced at the convention, depended on the actions and attitudes of the delegates. "Harmony and a united and determined purpose to make the college, in its new locality, a success," Ward believed, was essential to compel "such a leader of educational thought" to accept the position at Howard.[18]

J. L. Johnson sat among the delegates when the convention opened at Talladega Baptist Church on Friday, July 13, 1888. A "sentiment" of "division, if not discord," at the meeting, B. F. Riley wrote, was caused by the "college question." Following the call to order by President Jonathan Haralson and a devotional on Psalm 103, the gathering sang the hymn "How Firm a Foundation"—an ironic choice with Howard College having no foundations for a permanent building or a strong endowment. The future of the institution, one observer noted at the time, "rested heaviest" on the hearts of the delegates at the convention as they discussed supporting Howard in East Lake or "letting it die." While many of the speakers showed some optimism and held out "hope even against hope," a veil of gloom pervaded the gathering. "Whether the enthusiasm of some will infuse itself to all," an attendee wrote, was a "question that occasions doubt."[19]

Following the reading of Thomas J. Dill's report to the trustees and W. C. Ward's report from the board to the convention, Rev. John Pilgrim Shaffer offered his review of the fundraising efforts for Howard. He believed that the people of Birmingham were "warmer and firmer" in their support of Howard than "ever before" and were committed to donating even more money than they originally pledged to the college. But Shaffer's financial statement told a different story. Between January 1 and July 1888, he collected $712.27 for Howard and $403.96 for the endowment. Combined with the $19.85 rent on the president's house in Marion, Shaffer received a total of $1,136.08 for the college, but his salary and expenses amounted to $1,112.12—leaving the school with $23.96 cash on hand. The lack of money, he emphasized, "gave birth to a vast amount of misunderstanding of the real situation throughout the state, making it appear that the propositions and promises of Birmingham were false, and had not been complied with."[20]

There seemed little doubt that the discussion would soon turn to relocation, but L. W. Lawler offered a resolution that proclaimed ninety thousand Alabama Baptists should not allow Howard College to die. "The well-known usefulness of the College in the past forbade the thought of its abandonment," he continued, "and heroic efforts should be promptly made to place it upon a firm foundation." The supporters of Howard College and everyone who favored the "intellectual and moral training" of a Baptist school must consider the 'harmony" of the denomination and promote Howard, instead of "selfishness and local predilections." The convention needed to embrace the "Christian spirit" of James H. DeVotie, Edwin D. King, and the other founders of Howard and put aside "dissension and hurtful criticism" in favor of a "concert of action, prayer, and sound judgement." Lawler's resolution called for a new committee of thirteen to review the financial situation at Howard and report back to the convention with a "plan of action."[21]

The committee, which included Rev. B. F. Riley, discovered that the land and money promised by Birmingham were much less than what the boosters originally promised. In addition, some of the money already donated from Birmingham ($2,250) was used by the trustees to make up some of the deficit in faculty salaries from the previous academic year. The financial future of Howard appeared bleak, but the "Birmingham brethren" assured the committee that they would raise enough money to construct the $50,000 main college building. In their report to the convention, committee chairman Robert Whitfield Beck, an East Lake real estate developer, asserted that the "Baptist brotherhood of Alabama" would "rise up as one man and build God" and Christian education a "magnificent structure worthy of the name and the cause." In addition, the committee recommended that Alabama Baptists cover the deficits in salary and expenses for the president and faculty and raise $50,000 to build a permanent dormitory. Most importantly, the committee recommended to the convention that Howard continue to operate in East Lake.[22]

During a lengthy discussion following the committee's recommendations, the president of the Board of Trustees, William C. Ward, said he was grateful for the recommendation to leave the college in East Lake and that the issue was "now settled forever." Ward also apologized for Birmingham's failed promises and explained that waiting for the city to do more was futile. "If you determine by your vote tonight that East Lake shall be the home of your college," he said, "then bury tonight every disappointed, sore feeling forever; burn your bridges behind you! Don't wait on Birmingham! Go to work and endow your college!" Ward criticized Baptists for waiting too long before grasping an "advantageous situation." The rival Methodist churchgoers would never sit idly by and wait for Birmingham to build their college. The people of the Magic City possessed "get up and git" [sic] and never waited for others to do anything. "Build it!" Ward proclaimed in his soaring elocution. "Build! Build until it is the grandest college in the United States!"[23]

Likewise, Rev. David I. Purser, perhaps with a rare spirit of humility, said that "Birmingham was sorry, very sorry," in its failings and unfulfilled expectations. He blamed the city's (and Howard's) woes on the economic downturn throughout the mineral district. "Birmingham has not done what she could," he added, "but will do more."[24]

No doubt, when the pro-Marion delegates began speaking, the Birmingham faction braced for a firestorm. Former Howard fundraiser Gustavus Alonzo Nunnally said he almost began singing "Blest be the tie that binds" when he heard Purser and the other men from Birmingham begging the convention for forgiveness. Nunnally said that he "thought more of Birmingham than ever before," which brought forth laughter from the delegates. But before he sat down, he added, "Let's forgive 'em, brethren." In turn, Rev. Boardman Hartwell Crumpton argued that the convention never should have agreed to move Howard and that the college would be more successful if it returned to Marion. Yet he still supported Howard and "begged the Baptists of Alabama" to support the school like he was. B. F. Riley recalled that Crumpton was one of the "foremost opponents" of relocation in 1887, but at the convention in 1888, his "loyalty and devotion" remained with Howard College.[25]

Coswell Campbell Huckabee opposed the idea of bringing the institution back to Marion unless it was fully endowed. Birmingham must "keep the college now that she had it." Thomas G. Bush agreed that the convention should not question the location of Howard but ask, "how shall we build" the college? The Alabama Baptists gathered in Talladega possessed the power to let the institution live or "let it die." The love of Christian education should subordinate private views on location for the "good of the denomination" and in the spirit of cooperation of "all in a fraternal spirit." Even the acerbic editor of the *Montgomery Advertiser* admitted that the hope of restoring Howard to "our beloved Black Belt" was "gone and gone for good." The school was in Birmingham to stay, and there was only one thing left to do for all Alabamians: Support the college. "We are for Howard College," the paper emphasized, "where it is or wherever it may be."[26]

Professor John Lipscomb Johnson left the convention without giving the trustees a yes or a no on assuming the presidency of Howard College. He needed more time. Several more weeks passed before Johnson sent a telegram to the trustees and rejected the job offer. The *Clarion-Ledger* in Jackson, Mississippi, wrote that Johnson had a "long struggle" over whether to accept the position. "We believe," the paper added, Johnson "acted wisely." A few months later, however, Johnson accepted the presidency of Mary Sharp College in Winchester, Tennessee—a position he held for less than two years before returning to Mississippi.[27]

John L. Johnson's decision, coming just a few weeks before the start of the 1888–89 academic year, left the school's Board of Trustees desperate to hire a new president. For several days, the trustees "discussed and discarded" the names of many ministers and scholars for the job. At a board meeting, one downhearted Howard trustee announced that the college was "gone beyond the possibility of reclamation." The head of the board, W. C. Ward, offered an almost equally pessimistic solution to the institution's leadership void: Hire a young president; so if Howard closed, the person might salvage his career and "service the disaster." Rev. B. H. Crumpton put forward the name of a fellow board member, Benjamin Franklin Riley. On August 21, 1888, Crumpton, Ward, and the other trustees offered the presidency to Reverend Riley, a long-time Howard College supporter, and the popular pastor at Livingston First Baptist

Reverend Benjamin Franklin Riley assumed the Howard College presidency at a critical time in the institution's history in the wake of the broken promises of the New South that lured the school from Marion. (Samford University, Special Collection and University Archives)

Church. The thirty-nine-year-old Riley accepted the position but later recalled that the other trustees regarded him as a "makeshift" and "expedient" hire that "created no enthusiasm" or "roused any confidence."[28]

Despite B. F. Riley's gloomy assessment, a week before his hiring, the *Alabama Baptist* urged the trustees to hire the young preacher. Riley was an Alabamian, they argued, and "fully identified" with all the interests of the state's Baptists. "Let us honor our own men," the writer added. "Let us get beneath our young men and push them to the top, and then help to hold them there while they are blessing us." Publicly, when the trustees released the news of Riley's appointment, the state's secular papers hailed Riley's hiring. The *Tuskaloosa Gazette* believed Riley was a "Christian gentleman" who displayed the "vigor of manhood" to succeed in the job. In Montgomery, the *Weekly Advertiser* reported that Riley possessed the literary skills and executive talents to "capably administer the arduous duties" of president of Howard College. In the southwest part of the state, the *Clarke County Democrat* described Riley as a "good scholar, a good writer, a good preacher," and, in time, a "good college president." Privately, Riley received letters from individuals who warned him of the serious mistake he made in accepting the Howard presidency and vowing to offer Riley no support in his efforts. "You are destined to fail," one businessman wrote; "no college can succeed under such circumstances." Riley, however, determined to prove the naysayers wrong.[29]

Born July 16, 1849, in the small South Alabama hamlet of Pineville in Monroe County, Benjamin Franklin Riley was the son of Enoch and Sophronia Irvin Riley. A well-to-do small planter before the Civil War, the elder Riley migrated from Edgefield County, South Carolina—an area known for its widespread violence and ill-tempered, Scots-Irish residents. Enoch brought these hot-headed inclinations to Alabama, where he maintained a long-running feud with a Pineville neighbor, Jahiel B. Cotton, also an Edgefield native. In November 1871, the duo decided to settle their differences on the field of honor by brandishing shotguns in a bloody duel which neither man survived. No doubt the incident affected Enoch's son, Benjamin Franklin, who was at the time of the shooting a student at Erskine College, a South Carolina Presbyterian school. Two years earlier, the younger Riley was admitted to Erskine on a trial basis because his early education was "so defective" and "meager" that he was woefully insufficient as a student. Nonetheless, Riley worked hard and graduated in 1872—just a few months after his father's death. Riley had originally planned to study for the bar, but he abandoned those plans due to poor health and exhaustion—impacted by the violent duel and his heavy workload at Erskine.[30]

In July 1872, Riley received his ordination at Pineville Baptist Church and made plans to attend Southern Baptist Theological Seminary (SBTS) in Greenville, South Carolina. He applied for financial assistance, but the amount offered, he wrote John Albert Broadus, was "insufficient to have sustained me." Although Riley was in sympathy with the theological conservatism of the SBTS, he enrolled at Crozer Theological Seminary near Philadelphia, Pennsylvania, where the school covered all of his living expenses—and those of other southern students. Former Howard College president J. L. M. Curry wrote in 1874 that, if men like Riley were attracted to a northern school with liberal tendencies, then it was best for them to be "quarantined" outside the South so as to not contaminate southern theology. "I am sorry to say," Curry wrote, that Crozer was becoming a "sort of theological cholera hospital." Curry's conformist southern mindset was what W. J. Cash called the "Savage Ideal"—an ideal where "dissent and variety" of thought were so "completely suppressed" that every white southerner became in "all their attitudes, professions, and actions, virtual replicas of one another."[31]

Nonetheless, Riley attended Crozer for two years, never earning a degree, before returning to Alabama as minister at Carlowville Baptist Church, followed by pastorates in Albany, Georgia; Opelika, Alabama, and Livingston. While preaching in Livingston, the University of Alabama gave Riley an honorary doctorate of divinity in June 1885. On September 9, 1888, Riley preached his last sermon as pastor of Livingston First Baptist Church with a focus on 2 Corinthians 13:11, "Finally, brethren, farewell. Be perfect, be of good comfort, be of one mind, live in peace; and the God of love and peace shall be with you."[32]

By the middle of September, B. F. Riley and his family moved from their residence in the agrarian Black Belt to their new home in the industrial New South. When he arrived in Birmingham, Riley was already a strong booster for New South progress and economic development. Just a few months before accepting the Howard position, he published *Alabama as It Is: The Immigrants and Capitalists Guide Book,* to encourage interest in the state's mineral and agricultural resources. Funded with a $1,500 appropriation from the Alabama legislature, the state printed 5,000 copies in 1887 and an additional 25,000 of the revised edition in 1888. The book sold for ten cents per copy. In its pages, Riley wrote, were the truths of Alabama's greatness—the "inexhaustible resources of soil and mine, of field and forest, her balmy climate, her wonderful healthfulness, and her sweeps of extended beauty." No place on earth, he added, boasted more diverse resources than Alabama. The "profusion of her elements" for industry were "simply marvelous," and her cotton fields won worldwide distinction. Howard's new president, unlike his agrarian-bound predecessor,

ALABAMA

AS IT IS.

THE IMMIGRANTS AND CAPITALISTS

GUIDE BOOK.

James T. Murfee, fully embraced the New South and emerged as an important advocate for industrialism and urbanization.[33]

While most New South boosters supported the myth of the Lost Cause, Riley's views differed in two key areas. First, he rejected (rather than romanticizing) the entire economic and political order of the Old South based on the "baneful system" of African slavery. "The tendency of the institution of slavery," Riley said, "was detrimental to the full-orbed manhood and womanhood in the South." The system sapped the energy of the southern people, produced arrogance, and undermined moral obligations. "With its mingled elements of thousands of toiling slaves," he added, "seething tumults of political factions, the carnage and devastation of a most merciless war, and the deadly sway of a combined political military system that seemed destined to crush the spirits of our people, and to usher in a chaos" of darkness.[34]

Throughout the Old South, Civil War, and Reconstruction, the only means of economic progress was to till the soil, but with the "downfall of slavery" came the advancement of the "long slumbering resources" of a New South. The smoke of industry signified the move from an agricultural to an industrial economy in the region. Before the "knell of slavery" sounded, furnaces and foundries were almost unknown in Alabama and other areas of the South. "Now the nightly glare from the perpetual fires of thousands of plants," he added, was a common sight. Under the old cotton regime, the mountains in North Alabama were seen as obstacles to progress, but now they were "treasure houses." The so-called plantation aristocrats craved large tracts of land so they could "thrive upon the sweat and toil of the enslaved," boast that their enormous wealth gave them greatness and power, encourage "petty sectional hatred," and subordinate the "intellectual to the material." These ideas were gone, "hidden forever in the wreck of the ruin of an oblivious past.[35]

This included the end to the stereotypes of southern womanhood—Riley's second departure from the "Lost Cause" mythology. Women were "no longer the mere petted idol of the home of the charms of grace . . . [who] dared not

Facing page: Benjamin Franklin Riley published *Alabama as It Is: The Immigrants and Capitalists Guide Book* as a New South promotional guide for the state's industrial and agrarian resources. Unlike other New South boosters, Riley rejected the myth of the Lost Cause and loathed the institution of slavery. (Samford University, Special Collection and University Archives)

venture into the sphere of activity to contend with her sterner brother for the necessaries of life." The "southern side" of the women's rights question was the "right to labor" as women's "conscience, judgment, and self-regard may dictate." The gates were now opened to "spheres of activity hitherto closed against them." Whether for men or women, "the ability to conquer difficulties" was the "surest test of character."[36]

As he assumed his presidential duties, Riley confronted not only the significant financial deficit from the previous academic year, but also the "serious debt" owed the faculty: Thomas J. Dill, A. D. Smith, George W. Macon, B. F. Giles, and R. J. Waldrop. The faculty's salaries were derived solely from tuition income and were the last debts paid each year. During budget shortfalls, as in the 1887–88 academic year, the trustees simply left the faculty's salaries unpaid. Riley, however, in one of his first acts as president, called the faculty together and paid "these faithful men" out of his own personal funds. Riley also worked to lower the college's other expenditures by purchasing four milk cows, establishing a small dairy on the edge of campus, and planting a vegetable garden to supply at-cost food to the new mess hall that he opened in the old Ruhama Academy building.[37]

Unfortunately for B. F. Riley, the arrival of Howard College students to Birmingham in the fall of 1888 coincided with an outbreak of yellow fever in several southern towns, including Decatur, Alabama, and Meridian, Mississippi—both key stops along railroad lines leading into the Magic City. With yellow fever occurring north and south of Birmingham, officials took drastic measures to keep the virus from entering their city. Persistent rumors of the dreaded disease already spreading in Birmingham compelled Mayor Alexander Oscar Lane to order a citywide "shotgun quarantine" enforced by armed patrols stationed along public roads and near passenger-train stations. The patrols stopped every person entering Birmingham and forced everyone to give a "satisfactory account" of where they originated and why they desired to enter the Magic City. Many residents, however, complained about Lane's "over-strained precautions," leading one medical doctor to argue that the air in the city was so "permeated with the disinfecting fumes" of chemicals created by nearby blast furnaces that the "germs of the disease would be destroyed at once."[38]

Hysteria over yellow fever was at its peak in late September and early October, and many parents decided against sending their sons into an unsanitary town like Birmingham with the potential for a widespread epidemic. Many students that did travel to Birmingham avoided potential quarantine by disembarking at train stations outside the city's limits and sending telegraph wires to President Riley, who arranged for private carriages to ferry the young men to campus—traveling on routes to avoid passing through Birmingham. A few students stayed on the trains and arrived at Union Station in Birmingham and were detained by quarantine patrols. When Riley received word that several Howard boys were unable to leave the city, he decided to "run the blockade," enter Birmingham, and bring the students to campus. But rather than liberate the Howard captives, Riley found himself arrested by a quarantine patrol and taken to the city's jail. He appeared in Mayor's Court and offered a "frank statement" to Mayor Alexander Oscar Lane, who dismissed the charges and sent Riley to collect his students and return to East Lake.[39]

As classes began at Howard College on Monday, October 1, 1888, the impact of the "dreaded scourge" of yellow fever was obvious as fewer than expected students arrived to register for classes. In response, the trustees, the faculty, and President Riley assured uneasy parents that the virus would never reach Birmingham, much less East Lake. They urged them to "send their sons at once." Throughout early October, more and more young men enrolled at the college. "Each train," one cadet wrote at the time, "brought new accessions to our growing ranks" and in turn, the returning students taught the newcomers to be "laborious in their application, sunny hearted in [their spirit], and most manly in their deportment." During the academic year, 143 students enrolled at Howard (down from 157 the previous year), and the college continued to run a financial deficit.[40]

While many Baptists in East Lake and around the state grieved over Howard's fiscal and structural woes, the students living and learning in the rough-and-ready wood buildings remained upbeat. "The students," B. F. Riley observed, "cheerfully submitted to the abounding inconveniences, and were devoted to their duties." They encouraged the college's "friends and patrons" to come see for themselves the good work being done by the faculty and students. "Why should the college not succeed?" a student wrote in the October 1888 edition of the *Howard Collegian*. After all, he added, East Lake and its clean mountain air was the perfect location for a school that stimulated, motivated, and encouraged students. At the core of education at Howard, the writer emphasized, was "strengthening and fortifying" the virtue of each student and equipping them for the secular world's "rough encounters." The faculty accomplished this central goal by embracing the principles on which the institution was founded—training virtuous young men intellectually and "under the most wholesome Christian influences."[41]

As a "literary man" and advocate of classical education, Benjamin Franklin Riley affirmed Howard's mission, which emphasized four guiding principles: benevolence, virtue, faith, and intellect. As they had in the 1840s, students during the 1888–89 academic year continued to study Greek and Latin— reading Caesar, Virgil, Homer, Horace, Demosthenes, and others. In addition, the curriculum also included German and French. Students also studied history, English, natural sciences, mathematics, political economy, and moral science. As was the tradition, the college offered no systematic study of the Bible or theology (other than reading New Testament Greek), but all seniors still took a course on the evidence for Christianity in their final semester.[42]

Publicly, Benjamin F. Riley offered encouraging words to the college's students, faculty, and supporters. He emphasized that Howard's success was due, in no small part, to the faculty's constant attention to the "moral and social culture" of the students. The professors devoted "all their time" to their students— providing instruction during the day and visiting the dormitories at night. The faculty instilled the young men with the "correct views of life and duty" and expected that each cadet would conduct himself as both a gentleman and a scholar. Intellectual power meant little for a student whose "sentiments and habits" were corrupt. If a student lacked good character, they would find not only the "atmosphere of this institution uncongenial," Riley added, but the president would demand the student withdraw from the college. To keep the students focused, Riley introduced a program of "rigid discipline" that was "enforced to the letter." Board president W. C. Ward praised Riley's efforts and noted that his methods were "so rigid" that it gave the college grounds the "characteristics of a military camp." The board received several complaints from students about the president's inflexibility, but after a few months under Riley's watchful eye, they embraced the discipline—leading W. C. Ward to describe Riley as the "most popular president" in Howard's history. Riley demonstrated, Ward added, that the "board of trustees had accidentally chosen wisely" in his hiring.[43]

Privately, however, Riley communicated to a few "discreet friends" that the situation at Howard College "could scarcely have been worse" and that the academic year was one of "extreme embarrassment." During the fall, building crews laid the groundwork for the permanent main "Academic Hall" near the center of campus, but once finished, they learned Howard College was unable to pay them for their work. In turn, the contractors (presumably Allen & Taylor) decided to sell the foundation to recoup the costs of labor and materials—once again, the college was teetering on bankruptcy. "The college was on the verge of a collapse," Riley wrote, and no one seemed willing to "contribute to it, because confidence had perished." But one man stepped forward. Board member Felix Mercer Wood mortgaged his home for $2,300 to pay off the debt. "Even when things looked blackest," Wood once said, "I was never sorry that I advanced the money and saved the college." Although the debt was paid, the college still had no money to build the Academic Hall and, for months to come, the foundation stood as a testament to Birmingham's failure and Howard's tenuous future. That foundation just kept on "laying," quipped one Birmingham writer, and "don't ever hatch anything." The institution might soon "fly away," he predicted, and was already "pin-feathering for an everlasting flight."[44]

15

BAD BIRMINGHAM

"Bad Birmingham," newspaperman John R. Hornady wrote, was the "title the city won, and it was by this title that it became known far and wide." In 1887, when Howard College moved to the outskirts of Birmingham, promoters assured Alabama Baptists that the school's new location would be far removed from the city's crime, vice, and violence. But on December 4, 1888, a little girl's body was pulled from the waters of East Lake and placed in the pavilion, the site of Howard's commencement a few months before, for the public to identify. The girl was eight-year-old May Hawes. A Birmingham paper reported that her "little form" was "shrouded by a terrible crime." And it was. How she ended up in East Lake, far from her Birmingham home, was a mystery that only deepened when her mother and younger sister went missing. The father of the family, Richard Hawes, also disappeared and emerged as the obvious suspect when Birmingham investigators discovered that he had married another woman in Columbus, Mississippi—while still married to his missing wife. Police arrested Hawes when the newlyweds' train stopped in Birmingham. Soon afterward, the body of his first wife was found in another nearby lake. The other daughter would be pulled from the same waters a few days later. Allegedly, Hawes took little May on the dummy train to East Lake, intentionally drowned her in the lake's murky waters, and took the return train to Birmingham. Emotions reached a fever pitch in Birmingham, and a lynch mob descended on the jail and were met with a flurry of gunshots from law enforcement officials. In the aftermath, eleven men were dead or dying.[1]

On Howard's campus, there was talk of sending the cadets to Birmingham to help quiet the "Hawes' Riots," but as the rumor spread, one student later quipped, requests for sick leave were suddenly "on a boom." Yet, this murder, death, and mayhem occurred as the college continued to face disbandment or removal. One journalist argued that the school should stay put and arm the cadets with rifles to help "suppress the riots" in Birmingham. In the end, the unrest ended, and Hawes was tried, convicted, and hanged for the murders of his wife and two children. For President Benjamin F. Riley, the faculty, and students of Howard, "Bad Birmingham" was not so far away after all. Perhaps this incident, and economic factors, compelled Riley to seek a more "congenial home" for Howard College.[2]

The cadets, however, found East Lake itself a hospitable place filled with kind and sympathetic people. Residents opened their homes to the young men, as one student wrote, which relieved the "tedium of the leisure hours" and banished the "sadness that comes, now and then, to the heart of a boy, far away from home and loved ones." At Christmas, those students who remained in the dormitory were "constantly on the go" with invitations to dinners, parties, and other events. Ruhama Baptist served as a church home for most of the cadets, and the new pastor, Arthur Watkins McGaha, an 1881 Howard graduate, guided the young men spiritually and vocationally. "Taken altogether," a cadet wrote, "we doubt if a more homelike college can be found within the limits of the South."[3]

Yet, in December 1888, the economic outlook for Alabama Baptist higher education was bleak. In Marion, a fire destroyed Judson College in late November—leaving Alabama Baptists with the unenviable tasks of raising funds and erecting buildings on two college campuses. In East Lake, Benjamin Franklin Riley heard members of Howard College's Board of Trustees discuss "displacing the Baptist college with that of another denomination." These musings and the repeated predictions of Howard's inescapable failure compelled Riley to look north to Florence, Alabama—the latest New South economic boom town attracting the attention of investors—as the next home for Howard College.[4]

The visionary behind the economic boom was Joseph H. Field—a former Mississippi newspaperman and farmer who promoted Florence with passion, persistence, and unbounded energy. The *Florence Herald* described Field as among the "very best active elements of the New South," who threw himself into the "fight for industrial development and supremacy." He served as an officeholder or board member for more than a dozen companies and purchased advertising in publications across the country to sell Florence to potential investors. Field's marketing scheme boasted that this small Alabama town of 1,800 residents would soon become the "Philadelphia of the South" and an industrial stronghold along the navigable shores of the Tennessee River. The marketing and publicity worked. At the time, one observer called it the "best advertised boom of that boom period" that attracted speculators from across the United States. In three months, Florence's population swelled to 7,000 "speculative spirits" who were each "striving to get rich in a day."[5]

As news of this latest New South miracle spread, Rev. Washington Bryan Crumpton traveled to Florence to observe the frenzied excitement of the land boom and to take stock of the Baptists living in the area. Crumpton found the town filled with real-estate and industrial speculators but met only two Baptists. He also visited with a Presbyterian minister, who explained that Florence was a "Methodist town" with plenty of Presbyterians and "no Baptists." The preacher's musings convinced Crumpton that a Baptist church in the area was "worth more than an iron furnace." On return trips to Florence, Crumpton convinced land-company officials, most of whom were from out of state, that the nearly 100,000 Baptists in Alabama were a strong economic force. Perhaps J. H. Field had this in mind when he took a trip to Atlanta and met the pastor of First Baptist Church, James Boardman Hawthorne.[6]

Following his days as a Howard College student in the 1850s, Hawthorne pastored prominent Baptist churches in Mobile, Selma, Montgomery, New York, Baltimore, and Richmond. In Atlanta, Hawthorne partnered with Methodist evangelist Sam Jones and New South prophet Henry Grady to fight "saloons, gambling, and other forms of sin." Following a bruising battle with liquor interests, the temperance forces won a narrow victory and Atlanta went dry. Although he was at the "zenith of his power," Hawthorne was exhausted and decided to take a leave of absence from his church. According to Crumpton, as the minister was contemplating his next move, J. H. Field listened to him preach one of Hawthorne's last Sundays in the pulpit and had an epiphany: Invite the "great preacher, in search of rest," to spend his leave in the "fine climate" of Florence and "utilize his wide acquaintance with people of wealth and influence in the interest of the booms of Florence." When Field approached Hawthorne with the idea, he eagerly agreed. Hawthorne, however, said in 1889 he relocated to Florence because his two sons, Charles and Hartwell, were living there. Once there, Florence officials asked him to lead efforts to "establish a first-class educational institution."[7]

Whatever his motivations for moving, J. B. Hawthorne's arrival in Florence, Washington Bryan Crumpton wrote, sent "Baptist stock skyward" and

affirmed Field's hunch that the minister's presence would attract more investors. "Hawthorne's name," Field said, was "worth much to all our enterprises."
The newly organized Baptist church, where Hawthorne occasionally preached,
easily raised money to erect a permanent structure on a choice lot selected
by Crumpton. With the church built, the next task for the city's developers
was to establish elementary and secondary schools, and J. H. Field had another
idea: "Now let us complete our scheme," he said, "by building here a great
college." Hawthorne took charge of this new movement to build a "first-class
educational institution" in this New South boomtown. When Hawthorne met
with Florence's money men, he proclaimed that he was an "uncompromising
Baptist" and, if they financed education in Florence, the school would "come
under Baptist auspices." They agreed to his terms and deeded to Hawthorne:
thirty-five lots in Florence, 140 acres of land on the outskirts of town, and 1,000
acres of nearby iron ore land. Most of the people donating the land and money
were non-Baptists. "With them it is a plain matter of business," one journalist
observed, and all part of the "practical scheme" to build a "great and prosperous
city" along the Tennessee River.[8]

Into these flush times, Benjamin F. Riley arrived from East Lake—perhaps
searching for a better home for Howard College and assessing other economic
opportunities. According to Crumpton, Riley's initial trips were unknown to
W. C. Ward, the other members of the Board of Trustees, or Howard College's
financial agent, John Pilgrim Shaffer. When word spread of Riley's clandestine
activities, Shaffer asked him if he was "going to Florence again." When Riley
said yes, Shaffer replied, "Well, I want to go too." Crumpton recalled that the
two men traveled to North Alabama, but Riley prevented Shaffer from attending
meetings of economic investors or other Florence officials. Shaffer later confronted Riley. "I am the financial agent of Howard College," he said, "and I think
[that] I ought to go and see what is being done." In the end, Riley relented, and
Shaffer attended the meetings.[9]

Besides Riley and Shaffer, those in attendance likely included J. B. Hawthorne, J. H. Field, Porter King, and others—all of whom were "making overtures right straight" to move Howard College to Florence. With some measure
of irony, King came from Marion to not only participate in the economic boom
but to create a better home for Howard College. Birmingham was never going to
fulfill its promises, he said, and Howard must be moved to a new location. King
justified these furtive meetings that, in the end, would produce a relocation plan

for presentation at the next meeting of the Alabama Baptist State Convention—the only body that could authorize the removal of Howard College from East Lake. As part of their proposal, Riley, Hawthorne, Field, King, and two others formed the Florence Educational, Land and Development Company. Once they received a charter from the Alabama legislature, Hawthorne planned to deed the lots and lands to the company and begin collecting funds to erect buildings and to create an endowment. The board agreed that the company would pay Hawthorne a yearly salary of $5,000 (over $160,000 in 2023 dollars) to serve as president of the company's board. On January 23, 1888, the *Marion Standard* reported that Hawthorne was not president of Howard, but president of the board "controlling the college." Hawthorne was devoting himself to "building up the institution" and relocating it to Florence.[10]

As word of Howard's impending move entered the public discussion, newspapers reported that Florence officials were "bidding" for the college and offering a $100,000 building and $100,000 in cash for an endowment. "Birmingham will have to do some good work to prevent the removal of the college," one journalist noted. The *Marion Standard* proclaimed: "Poor old Howard! What a pity . . . that after living to a ripe old age, crowned with a life of honor and usefulness, you should now be found unhonored and without a home." The Baptists made a tremendous mistake moving the college from Marion and a greater mistake locating it in East Lake. The school was "practically cut off from the patronage of south Alabama" and now North Alabama was "working against" East Lake. Florence was a "more suitable place" for the college, and the Baptists would "do well to move the college again." Nonetheless, a writer in a Birmingham paper quipped that the only advantage for Baptists in Florence was all the water available for immersion in the Tennessee River.[11]

At a meeting of Howard's trustees in January 1889, a Birmingham paper reported, board president W. C. Ward "exploded the bugaboo" about the college's impending removal. "A mistaken idea has gone out," Ward said, "namely that we want to move the college. That's wrong." The trustees, he emphasized, were focused on completing the Academic Hall on the East Lake campus and not on moving to a new location. "No meeting has been called to consider the removal of the college," Ward explained to a newspaper reporter, "nor do I suppose that one will be called." To jump-start fundraising efforts, the trustees elected Rev. David I. Purser as the college's new financial agent to replace J. P. Shaffer. "This was done with the hope," Ward explained, that the vociferous minister would "take hold" of the situation and raise enough money to complete the main building. "If this money can be had," Ward added, then "everything will be settled," and the college will stay in East Lake. Purser, however, initially balked at the job offer, and state newspapers continued to advocate the college's move to Florence. In Birmingham, a writer for the *Evening News* concluded that "Neither Dr. Hawthorne nor fair Florence's fairy figures" would take Howard College from Birmingham, "for it will be kept here."[12]

Yet Howard's president, Benjamin Franklin Riley, was heavily involved in this latest removal scheme. When J. P. Shaffer told W. C. Ward of Riley's activities in Florence, Ward went to Riley and demanded an explanation. He reportedly asked: "What does it all mean?" In response, Riley explained to Ward that his activities were all part of an elaborate "sting" to scheme Florence's opportunistic schemers to compel Birmingham's reneging grifters to put up the money that they promised in 1887. In other words, use Florence as a ruse to obtain a big payout from the "people of Birmingham." If true, this was a crafty ruse on his part and one that took a great deal of time, energy, and deception.[13]

On Tuesday, February 26, 1889, the Alabama legislature passed an act incorporating the Florence Educational, Land and Development Company and "authorized and empowered" the new enterprise to establish and endow a college or colleges in, or near, Florence and to "perform . . . other acts as it may deem necessary and advisable for the advancement of the cause of higher education in the State of Alabama." Ironically, that same evening in Montgomery, around one hundred Alabama Baptist ministers and a handful of lay people held opening services for a special "Congress." The three-day, public event took place at First Baptist Church, where organizers planned to discuss a variety of topics relevant to preachers ("The Preacher with His Bible," "Preparation for the Pulpit," and so forth) and to explore ways to advance the denomination in Alabama. A large group of Howard College's supporters, detractors, and alumni were present, including David I. Purser, M. B. Wharton, Samuel Henderson, W. B. Crumpton, J. M. Frost, Washington Wilkes, E. B. Teague, John P. Shaffer, Z. B. Roby, G. A. Nunnally, Porter King, B. F. Riley, and J. B. Hawthorne.[14]

On the second day, J. B. Hawthorne stood before the Baptist Congress to explain why he moved to Alabama, to summarize his work, and to clear up any "unintentional misrepresentations made." Hawthorne discussed his vision of a "first-class" Baptist institution of higher education in Florence, the creation of the Florence Educational, Land and Development Company, and the donation of land and property. He emphasized that, if Howard College remained insufficiently "endowed to ensure success," once the building was completed in Florence and the company raised $100,000 in their treasury, his "first tender" of the property and money would be to Howard College. "If it cannot live and flourish in Birmingham," he said, then Alabama Baptists can "pick it up and plant it on new soil by the Tennessee." His statement brought a hardy round of applause from the congregation. Hawthorne, however, also went on to explain that a "good brother" just told him with "great warmth" that there was a sudden "ground swell" of support for Howard College in Birmingham and that buildings and an endowment were soon coming. "Glory to God in the highest!" Hawthorne replied to the man. "If I have done that much," he explained to the audience, "I shall never cease to be thankful."[15]

At the closing session of the Congress, Samuel Henderson stood, offered a resolution, and proclaimed that "here and now" was the time to help Howard College. Henderson announced that once again the college lacked the money to pay the faculty's salaries and proposed a resolution that the Alabama Baptist Congress promise to work on behalf of the faculty to "take up collections to meet this emergency" before April 15. He demanded that we "concentrate our energy, our labor, and our money on this line, right now!" If no one was willing, then "let's quit and bury" Howard College with no hope of a resurrection. "But if we intend to do anything for the rising generation, then the day and the hour has come to do it." By a unanimous vote, the Congress passed Henderson's resolution and then adjourned.[16]

Not long after the Congress adjourned, Benjamin F. Riley released a public statement to remove any "misapprehension" about his relationship with the Florence Educational, Land and Development Company. Even though Riley's name appeared on the company's charter, approved by the state legislature, he disavowed any "official relations" with the company. "I have persistently declined any connection" to the "movement" in Florence, he wrote, "because of my relation with Howard College." Privately, Riley wrote that his actions in Florence compelled Birmingham officials to "re-rally" their support for Howard and "renew" some of their previous promises to the college. Another observer said Riley's ploy resulted in a "wholesome effect" in Birmingham and changed the attitudes of many Alabama Baptists.[17]

Throughout the state, Alabama Baptist women stepped forward to raise funds for Howard College. In the South Alabama town of Brewton, churchwomen organized a "bazaar and festival" for the benefit of Howard—with "plenty of good music" and a door fee of ten cents. They served a variety of refreshments, including "oysters in every style" and offered many "fancy and useful" items for sale. Just up the road in Georgiana, a women's group made four quilts for the college with materials furnished by the town's merchants. In the Black Belt, Livingston's Annie Grace Tartt, the sister of Howard cadet Thomas M. Tartt, raised $500 to purchase bed frames and wire springs for the dormitories, while Avondale's Mary C. Etheridge purchased mattresses. Other women's groups provided additional bedding, support, and cash for the college. These efforts convinced B. F. Riley that, going forward, "there would be no difficulty about patronage."[18]

The greatest boost in giving came when David Ingram Purser resigned from the pulpit at First Baptist Church, accepted the position of financial agent, and devoted all his abundant energy to raising enough money to complete the Academic Hall. "This augured well for the success of Howard College," the *Birmingham Age-Herald* reported, "and caused a new wave of hope to rise in the breasts of its friends." If Birmingham citizens came through with the "necessities of the hour" and funded the school, then Howard would become a centerpiece in the Magic City. A writer for the rival *Evening News* agreed that Purser's qualifications as an "able financier" settled the question of removal—"as sure a thing as it could be"—and assured the completion of the building.[19]

In the Howard College fundraising (subscription) notebook passed down from J. P. Shaffer, Purser wrote that each person recorded in the book agreed to pay the pledged amount exclusively "for the purpose of completing the main building of Howard College at East Lake, Alabama." William H. Wood and Robert W. Beck, both members of the college's Board of Trustees, were the first two donors at $1,000 each; followed by Howard professors Robert J. Waldrop ($500), Thomas J. Dill ($100), and Benjamin F. Giles ($100). After several weeks on the job, a reporter for a Birmingham paper asked Purser how his fundraising was progressing. "Slowly sir, slowly," he answered. When he accepted the job, several Birmingham residents pledged $1,000 each to the college, but he had yet to receive a "single dime . . . from any of them." For some reason, these business leaders promised donations but then refused to part with any of their cash. Purser said that at least seventy-five men in Birmingham wanted to give, but none wanted to be the first. "They all wanted to be the last," he emphasized, "and how to make the whole seventy-five last is a mathematical problem I have as yet been able to solve, after days of thinking and working. . . . One of them has got to give in first, but they won't compromise."[20]

If Purser's efforts failed, however, then the Florence forces would bring their proposal to the state convention in November. A few days after Purser accepted the position as financial agent, J. B. Hawthorne spoke at O'Brien's Opera House in Birmingham on the economic boom in Florence. He told the audience that he hoped the Howard enterprise would succeed in East Lake and that his group had "no desire to interfere" with the college's efforts to remain there. But if those efforts failed, he added, then Florence was prepared to offer the school an "abiding place."[21]

While D. I. Purser raised funds, Howard's cadets attended classes and held military drills. The big event that spring was the April 30 celebration of the centennial of George Washington's inauguration as president. B. F. Riley invited Alabama's U.S. senator John T. Morgan to speak to the students on the history of the U.S. Constitution. Held at the East Lake Pavilion, Morgan offered a pedestrian speech on the history of the Constitution, but as he concluded the senator offered a full-throated justification of white supremacy that garnered widespread attention by the press. Whites were the "great race" that built the government at the state and federal levels and who will, when the time comes, "expurgate any unnatural element that disturbs the harmony of the country." As many whites of his generation believed, Blacks "never should have been accorded" the right to vote and now were a "menace" to American institutions. The *New York Times* reported that Morgan closed his speech by showing how the Constitution was flexible enough to "enable the people to rid themselves of the element of discord—negro suffrage—saying this was the ultimate solution of the race question." The *Montgomery Advertiser* reported that Morgan's concluding sentences were "tantamount to a declaration that sooner or later" the Fifteenth Amendment would be repealed. "Speed the day when it is so," the paper emphasized. On campus, one Howard College student wrote that Senator Morgan should not be lauded for his "greatness," but rather Alabamians should live in "honest emulation."[22]

A few weeks after Morgan's visit, Howard College held commencement before a large crowd gathered at the East Lake Pavilion. Seven "promising men" graduated: Charles G. Elliott, Henry R. Dill, William I. Chitwood, Graph J. Hubbard, Shem L. Tyson, William H. Owings, and John A. McCreary. Judging from their solid work at Howard, wrote one student, "They will prove a blessing

The Howard College faculty, circa 1890 (*standing left to right*): Robert Judson Waldrop, Capers Capehart Jones, and George Washington Macon; (*seated left to right*): Benjamin Franklin Giles, Thomas John Dill, Benjamin Franklin Riley, Albert Durant Smith. (Samford University, Special Collection and University Archives)

to their generation." Henry Reynolds Dill, the younger son of Professor Thomas J. Dill, graduated with first honors in 1889 and offered the valedictory address. Once the ceremony concluded, Riley marched the cadets back to campus and bid them all farewell. Unbeknownst to Riley, the students submitted a petition to the trustees—signed by every Howard student—urging the board to reappoint Riley as president of the college. At the board's meeting on the afternoon following commencement, the board unanimously reelected Riley and, when the news reached the cadets, they sent up a rousing cheer.[23]

In the two weeks leading up to the board's meeting—and in the weeks following—Howard College faced another push in several newspapers to move the school to a better location—especially after Jefferson County officials built a temporary convict labor camp near campus to house prisoners working on the new road from East Lake to Woodlawn. A writer for the *Montgomery Advertiser* argued that, since the college was "doing business in a woodshed near one of the convict camps," a good proposal might persuade the Baptists to move the school to the state capital. After all, Montgomery was the "best place in Alabama" for Howard, and the city deserved to have the college. An acerbic writer from Union Springs believed that Birmingham's promises to Howard were only equaled by the "devil when he made those vast promises to Christ on the high mountains, but Birmingham has made the devil ashamed of himself by the great success of her promises." The Magic City frauds convinced Alabama Baptists to abandon Marion, move to Birmingham, and then leave the college "lonely, squatting near the outskirts" of town; "destitute, deserted, her glory departed, striving against unmerited fate to preserve her character; fearfully but prayerfully waiting and hoping that the scholarly enterprising Florence may yet lift her out of the ashes of misfortune and foundries and the dust of coal mines, and set her upon the salubrious bank of the lovely Tennessee." The trustees responded with a statement condemning those advocating for another location for Howard College. "We deem its location at East Lake a finality," board members declared, "with no other place in consideration."[24]

By the summer of 1889, the feelings of the trustees and other Howard supporters was best reflected in one statement: "Birmingham may not build the college, but Alabama will." Following two difficult academic years in East Lake, the Howard College community finally accepted the reality that Birmingham would never fulfill its promises of cash and support. At the time, one newspaper reported that Alabama Baptists were "working among their members throughout the state for the means to make Howard College what it ought be." The work to support the college required unity among the Baptists of Alabama. A denominational house divided would result in the inevitable fall of Howard. The school was "at the bottom," another writer argued, and the state's Baptists must put aside the age-old sectional battle and join the fight to save the institution. Howard was neither a North nor a South Alabama institution, but a college that belonged to the entire state. "He who would run section lines through Christ's kingdom in Alabama," he added, "and let his beneficence stop on the border, was not worthy to claim himself a man in Christ Jesus."[25]

Benjamin Franklin Riley also hoped to receive the "prayerful cooperation" of Alabama Baptists during his five-thousand-mile student canvassing trip. With the assistance of professors B. F. Giles and R. J. Waldrop, Riley believed the key to a successful effort was to convince Baptist pastors to send the young men in their congregations to the college. "I should be glad to have brethren drop me a postal card at East Lake," he said, "calling attention to certain young men who may be induced to attend upon the college."[26]

On each of Riley's visits to towns, hamlets, and country crossroads throughout the state, he told prospective students and parents that the school completed a successful year and that everyone was "enthusiastic over the result." An education at Howard was "solid and thorough" and fully developed students both morally and intellectually. In the wake of the Hawes murders and riots, Riley reassured parents that the college was committed to respect, discipline, order, and was free of the "demoralizing influences" of Birmingham. "Whatever may occur in that city," he added, "does not in the least affect the students of Howard College." Riley also explained that the college required that all young men be "a gentleman and a student." Those not meeting this standard were "worthless" in his eyes and "not retained" at Howard. "It does him wrong to retain him," Riley added, because it misled parents into believing their son was on the right path, reinforced the young man's poor behavior, and imposed upon the college a "great pest" for those students attending Howard to study. Riley, Giles, and Waldrop's efforts resulted in an almost 20 percent increase in enrollment during the 1889–90 academic year.[27]

Classes began on September 16, 1889, two weeks earlier than normal. President Riley also added a Christmas break (beyond the one day off on December 25) and allowed those students who maintained "good behavior and diligence" the opportunity for a "brief respite." Cadet Robert Lee Curry of Monroeville believed that Howard College was giving him the training and discipline to be successful in any career path he chose. After a few months at the college, he told his friends back home that he was taking challenging courses to become a man who made wise choices and "attained a riper judgement." Howard's professors were also teaching him the "art of war as well as the quiet pursuit of peace." The temporary buildings on campus, however, were "not so elegantly situated," Curry added, but this would help them in the future to "appreciate our new home when we come to occupy it." On Thanksgiving Day, Curry and the other cadets enjoyed a sizable feast that was most likely prepared by the college's steward, William St. Clair—a native of England who was popular with the students. Following the meal, the afternoon was spent playing football, chasing greased pigs, picking up loose potatoes, and other games.[28]

Two weeks before the Thanksgiving celebration, the Alabama Baptist State Convention opened in Selma. Howard's board president W. C. Ward declared the college to be in a "prosperous state" due to the hard work of the faculty and the financial agent. Their endeavors, he said, demonstrated that through wisdom and effort the college can thrive without an endowment, stately buildings, or manicured lawns. Howard gave Alabama's young men an "education in fact, and not merely the means of education." Ward then appealed to everyone in the assembly to donate money to help in David I. Purser's "meritorious work" to complete the Academic Hall. "Purser had been everywhere," Ward added, "and had seen almost everybody" who might donate to the cause. He made appeals in Tuscaloosa, East Lake, Woodlawn, Avondale, Sylacauga, Selma, Jasper, Brundidge, Beech Grove, Eufaula, Greenville, Pine Apple, Tuskegee, Lineville, Mobile, Troy, and many other towns and churches. Most of Purser's cash and pledges came from the thirty-two local associations. After speaking to the Tuscaloosa and Coosa River associations, he raised $1,000 from each; Muscle Shoals Association gave $1,025; Union Baptist Association provided $1,100; Conecuh Baptist Association delivered $1,325; and Mobile Baptist Association donated $1,500. At a meeting of the Montgomery Association, Purser lectured on the importance of Christian higher education and called upon the audience to offer "financial support and moral suasion" to Howard College. The brethren responded by giving $2,240. It was "cheering news," a Montgomery paper reported, that the Baptists of Alabama were stepping forward in grand fashion to support the college.[29]

On Saturday evening, November 9, the convention gathered at the First Baptist Church of Selma and listened to speeches on behalf of Howard College from

W. C. Ward and D. I. Purser. Inspired by their appeals, the delegates gave
$14,415.51 in cash and pledges for construction of the main building. Baptists rep-
resenting every corner of the state gave to the cause—the largest, three $1,000
donations, came from laymen: T. Green Bush, an industrialist from Mobile;
Charles W. Collins, a planter from Hale County; and James T. Fitzgerald, a
Marion banker. After more than three years of division, the convention unified
to save Howard College. Rev. Washington Bryan Crumpton later suggested that
this change of attitude among the anti-removal forces was spearheaded by the
"level-headed Christian men at Marion" who were determined to stop an inescapable permanent split in the Alabama Baptist State Convention. Crumpton
credited James T. Murfee, Jesse B. Lovelace, and William W. Wilkerson for
changing the attitudes of many by deciding to put aside bitter feelings and offer
to support the college in its new location. Lovelace gave $100 toward the new
Howard building.[30]

With the additional donations from the state convention, David Ingram
Purser was nearing the goal of $50,000 for the Academic Hall. One Birmingham
paper praised Purser's efforts and noted that construction of the "handsomest
and best college" in Alabama was all but "assured." Soon the bricks would be
laid for a building which will be the pride of everyone who "felt an interest
in the education of young men of the state." But Purser continued to travel
and raise more money from individuals, churches, and associations. No doubt
Howard's financial agent was also looking ahead to the next "pile of buildings"
beyond the Academic Hall which, according to the plans, were to cost an additional $75,000. These included additional dormitories, a science building, and
a dining hall. He told one church congregation that Alabama Baptists were ob-
ligated to give their money to the college and raise the institution from its "em-
barrassments" by funding "suitable quarters" for students. Purser's emotional
appeals continued to work at the grassroots level—as most donors pledged or
gave between $25 and $100. Purser also received a letter from a convict who
pledged $10 for the building fund—made payable on April 1, 1890. "I am already
under obligation to Almighty God to contribute $2.60 per annum as long as my
prison life shall last," the convict wrote, "and $9.00 per annum thereafter, as long
as the Lord spares my life." The prisoner was closely following the "efforts and
success of the noble brethren" who worked for Howard College.[31]

On December 3, 1889, the Board of Trustees elected D. I. Purser, J. T. Fitzgerald of Marion, and W. T. Smith of Birmingham to a building committee to "ar-

range all necessary details." Purser deposited the cash he raised in the Jefferson County Savings Bank in Birmingham and turned over the pledges (subscriptions) to bank officials for collection. But David Ingram Purser and the members of his committee understood that constructing the new Academic Hall was but the beginning of Howard College's building projects. The school needed wealthy donors to provide more money for the additional buildings, but none of them were willing to step forward. "I like rich men," Purser quipped, but only those who had "big ways to do big things." A stingy rich man was "indeed a contemptible sight, whether he thinks so or not." With only small monetary donations trickling into Howard's bank account, college officials turned to banker brothers Burghard and Sigfried Steiner for an infusion of cash. History does not record who proposed the idea of working with the Steiner Brothers, but most likely it was Reverend Purser and Professor A. D. Smith. Purser was well connected with financial institutions throughout the city, and Smith maintained the college's internal business affairs. President B. F. Riley depended on Smith's advice in navigating Howard through the latest stormy winds. "I could not have succeeded without his aid," Riley wrote in 1909, and he knew "so much better than I what to do." Smith was "congenial and conciliatory" throughout the ordeal, and "his direction of affairs brought success more than anything which I did." Smith also had a long relationship with the Steiners, dating from the brothers' days as merchants in Hamburg, Alabama—some six miles from Marion.[32]

Jewish immigrants from Bohemia (then part of the Austro-Hungarian Empire), Burghard and Sigfried Steiner moved from Hamburg, Alabama, to Birmingham in 1888 and received a state charter to open a banking house—one that greatly impacted the city's economic prosperity in the decades to come. Newspapers reported that, on the morning of February 28, 1889, D. I. Purser met with the Steiner Brothers and began discussions on issuing bonds to "build the college with Philadelphia parties." By the end of March, the Union Trust Company of Philadelphia issued $40,000 worth of bonds (through the Steiner Brothers) in $1,000 denominations at 8 percent interest annually. The bonds were collateralized by a mortgage on Howard College's East Lake campus, with the debt to be paid back by 1894 at $10,000 a year plus interest. "Now let all who have pledged amounts be prompt in the payment of their notes," the *Alabama Baptist* urged its readers, "and those who have never pledged anything should come up and give the college assistance"[33]

Jewish immigrants Burghard and Sigfried Steiner had a long relationship with Howard College dating from their days in Perry County. In 1888, the duo opened the Steiner Brothers Bank in Birmingham and assisted in the issuing of bonds to fund the building of the new Howard campus in East Lake. When the college was unable to repay the debt, Burghard helped the institution avoid bankruptcy in 1896. One of the Steiner brothers is pictured on the left; the man at the right is unidentified. (Birmingham Public Library Department of Archives and Manuscripts)

As chairman of the building committee, Purser purchased advertisements in Birmingham papers to collect bids for the "erection of the main academic building of the college." Potential contractors could review the architectural plans in downtown Birmingham at the Eagle Hotel and submit a proposal to the building committee which would review and select the builder. The energetic Purser was wasting no time, one newspaper observed, by "rushing the business to a successful termination."[34]

The building committee received four bids: Figh & Williams ($39,740), Scully & Byrd ($37,700), C. F. Hardman ($36,660.70), and Matthew Talbert Richards ($32,000). The committee awarded the contract to Richards, who offered the lowest bid. "Mr. Richards thoroughly understands the construction of college buildings," the *Birmingham News* opined, having just completed the "magnificent structure" at Judson College. With limited funds and tight budgets, Richards apparently made every cost-savings change possible to the architectural designs for the Academic Hall. Struck from the plans were porticos, windows, ornate decorations, higher roof pitches, and a towering central spiral. His workers made bricks from clay on-site, rather than using a more refined brick from a manufacturer. Richards also used pine, instead of hardwood, for the interior architectural features—using a wood that was more prone to rot and termites. The cost-cutting measure resulted in an austere building with a diminished lifespan. Nonetheless, one Alabama newspaper reported, the Howard people were "feeling particularly happy" as the building was now guaranteed.[35]

On February 28, 1890, following the meeting with the Steiner brothers, Rev. David Ingram Purser made his way to the Jefferson County Jail—a brick-and-stone fortress on the corner of Fourth Avenue North and Twenty-First Street. Around noon, Purser and a Methodist minister entered the jail cell of Richard R. Hawes to "administer religious consolation" before his hanging. Although charged with all three murders, a jury convicted Hawes of murdering little Mae at East Lake and sentenced him to death. In his last hours of life, he asked Purser to pray for him so that God would give him "nerve and strength to go through the execution without breaking down." At 12:45 p.m., the sheriff and a deputy led Hawes from his cell and began the long walk to the scaffold with Purser and the other minister walking close behind. Hawes's final words to the crowd gathered inside the walls of the jail and on the streets beyond were: "Let liquor and vile women alone. You see where it has brought me." When the trapdoor opened, the people who had gathered outside the jail's walls cheered as Hawes's neck snapped at the end of the rope.[36]

A few years later, an 1890 Howard graduate, Joseph Davis Heacock, witnessed dozens of hangings behind the jail's stone walls. "A sordid, morbid sight," he later recalled. "Don't see why anyone would want to witness one. Yet they used to clamor for the privilege at the old Jefferson County Jail." Following graduation from Howard, Heacock attended medical school at Tulane University and returned to East Lake in 1894 to practice medicine. Looking to supplement his meager income, he also took on the job of Jefferson County physician—requiring him to attend all the county's executions. "I almost starved to death out there," he once said, as he made his house calls first on a saddle horse, then a horse and buggy, and in 1904, an automobile. Despite his simple beginnings as a physician, Heacock soon became one of the county's most prominent medical doctors. In 1908, he was appointed to the Howard

College Board of Trustees—a position he held for the next sixty-six years—until his death in 1974 at age of 105.[37]

At Heacock's graduation in 1890, Rev. Frank M. Ellis, pastor of Eutaw Place Baptist Church in Baltimore, delivered the commencement address based on 1 Corinthians 16:13: "Be Watchful, stand firm in the faith, act like men, be strong." Just because the Howard graduates were young, Ellis said, was no reason for them not to obtain "the full depth of the responsibility of being a Christian." Ellis called the men to obtain a mature faith and the "full depth of the responsibility of being a Christian." From Howard College, the student received "book learning," the development of a religious mind, and the foundation of good character.[38]

One attendee at graduation noted that, not only were Ellis's oratory skills strong, but so was Howard College as a whole. While the institution "struggled hard" through the difficulties of the previous three years, Benjamin Franklin Riley possessed the fortitude to hold the college together. "Too much praise cannot be given," he wrote. Riley came to Howard while the institution was "in the throes of death, and by his matchless energy and force of will, infused new life into it; and now it is on the high road to success." Riley, however, knew that the future of Howard College was still hanging by a thread.[39]

16

NO CROSS, NO CROWN

True to her motto, "No Cross, No Crown," she has made
adversities the stepping stones to higher things.

—WILLIAM L. SAMFORD, 1892

Following months of delay and with a crowd of onlookers nearby, M. T. Richards's
construction crew began erecting Howard College's main Academic Hall on
August 19, 1890. At midday, William Hamilton Wilson of nearby Huffman paid
five dollars for the privilege of laying the first brick on the new building. In turn,
David Ingram Purser, Felix M. Wood, Albert Durant Smith, and Williamson
Alfred Williams each paid five dollars to lay the second, third, fourth, and fifth
bricks. Then ten brickmasons stepped forward, and work "began in earnest" on
the long dormant building. Over the next few weeks, the *Alabama Baptist* observed, busy laborers covered rising walls, and "their shouts, mingled with the
rasping ring of the trowel," spoke to the "great work" that was in progress. "The
darkest days of Howard College, the paper supposed, "belonged to the past."[1]

But for the students, the Howard College campus still resembled a frontier
revival camp and not the grounds of a vibrant New South institution. "It has
been said that we are camping here now waiting for our house to be built," one
cadet wrote in 1890, "but if these 'sayers' will only come up here and take a peep
into our building they will see that we are living in 'ceiled houses,' painted too."
Nonetheless, the cramped temporary living spaces compelled D. I. Purser to
begin "stirring the Baptist hearts of Alabama" to give $20,000 to erect two small
dormitories for the students.[2]

A few weeks later, the large number of young men riding trains bound for
Birmingham and Howard College caught the attention of local newspapers and
suggested that the school was opening with "flattering prospects." During the

The new Howard College campus as proposed in 1887. As part of Robert Jemison's New South hyperbolic boosterism of selling East Lake to prospective investors and residents, the new Howard College would have splendid new buildings and "rank among the chief institutions of its kind in the South." The reality never matched the rhetoric. (Birmingham Public Library Department of Archives and Manuscripts)

summer months of 1890, President Benjamin Franklin Riley once again rambled about the state recruiting students. This time it resulted in a record-breaking 206 students enrolling in the college and overflowing the dormitories—so much so that the trustees rented five houses near campus to accommodate all the students. This was a "great matriculation," the *Birmingham News* reported, that Howard deserved because of its "excellent curriculum, a splendid faculty," and the "high literary and moral tone" of its location in the New South.[3]

Howard was entering its fourth academic year in Birmingham, and the impact of Benjamin F. Riley and the New South creed were evident. Inside the classroom, the faculty taught the traditional classical curriculum of Samuel Sterling Sherman, but outside the classroom, the students' oratorical skills were refined on contemporary issues. In 1890, cadet Manly Enos Weaver from Bibb County wrote that the "great men" of both the Old South and the New South were passing from the scene and a new generation of southerners needed to step forward and lead. His argument centered on a quote by Georgia politician Benjamin Hill: "There was a South of secession and slavery—that South is dead. There is a South of union and freedom—that South is living breathing, growing every hour." But Hill was now dead. Former Confederate president Jefferson Davis epitomized the South of "secession and slavery" who defended the cause he believed in. "He lived to see his plans and purposes thwarted, but he has fallen," Weaver added. Preeminently above all his predecessors, New South prophet Henry W. Grady represented the South of "union and freedom" and possessed a "philanthropic heart . . . filled with love, pride, and admiration." He fought to end the animosity between the North and South. "His career was brief," Weaver continued, but "it was brilliant." The student encouraged his classmates to "imitate his greatness" and embrace Grady's admonition to "catch the sunshine" of hope in the "bricks and mortar of our homes" and build no "ignoble prejudice" from the memory of the past. Some might build monuments to their memory, but "do they need to do this?" he asked. "Will not their deeds live longest when bequeathed through history to coming generations?"[4]

Writing in the Franklin Literary Society's publication, the *Franklin Advocate*, one recent graduate encouraged the cadets to use "sober, patient forethought" in choosing their life's occupation. This generation of students must "ventilate the subject," test the opportunities, weigh the options, and then make the choice with wisdom. Not everyone could become a George Washington, Jefferson Davis, or Henry W. Grady, but each Howard student could find his niche and become who God "designed" him to be. Some may lack the "push, pluck, and principle" to keep pace in an era which was "anything else than sleepy." These were "stirring times," and it was a student's duty to "make the most of life . . . to cultivate habits of industry, to learn diligence in business," and to pay close attention to the issues of each day. "The prime object in life was not to amass riches," he said, or "to win the bubble of reputation at the mouth of the cannon, or to gain the plaudits of an ignorant rabble, or to seek pleasure in things below, but to do good" through acts of "kindness and love" and to "elevate and enable . . . truth and integrity." In other words, a virtuous and benevolent person of strong faith, character, and intellect that the founders of Howard College envisioned, and John Howard exemplified.[5]

Just like James T. Murfee before him, Benjamin F. Riley also embraced the moral, mental, and physical discipline of the cadet corps. Even with no military background, Riley was perhaps more rigid in his discipline than Murfee and insisted that every cadet follow the regulations to the exact letter of the law. Allen Augustus Hutto of Lincoln, Alabama, reported to Riley's office during his freshman year and received a thorough inspection from the president. "Mr. Hutto," Riley said, you've earned "three demerits for having your hands locked behind you." The cadet was humiliated. "I was doing my best," he recalled, "but in my awkward way had shown . . . my worst." The demerits were later removed, but Hutto learned that Riley demanded not only adherence to the rules, but also required absolute perfection. Regularly the cadets attempted to get around the rules or the omnipresence of "Doc," as they called him. One evening two hungry students decided to steal a ham by climbing a tree and then onto the roof of the storage area, raising a window, and scampering inside. When they exited with the ham, they recognized Riley walking straight toward the tree they had just climbed. With no other way to escape, they lay flat against the roof as Riley sat on the tree's exposed roots. "The boys dared not move," another student recalled, "and hardly dared to breathe." After an hour or so, Riley stood and walked away, allowing the cadets to climb down the tree and scurry away with their prize. It was one of the few times the boys escaped from the president's watchful eyes."[6]

The placing of the cornerstone of the main Academic Hall was originally scheduled for Wednesday, October 22, but bad weather postponed the ceremony for a week. The delay prohibited the attendance of the "big men" who were scheduled to speak at the event, but a large crowd of students, faculty, and East Lake residents were on hand to witness the proceedings. Most of the onlookers stood about the cleared ground near the foundation or sat on stacked piles of lumber. At 10:30 a.m. on October 29, David I. Purser introduced Benjamin F. Riley, who read both Psalms 84 and 46, the latter which read: "God is our refuge and strength, a very present help in trouble. Therefore will not we fear, though the earth be removed and though mountains be carried into the midst of the seas. . . . Be still and know that I am God: I will be exalted among the heathen, I will be exalted in the earth." When Riley finished and a prayer was offered by Rev. Andrew Jackson Waldrop, Rev. William Lowndes Pickard, the new pastor of Birmingham's First Baptist Church, spoke to the gathering. What was the original purpose of Howard College, he asked, when there was "no brick, nor mortar, and few friends?" Howard College, Pickard continued, originated in the hearts and prayers of Alabama Baptists who "breathed for freedom of conscience." Howard was conceived by founders with a "deep devotion to truth" and through the sacrifices and contributions of "men of small earning." Loyalty to this truth, he emphasized, "laid the foundation of this building" and that same loyalty placed the cornerstone. "Truth, the whole truth, let the people honor it and be carried to the tomb clinging to it." The truth-seeking founders of Howard College believed an institution of learning would make the society of the Old South a better place.[7]

The next speaker, Mississippi educator Thaddeus Constantine Belsher, noted that Howard College was now part of Birmingham and the New South. "With all the city's vast shipments of iron," he added, "she could now ship trained intellects." He explained to the crowd that college was for affluent people, but not those wealthy in money or possessions. Howard College was for the rich man—"one rich in soul, rich in determination, [and] rich in a resolution to train his mind." When President Riley spoke, he emphasized that Howard was a Christian school that stressed the centrality of virtue and faith along with the discipline of "first class" military training. The success of the college was due to the compassion of the faculty. Any "pang in the student's heart" or any trouble in mind would always "find sympathy in the faculty."[8]

One such former student was Rev. Phillip Thomas Hale, the pastor of Southside Baptist Church in Birmingham, who spoke to the audience on the "Outlook of Howard College." An Alabama native, Hale graduated second in his class in 1879, received theological training at Southern Baptist Seminary in Louisville in 1883, and came to Birmingham in 1888 as the successor to J. J. D. Renfroe at Southside. Bespectacled and with a long handlebar mustache, Hale said that the building's cornerstone was laid when the convention hired D. I. Purser as the financial agent. "The outlook of the college was bright," he added, because of the faculty, the location, and the denomination. Some ninety-five thousand Baptists in Alabama loved the college and gave the institution "prayers, sympathies and money." Hale concluded by appealing to the students to "take a full diploma" at Howard because a "well-trained mind was of use in any occupation.[9]

When the speakers finished, workers spread a layer of mortar, and contractor Matthew T. Richards, subcontractors Patrick T. Fallon and S. McCullough, superintendent William Gabert, and others lowered the stone onto the foundation. Inside the cornerstone was sealed: flowers from Howard students, the college's charter and amendments, constitutions and bylaws from the Franklin and Philomathic societies, a list of cadets from the 1890–91 academic year, a history of Howard by Professor Thomas J. Dill, a picture of Howard College, a tract written by President B. F. Riley, a coin from Rev. W. L. Pickard, a sermon by J. J. D. Renfroe, names and addresses of all donors to the building fund, membership rolls of Ruhama, Avondale, and First Baptist Church of Birmingham, a Bible, a copy of the *Age-Herald* newspaper, and a flower from a person unable to attend the ceremony. Following the ceremonial breaking of the dirt, the gathering sang the Doxology and received a closing prayer from the pastor of East Lake Methodist Church.[10]

That October, the death of Howard College's former president Henry Talbird went largely unnoticed by Alabama Baptists and the Howard community. A short time later, the *Alabama Baptist* newspaper received a letter from Talbird's predecessor at Howard College, Samuel Sterling Sherman. "I have not seen in your esteemed paper," he wrote from his home in Chicago, "any notice of the death." Although Talbird left Alabama long ago, he was not forgotten, and Sherman believed that readers of the *Alabama Baptist* needed to remember his "life, work and character." As president of Howard College, Talbird was an "able and wise" administrator whose efforts led the state denomination to invest "more deeply" in the institution. After he resigned the presidency, he pastored churches in Alabama, Kentucky, Missouri, and Florida—retiring from full-time ministry in 1887 but continuing to preach an occasional sermon. Talbird believed that his "special mission" and "appointed work" were to preach and endeavor "to instruct men in the knowledge of the Lord and to persuade them to walk in his ways."[11]

But as his eyes grew dim and his strength faded, he wrote Sherman that he feared he might "outlive his usefulness" and that his mental and physical sharpness might "slowly waste away." Sherman, however, explained that Talbird's mind was "vigorous and active" to the end. Talbird spent his days reading René Descartes, Baruch Spinoza, Immanuel Kant, David Hume, and Victor Cousins. He rejected Thomas Henry Huxley's views on materialism as a form of infidelity. "Thanks to the good Lord," he wrote Sherman in July 1890, "I am delivered from this error. In my old age, I sometimes feel that I can live and talk with God; blessed be his name; Jesus is my savior and I humbly trust that the Holy Spirit is my enlightener." Talbird's death, Sherman believed, "came just as he wished, in the midst of useful labor, with mind unclouded and his hope of immortal life brightening as the scenes of earth faded from his sight." At the annual state convention in November, Alabama Baptists held a memorial service to honor Henry Talbird and the other stalwart brethren who passed away in 1890, including other benefactors of Howard College: Samuel Henderson, Porter King, and Robert H. Sterrett.[12]

On February 16, 1891, seventy-seven-year-old James Harvey DeVotie died at his home in Griffin, Georgia. He left Alabama in 1856 to become pastor of the First Baptist Church of Columbus, Georgia, where he continued his legacy of institution building and zealous support of missions and education. In 1870, he began a long association with the First Baptist Church of Griffin, Georgia, and later served as the secretary for the mission board of the state convention. A few months following his death, a few members of First Baptist organized a new church in Griffin named DeVotie Baptist Church. At Howard College, however, DeVotie's name and legacy faded from institutional memory.[13]

At Howard, during the spring term, the first death of a student on the East Lake campus shocked the faculty and cadets. Stephen Mathew Chitwood was a promising seventeen-year-old from Tuscumbia, Alabama, who was an honor roll student, a sergeant in his cadet corps company, and a popular friend to his peers. In the cold winter months of 1891, Chitwood fell ill with "la grippe" (influenza) and, as he recovered, was "smitten down" with the "alarming symptoms" of typhoid fever. According to college policy, sick students at Howard received close attention from President B. F. Riley, and, if they were extremely ill, were moved to Riley's nearby home and "nursed with care and tenderness." For a time, the young man rallied, but suddenly his symptoms returned and worsened, compelling Riley to summon Chitwood's mother from Tuscumbia. Campus physician Capers Capehart Jones attended Chitwood throughout the ordeal. A native of Carlowville, Jones received his early schooling at Thomas J. Dill's local school, graduated from the Philadelphia University of Medicine and Surgery in 1870, and later established a medical practice in East Lake. For Chitwood's case, Jones invited other medical professionals for consultation, but everyone agreed that he would never recover. With Chitwood's impending death, the cadet corps withdrew from a parade in downtown Birmingham in honor of President Benjamin Harrison's visit to the Magic City. "We shall always hold ourselves in readiness to assist you in the expression of patriotism," Professor George W. Macon wrote to Birmingham officials. Chitwood died on April 15, 1891, the evening before Harrison's visit.[14]

President Riley and twelve cadets brought Chitwood's remains home to Tuscumbia. Riley preached the funeral sermon at the First Presbyterian Church—since the local Baptist congregation had no building. When the service concluded, the twelve Howard cadets brought the coffin holding Chitwood's remains to nearby Oakwood Cemetery and carefully buried him in the ground. When they finished, the cadets sang a hymn, "The Sweet By-and-By." A writer in the *Alabama Baptist* noticed that the "young men wept over his untimely death as if he had been a brother beloved."[15]

On campus, a committee of cadets composed a "Tribute of Respect" to honor their fallen comrade, whose "manly bearing and generous conduct" made him a favorite of peers and faculty alike. "We sustain in his death," they wrote, one of Howard's best students and "one remarkable for the virtues which belong to an honorable gentleman." Chitwood would be missed in the classroom and among the corps. "While we deeply deplore his untimely end, we submit with resignation to the will of Him who doeth all things well." A writer in the *Alabama Baptist* noted that Chitwood's family rested on the hope of eternal salvation and were impressed with the tremendous value of Howard College. "The marked affection of the students and faculty for their poor boy won their deep affection." In the wake of Chitwood's death, a spiritual awakening and revival broke out on campus—the response of which was so great, students postponed the anniversary meetings of the literary societies.[16]

A few weeks later, as the term neared an end, workers completed most of the main Academic Hall, and the building was opened to faculty and students. On the first floor of the building was a glass-paneled room where the cadet corps "officer of the day" manned the post, President Riley's "large and handsome" office, faculty offices, "retiring rooms," and lecture rooms—the latter equipped with large pieces of slate the length of one wall. The second and third floors of the building included an over-five-hundred-seat chapel which occupied both floors in the center of the building. The "opera style" seating in the chapel was donated by John T. Davis, a member of the First Baptist Church of Columbia, Alabama. A writer for the *Birmingham Age-Herald* described it as a "superbly handsome hall." On the second floor, there were additional lecture rooms and, on the third, the literary society halls were on either end of the building.[17]

Kerosene oil lamps provided light in every room (but the building soon converted to electricity), and heating came from steam created by a Ruttan-Smead ventilating system. Water was accessible on each floor, but the only "toilet" in the building was on the third floor near the literary society rooms. Located in a closet, the four-seater was a direct drop-pit latrine with an open shaft emptying into a cesspool in the basement. For most faculty and students on campus, the privy was located several hundred yards southwest of the main building. This rough-hewn, jumbo-sized outhouse was, according to one writer, an "improvised structure" with a door at each end and accommodating fifteen to twenty individuals at a time squatting over the holes. In the campus lingo of the day, a trip to the latrine was called "going to congress."[18]

Howard College's main Academic Hall (seen here in 1892) was an austere building constructed with no redeeming architectural features. The hall (later called "Old Main")
and the other buildings on the East Lake campus were poorly built and prone to rot,
termites, and structural issues. After Howard abandoned the campus in 1957, all the
buildings were razed. (Samford University, Special Collection and University Archives)

On June 10, Howard College held the first commencement exercises in the
Academic Hall's new chapel. Fourteen students graduated—all going on to
middle-class professions—four pastors, three educators, two merchants, two
medical doctors, two civil engineers, and one lawyer. John Daniel Abernathy
graduated with first honors and went on to a prosperous legal career, and Henry
Jones Willingham received second honors—becoming a successful teacher,
later serving as the superintendent of education and president of the state normal school in Florence (now the University of North Alabama).[19]

With students home for the summer, workers completed final construction
on the Academic Hall and the two new brick dormitories. The new sleeping
quarters, which flanked the main building, resembled simple brick colonial
cottages with eight rooms each. All the new buildings contained long furnace
stacks—especially the enormous three-story chimney on the Academic Hall—

which attracted thousands of chimney swifts, more commonly called "sweeps," small gray-brown migratory birds that nest in chimneys. Each year for decades, the birds arrived in late August and took up residence at Howard; signaling to East Lake residents the college boys would soon arrive. "These peculiar little birds appeared at Howard College as the forerunners of college days," George W. Macon said. Down the hill from the new buildings, near Underwood Avenue, the wood-frame makeshift structures were renovated with "the barn" dormitory updated, the academic building converted to a dining hall ("the grub house"), and the Ruhama Academy building emptied and soon demolished.[20]

President Benjamin. F. Riley described the 1890–91 academic year as the "most remarkable" in the history of Howard College, with record enrollments and buildings completed—all pointing to a "buoyant hopefulness" for the future and "increasing prosperity." In the past, the days were "dark and many," Riley said in 1891. Resources at Howard were often "drained to the last cent and we knew not whither to turn, but like the widow's cruse, the oil was somehow present when it was needed." With this "educational uplift" at Howard, William C. Ward encouraged Alabama Baptists to keep supporting the college without hesitation. "There [was] no discharge in this war," Ward said, and the state's Baptists were enlisted in this conflict for "life and eternity." The college's advocates put their "hand to the plow," not looking back, and turning the page on "past failures, delinquencies, heart-burnings, and fault findings," praying for the greatest future success that "ever crowned the gifts, players and self-denials of God's poor—a posterity redeemed and glorified by saving grace and religious education." For Riley, Ward, and other Howard supporters, optimism abounded even as another stormy wind approached.[21]

Although the national financial Panic of 1893 was two years away, the economy in the South was already in steep decline with businesses failing "at a rate," historian Edward L. Ayers noted, "approaching depression levels." In Birmingham, another economic downturn only reinforced the local adage: "Hard times come here first and stay the longest." For Howard College, $4,262.44 was still owed to M. T. Richards, the building contractor, and several subcontractors. Once again, many people who pledged money to the college failed to honor their commitment. "This deficit must be provided for," W. C. Ward said. "Those who have given must give again." Even with the addition of the two new dormitories, the large enrollment still forced college officials to rent houses near campus. D. I. Purser arranged for contractor M. T. Richards to build two more dorms but wait until the spring of 1892 to receive payment for his services. With permanent campus buildings and a growing enrollment, Howard College was now "forged to the front," the *Alabama Baptist* opined, and was receiving praise from every direction. "The order, financial management, and good work done there make it a pride to our people."[22]

In September 1891, one visitor described Howard College's campus as "rugged, rocky out-of-doors," with no means of transporting the students' belongings from the College Station on the dummy line up the hill to the campus. When Baptist social activist Lida Bestor Robertson (Daniel Bestor's granddaughter) visited in 1891, she found the lack of conveyance a terrible inconvenience. The pragmatic Robertson "begged two generous Baptists" to give money to the college for the purchase of a horse. Once B. F. Riley bought the horse and hitched the animal to a wagon, the cadets dubbed it the "trunk dummy" that only made trips to the College Station and back to campus. Just before classes started, John James Finklea, a merchant from Buena Vista in Monroe County, arrived in Birmingham to enroll his son, Henry Lee, in Howard College. They disembarked from the East Lake dummy train at the College Station around midnight—too late for the "trunk dummy"—so they began the trek to campus. As they approached Underwood Avenue, Jack asked: "My boy, how much farther? Are we not about at the place?" Henry Lee responded, "Yes, Papa, this is the place." No doubt all Jack could see were a thick stand of tall trees and possibly the two makeshift buildings in the shadows. He said: "But I didn't know, my boy, that you were camped here in the woods." Henry Lee told his father to wait until the morning so he could see beyond the "pines and oaks" and view the new Academic Hall and the small dormitories. In the future, he added, "things will look entirely different" when more trees are cut, and the ground cleared. "It will present a beautiful appearance."[23]

At graduation in 1892, the college marked its fiftieth anniversary of the first class of students in 1842 and the forty-fifth anniversary of Howard moving from a boys' preparatory school to a men's college. J. B. Hawthorne returned to his alma mater and delivered the baccalaureate address. Hawthorne encouraged the Howard students to aspire to greatness by following the example of John the Baptist, who possessed "extraordinary discipline of body, mind, and spirit" to confront the troubles of his day. He was virtuous, strong, pure, intelligent, tender, noble, disciplined, faithful, and benevolent. John was, Hawthorne, believed, the perfect example of biblical manhood. He encouraged the graduates to go forth from Howard and confront the pressing issues of the 1890s. "If a pure gospel was to be preached," Hawthorne proclaimed, if religion were preserved; if hardened "bigotry of modern Phariseeism" were shattered; if "soul-degrading, home-debauching and villainy breeding infidelity" were destroyed; if "communism, socialism, free loveism," and other devilisms were snatched from American soil; if corruption of democracy through ballot fraud and bribery were overturned; if despotism of monopolies and moneyed elites were upended; if "infamous revenue laws" were repealed; if the "whiskey ring" were broken; if the defiled church were cleansed and made worthy; if any reforms were enacted, "they were made possible only through the devotion of the few who were dominated by the same spirit and purposes which made John the Baptist the matchless man and the peerless prophet that he was."[24]

The president of the Board of Trustees, W. C. Ward, invoked the Levitical Law of Jubilee as his justification for giving a "careful, scrutinizing" review of the history of Howard College. Through this, he supposed, the past would reveal the errors that brought displeasure to God and serve as a guide to the future and "a more perfect, acceptable, and glorious work." The middle-class parents of the first students at Howard refused to allow state institutions or cross-denominational schools to educate their sons. "They were Baptists," Ward said. "They were conscious of having the truth. They were conscious of love for the truth and fealty to the truth, the whole truth, free from contamination by error of any sort, from any source, under any circumstances." Their only choice was to establish a Baptist school for the training of their sons with the entire "weight and strength" of the influences of the "truths they held dear." Five decades ago, the college was founded, Ward said, and now looking back, Howard had lived "a checkered life" of irony and mixed emotions. The college survived fires, sectional conflict, and the "hazardous experiment of a violent transplantation." In 1892, the college was now "rejoicing in prosperity; buoyant with hope," but also "struggling in adversity for continued existence." Fifty years after the founding, all that was needed to make Howard a success was another effort by the members of the denomination with a "holy desire to uplift humanity." In the end, Ward asked, "Can the Baptists of Alabama be united in such an enterprise?"[25]

In his address, David G. Lyon of Harvard encouraged students to choose a profession which had the "best effect" on character. "A man's character was all he really had," Lyon said, and a "strong and upright" character was the only "permanent and truly valuable possession." Students must also be interested in their chosen professions to be happy and effective in their work. But the greatest requirement in choosing a profession was "serviceableness," Lyon emphasized. This was the "standard whereby we must choose what we will do with our lives, and, the choice once made, how we shall always act." College men must select those professions in which they can attain their best and "serve the most." Benevolent service to others, Lyon supposed, not material gain, was the true meaning of disciplined preparation. "This world was not a chaos, but a cosmos" guided by the "wise author of life who imparted its impulses, fixed its environs, and assigned its task." In conclusion, Lyon told the graduates of 1892 that they had more opportunities than those that came before them. The eyes of their older brothers were upon them, as were the "hopes and blessings" of Howard College. "In the love of men," he said, "and the fear of God, may your lives be marked by conscientious and effective service."[26]

William L. Sanford, an 1884 Howard graduate and a successful merchant in Sherman, Texas, gave the alumni address on the flavorless topic of the American credit system. Yet he began his speech with high praise for his alma mater. Howard was forged within the turmoil of the nineteenth century and endured many tribulations—never wavering from the college's motto: "No Cross, No Crown." Howard made "adversities the steppingstones to higher things," Sanford said, "and progress was written on her signet ring." The credit for Howard's "unsurpassed achievement and steady growth," he believed, was the result of the genius of the "master spirit" of one individual who served as a teacher and counselor. Although his presence was unseen following Sanford's graduation, he still "walked beside me through the years, whispering encouragement and infusing strength." In 1892, students still embraced the "illustrious" teaching and strong "Christian manhood" of Professor Thomas J. Dill.[27]

For over an hour, Sanford went on to outline his issues with the credit system and offering prophetic wisdom on the forthcoming national economic panic. The "tongueless testimony of privation" in the New South and the "stagnation and depression" throughout the region were facts that "no careful, posted man will dispute." Although the destruction of slavery brought beneficial change to the South, the peculiar institution was once again being "enthroned within her borders." This was not a slavery based on race or class, but a "slavery of condition" where the creditor served as master and the debtor the slave. "There was no bondage in the world so galling," he added, "so degrading as the servitude of debt." Debt stole the "flush from beauty's cheek; it hushed the song in the throat of childhood; it robbed of independence, ambition and manhood; it bred discontent, desperation and crime." And it was made worse with the coordinating evil of interest. A debtor worked from "sun to sun, but interest worked night and day—enriching the lender and impoverishing the borrower." It was unlikely that Sanford knew of Howard's mounting debt crisis and its increasing inability to meet the financial obligations to the Union Trust Company of Philadelphia—no doubt the irony was not lost on B. F. Riley, D. I. Purser, and W. C. Ward. Nonetheless, W. L. Sanford ended his speech with a direct appeal to the graduates: "Do not buy on credit that which will not afford you a corresponding ability to pay." Avoid all needless debt as you would hedonism; although the paths were different, they both ended in the same destruction. "Avoid it as you would pestilence," he said, "its breath was poison, and its touch was death."[28]

Arguably the best-known and most popular alumnus of Howard College, George Doherty Johnston, spoke to the literary societies on the "Existing Perils to Young Men." A member of Howard's second graduating class in 1849, Johnston went on to earn a law degree from Cumberland University (Lebanon, Tennessee) and was a member of the Alabama state legislature in the 1850s. He joined the Confederate Army, fought at the first Battle of Manassas (Bull Run) in 1861, and finished the war as a brigadier general. During Reconstruction, he practiced law in Marion, but in 1871, the same year James T. Murfee became president of Howard, Johnston was appointed to Murfee's old position as the commandant of cadets at the University of Alabama and was later hired as the superintendent at the Citadel (then known as the South Carolina Military Academy). President Benjamin Harrison later appointed him to the Civil Service Commission, where he served with Theodore Roosevelt, but he later resigned to run for a seat in the Alabama Senate.[29]

By 1892, the sixty-year-old Johnston was hailed as a "fluent and graceful" orator and a "gallant soldier of the Lost Cause." The focus of General Johnston's talk was on the evils of greed and its destructive power on someone's body, mind, and soul—a not-so-veiled critique of the New South and Gilded Age materialism. The pursuit of wealth, he believed, pervaded entire communities and served as the progenitor of the greatest evil of the age: skepticism. "God did not create you for this," Johnston said. "He had nobler purposes for you than to be a getter and lender of money." Passion for money impaired a person's usefulness and prevented them from reaching their true calling, to be in service to others. Johnston singled out one person in the audience who found his true calling in service to Johnston and other Howard students in the 1840s, Professor Amos Bailey Goodhue. A professor at Howard for over twenty years and interim president during the Civil War, the seventy-one-year-old Goodhue moved to East Lake to live with his daughter, Alice Goodhue Ward, and her husband, William C. Ward. In the fall of 1892, Goodhue rejoined the faculty of Howard College as an unpaid professor of elocution.[30]

When Benjamin Franklin Riley began his three-month-long vigorous canvassing throughout the state, he recognized a difference in prospective students. Riley concluded that the scarcity of money would diminish enrollment for the 1892–93 academic year. Throughout the decade of the 1890s, the financial Panic of 1893, and the debate over the monetary supply (gold vs. silver) fueled the political unrest throughout the country and drove the economy in the South into a deeper ferment. "The outlook," Riley wrote, "became one of discouragement from the beginning." As the fall semester approached, Riley began receiving letter after letter from prospective students and their parents who gave up on coming to college because of poor finances. Many of the young men who arrived on campus in September struggled to pay tuition in a timely manner, so the president made concessions to keep the students from leaving Howard. Riley spent the first weeks of the new academic year filled with anxiety and concern. He never wavered or despaired, he said, but the "ever increasing weight of responsibility," created a burden which grew "heavier and heavier" as the year advanced.[31]

Once again money was short, and the college struggled with debt payments and operating expenses. Riley's burden only increased when David Ingram Purser resigned as financial agent to accept the pastorate of Valence Street Church in New Orleans. That left Riley and the faculty to raise money to meet the college's financial obligations. Riley, however, explained that all fundraising avenues were "practically exhausted," which left the college in another dilemma. "I trust I may be pardoned," he wrote, "for respectfully suggesting" that the Board of Trustees could more successfully raise more money than the president and the faculty. Alumni were also critical of the board's inactivity. J. W. Willis, the valedictorian of 1892, asked: "Where was the enterprise of our board of trustees?" Why did they fail to advertise the college in communities unaware of what Howard offered?[32]

W. C. Ward and the trustees, however, were unamused by these and other criticisms. As "public servants who serve a cause without reward," Ward wrote, they expected criticism. Critics revealed their concern for Howard College. "We ask, however, that criticisms be so guarded as not to injure the college." Some of the recent complaints were unhelpful, Ward added, and if any of the Baptist brethren better know how to "build and operate" a college with no money and deep debt, then the board will "give back into the hands of the convention the trust committed to us." This might be a wise course of action, Ward supposed, to "discharge the old crew and put the institution in the hands of new men." In the end, the board authorized the college to borrow more money to stay afloat and carry forward, with no payments, the debt.[33]

Although Riley was exhausted from his efforts, the stormy present provided few opportunities for him to find rest or time to work on his next book project, a history of Alabama Baptists. Instead, Riley explored other avenues to increase students, money, and prestige. To free him from the heavy burden of recruiting students, Riley proposed that the Alabama Baptists establish academies throughout the state as preparatory schools for both Howard and Judson. This plan, he believed, would provide an ever-increasing number of students enrolling in the two colleges and a steady stream of income. The state convention, however, balked at the idea—arguing that Riley's plan would only spread resources too thin. "The contention was," Riley wrote, "that the colleges needed concentration, while the proposed plan meant dissipation."[34]

As was the case since the Civil War, Howard College still had no endowment to fall back on in difficult financial times. Riley proposed to the trustees either hiring a field agent to solicit funds and recruit students or giving Baptist women the opportunity to raise funds for "tenant houses" to be constructed on the back side of campus. His latter idea reflected the growing presence and power of women within the convention but also revealed his view that women's work should be done in a traditional framework. "Baptist mothers," he wrote, would be interested in contributing to Howard's "patronage." Rent from the "tenant houses" would provide a steady source of income for the endowment and increase the value of the college's property. Riley explained to the Board of Trustees that "any effort made might lead to something better" and at least "stimulate confidence."[35]

Benjamin F. Riley's most ambitious effort was his attempt to forge an alliance with the recently founded University of Chicago. The new Baptist institution already boasted a $600,000 endowment thanks to a donation from tycoon John D. Rockefeller. Although an alliance of Baptist colleges was a frequent topic of discussion in the early 1890s, Chicago president William Rainey Harper proposed a formal arrangement in early 1893. Mitchell Garrett reported that the University of Chicago would "fix the standard of instruction and scholarship" and provide a faculty exchange program, but no financial assistance to Howard or the other affiliated colleges. "This arrangement," Garrett wrote, "was to be something like a standardizing agency." In early May, Riley met with Harper at the annual meeting of the American Baptist Education Society which met concurrently with the Southern Baptist Convention in Nashville. Riley came away from the meeting impressed enough to travel to Chicago to meet again with Harper and to visit the recently opened World's Fair and Columbian Exhibition. Although Riley received no promises of financial assistance from Harper, Garrett wrote, he came away from the meeting "enthusiastic over the prospect of making Howard College an integral part of a great organization of Baptist colleges into which wealthy men, like the Rockefellers, might be expected to pour oceans of money." Riley would submit his proposal at the meeting of the Board of Trustees following graduation.[36]

Twenty-one students graduated in June 1883, the largest group in Howard's history. Leading the way was first-honor graduate (valedictorian) Jasper Fritz Thompson of Bibb County. Born December 7, 1872, near Centreville, some fifty miles south of Birmingham, Thompson went on to earn his law degree from the University of Alabama in 1896. That same year, he was admitted to the bar before Judge Rufus Hardy in eastern Texas. In February of 1897, Thompson returned to Bibb County and began practice at the county seat in Centreville—first in the firm of Ellison & Thompson and then in partnership with 1888 Howard College graduate William W. Lavender.[37]

Thompson was one of two representatives from Bibb County to the Alabama Constitutional Convention of 1901. Thompson's home county was a center for the agrarian uprisings of the 1890s (a Populist candidate had defeated his father in a race for probate judge in 1898), and this likely influenced some of his decisions at the convention on suffrage requirements, election of solicitors and county officers, and various taxation issues. Subsequently, Thompson served in the state legislature in 1903 and, in 1904, voters elected him the circuit solicitor for the Fourth Judicial Circuit. The rambling circuit included Bibb, Wilcox, Perry, Dallas, Greene, and Hale counties, and the new solicitor spent days traveling by horse and buggy throughout Alabama's Black Belt. The *Centreville Press*, at the time, proclaimed that "no man in Alabama" had risen so quickly in the legal profession. A remarkable trial lawyer, Thompson was an "earnest and fluent speaker" and managed each of his cases with "courage, integrity, and wisdom." The paper called him "one of the most progressive and liberal citizens in the county and no worthy cause is ever presented to him and turned away empty handed."[38]

Thompson, a "total abstainer" and Prohibitionist, was as "dry as they come," one journalist concluded, and a "liberal and tolerant companion." During the liquor wars of 1916, Alabama attorney general William Logan Martin asked Thompson to serve as a special prosecutor in one of the most sensational murder trials in Alabama history. The courtroom drama took place in Huntsville, where Dave Overton was on trial for the murder of probate judge W. T. Lawler. William Logan Martin later told colleagues that the Bibb County lawyer, without a single note, gave the "greatest courtroom summation he ever heard" and proved Overton's guilt beyond a reasonable doubt.[39]

In 1922, Thompson was still serving as circuit solicitor when Martin, now in private law practice, asked the forty-nine-year-old attorney to move to Birmingham to establish a new firm—Martin, Thompson, and Turner. Alabama attorney general Harwell G. Davis received Thompson's resignation on Thursday, September 28, 1922—effective on October 1. The Centreville newspaper reported that the new Martin firm was "securing the best talent in all lines that money can buy" and that Thompson regretted leaving "his friends throughout the circuit, but his present business opportunity was such that he considered it best to make the move." For the next decade, Thompson played a pivotal legal role in the expansion of the Alabama Power Company. He also served as one of Howard College's most active alumni in Birmingham.[40]

In June 1933, Alabama governor Benjamin M. Miller appointed Fritz Thompson to fill a vacancy on the circuit court bench in the state's Tenth Judicial Circuit (Jefferson County). Miller and Thompson had been friends for over thirty years, and the pair had worked with Logan Martin on the Dave Overton case in Madison County. "Governor Miller persuaded me to take it against my will," Thompson said at the time. The Birmingham papers gave "hearty approval" to the appointment of a "man of such recognized character." Thompson, one writer believed, possessed outstanding abilities and the "qualities of character and courage" which were essential to the "proper discharge of judicial duties." The next year, Jefferson County voters elected Thompson to the position and, in 1935, he became presiding judge in the district. During the 1930s, Judge Thompson improved judicial efficiency by making out dockets for all the courts in the circuit. When not on the bench, Thompson spent much of his time entertaining "lawyers and laymen who gathered in his office with stories of his court performances."[41]

Following Fritz Thompson's graduation from Howard College in June 1893, the Board of Trustees held their traditional meeting and reappointed all of the faculty, including President Benjamin Franklin Riley. Riley presented the findings of his Chicago visit and recommended that "such action be taken as would secure the bonds of affiliation between the two institutions." The trustees, however, refused to take any action on the proposal that Riley viewed as a matter of utmost importance. Instead, the board referred the matter to the state convention, which would not meet until November.[42]

For five years, Riley worked to save Howard College and place the institution on a stronger footing, both academically and financially. His work, just like that of D. I. Purser, was relentless. During the previous months, all his proposals to stabilize Howard were ignored, rejected, or postponed. And, with the financial crisis deepening in the United States and the debt situation continuing to spiral downward at Howard, Riley most likely believed that there was little more he could accomplish without additional funding and support. During the week following graduation and the board meeting, Riley resigned as president of Howard College and accepted a professorship of English at the University of Georgia in Athens. On June 20, 1893, a Birmingham paper praised Riley for raising the academic status of Howard College. "He took it as a puny infant," the writer believed, "and will leave it a strong man."[43]

Benjamin Franklin Riley was a pivotal figure in the history of Howard College. As a New South booster, Riley was uniquely prepared to guide the school through the difficult transition from the agrarian South to the industrial South. As a scholar, he reinforced the classical curriculum, studied social, economic, and racial dynamics in the state and region, and served as a prominent historian of Alabama Baptists. Rev. B. H. Crumpton believed that no one in Alabama ever "made himself more permanently felt in the social, moral, and political aspects of the state." As Crumpton wrote at the time, Riley "steered the institution safely and yet quietly through a stormy and perilous sea."[44]

17

THE BURDEN OF
HOWARD COLLEGE

The Howard College Board of Trustees looked across Underwood Avenue for the next president, Rev. Arthur Watkins McGaha, pastor of Ruhama Baptist Church. McGaha entered the pulpit at Ruhama just a few weeks after Benjamin F. Riley began his duties as president of the college in 1888. Under his pastorate, Ruhama became the campus church for Howard College with most of the faculty and students joining the congregation. The thirty-year-old pastor was popular with the students and invested much of his time looking after the cadets' spiritual needs. As Washington Bryan Crumpton observed at the time, McGaha's relationship with the cadets gave him an "advantage over any other man" considered by the Board of Trustees. A newspaper in McGaha's home state of Kentucky believed that Howard's new president would be a "blessing to his students" as they grew in "courage, truth, courtesy, and high sense of honor." Just seven years earlier, in 1881, McGaha graduated from Howard College and went on to take additional theological courses at the Southern Baptist Theological Seminary in Louisville, Kentucky. He pastored churches in Kentucky and in North Alabama before accepting the call to Ruhama. When Howard's board approached McGaha with the offer to serve as president, he hesitated to accept the position at an institution with such "difficulties and responsibilities." With great reluctance, however, he accepted the position.[1]

For the next three years, McGaha served as a caretaker president who embraced the classical curriculum and made but one significant change to the intellectual life of Howard College. Beginning in the fall of 1893, the evangelistic-minded McGaha required all students to take two courses on the Bible (Old Testament and New Testament). "No man," McGaha wrote, "can be properly

educated, who was not familiar with the literature of the Bible." In addition, he added, a Baptist college that ignored biblical studies offered no "sufficient reason for its existence." McGaha's addition most likely provided the groundwork for a campus-wide revival in 1894. Rev. L. O. Dawson and the new pastor at Ruhama Baptist, Joshua Hill Foster, preached a series of sermons at the East Lake church that sparked a spiritual awakening which spread throughout the community—especially on Howard's campus. McGaha reported that all the non-religious cadets living in the dormitories, except one, were converted. "The ground was already fallowed," W. C. Ward wrote, "and a great harvest was gathered." Howard, he added, was now the Lord's college.[2]

McGaha's years as president would be filled with Howard College's fruitless struggles against mounting debts. Compounding problems in the fall of 1893, enrollment fell to 151 students, and a combination of hostility and indifference from Alabama Baptists once again plagued the college. At the state convention that fall, former trustee Jesse B. Lovelace of Marion asked all the Howard College boys to stand and be seen. When both "gray-haired brethren" and young men stood, Lovelace said: "Let us resolve that Howard shall not die." The audience responded with a resounding "Amen." Nonetheless, neither the trustees nor the convention made any effort to replace D. I. Purser, and fundraising lagged far behind the previous years. However, the ever-present Lida B. Robertson suggested that the women of Alabama take over the task. This compelled W. C. Ward to offer a resolution to the Alabama Baptist State Convention to entrust the work to Robertson, "who, by pen and deed had shown great zeal on behalf of the college." The convention approved Ward's request but later reconsidered and tabled the resolution—as the delegates recommended that the trustees hire another full-time (male) financial agent and task Lida B. Robertson with fundraising to build a hospital "in connection" to Howard College.[3]

Although the notion of a Howard hospital was never mentioned again by the trustees, twenty of the college's alumni met at the convention and recommended that the trustees hire Rev. Walter Andrew Whittle as the financial agent. Whittle was well-known throughout the country for his vivid lectures

Facing page: One of the oldest churches in Alabama, Ruhama Baptist provided a spiritual home for Howard College's faculty and students from 1887 to 1957. In 1893, Reverend Arthur Watkins McGaha left the pulpit of Ruhama to serve as the eighth president of the institution. (Samford University, Special Collection and University Archives)

on his travels in Jerusalem and throughout the Middle East. A Michigan newspaper described Whittle as having no "superior on the American platform" and
"a wit, a humorist, a mimic, an orator, [and] an actor." The Howard alumni were
so confident that Whittle's effervescent personality (many knew him from his
days as a Howard student) would attract large donations, they decided to raise
enough money to pay the first year of his salary. Alumnus J. M. Thomas encouraged the gathering to "speak at once" and donate money to Howard. "Load me
down," Thomas exhorted, "with your name and money." J. R. Sampey, L. O.
Dawson, and P. T. Hale stepped forward with fifty-dollar contributions each.
Ultimately the plan worked, and Whittle began his solicitations in early 1894.[4]

Yet again, the pleas to save Howard College echoed across the state as Alabama Baptists endured another barrage of persuasive rhetoric, tailored mes-
sages, and attempts to invoke emotional responses through badgering, flattery,
guilt, shame, and humor. Rev. L. O. Dawson hoped to raise enthusiasm for
Whittle's fundraising efforts with several pro-Howard talks around the state.
"We of the South are poor," Dawson said, "but isn't it also true that we have
not yet learned the value of colleges and how to endow them?" In the North,
Christians gave millions to their schools because they saw the need to educate
their sons. The clarion call to "strike now or never" came loud and clear. Like
a college cheer, Dawson belted out: "Hands all round, fellows; hand all round!
You ought to have a deeper interest here than all others. Give to Howard College till you bleed; and out of the ground made right by your blood, will spring
a race of men who will keep your memory in deathless song."[5]

Poor health plagued President A. W. McGaha, and he said little publicly
about the college's finances, preferring to stay close to campus and focus on
the students. His greatest innovation during his tenure was the experiment
with coeducation. During the summer of 1894, the Board of Trustees asked
the Alabama Baptist State Convention to allow women to enroll for classes in
the fall term. To qualify for admission, the women must be prepared to enter
as juniors—a practice in keeping with other institutions. The board expected
that most of the enrollees would come from the neighborhoods adjacent to the
college and thus not adversely impact Judson College. The convention unanimously approved the measure. A few days later, however, the editor of the
Alabama Baptist criticized the endeavor as part of the trendy "Woman Craze"
sweeping through the state and claimed there was no real demand for coeducation. "Without claiming to be a prophet," he wrote, "we predict that, in the

South at least, the time will never come when any considerable number of our young women will attend the male colleges."[6]

Although no women officially enrolled as full-time students at Howard College before 1894, several took classes at both the East Lake and the Marion campuses. Most likely, the first female student was Maria Louisa "Lula" Bailey, whose father, Rev. T. M. Bailey, worked for the state mission board and served as a trustee at Howard College in Marion from 1875 to 1885. Following her graduation from Judson, Lula Bailey took several language classes at Howard. For years, her sister boasted that Lula was the "first woman ever admitted" to the college. In East Lake, according to one account, women may have taken classes as early as 1891, but the scant evidence from the time remains unclear. Regardless, in September 1894, two East Lake residents, Annie May Judge and Alice Eugenia Weatherly, became the first two full-time female students to enroll at Howard College. Judge and Weatherly's appearance on campus appeared to have little impact on the daily life of the male cadets at Howard. (The two women were excluded from participating in the corps.) "We expected that the girls' presence," one cadet wrote at the time, "would put an end to Dr. [Thomas J.] Dill's bountiful flow of laughable anecdotes, that we thought only suitable for us," but the men realized that Dill's stories rolled forth as "freely as ever" but now included an apology.[7]

At the opening ceremonies for the 1894–95 academic year, with Judge and Weatherly in the audience, McGaha announced that the male cadets were now required to purchase and wear "West Point regulation uniforms." These uniforms were "cadet gray," with a coat trimmed in black mohair braid, trousers with a black cloth stripe down both legs, a white high-collared shirt, and white gloves. While some locals praised the "Confederate-style" outfits, West Point "cadet gray" dated to the War of 1812 when the U.S. military faced a shortage of blue cloth. Nonetheless, references to the honored Confederate soldier and the myth of the Lost Cause were once again frequently used as a means of instructing students in faith, morality, and discipline. Speaking at the opening ceremonies, Rev. Phillip Thomas Hale, reminded the cadets to cultivate both their mind and their spiritual character. "Be prayerful," he said, "like Stonewall Jackson" whose prayers before each battle helped him go "fast and strong after the enemy."[8]

The primary adversary that Howard College faced that academic year was debt. On March 6, 1895, the Board of Trustees met to discuss the mortgage payments owed to the Union Trust Company of Philadelphia. W. A. Whittle gave the trustees a sobering report on the financial situation. He announced that he solicited no new subscriptions or collected any money from old subscribers. "Nothing had been accomplished," he said, "that was of benefit to the college." The general view among Alabama Baptists was that giving to Howard or even fulfilling donation subscriptions was a "useless waste of money" as the college teetered on insolvency. W. C. Ward reported that even some of Howard's most loyal supporters rejected the appeals to send money because they believed the "college must fail." Those who refused to pay, Ward added, were defaulters who would be liable if the college went under. "Will not all help tide over the shallows threatening us?" he asked.[9]

In turn, the trustees appointed board members William C. Ward (attorney), James M. Arnold (attorney), Edward Cabiness (attorney), and Eugene F. Enslen (banker) to negotiate an extension of the mortgage debt payments with the Union Trust Company. Following "considerable correspondence" with the company, the group received an extension for payments on $30,000 of the debt for three years, but they required the college to submit payment on the principal and the back interest by April 1—amounting to nearly $10,000. The trustees, however, were unable to pay the amount as the deadline passed. Ward warned the convention that paying no interest was inviting foreclosure, which would ruin the educational interests of Alabama Baptists and result in the loss of decades of work. "If we lost the college," he emphasized, "we lose the promise of these students as a basis for future development."[10]

At graduation in June 1895, Ward set a more optimistic tone for the students and parents—praising the college's successful year, the "high curriculum" of classical traditions, and the "best prospects" for another great year in 1895–96. Samuel James Ansley graduated with first honors. The Lowndes County native was unable to deliver his valedictory address because of a bout with the measles, so he made just a few comments that one observer described as "touching and tender and couched in beautiful language." Following the end of the ceremonies, the trustees informed the faculty that the students' tuition dollars once again failed to cover all the salaries of the faculty. The consistently short pay compelled faculty to look elsewhere for supplemental sources of income or new academic positions. Math Professor A. D. Smith started his own insurance business that grew into a full-time opportunity, and Professor George W. Macon accepted a faculty position in modern languages and biology at Mercer

University in Macon, Georgia. Following Macon's resignation from Howard, a writer for the *Birmingham News* complained that Georgia was not just satisfied with their "invaluable acquisition" of Benjamin F. Riley; they came back for "another invasion" and took "another eminent scholar" away from Alabama.[11]

With Arthur W. McGaha battling a serious illness, Professors Benjamin F. Giles, Albert D. Smith, and Jud Waldrop spent much of the summer of 1895 traveling the state and recruiting students. As classes opened in September, enrollment grew to 175 students, including three new women: Lillian Butler, Estelle Holloway, and Mattie Weldon. That same month, the usually reticent McGaha wrote to the Baptists of Alabama and encouraged the state's brethren to send their sons to Howard (he mentioned nothing of daughters) and there would be "no trouble" in paying the debt for years to come. But even with a 16 percent increase in enrollment in 1895–96, the financial situation only worsened.[12]

At the Alabama Baptist State Convention in November 1895, a bitter and disappointed William C. Ward offered his resignation as president of Howard College's Board of Trustees. Ward explained to the convention that he "bent his back" carrying the college's problems and had borne up under the heavy load the best he could. He chided the denomination for placing Howard's burdens on him and then heaping hot coals of criticisms on him and the college. He was now "bowed down by the weight of responsibility" and would "stay down" until the convention lifted him. Now that he placed the burdens back on the convention, he felt free to speak his mind—blasting the state's Baptist churches for failing to sympathize, contribute, or patronize Howard College. Ward prayed for the college the way he did for his own children but found the labor too great to continue. In response, an imprudent Rev. B. H. Crumpton told Ward that he had "too little faith" and that Howard College was "never in better financial condition." Despite Crumpton's musings, several individuals at the convention donated enough money to meet the interest payments on the debt for one year. Also, the convention asked Ward to reconsider his resignation and once again pick up Howard's burden—which he did.[13]

Just before the April 1, 1896, deadline for the next payment on the college's debt, Ward wrote an open letter to the Baptists of Alabama and made an urgent appeal for money. "I tried to lay down the burden of this college at your convention," he emphasized, "and you refused to accept my resignation." Now they must endure his demands. "You cannot afford," Ward added, to let Howard fail. But they did. Little or no money came, and the deadline passed again. On

April 18, 1896, the Union Trust Company of Philadelphia initiated foreclosure proceedings against Howard College.[14]

Two days later, the first notice of a mortgage sale appeared in the Birmingham newspapers—announcing that Howard had defaulted on the mortgage and the Jefferson County sheriff would sell the property on the courthouse steps to the highest bidder on a cash-only basis on June 22, 1896: "The sale will be made to satisfy the debt, principal and interest, and costs of foreclosure, including attorney's fees." The advertisement ran in the Birmingham papers almost every day for the next eight weeks. "This was extremely embarrassing to Baptists in Alabama," one historian wrote, "and especially to Baptists in Birmingham."[15]

Upon the request of W. C. Ward and the Board of Trustees, the directors of the Alabama Baptist State Convention met on May 29 at Selma to discuss how to save the college from the mortgage sale. If all of the directors attended the meeting, several Howard College supporters were present, including W. C. Cleveland, Eugene F. Enslen, B. D. Gray, and Colonel James T. Murfee. The group addressed a statement to all Baptists and friends of education in Alabama to come to Howard's rescue by organizing fundraising campaigns in churches throughout the state and for subscribers to send the $16,000 in unpaid donations to the college. "This must be done," they emphasized, or the Baptists of Alabama will write the word "failure" in large letters across the great work of Howard College. The meager response to the appeal did little to help Howard's dilemma.[16]

Howard College was not the only Baptist institution in the state struggling with finances during the lingering nationwide economic panic. Across Underwood Avenue, Ruhama hired Rev. William Andrew Hobson as pastor in 1896. Hobson found the church in debt for $5,000 to a Birmingham bank which was negotiating to sell Ruhama to a Black Baptist church. The church responded with "righteous wrath and stern purpose to make any sacrifice to redeem the meeting house." And the congregation did. To make the building unusable for any church services, an army of members moved all the pews and accoutrements from the sanctuary to a building on the Howard College campus—most likely into some of the unused space in the dining hall. As one witness later wrote, the zealous congregation presented an "unwavering front of defense" and defied the "money changers" at the bank to "come and get it." The bank backed down from selling the sanctuary, the pews and furnishings moved back to the sanctuary, and the congregation raised the $5,000 by the end of 1896—at the same time Howard was asking for donations.[17]

Anna "Annie" M. Judge, pictured in the second row above, was the first female graduate of Howard College in 1896. (Samford University, Special Collection and University Archives)

With no additional sources of income, the outlook for the college was grim as the school closed the 1895–96 academic year. At a two-day meeting of the Board of Trustees on June 8 and June 9—during commencement week—William C. Ward submitted his final resignation to the board. In turn, the trustees elected Rev. Phillip Thomas Hale of Southside Baptist Church in Birmingham as its new board president. In addition, Arthur McGaha refused to accept reelection to the presidency of the college, recommending instead that the board "dispense with the office" and abolish the presidency because of the "critical financial condition." Perhaps that was in the minds of the trustees when they appointed Albert Durant Smith as the "Chairman and Treasurer of the Faculty" and not the new president of Howard. At commencement, P. T. Hale wrote at the time, when Smith was announced as the de facto "president of the college, he received a perfect ovation from the students and the entire audience." Also, in one of Arthur McGaha's last acts as president, he presented a diploma to Anna Judge, the first female graduate of Howard College. Nonetheless, earlier that day, the trustees voted to end the experiment with coeducation because of the "lack of suitable arrangements for their accommodation," but those women already enrolled would be allowed to complete their degrees. It would take almost twenty years before the trustees agreed that women should be permanent students at Howard College.[18]

No doubt that Howard's new chairman/president was tasked with stopping the impending foreclosure on the college. At some point, A. D. Smith enlisted his banker friend, Burghard Steiner, to help stop the mortgage sale and assured him that Howard could pay the money if given more time. Steiner, who also served as an agent of the Union Trust Company of Philadelphia, successfully petitioned the company to delay their legal proceedings, and he personally "stood good for satisfaction of the mortgage." While some observers suggested that Smith and Steiner reached an agreement with Union Trust in April or May, most likely it occurred after McGaha resigned and the trustees hired, and empowered, A. D. Smith on June 9—evidenced by the advertisements that continued to run in the Birmingham papers until Saturday, June 20, just two days before the sell date on the courthouse steps.[19]

In Athens, Georgia, former president Benjamin Franklin Riley watched with "apprehensive interest" as the financial crisis deepened. In a letter to the *Alabama Baptist,* Riley wrote that Howard College was "destined to live" because the state's Baptists would refuse to let it suffer and die. "There will be a sufficient number found who will rally about it," he added, and "eventuate in the redemption of the college." Riley believed that the trustees showed wisdom in selecting A. D. Smith to lead Howard because of his vast management experience, masterful attention to details, and outstanding business acumen. Smith, however, would never succeed in ending Howard's burden without the cooperation of the Baptists of Alabama. "There was hard work ahead," Riley wrote, "and much of it."[20]

With W. A. Whittle's failed fundraising efforts, the Board of Trustees turned to two Birmingham ministers to "unburden" Howard College from debt or at least enough to prevent the Union Trust Company from resuming foreclosure proceedings. The two pastors, Baron DeKalb Gray of First Baptist and Phillip Thomas Hale of Southside, took leaves of absence from their pulpits and began rambling about the state, like barkers in a traveling medicine show, selling

Howard College. Throughout the summer and early fall, the preachers—later joined by William Andrew Hobson of Ruhama—raised $8,000 for the college. Most likely, A. D. Smith took the money to Burghard Steiner, who sent it to the Union Trust Company of Philadelphia. The good-faith effort impressed company officials.[21]

Just before the Alabama Baptist State Convention in November 1896, the college received a letter from the trust company's secretary and treasurer, D. Howard Foote, who promised to remit all back interest due on November 1 and deduct $1,000 from the principal. "Thus, the college was saved," Mitchell Garrett wrote, because the trust company saw more profit in waiting than forcing Howard "under the hammer of the sheriff." And, as another historian later explained, the dedicated work of a Jewish banker saved the Baptist Howard College from its second foreclosure.[22]

On campus, the frugal A. D. Smith announced that the college would be administered by stringent business values. "There will be a system and a method for everything and every man," Smith wrote at the time, "and everything and every man must fit into its or his place, like each piece of a complete machine." No doubt the trustees were pleased with Smith's commitment to cost savings. When the board offered Smith the position, it instructed him to accumulate no new debts and tasked him with making the college "self-sustaining." In turn, the new "president" planted a vast garden behind the main building; raised, milked, and butchered cows; hunted wild turkey in the woods beyond campus; cooked meals in the dining hall; and taught mathematics. "I attended to whatever chores there were to be done," Smith said.[23]

Born June 30, 1854, near Marietta, Georgia, Albert Durant Smith graduated from the University of Georgia in 1877 and taught in secondary schools in Georgia until 1881. That year, Colonel James T. Murfee wrote to Patrick H. Mell, chancellor of the university, and asked for his recommendations for a professor of mathematics at Howard College. Mell wrote that Smith was "a first-class mathematician, a first-class man in every respect," and a military expert. "Any institution obtaining his service would gain a prize." After fifteen years on the Howard faculty as a professor of mathematics, Smith was the board's obvious choice to provide leadership for the college and solve the financial crisis.[24]

During the summer of 1896, Smith busied himself making more campus improvements and recruiting students to the "old and honored institution." He attempted to overcome the negative publicity surrounding the debt by selling the virtues of "healthfulness and moral security" in East Lake. Saloons and other "demoralizing agencies" were excluded from the town—leaving a "cultured and religious society" surrounding Howard College. Students were free from wicked temptations and from the distractions of commercialism which brought "unwholesome social excitements." Attending Howard cost $188 per year, which included tuition, room, board, fuel, medical fee, and laundry. Ultimately, through A. D. Smith's efforts, 166 students enrolled for the 1896–97 academic year.[25]

One cadet described Smith as a man with hair as "black as a raven's wing," who "moved with the measured tread of the well-trained military man—truly a noble specimen of manhood." On assuming the "presidency," he explained to the cadets "that there should be a time for each duty, and that each duty should be performed at the proper time." A stern disciplinarian, he mandated that the students adhere to a strict schedule:

Study Hours	6 to 7 a.m.
Breakfast and Recreation	7 to 8:15 a.m.
Chapel Assembly and Prayer	8:15 to 8:30 a.m.
Recitations	8:30 a.m. to 12:30 p.m.
Dinner and Rest	12:30 p.m. to 2 p.m.
Recitations	2 to 4 p.m.
Military Drills	4 to 5 p.m.
Supper and Rest	5 to 7 p.m.
Study in Rooms	7 to 9:30 p.m.
Preparation to Retire	9:30 to 10 p.m.
Bell Taps and Lights Out	10 p.m.

Students were never allowed to leave the "quiet little town of East Lake" except on Saturday mornings from 8 a.m. to 12 p.m. On Sundays, students were required to attend the church services of their choice (either Baptist, Methodist, or Presbyterian) and participate in Sunday schools (if available). When one visitor arrived on campus, he expected to see cadets lined up outside Smith's office, offering excuses to avoid the rigid schedule, but what he found was "nothing but business through the whole day" and everything done in "systematic order."[26]

By April 1897, because of fundraising by the three pastors and the work of the new financial agent, M. M. Wood, the college made another sizable payment

Beginning in 1894, Howard College required male students to wear West Point "regulation uniforms" that were "cadet gray," with a coat trimmed in black mohair braid, trousers with a black cloth stripe down both legs, a white high-collared shirt, and white gloves. (Samford University, Special Collection and University Archives)

on the mortgage and renegotiated the remaining $20,000 at the reduced rate of 5 percent annually for the next five years. Board president P. T. Hale encouraged the convention to help pay off the remaining debt so the college could build an endowment, which stood at $88.36 in late 1897. With the college's financial situation improving (along with the national economy), A. D. Smith stepped aside as both the "president" of Howard and a professor of mathematics—severing his day-to-day ties to the institution after sixteen years of service. Smith did, however, remain active in the college as a trustee and donor until his death in 1943. In total, Albert Durant Smith served the school for sixty-two years and, as he once said, "Howard College has been my life-time hobby."[27]

At the meeting, the trustees reappointed several faculty members: Thomas John Dill in Greek and Latin, Robert Judson Waldrop in mathematics, and Amos Bailey Goodhue in elocution and French. Benjamin Franklin Giles left the college and was replaced in English by Edwin H. Foster. Howard graduate Edgar Poe Hogan replaced Willis Hilliard Payne in chemistry and natural history. The trustees turned to an experienced educator in Birmingham as the next president of the college. Francis Marion Roof was the principal at the local Henley School, where he gained a reputation as an excellent administrator. A Kentucky native, the forty-year-old Roof was hailed in Birmingham papers as a man of "scholastic attainments and high ideals" whose work endeared him to the residents of the Magic City. One observer described Roof as a stoop-shouldered, heavy-built man, nearly six feet tall, with black hair, and the odd habit of speaking out of the corner of his mouth.[28]

Roof was announced as the new president at commencement on June 9. That evening, Roof attended the alumni banquet in the dining room at the Florence Hotel on the corner of Nineteenth Street and Second Avenue North in Birmingham. With 104 men packed into the 96-seat dining room, one attendee described the raucous gathering as a "feast of reason and flow of soul" with unparalleled comradery—making the occasion "as near a venture towards conviviality as the orthodox tenets of the Baptist faith would permit." The engraved menu featured a quote from writer Edward Robert Bulwer-Lytton, who was best known for writing the often ridiculed sentence: "It was a dark and stormy night." But for this occasion, the banquet's planners chose Bulwer-Lytton's quote on *les cuisiniers:*

We may live without poetry, music, and art.
We may live without conscience and live without heart.
We may live without friends; we may live without books.
But civilized man cannot live without cooks.

Below the quote was the menu with appetizers, drinks, entrees, and desserts named after people and organizations associated with Howard College, including Giles's Lobster Croquets, Broiled Spring Chicken on Toast (à la Smith), Cold Smoked Tongue (à la Ward), Chicken Salad (à la Goodhue), Philomathic Ice Cream, and Fancy Franklin Cakes. The drink choices included water, black coffee, and (Willis Hilliard) Payne's Lemonade. Rev. W. A. Hobson of Ruhama Baptist served as the toastmaster for the festivities—leading a non-Baptist newspaper reporter to conclude that the "Payne" in Payne's Lemonade was a "misprint for spikes."[29]

Hobson and other Howard supporters offered scores of toasts and speeches throughout the evening—covering, one observer noted, the entire gambit of knowledge. "There were speeches by lawyers," the newspaper writer emphasized; "speeches by doctors, speeches by professors; speeches by everybody." The "genial influence" of Payne's Lemonade, he assumed, led to "chaste epigrams and *bon mots* . . . as plentiful as the water and kindred drinks which flowed liberally around the festive board." The writer seemed clueless to the fact that he was in a room filled with temperance reformers and devoted teetotalers. Rev. P. T. Hall responded to the first toast, "To the Outlook for the Future." Howard College, he said, "had its night—a dark and gloomy one, full of difficulties— but I think I can safely say the morning cometh." The state's Baptists now had faith in Howard and were offering more love than in years past. And the toasts continued for the alumni, graduates, college days, the new woman, the legal profession, and on and on. Responding to the toast, "Howard College on the Bench," Judge William Washington Wilkerson Jr., son of Howard's former trustee, praised the work of Professor Thomas J. Dill, who showed "a thousand men the way to honor and the nobility of true manhood." Howard's new president, Frank M. Roof, received thunderous applause when he responded to the toast, "Howard College in Its Relation to Birmingham." Roof made a "thoughtful speech," the newspaper writer noted, given the "weight" of his new position. After the last toast and speech were given, "Reverend Toastmaster" Hobson closed the banquet. "Gentleman," he said, "I wish you good morning."[30]

As Frank Roof entered his first academic year as president, he made few changes to the content of the classical curriculum, but he did add a pedagogy course to meet the needs of Howard students entering the teaching profession. Roof explained that Howard was unable to fill all the requests from schools needing teachers. Trained teachers, he wrote, were "always in demand at good salaries." With Roof's connections in the Birmingham public schools, he arranged for students to observe the work of teachers. In addition, the new president placed more of an emphasis on physical education and support for fledgling athletic teams in track, baseball, football, and most recently, basketball. He also adopted several new textbooks in efforts to make the curriculum more "progressive and interesting."[31]

CONCLUSION
Laurel Wreaths of Victory

In June 1898, Rev. P. T. Hale stepped down as president of the Board of Trustees upon accepting the pastorate of Calvary Baptist Church in Roanoke, Virginia. Hale's fundraising partner, Rev. Baron D. Gray of First Baptist Church, was elected his successor. By the fall, Gray, Frank M. Roof, A. D. Smith, E. F. Enslen, and other board members met to discuss paying off Howard's debt by asking the over fifty Baptist associations in the state to pay the $20,000 in bonded debt and $13,612 in floating debt. At the Alabama Baptist State Convention, Gray announced that the board was convinced that the "entire indebtedness" of Howard must be paid off as soon as possible. He set a goal to see the college debt free within two years, and the convention delegates agreed to support the effort.[1]

In January 1899, the First Baptist Church of Birmingham agreed to allow Gray a leave of absence to raise funds to settle Howard's debt. Gray also elicited the help of the pastor of Southside Baptist, Augustus Cleveland Davidson, to assist in the challenging drive. This fundraising campaign, however, was different. With the economy growing once again and many churches eliminating their own debt, more money was available to give to Howard College. Gray and Davidson embarked upon their campaign with the zeal and determination of their predecessor, David I. Purser (who died in 1897 during a yellow fever epidemic in New Orleans), and with the help of other Baptist pastors, Howard alumni, and college supporters. Throughout 1899, the money flowed in—some small donations and some large. The Baptists of Tuskegee gave $60; those in Mobile donated $3,000, while members of First Baptist Church of Montgomery provided $4,000. Several individuals also contributed sizable sums, including $1,000 from Martha Matilda Tyson, the mother of Alabama Supreme Court Justice John R. Tyson, an 1877 Howard graduate; and cotton gin owner Dorsey L. Lewis gave $6,000.[2]

In early June, Rev. W. B. Crumpton told the congregation at First Baptist Church of Birmingham that Gray-Davidson raised so much money that Howard's debt was down to $6,000. At commencement on June 14, twelve cadets graduated, including Elred M. Stewart, who earned first honors. Eventually, all twelve would enter middle-class professions: three doctors, three pastors, a postmaster, a clerk, a salesman, a merchant, a grocer, and a teacher. But their accomplishments while students at Howard College were overshadowed that day when the president of the Board of Trustees, Baron Gray, announced that only $1,000 of Howard's burdensome debt remained and that he expected the remaining amount would be "quickly wiped out."[3]

At the end of the month, the Union Trust Company returned the bonds from Philadelphia and newspapers reported that a Howard official would sign a check in a few days to "make Howard College debt free." By July, the Steiner brothers wrote Baron Gray a letter recognizing his "enormous labors" in paying off the debt of First Baptist Church and raising the money to pay off the college's debt. "We think you are entitled to a vacation and rest," they added, offering Gray an all-expense-paid "first-class passage on a first-class steamer" to Europe and back. Gray accepted the "thoughtful and generous" offer to recognize his "excessive labor."[4]

Two weeks later, at 1 p.m. on Friday, July 14, Gray, A. C. Davidson, W. A. Hobson, Dorsey L. Lewis, Dr. C. C. Jones, W. B. Crumpton, Robert Jemison, and Burghard Steiner gathered in the offices at the Steiner Brothers Bank to "eliminate and annihilate" the debts of Howard College. The gathering deserved, a writer noted at the time, the "laurel wreaths of victory" to be placed upon their heads. The debt was now "wiped out," and a celebratory "love feast" by the Baptists of Alabama would mark the occasion. "It ought to rain hard," a *Birmingham News* reporter emphasized, "to cool the atmosphere and flood Alabama" with proof that "immersion was not only right, but at hand."[5]

On Sunday, July 16, W. A. Hobson stood in the pulpit of Ruhama Baptist and offered a sermon from Psalms 112:6: "There ariseth light in the darkness." The minister said that "light and darkness" were "symbols of moral conditions" and that only light could dispel the darkness. The Baptists of Alabama lived through a dark time as the millstone of debt hung around the neck of Howard College for decades. "Darker and darker grew the night," he said, until even the confident "lost heart" and gave up in despair. Quoting Isaiah, he asked, "Watchmen, what of the night?" The question rang out from the darkness, but to the watchmen standing in the tower, dawn never seemed to rise. But a new light arose from the dark, and on July 14, "every dollar" of the college's debt was paid and, like the veil in the tabernacle, the "bonds and mortgages were rent in twain from top to bottom." Alabama Baptists were now free of debt and here to stay. "Let country and hamlet and city ring out the glad refrain." Now "freed from the fetters of debt," Howard College was moving into a new period of success with unity, fraternity, confidence, and cooperation.[6]

Although problems remained, the end of the century proved a major turning point in the history of Howard College. The stormy winds of debt that had enveloped the college for six decades finally eased—leading to a sustained period of unprecedented growth and expansion. When Frank M. Roof resigned in 1902, the college lured experienced educator Andrew Phillip Montague away from the presidency of Furman—an older and more prestigious institution. A "literary man" and scholar of Cicero, Montague reinforced the commitment to the classical curriculum while proving to be an excellent fundraiser and student recruiter. "Dr. Andrew Philip Montague," Mitchell Garrett wrote, "was a man of scholarship, energy and personality. With his *entrée en scène,* Howard College entered upon a distinctly new era."[7]

Perhaps no one since Samuel Sterling Sherman and James H. DeVotie understood the mission and purpose of Howard College better than the outsider Montague. The founders established the college, he wrote, to provide the state of Alabama with better-trained ministers. "An ignorant preacher," Montague wrote, "cannot guide an uneducated people." But the founders were thoughtful and "far-seeing" individuals who knew that preachers needed to find educated laypeople occupying their church pews. Howard, he added, possessed a much wider educational breadth than some people understood. The college's purpose was to educate everyone—preacher and layperson alike—to provide a foundation upon which "lives might be built, whose influences would avail for better homes, larger civic righteousness, and broader more progressive service" in the church.[8]

Howard was founded, Montague emphasized, to teach others that "material things" needed the "guidance of the mind," if civilization was to survive. And the mind must "yield obedience to the spiritual," if humanity was to "reach its best" and "look above the ways of time to eternity with God." The college's mission was to show, in educating people, what education was: "the development of the physical, mental, and spiritual faculties" to "make the world better and brighter" and to serve others and to serve God. To illustrate his point, Montague turned to a classical example. In *The Aeneid,* Virgil wrote that Aeneas, who was "storm-tossed and at last cast upon the shores of Africa," stood with Achates below the walls of Carthage and saw sculptured the "embattled hosts of Troy and Greece," and the "wreck of Trojan hope" and the "downfall of Trojan power." Stirred by memory and sorrow, Aeneas cried, "What land, O Achates, what place in all the world was not full of the story of our misfortunes?"[9]

Now was the time, Montague supposed, for Baptists of the South to make a "nobler cry" and tell the stories of "Baptist struggles" and triumphs. In Alabama, Baptists should tell of the "toils and triumphs" of "our grand old college" and the "large and splendid" influence the institution played—in both Marion and Birmingham—in the lives of so many.[10]

EPILOGUE

In September 1919, Howard College installed Charles Bray Williams as the institution's thirteenth president. In the wake of the Great War and a lingering global epidemic, the theme of the new president's inauguration ceremony was a "New Era in Education." Throughout his address, Williams spoke of his grand vision of a new Howard College with a modern campus, expanded programs, and a fat endowment to pay for it all. Also speaking that day were college and university presidents from throughout the state who were invited to offer their perspectives on the future of Howard College. Before the large crowd gathered in the auditorium on the East Lake campus, each speaker, one by one, focused more on the college's past than on the imagined future—encouraging Charles Bray Williams to move guardedly into the new era and not leave behind the idea and mission of Howard College.[1]

University of Alabama president George Denney argued that, as a Christian school, Howard College stood "distinctly and distinctively" for an education that subordinated the accumulation of wealth to virtue, faith, and moral character. This was especially needed in an era when so many people regarded brains as "mere merchandise" and educational institutions as "mere mills to coin them into money." Vocational training was needed, Denny added, to allow people to perform specific tasks, but Howard College educated young men and women who were "bigger than any task" and trained in "sober discipline, moral efficiency, and catholic vision." If Howard kept the faith of its founders and its Christian intellectual traditions, he said, then the institution would have "greater ultimate value to humanity" than if the college acquired "vast riches" and betrayed its core values. Howard must continue to address the souls of young men and women, give them an opportunity to grow, teach them that life is more than material goods and the accumulation of wealth, convince them that a brilliant mind works in harmony with virtue and morality, and persuade them that God serves as the beginning and the end of correct thinking and living. These were the "real and abiding principles" of an educational philosophy relevant for any era. Denny concluded with a boisterous *"Sicut patribus, sit deus nobis!"* [God be with us, as he was with our fathers!][2]

President Mifflin Wyatt Swartz of the Women's College of Alabama (later Huntington College) agreed that the "time honored and time proven" Christian liberal arts curriculum provided Howard students with a "broad, clear, vigorous, and active" intellect that prepared them for any calling. Vocational and practical training, however, was secondary to the central goal of higher education: to be "liberally educated" and not vocationally trained. Students did not come to Howard College to learn how to "sharpen a saw," or other utilitarian tasks, but to become useful and enlightened citizens who exerted a "wholesome influence upon all." At Howard College, education offered no specialized training in specific tasks but produced disciplined minds with "sound and accurate judgement" and the talent to succeed in any job.[3]

Birmingham-Southern College president Cullen Coleman Daniels, a one-time Howard student, regretted that many parents sent their children to college to "learn to make money," which sacrificed everything "along the pathway of life" that stood in the way of achieving that goal. Echoing the words of writer and poet John Milton, Daniels believed that the "end of learning" for students was knowing God with such depth that it brought them closer to possessing a soul of "true virtue." Reflecting his intellectual and theological predisposition toward romanticism and free will, Daniels argued that character was created in the "moral realm (the realm of will)" and that a disciplined will was the primary "architect of character." Although Daniels never mentioned his name, this was the type of character and enlightened citizenry embodied in John Howard.[4]

After his inauguration in 1919, Charles Bray Williams charged forward in creating a "Greater Howard" but was soon met such recalcitrant opposition that he resigned in less than two years. It was clear in the decade that followed that the college's ties to John Howard were all but lost. Alumnus, professor, and historian Mitchell Garrett discovered only the "tradition," and no documentation, that the institution was named after "probably Baptist" John Howard—that possibility mentioned in a brief footnote. After Garrett left Howard College, religious-education professor James H. Chapman spent the next two decades searching for evidence that connected the institution to John Howard. He found it in January 1946. Reuben E. E. Harkness, president of the American Baptist Historical Society, wrote a letter to Chapman that began with the salutation "EUREKA!" What followed was the documentation that linked Howard College to John Howard. He pointed to the March 1842 edition of the *Baptist Memorial and Monthly Chronicle* announcing that the college established in Marion, Alabama, was named in honor of the "distinguished philanthropist" John Howard. "I am happy to have discovered this," Harkness wrote.[5]

While the institution rediscovered the connection with John Howard, the prison reformer, they never reconnected Howard's faith, benevolence, virtue, and intellect to the identity and mission of the college. They neglected to understand that it was less about what John Howard *did* and much more about who he *was* as a person and an enlightened Christian. Over the next few years, the faculty held fast to the Christian mission and liberal arts traditions, but continued professionalization, vocational training, progressive philosophies, societal upheaval, and secular influences further loosened the connection with John Howard and the idea of Howard College.

In 1957, Howard College moved from its decaying "New South" college grounds in East Lake to a new campus in the suburbs—far away from the rising economic and racial tensions in Birmingham. With increased room for physical and programmatic growth, Howard officials expanded course offerings, reorganized professional programs, and, in 1961, purchased a law school from Cumberland University in Lebanon, Tennessee, and moved it to campus. That same year, Howard president Leslie Wright announced a $10 million "expansion campaign" to construct eighteen new buildings on campus by the end of the decade. With this unprecedented growth in resources, professional programs, and students, the president also pronounced that Howard was no longer a liberal arts college.[6]

When colleges separate from their liberal arts traditions, they often lose their unity, focus, and missional identity. Quite often these institutions reduce the common liberal arts curriculum—based on the liberating ideas needed for free citizens—into a random collection of general education classes with no unifying purpose other than their utilitarian value to a student's vocational training. As one writer suggested, a liberating education was defined by its aims rather than its content and methods. A narrow utilitarian education was vocational training, but if students sought to develop their minds in the pursuit of truth, then all knowledge, as Aristotle wrote, contained "liberating potential." In other words, if students studied to gain employment, they sought vocational training, but if students studied to gain knowledge, they received a liberating education.[7]

At most schools, the traditional liberating arts sustained and strengthened an institution's ties with the past and served as the guardian of the Christian mission. Although Wright believed that Howard had outgrown its liberal arts traditions, neither he nor the board articulated what unifying theme would take its place. Institutions that separated the liberal arts from the Christian mission were left without a clearly defined or easily articulated organizing principle that allowed others to reimagine the community's identity and mission. Over time, new hires who supported liberal arts concepts but found evangelicalism and intellectualism incompatible replaced the missional ambiguity with an ill-defined, desacralizing view that minimized and marginalized Christianity in favor of their own secular perspectives.[8]

Leslie Wright and the board further separated the liberal arts from the Christian identity and educational goals of the institution during the 1964–65 academic year by suggesting that Howard College change its name and attain university status. The impetus behind the name change came during a meeting of the board's executive committee on September 3, 1964. The members gathered, in part, to discuss ways that Howard College could avoid compliance with the Civil Rights Act of 1964—legislation that prohibited racial discrimination in public accommodations and federally funded programs. If the college rejected all federal funding, they supposed, then Howard College could avoid integration. Near the end of the meeting, board chairman Frank Park Samford expressed his displeasure over the continued confusion between the all-white Howard College in Birmingham and the all-Black Howard University of Washington, DC. "Some thought should be given," Samford said, to changing the name of the institution. Given Frank P. Samford's staunch support of segregation, race appeared to be one of the primary motivating factors in renaming the institution. A committee was formed to study the possibility of changing the college's name.[9]

In May 1965, the committee recommended that Howard College become a university and that the name be changed to either Howard-Samford University or Samford University. With little fanfare and minimal discussion, the trustees voted unanimously in favor of Samford University in honor of both Frank P. Samford and the Samford family's contributions to Alabama. A wealthy insurance mogul, Frank Park Samford served as chairman and president of the Howard College Board of Trustees for a quarter-century and was the institution's most generous benefactor. Stalwarts in Alabama politics for generations, the Samfords were elite, Bourbon-class Democrats with an affinity for oration and fervent support for the state's status quo. Frank P. Samford's great-grandfather was an outspoken planter-class secessionist who made two unsuccessful runs for governor in the 1850s; his grandfather served as a governor when the 1901 constitutional convention was called, and his father was a delegate to that convention, which ratified the Alabama Constitution of 1901—imposing a regressive tax system and disenfranchising most Black and many poor white voters in the state.[10]

President Leslie Wright was tasked with convincing both skeptical alumni and Alabama Baptists that the name change was justified and necessary. While speaking across the state, Wright insisted that the John Howard name meant nothing to the institution. Howard never visited the United States, donated no money to the school, and in general did nothing for the college that bore his name. If this was not enough justification to strike his name from the institution, Wright proclaimed, then the fact that Howard was "not even a Baptist" was the unpardonable sin. The president seemed uninformed of who John Howard was, how he embodied the college's founding principles, that the historical record suggested he was Baptist, and that he died fifty years before the founding of Howard College. The president's hyperbolic rhetoric attracted the attention of the media around the state, and newspapers promoted Wright's narrative about John Howard. The *Montgomery Advertiser* reported that the college was named after a "prison reformer" who never made a financial contribution of "any sort" to the school. "He just happened to be famous at the time," the writer concluded, "and the Baptists needed a name."[11]

Despite Leslie Wright's vigorous public relations campaign to "sell" the new name, many Alabama Baptists and Howard College alumni opposed the change. The Howard name, one alumnus wrote, "means so much to Alabama Baptists" and to the work of Christ "around the globe." The publicity over the name change, another former student argued, gave the impression that friends, alumni, and pastors throughout the state supported the proposal. "Our findings," Rev. Robert G. Hood wrote, indicated that many of this group opposed changing the name of the "revered institution." For almost 125 years, Howard College stood as a "lighthouse to the Christian faith" by training leaders who "carried her banner to the four corners of the earth." To change the name, he emphasized, would destroy both the institution's identity and the great work done by those leaders. The "priceless" Howard name was "endeared in the hearts and minds of our people," and neither money nor publicity would ever "compensate for its loss." Changing the name, he added, would also break the college's ties with its "glorious past." Leslie Wright, however, dismissed the opposition as the work of rural Alabama Baptists with little understanding of higher education. The vote at the Alabama Baptist State Convention, however, was surprisingly close—as delegates approved the name change 593 to 512.[12]

During the nineteenth century, Howard College struggled with the deep tensions between those Alabama Baptists who believed that the mission of the institution was to provide a classical education for the whole person and those who wanted the college to offer only theological and vocational training for would-be preachers. While the stormy financial winds tossed the institution to and fro for decades, in the end the liberal arts forces won the argument, and the school retained its missional identity rooted in virtue, benevolence, intellect, and faith. Even through rebellion, Reconstruction, "Redemption," and relocation, the educational mission, Christian identity, and curricular focus changed little at the college.

In the twentieth century, the institution lost most connections to John Howard and its past. The college's historical amnesia coincided with changes in higher education as most schools moved away from Common Sense philosophy to more secular ideas. By the time faculty members began pondering the forgotten origins of the name "Howard College," the institution was increasingly embracing professionalization. Although faculty rediscovered John Howard, administrators came to see little value in the name or idea behind Howard College. President Leslie Wright summed up the unimportance of the institution's historical identity by asking the simple question: "What did John Howard ever do for Howard College?"[13]

In short, John Howard's life was intrinsically bound with the identity of the college that once bore his name. Wright's pronouncement that the school was no longer a liberal arts college, combined with an improvident name change, symbolically shifted Howard's focus from creating enlightened Christian citizens to training money-focused elites in a Christian environment. While John Howard embodied the former, Frank Park Samford symbolized the latter. "We believe," one alumnus wrote Leslie Wright, that it is unfitting to "name an institution after a living individual. Only time can prove the abiding worth of a man."[14]

NOTES

INTRODUCTION: USEFUL AND ENLIGHTENED CHRISTIAN CITIZENS

1. "A Narrative of the Revival of Religion, in the County of Oneida: Particularly in the Bounds of the Presbytery of Oneida, in the Year 1826" (Utica, NY: Hastings & Tracy, 1826), 3–5, 24; James H. DeVotie, "Memoirs," vol. 1:13–28, Special Collection, Samford University Library, Birmingham (hereafter referred to as SUSC); Chris Peters, "James H. DeVotie, Leading the Transformation and Expansion of Baptists in Alabama and Georgia: 1830–1890" PhD diss., University of Alabama, 2014, 23–30.

2. DeVotie, "Memoirs," vol. 1: 13–28.

3. DeVotie, "Memoirs," vol. 1: 13–28; Peters, "James H. DeVotie," 23–30; David W. Bebbington, *Baptists Through the Centuries: A History of a Global People* (Waco, TX: Baylor University Press, 2010), 84; David Bebbington, *Victorian Religious Revivals: Culture and Piety in Local and Global Contexts* (New York: Oxford University Press, 2012), 1–3; George Marsden, *The Evangelical Mind and the New School Presbyterian Experience: A Case Study of Thought and Theology in Nineteenth-Century America* (New Haven, CT: Yale University Press, 1970), 2–4; Perry Miller, *The Life of the Mind in America, from the Revolution to the Civil War* (New York: Harcourt, Brace & World, 1965), 3–9; George Marsden, *Religion and American Culture* (New York: Harcourt, Brace, Jovanovich, 1990), 48–49; Alvin Reid, *Introduction to Evangelism* (Nashville: Broadman & Holman, 1998), 72–73.

4. "Narrative of the Revival," 3–5; DeVotie, "Memoirs," vol. 1: 13–28; Peters, "James H. DeVotie," 23–30.

5. Charles G. Finney, *The Memoirs of Charles G. Finney: Written by Himself* (New York: Fleming H. Revel Co., 1876), 36, 46, 112, 116, 127, 175, 199, 222, 229, 310; Samuel Boykin, *History of the Baptist Denomination in Georgia: With Biographical Compendium and Portrait Gallery of Baptist Ministers and Other Georgia Baptists* (Atlanta: Jas. P. Harrison & Co., 1881), 604–6; Timothy James Lockley, *Lines in the Sand: Race and Class in Lowcountry Georgia, 1750–1860* (Athens: University of Georgia Press, 2001), 229n46; Jesse Harrison Campbell, *Georgia Baptists: Historical and Biographical* (Macon, GA: G. W. Burke & Co., 1874), 326–33; DeVotie, "Memoirs," vol. 1: 13–28; Peters, "James H. DeVotie," 23–30.

6. DeVotie, "Memoirs," vol. 1: 13–28; Peters, "James H. DeVotie," 23–30.

7. Lee N. Allen, *The First 150 Years: Montgomery First Baptist Church, 1829–1979* (Montgomery, AL: First Baptist Church, 1979), 20–21; Hosea Holcombe, *A History of the Rise and Progress of the Baptists in Alabama . . .* (Philadelphia: King and Baird Printers, 1840), 45–46; *South Western Baptist*, September 16, 1853; Peters, "James H. DeVotie," 23–30.

8. Luther Quentin Porch, *History of the First Baptist Church, Tuscaloosa, Alabama* (Tuscaloosa: Drake Printers, 1968), 15–19; R. L. Guffin, *A Lasting Legacy: First Baptist Church, Tuscaloosa Alabama, 1818–2008* (Tuscaloosa: First Baptist Church, 2008), 3–4; A. James Fuller, *Chaplain to the Confederacy: Basil Manly and Baptist Life in the Old South* (Baton Rouge: Louisiana State University Press, 2000), 208–9.

9. DeVotie, "Memoirs," vol. 1: 13–28.

10. Elton Trueblood, *The Idea of a College* (New York: Harper & Brothers, 1959), 8; Donald G. Tewksbury, *The Founding of American Colleges and Universities before the Civil War, with Particular Reference to the Religious Influences Bearing upon the College Movement* (New York: Teachers College, Columbia University, 1932), 1–4; Page Smith, *Killing the Spirit: Higher Education in America* (New York: Penguin Books, 1991), 39.

11. Yale University, "Yale University. University Catalogue, 1835" (1835). elischolar.library.yale.edu/yale_catalogue/21; Middlebury College, "Middlebury College Catalogue, 1837" (1837). jstor.org/stable/community.28478362; Gregory Clark, "Timothy Dwight's Moral Rhetoric at Yale College, 1795–1817," *Rhetorica* 5, no. 2 (1987): 151–54; Edward Farwell Hayward, *Lyman Beecher* (Boston: Pilgrim Press, 1904), 11; Heman Humphrey, *Revival: Sketches and Manual in Two Parts* (New York: American Tract Society, 1859), 198.

12. Samuel Sterling Sherman, *Autobiography of Samuel Sterling Sherman, 1815–1910* (Chicago: M. A. Donohue & Co., 1910), 20.

13. Randolph Roth, "Can Faith Change the World? Religion and Society in Vermont's Age of Reform." *Vermont History* 69, Supplement (Winter 2001): 7–18; Joshua Bates, "Revivals of Religion in Middlebury College," *Journal of the American Education Society* 12, no. 3 (February 1840): 49–67.

14. Marsden, *The Evangelical Mind*, 83; Smith, *Killing the Spirit*, 39.

15. Alexander Broadie, *A History of Scottish Philosophy* (Edinburgh: Edinburgh University Press, 2009), 236–323; Mark Noll, *America's God: From Jonathan Edwards to Abraham Lincoln* (Oxford, UK: Oxford University Press, 2002), 220.

16. Joseph Esmond Riddle, *A Complete English-Latin Dictionary: For Use of Colleges and Schools* (London: Longman, Ord, Brown et al., 1838), 16, 136, 223; Michael Lind, "Why the Liberal Arts Still Matter," *Wilson Quarterly* 30, no. 4 (Autumn 2006): 54.

17. George Marsden, *The Soul of the American University: From Protestant Establishment to Established Nonbelief* (Oxford, UK: Oxford University Press, 1994), 81–82; Samuel Sterling Sherman, *The Bible a Classic: A Baccalaureate Address* (Tuskaloosa, AL: M. D. J. Slade, 1850), 3; Melvin I. Urofsky, "Reforms and Response: The Yale Report of 1828," *History of Education Quarterly* 5, no. 1 (March 1965): 59, 64–65.

18. Sherman, *The Bible a Classic*, 4, 5, 20, 25.

19. Bill J. Leonard, *Baptist Ways: A History* (Valley Forge, PA: Judson Press, 2003), 170; David B. Potts, "American Colleges in the Nineteenth Century: From Localism to Denominationalism," *History of Education Quarterly* 11, no. 4 (Winter 1971): 366–67; Natalie A. Naylor, "The Ante-Bellum College Movement: A Reappraisal of Tewksbury's *Founding of American Colleges and Universities*," *History of Education Quarterly* 13, no. 3 (Autumn 1973): 269–70.

20. Potts, "American Colleges," 367.

21. Miller, *The Life of the Mind*, 95.

22. Lynn R. Buzzard, "A Christian Law School: Images and Vision," *Marquette Law Review* 78, no. 2 (1995): 267–82.

23. James Axtell, *The Making of Princeton University: From Woodrow Wilson to the Present* (Princeton, NJ: Princeton University Press, 2006), xiii.

1. *DUM VIVIMUS, VIVAMUS*

1. Samuel A. Townes and Lee N. Allen, *The History of Marion, Alabama* (Birmingham: A. H. Cather Publishing Co., 1985), 25–29; *Marion Times-Standard*, February 12, 19, 26; March 5, 12, 19; April 23, 1909; William Garrott Brown, "Marion," in *Northern Alabama: Historical and Biographical* (Birmingham: Smith & Deland, 1888), 701–2; W. Stuart Harris, "Rowdyism, Public Drunkenness, and Bloody Encounters in Early Perry County," *Alabama Review* 33, no. 1 (January 1980): 17.

2. Townes and Allen, *History of Marion*, 5–9; *Marion Times-Standard*, February 26, 1909; Harris, "Rowdyism," 18.

3. *Marion Standard*, February 19, 1909; Brown, "Marion," 701–2.

4. *Marion Standard*, February 19, 1909.

5. Ted Ownby, *Subduing Satan: Religion, Recreation, and Manhood in the Rural South, 1865–1920* (Chapel Hill: University of North Carolina Press, 1990), 13, 40; Brown, "Marion," 702; *quotes* from *Marion Standard*, March 19, 1909.

6. *Marion Standard*, April 9, 1909; W. J. Cash, *The Mind of the South* (1941; New York: Vintage Books, 1991), 50; *Marion Times-Standard*, November 16, 1930.

7. Townes and Allen, *History of Marion*, 26–28; Harris, "Rowdyism," 18; W. Stuart Harris, *Perry County Heritage* (Marion, AL: Perry County Historical and Preservation Society, 1991), 57–58.

8. Samuel A. Townes to George F. Townes, Greenville, SC, February 20, 1837, Townes Family Papers, 1784–1967, University of South Carolina, Columbia.

9. *Marion Standard*, March 19, 1909; Brown, "Marion," 702.

10. *Marion Standard*, April 9, 1909; Thomas Perkins Abernethy, *The Formative Period in Alabama, 1815–1828* (Tuscaloosa: University of Alabama Press, 1990), 57–58; quotes from the *Alabama Mercury* rpt. in *Free Selma Press*, July 23, 1836.

11. Daniel R. Hundley, *Social Relations in our Southern States* (1860; Baton Rouge: Louisiana State University Press, 1979), 139–46; *Marion Standard*, April 9, 1909; William Garrott Brown, *A History of Alabama* (New York: University Publishing Co., 1900), 178.

12. Ownby, *Subduing Satan*, 1.

13. Wayne Flynt, *Alabama Baptists: Southern Baptists in the Heart of Dixie* (Tuscaloosa: University of Alabama Press, 1998), 49; *Marion Standard*, June 10, 1885.

14. Alabama Baptist State Convention Annual Report, 1837, SUSC.

15. "Rules of Decorum," Siloam Baptist Church Records, SUSC; Flynt, *Alabama Baptists*, 36.

16. Robert Elder, *The Sacred Mirror: Evangelicalism, Honor, and Identity in the Deep South, 1790–1860* (Chapel Hill: University of North Carolina Press, 2016), 45–46.

17. Alabama Baptist State Convention Annual Report, 1835.

18. Samuel Henderson, "Our Worthy Dead: Rev. Daniel P. Bestor, D.D.; Sketch of a Pioneer Baptist Preacher of Alabama," archive.org/details/ourworthydeadrevoohend.

19. Mitchell Garrett, "Sixty Years of Howard College," *Howard College Bulletin* 85, no. 4 (October 1927): 7; Flynt, *Alabama Baptists*, 55.

20. William Warren Rogers et al., *Alabama: The History of a Deep South State* (Tuscaloosa: University of Alabama Press, 1994), 120; Lori Glover, *Southern Sons: Becoming Men in the New Nation* (Baltimore: Johns Hopkins University Press, 2007), 64–82.

21. Phillip Henry Gosse in Rogers et al., *Alabama*, 118.

22. *Marion Standard*, April 2, 1909.

23. Garrett, "Sixty Years of Howard College," 7.

24. Ibid., 9–12; Flynt, *Alabama Baptists*, 56; Dan Frost, *Thinking Confederates: Academia and the Idea of Progress in the New South* (Knoxville: University of Tennessee Press, 2000), 7–8.

25. Garrett, "Sixty Years of Howard College," 13.

26. Ibid., 10–15; Flynt, *Alabama Baptists*, 56; Benjamin Franklin Riley, *History of the Baptists of Alabama: From the Time of Their First Occupation of Alabama in 1808 until 1894* (Birmingham: Roberts & Son, 1895), 68; Chriss H. Doss, "The Original Fifteen Trustees of Howard College," *Alabama Baptist Historian* 28, no. 2 (July 1992): 4; Harris, *Perry County Heritage*, 97; Frost, *Thinking Confederates*, 8.

27. Townes and Allen, *History of Marion*, 35–43; *Sixth Census of the United States, 1840*, Perry, Alabama, roll 11, p. 257, National Archives, Washington, DC; Doss, "Original Fifteen Trustees," 3.

28. Harris, *Perry County Heritage*, 65; Riley, *History of the Baptists of Alabama*, 71; Flynt, *Alabama Baptists*, 58.

29. Flynt, *Alabama Baptists*, 56–58; Harris, *Perry County Heritage*, 65–66; *Sixth Census of the United States, 1840*, Record Group 29; *Marion Times-Standard*, March 12, 1909.

30. Flynt, *Alabama Baptists*, 58; Harris, *Perry County Heritage*, 66–67; Riley, *History of the Baptists of Alabama*, 70–72; Brown, "Marion," 703; Washington Bryan Crumpton, *A Book of Memories, 1842–1920* (Montgomery: Baptist Mission Board, 1921), 176–77.

2. HOWARD ENGLISH AND CLASSICAL SCHOOL

1. DeVotie, "Memoirs," vol. 1: 55–77; Garrett, "Sixty Years of Howard College," 18–19; Flynt, *Alabama Baptists*, 54–60.

2. Alabama Baptist State Convention Annual Report, 1841; Garrett, "Sixty Years of Howard College," 19–20.

3. Doss, "Original Fifteen Trustees," 3–36.

4. DeVotie, "Memoirs," vol. 1: 76–77; *South Western Baptist*, June 10, 1853.

5. Edmund Burke, *The Works of the Right Honourable Edmund Burke* (London: John H. Nimmo, 1887), vol. 2: 387–88; Samuel Stennett, *A Sermon Occasioned by the Decease of John Howard, Esq* (London: Printed for T. Cadell [et al.], 1790 [*sic*]), 30, 33. Gertrude Himmelfarb, *The Roads to Modernity: The British, French, and American Enlightenments* (New York: Vintage, 2005), 33, 73, 134.

6. *Boston Recorder*, July 19, 1834; *Alabama Baptist*, January 2, 1850; John Aikin, *A View of the Character, and Public Services of the Late John Howard* (London: Printed for J. Johnson, 1792), 208.

7. John G. Deal, "Middle Class Benevolent Societies in Antebellum Norfolk, Virginia," in Jonathan Daniel Wells and Jennifer R. Green, eds., *The Southern Middle Class in the Long Nineteenth Century* (Baton Rouge: Louisiana State University Press, 2011), 84–103, 104n6; Howard Benev-

olent Society, www.howardbenevolentsociety.org (accessed May 21, 2023); Jeanette Keith, *Fever Season: The Story of a Terrifying Epidemic and the People Who Saved a City* (New York: Bloomsbury Press, 2012), 53.

8. Sherman, *Autobiography*, 49–50; Fuller, *Chaplain to the Confederacy*, 208–9.

9. Sherman, *Autobiography*, 28; Garrett, "Sixty Years of Howard College," 21.

10. Sherman, *Autobiography*, 44, 49.

11. Ibid., 51–52.

12. Ibid.

13. Garrett, "Sixty Years of Howard College," 22–23.

14. Sherman, *Autobiography*, 52; Garrett, "Sixty Years of Howard College," 23.

15. *Alabama Baptist*, June 6, 1843. In addition, Sherman used the complete West Point Mathematics course and Charles Anthon's Classical Series on Greek and Latin.

16. Sherman, *The Bible a Classic*, 18; *Alabama Baptist* June 6, 1843.

17. *Alabama Baptist*, June 6, 1843.

18. Sherman, *Autobiography*, 54–55; Garrett, "Sixty Years of Howard College," 23–24.

19. Alabama Baptist State Convention Annual Report, 1842.

20. *Alabama Baptist*, June 24, July 1, 1843. Two of the award winners announced in the *Alabama Baptist* were John Calhoun Hornbuckle (September 11, 1839, to December 6, 1860) and Lemuel Augustus West (March 7, 1831, to October 3, 1906).

21. Alabama Baptist State Convention Annual Report, 1843; *South Western Baptist*, September 16, 1853. During the summer break, Samuel Sterling Sherman traveled to visit family in Wisconsin and Vermont. See Sherman, *Autobiography*, 56–58.

22. Alabama Baptist State Convention Annual Report, 1843; Garrett, "Sixty Years of Howard College," 24–26; *Alabama Baptist*, July 1 and September 2, 1843.

23. *Alabama Baptist*, September 2, 1843; "Guide to the Hartwell Family Papers," Record Group Four, Yale University Divinity School Library, drs.library.yale.edu/fedora/get/divinity004/PDF; *Baptist Missionary Magazine* 17, no. 6 (June 1837): 144.

24. *Alabama Baptist*, October 7, 1843.

25. Garrett, "Sixty Years of Howard College," 26; Flynt, *Alabama Baptists*, 60; Alabama Baptist State Convention Annual Report, 1844.

26. *Alabama Baptist*, May 18, 1844.

27. Sherman, *Autobiography*, 60; Alabama Baptist State Convention Annual Report, 1843; Garrett, "Sixty Years of Howard College," 27.

28. *Alabama Baptist*, July 27, 1844.

29. *Alabama Baptist*, January 20 and 27, 1844; James Frederick Sulzby, *Toward a History of Samford University* (Birmingham: Samford University Press, 1986), vol. 1: 13; Sulzby incorrectly attributed this quote to Samuel Sterling Sherman.

3. A DILIGENT WATCH OVER MORALS

1. Flynt, *Alabama Baptists*, 106–7; David E. Harrell Jr. et al., *Unto a Good Land: A History of the American People* (Grand Rapids, MI.: William B. Eerdmans, 2005), 322–23; *1850 U.S. Federal*

Census—Slave Schedules [Alabama] (Provo, UT: Ancestry.com Operations Inc., 2004); Bertram Wyatt-Brown, *Southern Honor: Ethics and Behavior in the Old South* (Ann Arbor, MI: Scholarly Publishing Office, University of Michigan, 2010), 3.

2. Flynt, *Alabama Baptists*, 106–7; Harrell et al., *Unto a Good Land*, 322–23; *1850 U.S. Federal Census—Slave Schedules* [Alabama]; Wyatt-Brown, *Southern Honor*, 3.

3. Alfred L. Brophy, "The Southern Scholar: Howard College Before the Civil War," *Cumberland Law Review* 46, no. 2 (2015–16): 289–309; Alfred L. Brophy, "Proslavery Political Theory in the Southern Academy, 1832–1861," in *Slavery and the University: Histories and Legacies*, ed. Leslie M. Harris, James T. Campbell, and Alfred L. Brophy (Athens: University of Georgia Press, 2019), 67; Patrick C. Jamieson, "Making Their Case: Religion, Pedagogy, and the Slavery Question at Antebellum Emory College," in *Slavery and the University*, ed. Harris, Campbell, and Brophy, 102–5; A. James Fuller, "'I Whipped Him a Second Time, Very Severely': Basil Manly, Honor, and Slavery at the University of Alabama," in *Slavery and the University*, ed. Harris, Campbell, and Brophy, 118; Ellen Griffith Spears and James C. Hall, "Engaging the Racial Landscape at the University of Alabama," in *Slavery and the University*, ed. Harris, Campbell, and Brophy, 305.

4. Alabama Baptist State Convention Annual Report, 1846.

5. Catalogue of Howard College, 1845–46, 1846–47, 1847–48, 1848–49, SUSC. For more on classical education on the frontier, see Carl J. Richard, *The Golden Age of the Classics in America: Greece, Rome, and the Antebellum United States* (Cambridge, MA: Harvard University Press, 2009), xi.

6. Francis Wayland, *The Elements of Moral Science* (Boston: Gould, Kendall, and Lincoln, 1843), 29, 75; Noll, *America's God*, 217.

7. Garrett, "Sixty Years of Howard College," 28–29.

8. "Laws of Howard College" (1846), SUSC.

9. Ibid.

10. Edward Baptist, "Address Delivered before the Trustees, Faculty, and Students, Howard College," November 16, 1846 (pamphlet, Tuskaloosa: D. J. Slade, 1846); *Marion Review*, rpt. in *Alabama Baptist*, November 26, 1846.

11. Alabama Baptist State Convention Annual Reports, 1847, 1850; J. D. B. DeBow, *Statistical View of the United States: Embracing Its Territory, Population—White, Free Colored, and Slave* (Washington, DC: Beverley, Tucker, Senate Printer, 1854), 191.

12. Kolan Thomas Morelock, *Taking the Town: Collegiate and Community Culture in the Bluegrass, 1880–1917* (Lexington: University Press of Kentucky, 2008), 4; Waldo Warder Braden, *The Oral Tradition in the South* (Baton Rouge: Louisiana State University Press, 1983), ix; Charles S. Sydnor, *The Development of Southern Sectionalism, 1819–1848* (Baton Rouge: Louisiana State University Press, 1948), 68; Ryan Lally, "Collegiate Literary Societies: Moral Intellect in Action," freshman thesis, Samford University, 2014, 2–12.

13. T. G. Keen, *Characteristics of the Times, Strong Incentives to Intellectual Effort: An Address Delivered before the Franklin & Adelphi Societies of Howard College at Their Anniversary, Held at Marion, Alabama, July 24, 1850* (Tuskaloosa, AL: Franklin & Adelphi Societies / M. D. J. Sledge, 1850).

14. William Garrott Brown, *The Lower South in American History* (New York: Macmillan Co., 1902), 125–29.

15. Cash, *Mind of the South*, 51; Sydnor, *Development of Southern Sectionalism*, 68; Catalogue of Howard College, 1847–48. Of the nine boys who began classes on January 3, 1842, only Barron, Blassingame, and Booth graduated.

16. William S. Blassingame diploma, copy in possession of author.

17. *Alabama Baptist*, January 2, 1850. Hartwell founded the Camden Female Institute in Arkansas and helped organize the Arkansas Baptist Convention. In 1857, he became president and professor of theology at Mt. Lebanon University in Louisiana. He died there in 1859.

18. Flynt, *Alabama Baptists*, 78; *Alabama Baptist*, March 2, 1849.

19. Riley, *History of the Baptists of Alabama*, 110. For more on Curtis's views on ministerial education, see the series of articles in the *Alabama Baptist* on November 14 and 21, December 5 and 12, 1849.

20. *South Western Baptist*, October 23 and 30, 1850; Alabama Baptist State Convention Annual Report, 1850.

21. Garrett, "Sixty Years of Howard College," 33–34.

4. SHALL HOWARD COLLEGE LIVE OR DIE?

1. *Memorial Record of Alabama: A Concise Account of the State's Political, Military, Professional and Industrial Progress* (Madison, WI: Brant & Fuller, 1893), vol. 2: 992–93; *Alabama Baptist*, July 30, 1851.

2. *The United States Biographical Dictionary and Portrait Gallery of Eminent and Self-Made Men: Missouri Volume* (New York: United States Biographical Publishing Co., 1878), 236–37. Talbird was no stranger to Marion or Howard College—serving on the college's board of trustees. On January 14, 1845, he married Julia Barron's widowed sister, Mary C. Griffin, in a ceremony conducted by Rev. James H. DeVotie.

3. Sherman, *Autobiography*, 55–68; Garrett, "Sixty Years of Howard College," 38; William Cathcart, *The Baptist Encyclopedia: A Dictionary of the Doctrines, Ordinances . . . and . . . History of the Baptist Denomination in All Lands* (Philadelphia: Louis H. Everts, 1881), 1130–31; *United States Biographical Dictionary and Portrait Gallery*, 236–37; Flynt, *Alabama Baptists*, 59–60; J. S. Dill, *Lest We Forget: Baptist Preachers of Yesterday That I Knew* (Nashville: Broadman Press, 1938), 76–80.

4. *South-Western Baptist*, July 12, 1851; *Alabama Planter* (Mobile), July 29, 1851, August 1, 1851; Alabama Baptist State Convention Annual Reports, 1851; Elam Franklin Dempsey, "Life and Services of Albert Durant Smith, LL.D.: A Memorial Volume Published by His Sons as an Expression of Their Filial Love and Honor," 117, SUSC.

5. Alabama Baptist State Convention Annual Report, 1852; Garrett, "Sixty Years of Howard College," 39; Sulzby, *Toward a History of Samford University*, 22–23; Sherman, *Autobiography*, 60; *South Western Baptist*, October 28, 1853.

6. Riley, *History of the Baptists of Alabama*, 205. In addition, Wayne Flynt argued that preachers who advocated separation of ministerial students from classical students forced Sherman to leave Howard. See Flynt, *Alabama Baptists*, 60.

7. Sherman, *Autobiography*, 67–68.

8. *South Western Baptist,* November 29, 1855.

9. James Grant Wilson and John Fiske, eds., *Appleton's Cyclopedia of American Biography* (New York: D. Appleton and Co., 1887), vol. 2: 106.

10. Catalogue of Howard College, 1854–55; George Braxton Taylor, *Virginia Baptist Ministers: 5th Series, 1902–1914* (Lynchburg, VA: J. P. Bell, 1915), 244–45.

11. Catalogue of Howard College, 1854–55; Alabama Baptist State Convention Annual Report, 1852; Garrett, "Sixty Years of Howard College," 40.

12. Catalogue of Howard College, 1853–54; Garrett, "Sixty Years of Howard College," 40–45.

13. Catalogue of Howard College, 1853–54; *South Western Baptist,* October 27, 1853; Garrett, "Sixty Years of Howard College," 73–74.

14. *South Western Baptist,* October 28, 1853; Alabama Baptist State Convention Annual Report, 1853.

15. Alabama Baptist State Convention Annual Report, 1853.

16. Ibid.

17. Alabama Baptist State Convention Annual Reports, 1854, 1855.

18. Garrett, "Sixty Years of Howard College," 42–50; Alabama Baptist Convention Annual Reports, 1854, 1855.

19. Garrett, "Sixty Years of Howard College," 42–50; *The Appeal* (St. Paul, MN), August 2, 1890.

20. Garrett, "Sixty Years of Howard College," 42–50; *Marion Standard,* December 12, 1895.

21. Garrett, "Sixty Years of Howard College," 42–50.

22. Ibid., 46–48; *Daily Advocate* (Baton Rouge), December 14, 1854.

23. "Account of the Fire at Howard College," n.d., Marion Military Institute Archives, Marion, Alabama.

24. Alabama Baptist State Convention Annual Report, 1854.

25. Sulzby, *Toward a History of Samford University,* 32–33; Alabama Census, 1855.

26. Alabama Baptist State Convention Annual Report, 1854.

27. Alabama Baptist State Convention Annual Report, 1855.

28. Ibid.

29. J. H. DeVotie to the president and board of trustees of Howard College, December 24, 1855, Helmbold Collection, SUSC; *South Western Baptist,* May 15, 1856. At the end of 1855, DeVotie resigned his position and later moved to Columbus, Georgia, where he pastored the First Baptist Church for several years.

30. *South Western Baptist,* October 18, 1855.

31. Garrett, "Sixty Years of Howard College," 60–71.

32. Ibid., 53–57. According to J. O. Bailey, Noah Davis later gave this small cabinet to his father, Richard, because "Howard College was growing and expanding" so much that the little box was too small to house all the chemicals needed. See. J. O. Bailey, signed affidavit, January 29, 1930, Helmbold Collection. The telescope was purchased from Alvan Clark and Sons of Cambridge, Massachusetts, and had an aperture of six inches, a focal length of eight feet by five-and-a-half inches, was mounted on a three-hundred-pound cast-iron stand, and contained a driving clock so the instrument could "follow the motions of a star or other object." *South Western Baptist,* November 29, 1855; "Catalogue of the Officers and Students of Howard College 1855–1856" (Marion,

AL: Dennis Dykous, 1856). The scheduled February completion of the main building was delayed several months because of an unusually harsh winter.

33. Thomas [Espy] to father, November 25, 1858, SUSC; *South Western Baptist,* December 17, 1857.

34. Taylor, *Virginia Baptist Ministers,* 257–58. The sketch of J. B. Hawthorne that appeared in Taylor's book was written by Benjamin Franklin Riley; Riley, *A Memorial History of the Baptists of Alabama* (Philadelphia: Judson Press, 1923), 140.

5. OUR PECULIAR PROPERTY

1. *1850 U.S. Federal Census,* Ward 1, Montgomery, Alabama, roll 12, p. 121a.

2. Christopher Lyle McIlwain Sr., "Harry: Faithful unto Death" *Alabama Heritage* 116 (Spring 2015): 28–29; *Marion American* qtd. in *African Repository and Colonial Journal* (American Colonization Society), vol. 33 (1857): 212; *South Western Baptist,* April 30, 1857.

3. *The National Era* (Washington, DC), June 11, 1857; *Pittsburgh Gazette,* May 8, 1857.

4. *South Western Baptist,* July 30, August 13, 1857; Henry Talbird to Basil Manly, April 25, 1858, Manly Family Papers, University of Alabama Libraries Special Collections, Tuscaloosa.

5. "Henry Talbird Sketch," William Jewell College Archives, Liberty, MO.

6. Thomas [Espy] to father, November 25, 1858, SUSC; Henry Talbird, "Report on Temperance," Cahaba Baptist Association, 1858; Sulzby, *Toward a History of Samford University,* 35–36.

7. *Howard College Magazine,* March 1860.

8. Ibid.

9. Ibid. Glover, *Southern Sons,* 86. See also Timothy J. Williams, *Intellectual Manhood: University, Self, and Society in the Antebellum South* (Chapel Hill: University of North Carolina Press, 2015).

10. Rogers et al., *Alabama,* 182.

11. Catalogue of Howard College, 1860–61; Alabama Baptist State Convention Annual Report, 1861; Riley, *History of the Baptists of Alabama,* 282.

12. Alabama Baptist State Convention Annual Report, 1860; Riley, *History of the Baptists of Alabama,* 279–80; Flynt, *Alabama Baptists,* 112.

13. *South Western Baptist,* January 17, 1861.

14. *Baptist Correspondent,* April 27, 1861.

15. Alabama Baptist State Convention Annual Report, 1861; *South Western Baptist,* April 4, 1861.

16. *South Western Baptist,* May 16, 1861.

17. *Daily Dispatch* (Richmond), November 21, 1861; Drew Gilpin Faust, "Christian Soldiers: The Meaning of Revivalism in the Confederate Army," *Journal of Southern History* 53, no. 1 (February 1987): 65. *South Western Baptist,* September 12, 1861.

18. *South Western Baptist,* September 12, 1861.

19. Ibid., March 26, 1863.

20. Henry Talbird to General Samuel Cooper, May 25, 1863, Henry Talbird, Alabama Confederate Pension Applications and Service Records, 1865–1940, Alabama Department of Archives

and History, Montgomery [hereafter CPASR]. James T. Murfee was selected lieutenant colonel under Talbird but declined the appointment to stay at the University of Alabama to train cadets. See James T. Murfee, CPASR.

21. Kate Cumming, *A Journal of Hospital Life in the Confederate Army of Tennessee* (Louisville, KY: John P. Morton & Co., 1866), 46.

22. Garrett, "Sixty Years of Howard College," 72–73; Flynt, *Alabama Baptists*, 132; Ann D. England, "A Compilation of Documented Information About the Confederate Hospital in Marion, Alabama, May 20, 1863–May 20, 1865" (n.p.: Marion Military Institute, n.d.), 4.

23. Alabama Baptist State Convention Annual Report, 1863; Garrett, "Sixty Years of Howard College," 73. In July 1863, the trustees received notice that board president Isham W. Garrott had been shot and killed at Vicksburg.

24. England, "A Compilation of Documented Information About the Confederate Hospital in Marion, Alabama," 10–14.

25. Sherman, *Autobiography*, 81; John Moore, CPASR; William Stanley Hoole, ed., "Letters from Johnson's Island Prison," *Alabama Review* 12, no. 3 (July 1959): 222–25.

26. Hoole, ed., "Letters from Johnson's Island Prison," 222–25.

27. Ibid.

28. Ibid.

29. Sulzby, *Toward a History of Samford University*, 51.

30. John B. Lundstrom, *One Drop in a Sea of Blue: The Liberators of the Ninth Minnesota* (St. Paul: Minnesota Historical Society Press, 2012), 387; "On the Historical Horizon," *Minnesota History* 38, no. 1 (1962): 41–43, www.jstor.org/stable/20176435 (accessed March 19, 2018).

31. Alabama Baptist State Convention Annual Report, 1866; Lundstrom, *One Drop in a Sea of Blue*, 386; Minnesota Historical Society, *Minnesota in the Civil and Indian Wars, 1861–1865* (St. Paul: Pioneer Press, 1890), vol. 1: 435–36.

32. Lundstrom, *One Drop in a Sea of Blue*, 387.

33. Ibid. Sulzby, *Toward a History of Samford University*, 52.

34. Thomas S. Hawley, *This Terrible Struggle for Life: The Civil War Letters of a Union Regimental Surgeon*, ed. Dennis W Belcher (Jefferson, NC: McFarland, 2013), 234.

35. Ibid.

36. *Livingston Journal*, September 23, 1865; Bertis English, "Civil Wars and Civil Beings: Violence, Religion, Race, Politics, Education, Culture, and Agrarianism in Perry County, Alabama, 1860–1875," PhD diss., Auburn University, 2006, 204.

37. Alabama Baptist State Convention Annual Report, 1865; Sulzby, *Toward a History of Samford University*, 54–55.

6. A WILD AND STORMY SEA OF DISORDER

1. Riley, *History of the Baptists of Alabama*, 307; Robert H Wiebe, *The Search for Order: 1877–1920* (New York: Hill and Wang, 1966), 5.

2. Rogers et al., *Alabama*, 225–26; Riley, *History of the Baptists of Alabama*, 307.

3. Rogers et al., *Alabama*, 230; Dan T. Carter, *When the War Was Over: The Failure of Self-Reconstruction in the South, 1865–1867* (Baton Rouge: Louisiana State University Press, 1985), 25; Walter Fleming, *Civil War and Reconstruction in Alabama*. (New York: Peter Smith, 1949), 350.

4. "William P. Chilton Amnesty," Ancestry.com, U.S., Pardons Under Amnesty Proclamations, 1865–69 [database online]. Provo, UT.

5. "J. L. M. Curry Amnesty, "Ancestry.com, U.S., Pardons Under Amnesty Proclamations, 1865–69; Edwin Anderson Alderman and Armistead Churchill Gordon, *J. L. M. Curry: A Biography* (New York: MacMillan Co., 1911), 191–93.

6. Alabama Baptist State Convention Annual Report, 1865.

7. Ibid.

8. Flynt, *Alabama Baptists*, 152.

9. Walter Belt White, "J. L. M. Curry—Alabamian," MA thesis, Samford University, 1971, 9, 14–15.

10. Ibid., 17.

11. Ibid., 324–25; Alderman and Gordon, *J. L. M. Curry*, 195; Flynt, *Alabama Baptists*, 146.

12. Flynt, *Alabama Baptists*, 146–47.

13. Caroline Janney, "The Lost Cause" *Encyclopedia Virginia*, last modified December 7, 2020, encyclopediavirginia.org/entries/lost-cause-the/.

14. Bertis English, *Civil Wars, Civil Beings, and Civil Rights in Alabama's Black Belt: A History of Perry County* (Tuscaloosa: University of Alabama Press, 2020), 81–83.

15. Charles Reagan Wilson, *Baptized in Blood: The Religion of the Lost Cause, 1865–1920* (Athens: University of Georgia Press, 1980), 7, 11–13, 47, 142; White, "J. L. M. Curry," 313, 320, 356.

16. *Religious Herald*, n.d.; White, "J. L. M. Curry," 324–25; Alderman and Gordon, *J. L. M. Curry*, 195; Flynt, *Alabama Baptists*, 146.

17. Alabama Baptist State Convention Annual Reports, 1865, 1866; John Witherspoon Dubose and James K Greer, *Alabama's Tragic Decade: Ten Years of Alabama, 1865–1874* (Birmingham: Webb Book Co., 1940), 252–53; *Christian Index & South-Western Baptist*, n.d.; *Selma Times*, September 18, 1865; *Jacksonville Republican*, January 27, 1866.

18. Sherman, *Autobiography*, 93, 94; Sulzby, *Toward a History of Samford University*, 53–54.

19. Alabama Baptist State Convention Annual Reports, 1865, 1866.

20. Ibid., 1865, 1866.

21. Crumpton, *Book of Memories*, 138; Alabama Baptist State Convention Annual Reports, 1866, 1867, 1868.

22. Rogers et al., *Alabama*, 239.

23. White, "J. L. M. Curry," 339.

24. Samuel L. Webb and Margaret E. Armbrester, *Alabama Governors: A Political History of the State* (Tuscaloosa: University of Alabama Press, 2014), 85–86; Riley, *History of the Baptists of Alabama*, 311.

25. Alderman and Gordon, *J. L. M. Curry*, 209–10; Garrett, "Sixty Years of Howard College," 77–79.

26. Catalogue of Howard College, 1860–61.

27. Tuomey assigned Thornton "the duty of tracing the Northern and Southern boundaries of the great Cretaceous formation of the State; in doing which, he not only defined the limits of the formation as a whole, enabling its position to be laid down upon the map with greater exactness than was before possible, but also examined the space occupied by the various beds of which the formation is composed, determined the relative position of these beds, and collected specimens of fossils, rocks, and soils characteristic of the districts passed over." See M. Tuomey, *Second Biennial Report of the Geology of Alabama* (Montgomery: N. B. Cloud, State Printer, 1858), 223–52.

28. Alabama Baptist State Convention Annual Report, 1868.

29. Garrett, "Sixty Years of Howard College," 80–82.

30. Ibid.

31. Alabama Baptist State Convention Annual Report, 1869.

32. S. Jonathan Bass, "'How 'Bout a Hand for the Hog': The Enduring Nature of the Swine as a Cultural Symbol in the South," *Southern Cultures* 1, no. 3 (1995): 301–20; Dill, *Lest We Forget,* 81–84.

33. Dill, *Lest We Forget,* 81–84; Garrett, "Sixty Years of Howard College," 82–87.

34. Dill, *Lest We Forget,* 81–84; Garrett, "Sixty Years of Howard College," 82–83.

35. Alabama Baptist State Convention Annual Report, 1869.

36. Ibid.

37. Garrett, "Sixty Years of Howard College," 84–87; Dill, *Lest We Forget,* 81–84.

38. Garrett, "Sixty Years of Howard College," 83–84. Garrett also wrote that Dill later found a "better way" than corporal punishment and instituted a system of rewards.

39. Catalogue of Howard College, 1869–70.

40. *Christian Index and South-Western Baptist,* n.d.

41. Alabama Baptist State Convention Annual Report, 1869.

42. Rev. Samuel R. Freeman clippings (ca. 1872), copies in possession of author.

43. Wiebe, *Search for Order,* xiii; Catalogue of Howard College, 1869–70; Rogers et al., *Alabama,* 278.

7. COLONEL MURFEE'S SCHOOL

1. James Sellers, *History of the University of Alabama, vol. 1: 1818–1902* (Tuscaloosa: University of Alabama Press, 2014), 197, 225, 257–61, 265; James Thomas Murfee, *A New Scheme of Organization, Instruction, and Government for the University of Alabama, with Report on Construction of Building* (Tuskaloosa: Printed by J. F. Warren, 1867), 10, 13; *Independent Monitor* (Tuscaloosa), April 28, 1868.

2. Francis Smith to Major O. M. Crutchfield, July 13, 1859, Virginia Military Institute Archives (hereafter VMIA), Lexington; VMI Catalog, 1854, VMIA.

3. James T. Murfee to Francis Smith, May 14, 1855, VMIA; W. Harrison Daniel, "Madison College, 1851–1858: A Methodist Protestant School," *Methodist History* 17, no. 2 (January 1979): 101.

4. *Richmond Whig,* July 14, 1857; February 14, 1860. *Alexandria Gazette,* August 12, 1858. Taylor, *Virginia Baptist Ministers,* 278.

5. James T. Murfee, CPASR; Sellers, *History of the University of Alabama* 1: 265–72, 284.

6. *Christian Index and South-Western Baptist,* November 2, 1871; Garrett, "Sixty Years of Howard College," 98; *Marion Commonwealth,* August 24, 1871.

7. J. Williams Jones, *Personal Reminiscences, Anecdotes, and Letters of Gen. Robert E. Lee* (New York: D. Appleton and Co., 1875), 84.

8. Frost, *Thinking Confederates,* 50.

9. Murfee, *A New Scheme of Organization,* 13–15, 23.

10. Ibid.

11. Howard College Minutes of the Board of Trustees, June 17, 1871, SUSC.

12. James A. Pate, "The Development of the Instructional Program at Howard College, 1842–1957," PhD diss., 1959, 67–68; Murfee, *A New Scheme of Organization,* 15, 23.

13. Howard College Minutes of the Board of Trustees, June 17, 1871.

14. *Marion Commonwealth,* August 24, 1871.

15. Catalogue of Howard College, 1871–72; *Marion Commonwealth,* August 24, 1871; Flynt, *Alabama Baptists,* 147.

16. Howard College Minutes of the Board of Trustees, June 17, 1871.

17. Garrett, "Sixty Years of Howard College," 92–94.

18. Ibid., 102.

19. Ibid. *Marion Standard,* October 1, 1909.

20. Howard College Minutes of the Board of Trustees, February 15, 18, 1873; Alabama Baptist State Convention Annual Report, 1873, SUSC.

21. *Montgomery Advertiser,* September 19, 1872; Howard College Minutes of the Board of Trustees, n.d.

22. *Eufaula Daily Times,* June 22, 1872.

23. *Times-Argus* (Selma), July 11, 1873; Catalogue of Howard College, 1871–72.

24. *Montgomery Advertiser,* June 25, 1873.

8. HOW LIFELESS OUR COUNTRY LOOKS

1. David Gordon Lyon, Diary (1873–74, 1876), Papers of David Gordon Lyon, HUG 1541, box 6, vol. 2, Harvard University Library, Cambridge, MA. iiif.lib.harvard.edu/manifests/view /drs:47567736$1iAU.

2. Ibid.

3. Ibid.

4. Ibid.

5. Ibid.

6. Ibid.

7. Ibid.

8. Ibid.

9. Howard College Minutes of the Board of Trustees, June 17, 1873; Alabama Baptist State Convention Annual Report, 1873.

10. Catalogue of Howard College, 1872–73 and 1873–74; Alabama Baptist State Convention Annual Report, 1873.

11. Catalogue of Howard College, 1874–75; Alabama Baptist State Convention Annual Reports, 1874 and 1875.

12. *Marion Commonwealth,* January 2, 1875; "David Gordon Lyon: In Memoriam," *Bulletin of the American Schools of Oriental Research* 62 (April 1936): 2–4; Gregory A. Wills, *Southern Baptist Seminary, 1859–2009* (New York: Oxford University Press, 2009), 145–46; George Huntston Williams and Rodney L. Petersen, *Divinings: Religion at Harvard : From Its Origins in New England Ecclesiastical History to the 175th Anniversary of the Harvard Divinity School, 1636–1992* (Göttingen: Vandenhoeck Et Ruprecht, 2014), 140–41; Israel Finestein, "The Jews in Hull, between 1766 and 1880," *Jewish Historical Studies* 35 (1996–98): 38–40.

13. Alabama Baptist State Convention Annual Report, 1874.

14. *Montgomery Advertiser,* February 3, 1872; *Clarke County Democrat* (Grove Hill, AL), February 8, 1872; *Alabama Beacon* (Greensboro, AL), September 30, 1871; *Marion Commonwealth,* October 19, 1871.

15. James Mallory, *Fear God and Walk Humbly: The Agricultural Journal of James Mallory, 1843–1877* (Tuscaloosa: University of Alabama Press, 2013), 526; *Troy Messenger,* April 4, 1872; *Alabama Baptist,* n.d.

16. Wiebe, *Search for Order,* xiii, 4.

17. Riley, *History of the Baptists of Alabama,* 346.

18. Ibid., 353; Garrett, "Sixty Years of Howard College," 96–97.

19. Riley, *History of the Baptists of Alabama,* 355; B. Dwain Waldrep, "J. J. D. Renfroe," *Encyclopedia of Alabama,* www.encyclopediaofalabama.org/article/h-1172 (accessed May 15, 2007); Cathcart, *Baptist Encyclopedia,* 969–70.

20. Crumpton, *Book of Memories,* 265–68.

21. Ibid.; *Alabama Baptist,* October 7, 1886.

22. Crumpton, *Book of Memories,* 265–68; *Alabama Baptist,* October 7, 1886; Howard College Minutes of the Board of Trustees, June 17, 1879.

23. Rod Andrew, *Long Gray Lines: The Southern Military School Tradition, 1839–1915* (Chapel Hill: University of North Carolina Press, 2004), 45.

24. Howard College Minutes of the Board of Trustees, June 17, 1879.

25. *Franklin Advocate,* March 1885, May 1885.

26. Garrett, "Sixty Years of Howard College," 96.

27. *Marion Commonwealth,* May 30, 1878.

28. *Alabama Baptist,* July 5, 1883.

29. Catalogue of Howard College, 1877–78; Garrett, "Sixty Years of Howard College," 96–97.

9. TO THE HIGHEST BIDDER

1. Chriss H. Doss, "In the Shadows of Foreclosure: Three Financial Crises That Threatened the Existence of Howard College," *Alabama Baptist Historian* 28, no. 1 (January 1992): 5; Alabama Baptist State Convention Annual Report, 1866.

2. Doss, "In the Shadows of Foreclosure," 5–7.

3. *The Sun* (Talladega), August 30, October 11, 1870; *Turner v. Turner* (June 1870) in *Reports of Cases Argued and Determined in the Supreme Court of Alabama* (n.p.: West Publishing Co., 1871), 437–58.

4. *Turner v. Turner* (June 1870) in *Reports of Cases Argued and Determined in the Supreme Court of Alabama* (n.p.: West Publishing Co., 1871), 437–58.

5. *Trustees of Howard College v. Turner* (December 1882) in *Reports of Cases Argued and Determined in the Supreme Court of Alabama* (Montgomery: Joel White, 1884), 429.

6. Thomas McAdory Owen, *History of Alabama and Dictionary of Alabama Biography* (Chicago: S. J. Clarke Publishing Co., 1921), vol. 3: 412; *Times-Argus* (Selma), January 21, 1876.

7. Owen, *History of Alabama and Dictionary of Alabama Biography* 4: 1706; Doss, "In the Shadows of Foreclosure," 6.

8. *Greensboro Watchman*, July 8, 1880; Doss, "In the Shadows of Foreclosure," 6.

9. Doss, "In the Shadows of Foreclosure," 5–8; Owen, *History of Alabama and Dictionary of Alabama Biography* 3: 223–24.

10. Doss, "In the Shadows of Foreclosure," 5–8; Howard College Board of Trustees Minutes, September 26, 1882, SUSC.

11. Doss, "In the Shadows of Foreclosure," 5–8; *Trustees of Howard College v. Turner* (December 1882) in *Reports of Cases Argued and Determined in the Supreme Court of Alabama* (1884), 429–36; Garrett, "Sixty Years of Howard College," 95–96, 103.

12. Howard College Board of Trustees Minutes, July 23, August 1, 1884; *Marion Standard*, March 12, 1884; Doss, "In the Shadows of Foreclosure," 5–8; Garrett, "Sixty Years of Howard College," 95–96, 103.

13. Doss, "In the Shadows of Foreclosure," 5–7; *Our Mountain Home* (Talladega), April 2, 1884.

14. Howard College Board of Trustees Minutes, July 23, 1884; Doss, "In the Shadows of Foreclosure," 8–9.

15. Catalogue of Howard College, 1872–73, 1873–74, 1874–75, 1875–76, 1876–77, 1877–78, 1878–79, 1879–80, 1880–81, 1881–82, 1882–83, 1883–84, 1884–85, 1885–86, 1886–87, 1900–1901.

16. *Charleston Daily News*, July 6, 1872; *The Intelligencer* (Anderson, SC), January 4, 1872; Nicholas Cords and Patrick Gerster, eds., *Myth and Southern History: The Old South* (Champagne: University of Illinois Press, 1989), vol. 1: 189–92; Cathcart, *Baptist Encyclopedia*, 17; John Julian, *A Dictionary of Hymnology: Setting Forth the Origin and History of Christian Hymns of All Ages and Nations* (New York: Charles Scribner's Sons, 1892), 1287; E. T. Winkler, *The Sacred Lute: A Collection of Popular Hymns, with Choruses and Forms for Special Occasions* (n.p.: Southern Baptist Publication Society, 1861); Henry S. Burrage, *Baptist Hymn Writers and Their Hymns* (Portland, ME: Brown Thurston & Co., 1888), 416–19.

17. *Alabama Baptist*, August 4, 1881.

18. Ibid.

19. John R. Sampey, *The Memoirs of John R. Sampey* (Nashville: Broadman Press, 1947), 15.

20. Ibid., 1–2, 12.

21. Ibid., 12–13.

22. Ibid., 13.

23. Ibid., 14.

24. Garrett, "Sixty Years of Howard College," 150–57.

25. Ibid., 152–54; Sulzby, *Toward a History of Samford University*, 98–100.

26. Sulzby, *Toward a History of Samford University*, 84.

27. *Marion Times-Standard*, March 16, 1881. Catts left Howard College at the end of the year and graduated with a law degree from Cumberland College in Lebanon, Tennessee. Years later, Sampey mistakenly recalled that "my colleague and I were happy when we won the decision." See Sampey, *Memoirs*, 16.

28. *Marion Times-Standard*, March 1, 1882; John R. Sampey, "The Proper Attitude of Young Ministers toward Issues of the Day," Southern Baptist Theological Seminary Archives and Special Collections.

10. AWAKE, ARISE, OR BE FOREVER FALLEN

1. Woodward, *Origins of the New South*, 107.

2. Howard College Board of Trustees Minutes, March 1, 1883; Alabama Baptist State Convention Annual Report 1883.

3. Howard College Board of Trustees Minutes, June 11, 1883.

4. Ibid.

5. *Alabama Baptist*, January 17 and 24, 1884.

6. Alabama Baptist State Convention Annual Report, 1883.

7. *Troy Messenger*, April 14, 1887; *Southern Aegis* (Ashville, AL), October 28, 1897.

8. Garrett, "Sixty Years of Howard College," 102–3.

9. Ibid.; *Alabama Baptist*, August 28, 1884.

10. *Alabama Baptist*, September 4, 1884.

11. Ibid., April 16, 1885.

12. Crumpton, *Book of Memories*, 277–79; Garrett, "Sixty Years of Howard College," 103; *Montgomery Advertiser*, July 15, 1887.

13. Garrett, "Sixty Years of Howard College," 103; Sulzby, *Toward a History of Samford University*, 115.

14. *Alabama Baptist*, August 27, 1885; *Our Mountain Home*, July 22, 1885; Crumpton, *Book of Memories*, 262.

15. *Alabama Baptist*, August 27, 1885.

16. Ibid., September 10 and 17, 1885.

17. Ibid., July 8, 1886.

18. Ibid. Board president W. W. Wilkerson agreed that the faculty's "constant presence" promoted good discipline and imprinted a professor's Christian character and intellect upon the students. Wilkerson told the Alabama Baptist State Convention that each faculty member was doing the work of two or more professors at other institutions.

19. *The Philomathian*, March 1, 1885.

20. Ibid.

21. *Marion Standard*, June 2, 1886.

22. *Mountain Eagle* (Jasper, AL), June 2, 1886; *Troy Messenger*, June 17, 1886.

23. Wendell H. Stephenson, "William Garrott Brown: Literary Historian and Essayist," *Journal of Southern History* 12 (August 1946): 313–15; *Daily News* (Birmingham), June 17, 1891.

24. John Spencer Bassett, "My Recollections of William Garrott Brown," *South Atlantic Quarterly* 16 (April 1917): 97–107; Stephenson, "William Garrott Brown," 319.

25. Theodore Roosevelt, *The Letters of Theodore Roosevelt: The Big Stick, 1905–1909* (Cambridge, MA: Harvard University Press, 1952), 1201.

26. Brown, *The Lower South*, viii–ix.

27. Harvard College: Class of 1891, *Secretary's Report, No. IV* (Boston: Rockwell & Churchill Press, 1906), 33; Harvard College: Class of 1891, *Secretary's Report. No. V* (Boston: Rockwell & Churchill Press, 1911), 33–34.

28. *Harper's Weekly*, November 15, 1913; *South Atlantic Quarterly*, January 1914, 69–74.

29. Garrett, "Sixty Years of Howard College," 104.

11. RACE, REBELLION, AND RELOCATION

1. Doss, "In the Shadows of Foreclosure," 8–9; *Marion Standard*, July 21, 1886.

2. Riley, *History of the Baptists of Alabama*, 405–6; Garrett, "Sixty Years of Howard College 106–7; *Montgomery Advertiser*, July 18, 1886; *Alabama Baptist*, August 5, 1886; Eldred Burder Teague Papers, University of Alabama Libraries Special Collections, Tuscaloosa. Rev. Washington Bryan Crumpton later wrote: "Those who knew Dr. E. B. Teague, would never accuse him of doing a selfish or unkind thing. He was as modest as a woman and never had the slightest disposition to thrust himself forward. Yet he was the man who with tremulous words moved that the Convention consider the removal of the College. Probably if he had not offered the resolution, it never would have been mentioned and, by the next Convention the work of endowment would have been so far advanced its removal could not have been accomplished." See Crumpton, *Book of Memories*, 181.

3. Riley, *History of the Baptists of Alabama*, 406; Garrett, "Sixty Years of Howard College," 106–7; *Alabama Baptist*, July 29, 1886.

4. Riley, *Memorial History*, 106; Garrett, "Sixty Years of Howard College," 107.

5. Garrett, "Sixty Years of Howard College," 108.

6. *Marion Times-Standard*, July 28, 1886, January 26, 1887; *Greensboro Watchman*, July 29, 1886.

7. *Alabama Baptist*, August 5, 1886.

8. Ibid., August 26, October 14, 1886; *Northern Alabama Historical and Biographical*, 477–78; Riley, *History of the Baptists of Alabama*, 407; Garrett, "Sixty Years of Howard College," 109.

9. *Alabama Baptist*, October 21, November 4, 1886.

10. Riley, *History of the Baptists of Alabama*, 407; Garrett, "Sixty Years of Howard College," 109; *Alabama Baptist*, August 5 and 26, October 7 and 21, November 4, December 16, 1886.

11. John Evans Barnes Jr., "My Autobiography as I Recall It," Wayne Flynt Papers, SUSC.

12. Ibid.

13. Ibid.

14. Ibid.

15. *Marion Standard*, October 6, 1886.

16. Ibid., June 16, 1886.

17. Bertis English, "A Black Belt Anomaly: Biracial Cooperation in Reconstruction-era Perry County, 1865–1874" *Alabama Review* 62, no. 1 (January 2009): 6, 27.

18. *Marion Standard,* August 3, 1881; *Selma Times,* July 24, 1881.

19. See Joseph D. Caver, *From Marion to Montgomery: The Early Years of Alabama State University, 1867–1925* (Montgomery: New South Books, 2020), and English, *Civil Wars, Civil Beings.*

20. Stephen A Berrey, *The Jim Crow Routine: Everyday Performances of Race, Civil Rights, and Segregation in Mississippi* (Chapel Hill: University of North Carolina Press, 2015), 41.

21. English, "Civil Wars and Civil Beings," 522–23; *Marion Commonwealth,* January 15, 1874.

22. Caver, *From Marion to Montgomery,* 49.

23. *Alabama Baptist,* March 3, 1887.

24. *Montgomery Advertiser,* December 14, 1886; *Marion Standard,* January 5, February 16, 1887; *Alabama Baptist,* March 3, 1887; *Evening Star* (Washington, DC), December 18, 1886; *New York Times,* December 17, 1886; Caver, *From Marion to Montgomery,* 49–54; English, *Civil Wars, Civil Beings,* 235–36.

25. *Marion Standard,* February 16, 1887; William B. Paterson to Booker T. Washington, January 5, 1887, in *Booker T. Washington Papers* (Urbana: University of Illinois Press, 1972), vol. 2: 319; Valerie Pope Burns, "From Pre–Civil War to Post–Civil Rights: The Political Lives of African-Americans from Slavery to the 21st Century in Perry County, Alabama," MA thesis, Auburn University, 2012, 101; Caver, *From Marion to Montgomery,* 49–54.

26. *The Herald* (Montgomery), January 8, 1887; Caver, *From Marion to Montgomery,* 49–54.

27. *The Herald* (Montgomery), January 8, 1887; *Marion Standard,* February 16, 1887; William B. Paterson to Booker T. Washington, January 5, 1887, in *Booker T. Washington Papers* 2: 319; Caver, *From Marion to Montgomery,* 49–51; *1880 U.S. Federal Census,* Marion, Perry, Alabama, roll 27, p. 231B, Enumeration District 078; *1870 U.S. Federal Census,* Jones Bluff, Sumter, Alabama, roll M593-40, p. 358A; Ancestry.com, U.S., Find a Grave Index, 1600s–Current, online database, www.findagrave.com/cgi-bin/fg.cgi; Daniel Webster Brown, 1923, "Alabama Deaths, 1908–1974," database, FamilySearch, familysearch.org/ark:/61903/1:1:JKQG-CZ9 (accessed August 5, 2019).

28. Howard College Minutes of the Board of Trustees, December 17, 1886; Caver, *From Marion to Montgomery,* 49–54.

29. *Marion Standard,* March 23, 1887; Caver, *From Marion to Montgomery,* 49–54.

30. *Marion Standard,* April 6, 1887; *Alabama Beacon* (Greensboro), June 28, 1887; Caver, *From Marion to Montgomery,* 49–51.

31. *Huntsville Gazette,* March 26, 1887; *Alabama Beacon* (Greensboro), June 28, 1887. In the last week of November 1888, Jewett Hall on Judson's campus burned. Just over a week later, a fire burned a Lincoln School building. See the *Greenville Advocate,* December 12, 1888.

32. Riley, *History of the Baptists of Alabama,* 399.

33. Howard College Minutes of the Board of Trustees, June 13, 1887; *Wilcox Progressive Era,* May 18, 1887.

34. Riley, *History of the Baptists of Alabama,* 399.

12. THEY OUT FIGURED US

1. *Montgomery Advertiser,* November 14, 1886.

2. Ayers, *Promise of the New South,* 63, 163.

3. *Montgomery Advertiser,* March 30, April 3, 1887; *Weekly Advertiser* (Montgomery), May 5, 1887; *Troy Messenger,* April 14, 1887; *Union Springs Herald,* July 20, 1887; Crumpton, *Book of Memories,* 279; Riley, *Memorial History,* 240.

4. *Troy Messenger,* April 14, 1887; Crumpton, *Book of Memories,* 279.

5. Ibid.

6. Crumpton, *Book of Memories,* 279; *Troy Messenger,* April 14, 1887; Florence Hawkins Wood Moss, *Building Birmingham and Jefferson County* (Birmingham: Birmingham Printing Co., 1941), 205; Louise Crenshaw Ray, *The Color of Steel* (Chapel Hill: University of North Carolina Press, 1932), 51.

7. Crumpton, *Book of Memories,* 279; James C Cobb, *Away Down South: A History of Southern Identity* (New York: Oxford University Press, 2007), 76.

8. *Weekly Advertiser* (Montgomery), May 5, 1887.

9. *Birmingham Age* qtd. in *Greensboro Watchman,* May 1887; *Weekly Advertiser* (Montgomery), May 5, 1887.

10. *Montgomery Advertiser,* May 19, 25; July 28, 1887.

11. *Alabama Baptist,* May 12, June 30, 1887.

12. Ibid., July 7, 1887.

13. Ibid., July 14, 1887.

14. Ibid.; Garrett, "Sixty Years of Howard College," 109–10.

15. *Union Springs Herald,* July 20, 1887; *Montgomery Advertiser,* July 16, 1887; Riley, *Memorial History,* 241.

16. *Union Springs Herald,* July 20, 1887; George W. Lasher, ed., *The Ministerial Directory of the Baptist Churches in the United States of America* (Oxford, OH: Press of the Oxford News Co., 1899), 623; *Alabama Baptist,* July 7, 1887.

17. *Union Springs Herald,* July 20, 1887.

18. Ibid.

19. Ibid.

20. Alabama Baptist State Convention Annual Report, 1887; Garrett, "Sixty Years of Howard College," 111.

21. Benjamin Franklin Riley, *Makers and Romance of Alabama History* (Birmingham: B. F. Riley, 1921), 342–45; Crumpton, *Book of Memories,* 251–52; Emir Fethi Caner and Ergun Mehmet Caner, *The Sacred Trust: Sketches of the Southern Baptist Convention Presidents* (Nashville: Broadman & Holman, 2003), 24–25.

22. James Sanders Day, "Henry DeBardeleben," *Encyclopedia of Alabama,* www.encyclopediaofalabama.org/article/h-3675; John Witherspoon DuBose, *Jefferson County and Birmingham, Alabama: Historical and Biographical* (Birmingham: Teeple & Smith, 1887), 263–64; Margaret E. Armbrester, *Samuel Ullman and "Youth": The Life, the Legacy* (Tuscaloosa: University of Alabama Press, 1993), 113; Garrett, "Sixty Years of Howard College," 111; *Union Springs Herald,* July 20, 1887; Alabama Baptist State Convention Annual Report, 1887.

23. Garrett, "Sixty Years of Howard College," 110; *Alabama Baptist,* July 21, 1887.

24. Lucina Boyd, *The Irvines and Their Kin* (Chicago: R. R. Donnelley and Sons Co., 1908), 191; S. A. Cunningham, ed., *Confederate Veteran* (Nashville: S. A. Cunningham, 1893), vol. 12:

431; Garrett, "Sixty Years of Howard College," 34–35. Wharton also wrote the lyrics: "The land where rules the Anglo-Saxon; The Land of Davis, Lee, and Jackson; Look away, look away, look away, Dixie land."

25. Alabama Baptist State Convention Annual Report, 1887; *Montgomery Advertiser,* July 20, 1887; *Union Springs Herald,* July 20, 1887; Riley, *History of the Baptists of Alabama,* 410–15; Garrett, "Sixty Years of Howard College," 110–14.

26. *Montgomery Advertiser,* July 20, 1887; *Union Springs Herald,* July 20, 1887; Riley, *History of the Baptists of Alabama,* 410–15; Garrett, "Sixty Years of Howard College," 110–14; Gray Sprayberry, "Anniston," in *Encyclopedia of Alabama,* www.encyclopediaofalabama.org/article/h-1464 (accessed February 1, 2020); Alabama Baptist State Convention Annual Report, 1887; *Alabama Baptist,* July 21, 1887.

27. "John Pertiller Hubbard," Alabama Surname Files (surname range: Hoxie–Huddleston), Alabama Department of Archives and History, Montgomery (hereafter ADAH).

28. *Alabama Baptist,* July 21, 1887.

29. Riley, *History of the Baptists of Alabama,* 414; Garrett, "Sixty Years of Howard College," 114; *Alabama Baptist,* July 21, 1887.

30. *Union Springs Herald,* July 20, 1887; *Marion Standard,* July 20, 1887.

31. Riley, *History of the Baptists of Alabama,* 414.

13. ALL NATIONS WERE GATHERING IN BIRMINGHAM

1. *Weekly Iron Age,* July 21, 1887.

2. *Tuskegee News,* July 21, August 18, 1887.

3. *Birmingham City Directory,* 1887.

4. Ayers, *Promise of the New South,* 64; Robert Jemison Papers, Birmingham Public Library Department of Archives and Manuscripts.

5. East Lake Land Company Brochure, SUSC.

6. Ibid.

7. Thomas E Huey, *Ruhama, the Story of a Church, 1819–1945* (Birmingham: Birmingham Printing Co., 1946), 42; *Birmingham Iron Age,* July 6, 1881.

8. Huey, *Ruhama,* 42–48; *Birmingham Iron Age,* July 6, 1881. No doubt this influenced the academy becoming an "authorized church school" in 1874.

9. *Birmingham Iron Age,* July 6, 1881; Garrett, "Sixty Years of Howard College," 115.

10. Riley, *Memorial History,* 248.

11. *Birmingham Iron Age,* July 6, 1881.

12. *Montgomery Advertiser,* August 4, 1887.

13. Ibid., July 30, 1887; *Alabama Beacon,* August 2, 1887; *Birmingham Age,* July 31, 1887; Garrett, "Sixty Years of Howard College," 114–16; *Tuskegee News,* August 18, 1887.

14. *Birmingham Age,* August 3, 1887; *Montgomery Advertiser,* August 3, 1887.

15. Garrett, "Sixty Years of Howard College," 115–20; *Wilcox Progressive Era,* August 10, 1887; *Marion Standard,* August 17, 1887.

16. Garrett, "Sixty Years of Howard College," 115–20; *Marion Standard,* August 10, 1887.

17. *Tuskegee News,* August 18, 1887; *Our Mountain Home* (Talladega), August 10, 1887.

18. *Weekly Iron Age,* August 4, 1887; *Hartford Courant* (CT), August 5, 1887; *Times-Picayune* (New Orleans), August 3, 1887.

19. *Weekly Advertiser,* August 3, 1887; Sulzby, *Toward a History of Samford University,* 134.

20. *Marion Standard,* July 27, 1887; Catalogue of Howard College, 1886–87, 1887–88.

21. *Marion Standard,* August 3, 1887; June 3, 1888. Garrett, "Sixty Years of Howard College," 116–20; Riley, *Memorial History,* 249.

22. Garrett, "Sixty Years of Howard College," 116–20; *Marion Standard,* August 10, 1887.

23. *Montgomery Advertiser,* July 14, 1910; *Birmingham News,* July 14, 1910.

24. "Thomas J. Dill," Alabama Surname Files (range: Dickson–Dingwall), ADAH.

25. *Marion Standard,* August 24, October 12, 1887; *Bibb Blade,* October 27, 1887; *Montgomery Advertiser,* October 14, 1887; *Our Mountain Home* (Talladega), June 20, 1888.

26. *Union Springs Herald,* August 31, 1887; Howard College Catalogue, 1887–88.

27. Garrett, "Sixty Years of Howard College," 120–21.

28. Ibid., 122.

29. Catalogue of Howard College, 1859–60, 1860–61, 1869–70, 1870–71, 1871–72, 1872–73, 1873–74, 1874–75, 1875–76, 1876–77, 1877–78, 1878–79, 1879–80, 1880–81, 1881–82, 1882–83, 1883–84, 1884–85, 1885–86, 1886–87, 1887–88, 1888–89; *Birmingham Age,* October 5, 1887.

30. Garrett, "Sixty Years of Howard College," 123.

31. J. E. McClurkin to M. E. Miller, October 8, 1887, SUSC; Wayne Flynt and Gerald W. Berkley-Coats, *Taking Christianity to China: Alabama Missionaries in the Middle Kingdom, 1850–1950* (Tuscaloosa: University of Alabama Press, 1997), 21–22.

32. Sulzby, *Toward a History of Samford University,* 135; *Birmingham Age,* October 5, 1887; *Alabama Enquirer* (Hartselle), October 13, 1887.

33. Alabama Baptist State Convention Annual Report, 1888; *Montgomery Advertiser,* October 6, 1887; Riley, *Memorial History,* 414.

34. Riley, *History of the Baptists of Alabama,* 419; Riley, *Memorial History,* 249; Garrett, "Sixty Years of Howard College," 123–24.

35. *Bibb Blade,* October 13, 1887; *Clarke County Democrat* (Grove Hill), November 3, 1887; Riley, *Memorial History,* 249; Garrett, "Sixty Years of Howard College," 124.

14. AN EMBARRASSING PILE OF BUILDINGS

1. Riley, *History of the Baptists of Alabama,* 420–21; *South Alabamian* (Jackson), May 25, 1889.

2. *Marion Standard,* January 25, February 1, 1888; *Our Mountain Home* (Talladega), June 30, 1937.

3. *Montgomery Advertiser,* July 18, 1888; Sulzby, *Toward a History of Samford University,* 139–40; *Monroe Journal* (Claiborne, AL), June 6, 1888.

4. *Montgomery Advertiser,* July 18, 1888; Sulzby, *Toward a History of Samford University,* 139–40; *Monroe Journal* (Claiborne, AL), June 6, 1888.

5. *Troy Messenger,* June 7, 1888; Owen, *History of Alabama and Dictionary of Alabama Biography* 4: 1533; *Weekly Advertiser,* July 7, 1875; *Clay County Watchman,* January 6, 1888; *Birmingham Herald* qtd. in *Troy Messenger,* January 12, 1888; Garrett, 125–26.

6. Sulzby, *Toward a History of Samford University,* 137–39.

7. Owen, *History of Alabama and Dictionary of Alabama Biography* 4: 1533; *Weekly Advertiser* (Montgomery), July 7, 1875; Garrett, "Sixty Years of Howard College," 125–26.

8. Riley, *History of the Baptists of Alabama,* 421; Riley, *Memorial History,* 253; Garrett, "Sixty Years of Howard College," 124–26; *Our Mountain Home,* May 30, 1888.

9. Sulzby, *Toward a History of Samford University,* 139–40; *Monroe Journal* (Claiborne, AL), June 6 and 20, 1888.

10. *Monroe Journal* (Claiborne), June 20, 1888; Garrett, "Sixty Years of Howard College," 119; Sulzby, *Toward a History of Samford University,* 137–39.

11. *Canebrake Herald* (Uniontown), December 3, 1902; *Montgomery Advertiser,* June 13, 1888.

12. *Montgomery Advertiser,* June 13, 1888.

13. Catalogue of Howard College, 1887–88; *Birmingham Herald* qtd. in *Our Mountain Home* (Talladega), June 20, 1888. William Webb Lavender graduated with first honors and went on to serve as a prosecutor in Bibb County for many years.

14. Richard Guy, "Architecture and the Reinterpretation of the Past in the American Renaissance." *Winterthur Portfolio* 18, no. 1 (Spring 1983): 69–87.

15. *Tuskaloosa Gazette,* June 21, 1888; *Weekly Advertiser* (Montgomery), June 21, 1888; *Birmingham Herald* qtd. in the *Marion Standard,* June 27, 1888; Crumpton, *Book of Memories,* 181.

16. *Birmingham Herald* qtd. in *Our Mountain Home* (Talladega), June 20, 1888; L. S. Foster, *Mississippi Baptist Preachers* (St. Louis, MO: National Baptist Publishing Co., 1895), 396–407.

17. Foster, *Mississippi Baptist Preachers,* 396–407; *Weekly Advertiser* (Montgomery), June 21, 1888.

18. Alabama Baptist State Convention Annual Report, 1888.

19. Riley, *History of the Baptists of Alabama,* 428; *Montgomery Advertiser,* July 17, 1888.

20. Alabama Baptist State Convention Annual Report, 1888.

21. Ibid.; *Weekly Advertiser* (Montgomery), July 19, 1888.

22. Alabama Baptist State Convention Annual Report, 1888; *Birmingham City Directory,* 1890, 90.

23. *Alabama Baptist,* July 26, 1888; Garrett, "Sixty Years of Howard College," 128.

24. *Alabama Baptist,* July 26, 1888; Garrett, "Sixty Years of Howard College," 128.

25. *Alabama Baptist,* July 26, 1888; Garrett, "Sixty Years of Howard College," 128. Riley, *History of the Baptists of Alabama,* 428.

26. *Alabama Baptist,* July 26, 1888; Garrett, "Sixty Years of Howard College," 119, 128; *Montgomery Advertiser,* July 15, 1888.

27. *Clarion-Ledger* (Jackson, MS), August 23, 1888; Tara Mitchell Mielnik, "Mary Sharp College," Tennessee Historical Society, *Tennessee Encyclopedia,* tennesseeencyclopedia.net/entries/mary-sharp-college/ (accessed: April 12, 2020).

28. Riley, *Memorial History,* 253; Garrett, "*Sixty Years of Howard College,*" 129–30; *Our Mountain Home* (Talladega), August 22, 1888.

29. *Alabama Baptist* qtd. in Sulzby, *Toward a History of Samford University,* 146; *Clarke County Democrat,* August 23, 1888; Riley, *Memorial History,* 253–54; Riley, *History of the Baptists of Alabama,* 430.

30. Orville Vernon Burton, *In My Father's House Are Many Mansions: Family and Community in Edgefield, South Carolina* (Chapel Hill: University of North Carolina Press, 2000), 5–6; Kevin O.

McKinley, *Shadows and Dust III: Legacies* (Morris, NC: Lulu Publications, 2018), 226; *Northern Alabama: Historical and Biographical,* 217.

31. Wills, *Southern Baptist Theological Seminary,* 76–77; *General Catalog of the Crozer Theological Seminary* (1918), 47–48; Cash, *Mind of the South,* 93–94.

32. Owen, *History of Alabama and Dictionary of Alabama Biography* 4: 1440; *Montgomery Advertiser,* June 18, 1885; *Troy Messenger,* December 14, 1871; *Monroe Journal* (Claiborne, AL), June 5, 1913; *Evening News* (Birmingham), September 15, 1888; 2 Corinthians 13:11 (KJV).

33. Benjamin Franklin Riley, *Alabama as It Is; Or, The Immigrant's and Capitalist's Guide Book to Alabama* (Atlanta: W. C. Holt, 1887), 5–6; James C. Cobb, *The Selling of the South: The Southern Crusade for Industrial Development, 1936–1980* (Baton Rouge: Louisiana State University Press, 1980), 2–3; *Eutaw Whig and Observer,* June 28, 1888; *Guntersville Democrat,* September 22, 1887; *Times* (Opelika), November 27, 1886; *Alabama Courier* (Athens), September 22, 1887; *Montgomery Advertiser,* December 4, 1886; *Eufaula Daily Times,* November 28, 1886.

34. *Florence Herald,* May 31, 1890.

35. Ibid.

36. Ibid.

37. Riley, *Memorial History,* 254; Garrett, "Sixty Years of Howard College," 131–33; Sulzby, *Toward a History of Samford University,* 149.

38. *Our Mountain Home* (Talladega), September 19, 1888; *Montgomery Advertiser,* September 22 and 23, October 9 and 25, 1888; John H. Ellis, *Yellow Fever and Public Health in the New South* (Lexington: University Press of Kentucky, 1992), 121; *Evening News* (Birmingham), September 15 and 24, 1888; *Tuskaloosa Gazette,* September 20 and October 4, 1888. The *Gazette* reported: "Birmingham is enforcing a most rigid quarantine against all fever infected points. Even the public roads as well as the railroads are carefully guarded by quarantine officers."

39. Terry Lawrence Jones, "Benjamin Franklin Riley: A Story of His Life and Work," PhD diss., Vanderbilt University, 1974, 44; Riley, *Memorial History,* 254.

40. Jones, "Benjamin Franklin Riley," 44; Riley, *Memorial History,* 254. *Howard Collegian,* October 1888.

41. Riley, *History of the Baptists of Alabama,* 430; *Howard Collegian,* October 1888.

42. Howard College Catalogue, 1888–89.

43. Ibid.; Riley, *History of the Baptists of Alabama,* 430; *Alabama Baptist,* n.d.

44. *Evening News* (Birmingham), January 28, 1889.

15. BAD BIRMINGHAM

1. John R. Hornaday, *The Book of Birmingham* (New York: Dodd, Mead, and Co., 1921), 5; Riley, *History of the Baptists of Alabama,* 430; *Our Mountain Home* (Talladega), January 23, 1889.

2. Riley, *History of the Baptists of Alabama,* 430; *Our Mountain Home* (Talladega), January 23, 1889.

3. *Howard Collegian,* June 1889.

4. Riley, *History of the Baptists of Alabama,* 430.

5. "The Last of the Florence Boom," in *Bulletin of the American Iron and Steel Association* (Philadelphia), vol. 31, no. 23 (August 10, 1897): 179.

6. Crumpton, *Book of Memories*, 207–8.

7. *Weekly Advertiser* (Montgomery), March 7, 1889.

8. Ibid.

9. Ibid.; Garrett, "Sixty Years of Howard College," 132–33.

10. *Marion Standard*, January 23, 1889; Crumpton, *Book of Memories*, 210–11; *Shelby Chronicle* (Columbiana), January 24, 1889.

11. *Marion Standard*, January 23, 1889; Crumpton, *Book of Memories*, 210–11; *Shelby Chronicle* (Columbiana), January 24, 1889; *Evening News* (Birmingham), January 16, 1889).

12. *Evening News* (Birmingham), January 31, 1889.

13. Crumpton, *Book of Memories*, 210–11.

14. Act to Incorporate the Florence Educational, Land and Development Company, *Acts of the General Assembly of Alabama* (1888–89), 746–48; *Montgomery Advertiser*, February 26, 1889.

15. *Weekly Advertiser* (Montgomery), March 7, 1889; *Clarke County Democrat* (Grove Hill), March 7, 1889.

16. *Weekly Advertiser* (Montgomery), March 7, 1889.

17. *Montgomery Advertiser*, March 29, 1889; Riley, *History of the Baptists of Alabama*, 430; Garrett, "Sixty Years of Howard College," 133.

18. *Standard Gauge* (Brewton), February 28, 1889; *Birmingham City Directory*, 1905, 413; *Sumter County Sun* (Livingston), May 2, 1889; *Livingston Journal*, November 15, 1889; *Montgomery Advertiser*, October 8, 1889; Sulzby, *Toward a History of Samford University*, 151; Riley, *History of the Baptists of Alabama*, 433–34; Riley, *Memorial History*, 255; Garrett, "Sixty Years of Howard College," 134.

19. *Birmingham Age-Herald* qtd. in Garrett, "Sixty Years of Howard College," 133; *Evening News* (Birmingham), April 4, 1889.

20. Sulzby, *Toward a History of Samford University*, 151–52; Riley, *History of the Baptists of Alabama*, 434; Garrett, "Sixty Years of Howard College," 134; David I. Purser Notebooks, 1889–90, SUSC.

21. *Birmingham Age-Herald* qtd. in Garrett, "Sixty Years of Howard College," 133; *Evening News* (Birmingham), April 4, 1889.

22. *Montgomery Advertiser*, April 28, May 2, 1889; *Weekly Advertiser* (Montgomery), May 9, 1889; *New York Times*, May 1, 1889; *Our Mountain Home* (Talladega), May 1, 1889; *Baltimore Sun*, May 1, 1889; *New York Tribune*, May 1, 1889; *Norfolk Landmark* (Virginia), May 1, 1889; *Evening News* (Anniston), May 2, 1889; *Howard Collegian*, June 1889.

23. *Weekly Age-Herald* (Birmingham), June 18, 1889.

24. *Evening News* (Birmingham), July 13, 1889; *Weekly Advertiser* (Montgomery), May 23, 1889; *Our Mountain Home* (Talladega), May 29, 1889; *Eufaula Weekly Times and News*, June 20, 1889; *Alabama Baptist* qtd. in *Evening News* (Birmingham), June 29, 1889.

25. *Montgomery Advertiser*, June 25 and 28, 1889.

26. *Evening News* (Birmingham), July 6, 1889.

27. Ibid.

28. *Monroe Journal*, April 11, 1890; Sulzby, *Toward a History of Samford University*, 154.

29. *Alabama Enquirer* (Hartselle), October 10. 1889; *Montgomery Advertiser*, September 22, October 20 and 25, 1889; *West Alabamian* (Carrolton), October 16, 1889; *Daily News* (Birmingham), December 13, 1889; *Tuscaloosa Times*, April 3, August 21, 1889; *Evening News* (Birmingham),

April 18, July 20, 1889; *Our Mountain Home* (Talladega), September 11, 1889; *Times-Democrat* (Wetumpka), October 24, 1889.

30. "T. G. Bush," Alabama Surname Files (range: Bush–Butler), ADAH; "Charles W. Collins," Alabama Surname Files (range: Colley–Collins); *Weekly Advertiser* (Montgomery), November 21, 1889; *Montgomery Advertiser,* November 12, 1889; Garrett, "Sixty Years of Howard College," 119.

31. *Daily News* (Birmingham), November 27, 1889; Sulzby, *Toward a History of Samford University,* 154–55; *Eufaula Daily Times,* January 18, 1890; *Montgomery Advertiser,* January 20, 1890.

32. B. F. Riley to Mamie Mell Smith, May 26, 1909, SUSC; Doss, "In the Shadows of Foreclosure," 9–10; Sulzby, *Toward a History of Samford University,* 152. Several sources identify the brothers as Burghard and Leo Steiner. Leo, however, was Burghard and Sigfried's eighteen-year-old cousin, who worked as a clerk at the banking house. Leo, however, would be named president of the Steiner Brothers Bank in 1901. See Mark H. Elovitz, *A Century of Jewish Life in Dixie: The Birmingham Experience* (Tuscaloosa: University of Alabama Press, 2003), 31–33.

33. *Montgomery Advertiser,* February 28, 1890; Doss, "In the Shadows of Foreclosure," 9–10; Sulzby, *Toward a History of Samford University,* 152. The *Alabama Baptist* reported: "Our information is that he has negotiated the notes held and has thereby gotten $50,000 in clean cash . . . to complete main building." The "clean cash" was used to pay for the new Administrative Hall, and Purser's money was used for the additional buildings, or vice versa. *Alabama Baptist* qtd. in *Montgomery Advertiser,* March 25, 1890.

34. *Daily News* (Birmingham), April 10, 1890; *Standard Gauge* (Brewton), March 20, 1890; *Montgomery Advertiser,* December 4, 1889; *Tuscaloosa Gazette,* December 12, 1889.

35. Sulzby, *Toward a History of Samford University,* 163–64; *Daily News* (Birmingham), April 30, 1890; *Standard Gauge* (Brewton), March 20, 1890; *Birmingham Age-Herald* qtd. in *Our Mountain Home* (Talladega), May 7, 1890. The *Age-Herald* reported that P. J. Gillam put in a sixth bid, but "it was based on misinformation as to specifications and was to[o] high to be considered."

36. *Montgomery Advertiser,* March 1, 1890; *Troy Messenger,* March 6, 1890.

37. *Montgomery Advertiser,* March 1, 1890; *Troy Messenger,* March 6, 1890; Samford University, *Seasons,* Summer 2004, 9.

38. *Baltimore Sun,* September 18, 1886; *Choctaw Advocate* (Butler County, AL), June 25, 1890; *Montgomery Advertiser,* June 10, 1890; 1. Corinthians 16:13 (ESV); John F. Weishampel and George F. Adams, *History of Baptist Churches in Maryland Connected with the Maryland Baptist Union Association* (Baltimore: John F. Weishampel Jr., 1885), 169–70.

39. *Choctaw Advocate* (Butler County, AL), June 25, 1890.

16. NO CROSS, NO CROWN

1. *Birmingham News,* August 21, September 13, 15, 16, 1890; September 6, 1928. *Alabama Baptist,* August 28, 1890 *Our Mountain Home* (Talladega), October 1, 1890.

2. *Franklin Advocate,* January 1890; *Our Mountain Home* (Talladega), October 1, 1890.

3. *Birmingham News,* August 21; September 13, 15, 16, 1890.

4. *Franklin Advocate,* January 1890.

5. Ibid.

6. Garrett, "Sixty Years," 142; *Birmingham News,* January 31, 1946.

7. Sulzby, *Toward a History,* 158–60.

8. Ibid.

9. Ibid.

10. Ibid.

11. *Alabama Baptist,* November 20, 1890.

12. Ibid.

13. "Devotie's History," DeVotie Baptist Church, www.devotie.com/our-history.html (accessed May 20, 2023).

14. *Alabama Baptist,* April 23, 1891; *Daily News* (Birmingham), April 16, 1891.

15. *Alabama Baptist,* April 23, 1891; *Daily News* (Birmingham), April 16, 1891.

16. *Moulton Advertiser* (AL), May 7, 1891; *Daily News* (Birmingham), April 23, 1891.

17. *Birmingham Age-Herald* qtd. in *Alabama Baptist,* June 4, 1891; Sulzby, *Toward a History of Samford University,* 163–64; Riley, *History of the Baptists of Alabama,* 451.

18. Sulzby, *Toward a History of Samford University,* 163–64; Catalogues of Howard College, 1891, 1903.

19. Catalogues of Howard College, 1891, 1903.

20. Ibid.; Riley, *History of the Baptists of Alabama,* 451–52; Garrett, "Sixty Years of Howard College," 136; *Birmingham News,* September 1, 1915.

21. Riley, *History of the Baptists of Alabama,* 451–52; Garrett, "Sixty Years of Howard College," 136–37; Alabama Baptist State Convention Reports, 1891; *Alabama Baptist,* November 26, 1891.

22. Alabama Baptist State Convention Annual Report, 1891.

23. Garrett, "Sixty Years of Howard College," 136–37; *Alabama Baptist,* July 9, 1891; Flynt, *Alabama Baptists,* 372–73.

24. J. B. Hawthorne, "John the Baptist," Catalogue of Howard College, 1892. Most of the speeches were published in the 1891–92 Howard College Catalogue. In newspapers, William Garrott Brown was announced as offering an alumni poem, but the one printed in the catalog was by George W. Macon. General George D. Johnson offered his remarks from memory, and no transcript of his talk, entitled "Existing Perils to Young Men," was available for publication.

25. W. C. Ward, "A Historical Summary from the Speech of Hon. W. C. Ward, LL. D.," Catalogue of Howard College, 1892.

26. D. G. Lyon, "The College Man's Choice of a Profession," Catalogue of Howard College, 1892.

27. W. L. Sanford, "The Credit System," Catalogue of Howard College, 1892.

28. Ibid. Tragically, heart issues and depression compelled William L. Sanford to commit suicide on May 21, 1915. See *American Artisan and Hardware Record,* May 29, 1915.

29. *Montgomery Advertiser,* December 8, 1910; February 7, 1904.

30. *Daily News* (Birmingham), June 7, 1892; *Montgomery Advertiser,* December 8, 1910.

31. Sulzby, *Toward a History of Samford University,* 170–71.

32. Ibid., 172; *Alabama Baptist,* February 16, 1893.

33. Alabama Baptist State Convention Annual Report, 1893.

34. Riley, *Memorial History,* 261.

35. Sulzby, *Toward a History of Samford University,* 173.

36. *Montgomery Advertiser,* June 1, 1893; Garrett, "Sixty Years of Howard College," 137–38; Riley, *History of the Baptists of Alabama,* 463–64; Sulzby, *Toward a History of Samford University,* 174–75.

37. *Alabama Blue Book and Social Register, 1929* (Birmingham: Blue Book Publishing, 1929), 199–200; *The Book of Birmingham and Alabama* (Birmingham: Birmingham Ledger, 1914), 113; "Birmingham Judges," Newspaper Clipping Files, Southern History Department, Birmingham Public Library (hereafter SHDBPL).

38. *Official Proceeding of the Constitutional Convention of the State of Alabama, May 21, 1901 to September 3, 1901* (Wetumpka, AL: Wetumpka Printing Co., 1940), 1704–7; "Birmingham Judges," Newspaper Clipping Files, SHDBPL; *Centreville Press,* January 14, 1904.

39. Eason Balch, interview by author, Birmingham, August 18, 2007.

40. *Centreville Press,* October 5, 1922; *Birmingham News,* September 29, 1922; "Birmingham Judges," Newspaper Clipping Files, SHDBPL.

41. "Judges," Newspaper Clipping Files, SHDBPL; "Fritz Thompson," Newspaper Clipping Files, DSHL.

42. Riley, *History of the Baptists of Alabama,* 463–64.

43. Ibid., 464; *Daily News* (Birmingham), June 20, 1893.

44. Sulzby, *Toward a History of Samford University,* 176.

17. THE BURDEN OF HOWARD COLLEGE

1. *Alabama Baptist,* July 13, August 3, December 7, 1893.

2. Alabama Baptist State Convention Annual Report, 1894; Huey, *Ruhama,* 106–7; *Alabama Baptist,* September 13, 1894.

3. *Alabama Baptist,* n.d.

4. *Russell Register* (Seale, AL), November 10, 1894; *Alabama Baptist,* November 23, 1893.

5. *Alabama Baptist,* January 25, 1894.

6. Alabama Baptist State Convention Annual Report, 1894; *Alabama Baptist,* July 19, 1894; Sulzby, *Toward a History of Samford University,* 187.

7. Maria Louisa "Lula" Bailey Materials, SUSC; *Howard Alumnus,* March 1958; Sulzby, *Toward a History of Samford University,* 187.

8. *Alabama Baptist,* October 4, 1894; *Scribner's Monthly,* July 1872.

9. *Alabama Baptist,* March 6, 1895; Alabama Baptist State Convention Annual Report, 1894.

10. Garrett, "Sixty Years of Howard College," 144; Sulzby, *Toward a History of Samford University,* 187–88; *Alabama Baptist,* September 12, 1895.

11. *Birmingham News,* September 11, 1896.

12. *Alabama Baptist,* September 19, 1895; Sulzby, *Toward a History of Samford University,* 195–96; Samford *Seasons,* Winter 2003.

13. *Birmingham News,* November 15, 1895.

14. *Alabama Baptist,* March 19, 1896.

15. *Birmingham News,* April 20, 1896; Doss, "In the Shadows of Foreclosure,"10.

16. Alabama Baptist State Convention Annual Report, 1896.

17. Huey, *Ruhama,* 110.

18. *Alabama Baptist,* July 9, 1896; Alabama Baptist State Convention Annual Report, 1896.

19. Doss, "In the Shadows of Foreclosure,"10–11; Sulzby, *Toward a History of Samford University,* 203.

20. Sulzby, *Toward a History of Samford University,* 204–5; *Alabama Baptist,* July 9, 1896.

21. *Montgomery Advertiser,* November 12, 1898; Garrett, "Sixty Years of Howard College," 144; Doss, "In the Shadows of Foreclosure," 10–11.

22. Alabama Baptist State Convention Annual Report, 1896; Garrett, "Sixty Years of Howard College," 144; Doss, "In the Shadows of Foreclosure," 10.

23. Dempsey, "Life and Services of Albert Durant Smith," 171–72.

24. Ibid., 168; *Howard College Bulletin,* October 1927.

25. Sulzby, *Toward a History of Samford University,* 206–7.

26. Dempsey, "Life and Services of Albert Durant Smith," 200; *Alabama Baptist,* October 29, 1896; Garrett, "Sixty Years of Howard College," 145–46.

27. Dempsey, "Life and Services of Albert Durant Smith," 158; *Birmingham News,* June 17, 1897; *Pine Belt News* (Brewton), September 17, 1896.

28. Sulzby, *Toward a History of Samford University,* 213.

29. *Birmingham News,* June 15, 1897; Sulzby, *Toward a History of Samford University,* 211–13.

30. *Birmingham News,* June 15, 1897; Sulzby, *Toward a History of Samford University,* 211–13.

31. *Birmingham News,* June 15, 1897; Sulzby, *Toward a History of Samford University,* 211–13.

CONCLUSION: LAUREL WREATHS OF VICTORY

1. Alabama Baptist State Convention Annual Report, 1898; *Birmingham News,* November 10, 1898; *Weekly Advertiser* (Montgomery), November 18, 1898; *Tuskegee News,* November 17, 1898.

2. *Montgomery Advertiser,* January 22, 1899; *Tuskegee News,* June 1, 1899; *Birmingham News,* May 30, 1999.

3. *Birmingham News,* June 5, 1899.

4. *Montgomery Advertiser,* July 9, 1899; *Birmingham News,* July 15, 1899.

5. *Birmingham News,* July 15, 1899; *Our Mountain Home* (Talladega), July 19, 1899.

6. *Birmingham News,* July 18, 1899.

7. Garrett, "Sixty Years of Howard College," 149–50.

8. W. B. Crumpton, *Our Baptist Centennials, 1808–1923 (Montgomery: Paragon Press, 1923),* 22–28.

9. Ibid.

10. Ibid.

EPILOGUE

1. Charles B. Williams, "Christian Colleges and the Re-Creation of the World," speech at Installation Service of Charles B. Williams, September 26, 1919, SUSC; *Birmingham News,* September 17, 1919.

2. George H. Denny, "The Denominational College and the New Era in Education," speech at Installation Service of Charles B. Williams, September 26, 1919, SUSC; *Birmingham News,* September 17, 1919.

3. Mifflin Wyatt Swartz, "The New Era in Education—Liberal Education" speech at Installation Service of Charles B. Williams, September 26, 1919, SUSC.

4. C. C. Daniels, "The New Era in Education—Christian Education," speech at Installation Service of Charles B. Williams, September 26, 1919, SUSC; *Howard Crimson,* October 3, 1919.

5. Garrett, "Sixty Years of Howard College," 20; Reuben E. E. Harkness to James H. Chapman, January 1946, James H. Chapman Collection, SUSC.

6. *Union Banner* (Clanton, AL), June 29, 1961; *Anniston Star (AL),* June 18, 1961; *Montgomery Advertiser,* November 10, 1965.

7. Wayne Willis, "Liberating the Liberal Arts: An Interpretation of Aristotle," *Journal of General Education* 39, no. 4 (1988): 201.

8. Trueblood, *The Idea of a College,* 16–17; Urofsky, "Reforms and Response," 65; Gilman M. Ostrander, "Review: Accreditations for the Old-Time American College," *Historical Reflections / Réflexions Historiques* 10, no. 3 (Fall 1983): 406.

9. Minutes of the Executive Committee of the Howard College Board of Trustees, September 3, 1964, copies in possession of the author.

10. Minutes of the Executive Committee of the Howard College Board of Trustees, May 19, 1965, and Annual Meeting of the Howard College Board of Trustees, May 28, 1965, copies in possession of the author; "Frank Park Samford," Alabama Surname Files (range: Ryan–St. John); "William Hodges Samford," Alabama Surname Files (range: Ryan–St. John); "William James Samford," Alabama Surname Files (range: Ryan–St. John).

11. *Montgomery Advertiser,* November 7–10, May 30, 1965; *Tennessean,* November 18, 1965; *Anniston Star,* August 3, 1965, November 10, 1965; *Alabama Journal,* November 4 and 10, 1965; *Selma Times-Journal,* November 10, 1965.

12. *Montgomery Advertiser,* November 7, 1965, November 10, 1965.

13. Ibid., November 7, 1965.

14. Ibid.

BIBLIOGRAPHY

PRIMARY SOURCES

Manuscript Collections

Alabama Department of Archives and History, Montgomery (ADAH).
    Alabama Confederate Pension Applications and Service Records, 1865–1940 (CPASR).
    Alabama State Census, 1820, 1850, 1855, 1866.
    Alabama Surname Files.
Birmingham Public Library Department of Archives and Manuscripts.
    Robert Jemison Papers.
    Birmingham Public Library Southern History Department.
    Newspaper Clipping Files.
    Birmingham City Directory, 1887, 1890, 1905.
Furman University Special Collections and Archives, James B. Duke Library.
Hargrett Rare Book and Manuscript Library, University of Georgia, Athens.
    James Henry Lumpkin Papers.
Harvard University Library. Cambridge, MA.
    Papers of David Gordon Lyon.
Hofstra University Special Collections. Hempstead, NY.
Library of Congress. Washington, DC.
    J. L. M. Curry Papers, 1637–1939.
Marion Military Institute Archives. Marion, AL.
    Documents Related to Howard College.
Middlebury College.
    Middlebury College Catalogue, 1837.
Morgan Library and Museum. New York.
    John Howard Letters.
Samford University, Special Collection and Archives, Birmingham, AL (SUSC)
    Alabama Baptist State Convention Annual Reports, 1834–1913.
    Bailey, Maria Louisa "Lula," Materials.
    Burns, Percy Pratt, Collection.
    Cahaba Baptist Association Minutes.
    Catalogue of Howard College, 1847–61, 1865–1910.

Chapman, James H., Collection.

Davis, Harwell G., Papers.

Dempsey, Elam Franklin. "Life and Services of Albert Durant Smith, LL.D.: A Memorial Volume Published by His Sons as an Expression of Their Filial Love and Honor."

DeVotie, James H. "Memoirs."

First Baptist, Tuscaloosa, Records.

Flynt, Wayne, Papers.

Helmbold, Wilbur F., Collection.

Howard College Minutes of the Board of Trustees, 1871–87.

"Journal of the Proceedings of the Baptist State Convention in Alabama at Its Eighteenth Anniversary." Marion, AL: Marion Herald, 1841.

Judson College Collection.

"Laws of Howard College," 1846.

Purser, David I., Notebooks.

Sesquicentennial Files.

Siloam Baptist Church Records.

Wright, Leslie, Papers.

Southern Baptist Theological Seminary Archives and Special Collections. Louisville, KY.

Thomas Treadwell Eaton Papers.

Tennessee Department of Archives. Nashville.

John Trotwood Moore Papers.

University of Alabama Libraries Special Collections, Tuscaloosa.

King Family Papers.

Manly Family Papers.

Teague, Eldred Burder, Papers.

University of North Carolina, Wilson Special Collection Library. Chapel Hill.

Lockett, Samuel Henry, Papers, 1820–1972.

Spring Family Papers.

University of South Carolina Libraries Special Collections. Columbia.

Townes Family Papers, 1784–1967.

Virginia Military Institute Archives. Lynchburg (VMIA).

Smith, Francis H., Administration Records.

William Jewell College Archives, Liberty, MO.

Henry Talbird Sketch.

Yale University Divinity School Library. New Haven, CT.

Hartwell Family Papers.

Yale University Catalogue, 1835.

Published Primary Sources

African Repository and Colonial Journal (American Colonization Society), vol. 33 (1857).

Baptist, Edward. "Address Delivered before the Trustees, Faculty, and Students, Howard College." November 16, 1846. Pamphlet. Tuskaloosa: D. J. Slade, 1846.

Bates, Joshua. "Revivals of Religion in Middlebury College." *Journal of the American Education Society* 12, no. 3 (February 1840): 49–67.

Cathcart, William. *The Baptist Encyclopedia: A Dictionary of the Doctrines, Ordinances . . . and . . . History of the Baptist Denomination in All Lands.* Philadelphia: Louis H. Everts, 1881.

Crumpton, Washington Bryan. *A Book of Memories, 1842–1920.* Montgomery: Baptist Mission Board, 1921.

———. *Our Baptist Centennials, 1808–1923.* Montgomery: Paragon Press, 1923.

Cumming, Kate. *Hospital Life in the Confederate Army of the Tennessee.* Louisville, KY: John P. Morton & Co., 1866.

DeBow, J. D. B. *Statistical View of the United States: Embracing Its Territory, Population— White, Free Colored, and Slave. . . .* Washington, DC: Beverley, Tucker, Senate Printer, 1854.

Harvard College. Class of 1891. *Secretary's Report, No. IV.* Boston: Rockwell & Churchill Press, 1906.

———. Class of 1891. *Secretary's Report, No. V.* Boston: Rockwell & Churchill Press, 1911.

Humphrey, Heman. *Revival: Sketches and Manual in Two Parts.* New York: American Tract Society, 1859.

Keen, T. G. *Characteristics of the Times, Strong Incentives to Intellectual Effort: An Address, Delivered before the Franklin & Adelphi Societies of Howard College at Their Anniversary, Held at Marion, Alabama, July 24, 1850.* Tuskaloosa, AL: Franklin & Adelphi Societies / M. D. J. Sledge, 1850.

Lasher, George William, ed. *The Ministerial Directory of the Baptist Churches in the United States of America: Together with a Statement of the Work of the National Missionary Publication and Young People's Societies, with the Names and Location of Educational Institutions and Church Papers.* Oxford, OH: Press of the Oxford News Co., 1899.

Murfee, James Thomas. *A New Scheme of Organization, Instruction, and Government for the University of Alabama, with Report on Construction of Building.* Tuskaloosa: Printed by J. F. Warren, 1867.

"A Narrative of the Revival of Religion, in the County of Oneida: Particularly in the Bounds of the Presbytery of Oneida, in the Year 1826." Utica, NY: Hastings & Tracy, 1826.

Sampey, John. *The Memoirs of John R. Sampey.* Nashville: Broadman, 1947.

Sherman, Samuel Sterling. *Autobiography of Samuel Sterling Sherman, 1815–1910.* Chicago: M. A. Donohue & Co., 1910.

———. *The Bible a Classic: A Baccalaureate Address.* Tuskaloosa, AL.: M. D. J. Slade, 1850.

Stennett, Samuel. *A Sermon Occasioned by the Decease of John Howard, Esq.* London: Printed for T. Cadell [et al.], 1790 [*sic*].

Tuomey, M. *Second Biennial Report on the Geology of Alabama.* Montgomery: N. B. Cloud, State Printer, 1858.

Washington, Booker T. *The Booker T. Washington Papers,* ed. Louis R. Harlan and Raymond Smock. Urbana: University of Illinois Press, 1972.

Government Documents

1850 U.S. Federal Census—Slave Schedules. Online database. Provo, UT: Ancestry.com Operations Inc., 2004.

Acts of the General Assembly of Alabama, Passed at the Session of 1888–89. Montgomery: Brown Printing Co., 1889.

Amnesty, Ancestry.com. U.S., Pardons Under Amnesty Proclamations, 1865–1869. Online database. Provo, UT.

Official Proceedings of the Constitutional Convention of the State of Alabama. Montgomery: Brown Printing Co., 1901.

Sixth Census of the United States, 1840. NARA microfilm publication M704, 580 rolls. Records of the Bureau of the Census, Record Group 29. National Archives, Washington, DC.

Alabama Newspapers and Periodicals

Alabama Baptist.
Alabama Beacon.
Baptist Correspondent.
Bibb Blade.
Birmingham Age.
Birmingham Age-Herald.
Birmingham Iron Age.
Birmingham News.
Canebrake Herald (Uniontown).
Christian Index and South-Western Baptist.
Clarke County Democrat.
Eufaula Daily Times.
Florence Herald.
Franklin Advocate.
Greensboro Watchman.

Howard College Magazine.
Howard Collegian.
Independent Monitor (Tuscaloosa).
Livingston Journal.
Marion Commonwealth.
Marion Standard.
Marion Times Standard.
Monroe Journal.
Montgomery Advertiser.
Mountain Eagle (Jasper).
Our Mountain Home (Talladega).
Philomathian.
South Western Baptist.
Southern Aegis.
The Sun.
Talladega News.
Times-Argus.
Troy Messenger.
Tuskaloosa Gazette.
Union Springs Herald.
Weekly Iron Age.
Weekly Messenger.
Wilcox Progressive Era.

Non-Alabama Newspapers and Periodicals

Alexandria Gazette (Richmond, VA).
Appeal (St. Paul).
Boston Recorder.
Charleston Daily News (SC).
Daily Advocate (Baton Rouge).
Daily Dispatch (Richmond, VA).
Harper's Weekly (New York).
Intelligencer (Anderson, SC).
National Era (Washington, DC).
New York Times.
Pittsburgh Gazette.
Religious Herald (Richmond, VA).
Richmond Whig.

South Atlantic Quarterly (Durham, NC).

Times-Picayune (New Orleans).

SECONDARY SOURCES

Books and Articles

Abernethy, Thomas Perkins. *The Formative Period in Alabama, 1815–1828*. Tuscaloosa: University of Alabama Press, 1990.

Adams, George F. *History of Baptist Churches in Maryland Connected with the Maryland Baptist Union Association*. Baltimore: John F. Weishampel Jr., 1885.

Aikin, John. *A View of the Character and Public Services of the Late John Howard*. London: Printed for J. Johnson, 1792.

Alderman, Edwin Anderson, and Armistead Churchill Gordon. *J. L. M. Curry: A Biography*. New York: Macmillan Co., 1911.

Allen, Lee N. *The First 150 Years: Montgomery First Baptist Church, 1829–1979*. Montgomery: First Baptist Church, 1979.

Andrew, Rod. *Long Gray Lines: The Southern Military School Tradition, 1839–1915*. Chapel Hill: University of North Carolina Press, 2004.

Armbrester, Margaret E. *Samuel Ullman and "Youth": The Life, the Legacy*. Tuscaloosa: University of Alabama Press, 1993.

Askew, Thomas. "The Founding of Church Colleges, 1820–1860." In Noll et al., eds., *Eerdmans' Handbook to Christianity in America*.

Axtell, James. *The Making of Princeton University: From Woodrow Wilson to the Present*. Princeton, NJ: Princeton University Press, 2006.

Ayers, Edward L. *The Promise of the New South: Life after Reconstruction*. New York: Oxford University Press, 1992.

Bass, S. Jonathan. "'How 'Bout a Hand for the Hog': The Enduring Nature of the Swine as a Cultural Symbol in the South." *Southern Cultures* 1, no. 3 (1995): 301–20. doi.org/10.1353/scu.1995.0106.

Berrey, Stephen A. *The Jim Crow Routine: Everyday Performances of Race, Civil Rights, and Segregation in Mississippi*. Chapel Hill: University of North Carolina Press, 2015.

Bebbington, David W. *Baptists Through the Centuries: A History of a Global People*. Waco, TX: Baylor University Press, 2010.

———. *Victorian Religious Revivals: Culture and Piety in Local and Global Contexts*. New York: Oxford University Press, 2012.

Berton, Orville Vernon. *In My Father's House Are Many Mansions: Family and Community in Edgefield, South Carolina*. Chapel Hill: University of North Carolina Press, 2000.

Boyd, Lucina. *The Irvines and Their Kin*. Chicago: R. R. Donnelley and Sons Co., 1908.

Boykin, Samuel. *History of the Baptist Denomination in Georgia: With Biographical Compendium and Portrait Gallery of Baptist Ministers and Other Georgia Baptists.* Atlanta: Jas. P. Harrison & Co., 1881.

Braden, Waldo Warder. *The Oral Tradition in the South.* Baton Rouge: Louisiana State University Press, 1983.

Broadie, Alexander. *A History of Scottish Philosophy.* Edinburgh: Edinburgh University Press, 2009.

Brophy, Alfred L. "Proslavery Political Theory in the Southern Academy, 1832–1861." In *Slavery and the University,* ed. Harris, Campbell, and Brophy, 65–83.

———. "The Southern Scholar: Howard College Before the Civil War." *Cumberland Law Review* 46, no. 2 (2015–16): 289–309.

Brown, William Garrott. *A History of Alabama.* New York: University Publishing Co., 1900.

———. *The Lower South in American History.* New York: Macmillan Co., 1902.

Burke, Edmund. *The Works of the Right Honourable Edmund Burke. Vol. 2.* London: John H. Nimmo, 1887.

Burrage, Henry S. *Baptist Hymn Writers and Their Hymns.* Portland, ME: Brown Thurston & Co., 1881.

Buzzard, Lynn R. "A Christian Law School: Images and Vision." *Marquette Law Review* 78, no. 2 (1995): 267–82.

Campbell, Jesse Harrison. *Georgia Baptists: Historical and Biographical.* Macon, GA: G. W. Burke & Co., 1874.

Caner, Emir Fethi, and Ergun Mehmet Caner. *The Sacred Trust: Sketches of the Southern Baptist Convention Presidents.* Nashville: Broadman & Holman, 2003.

Carter, Dan T. *When the War Was Over: The Failure of Self-Reconstruction in the South, 1865–1867.* Baton Rouge: Louisiana State University Press, 1985.

Cash, W. J. *The Mind of the South.* 1941. New York: Vintage Books, 1991.

Caver, Joseph D. *From Marion to Montgomery: The Early Years of Alabama State University, 1867–1925.* Montgomery: New South Books, 2020.

Clark, Gregory. "Timothy Dwight's Moral Rhetoric at Yale College, 1795–1817." *Rhetorica: A Journal of the History of Rhetoric* 5, no. 2 (1987): 149–61.

Cobb, James C. *Away Down South: A History of Southern Identity.* New York: Oxford University Press, 2007.

———. *The Selling of the South: The Southern Crusade for Industrial Development, 1936–1980.* Baton Rouge: Louisiana State University Press, 1980.

Cords, Nicholas, and Patrick Gerster, eds. *Myth and Southern History: The Old South.* Champagne: University of Illinois Press, 1989.

Daniel, W. Harrison. "Madison College, 1851–1858: A Methodist Protestant School." *Methodist History* 17, no. 2 (January 1979): 90–105.

Dill, J. S. *Lest We Forget: Baptist Preachers of Yesterday That I Knew.* Nashville: Broadman Press, 1938.

Doss, Chriss H. "In the Shadows of Foreclosure: Three Financial Crises That Threatened the Existence of Howard College." *Alabama Baptist Historian* 28, no. 1 (January 1992): 3–17.

———. "The Original Fifteen Trustees of Howard College." *Alabama Baptist Historian* 28, no. 2 (July 1992): 3–36.

DuBose, John Witherspoon. *Jefferson County and Birmingham, Alabama: Historical and Biographical.* Birmingham: Teeple & Smith, 1887.

———, and James K Greer. *Alabama's Tragic Decade: Ten Years of Alabama, 1865–1874.* Birmingham: Webb Book Co., 1940.

Elder, Robert. *The Sacred Mirror: Evangelicalism, Honor, and Identity in the Deep South, 1790–1860.* Chapel Hill: University of North Carolina Press, 2016.

Elovitz, Mark H. *A Century of Jewish Life in Dixie: The Birmingham Experience.* Tuscaloosa: University of Alabama Press, 2003.

Encyclopedia of Alabama. Alabama Humanities Alliance and Auburn University Outreach. www.encyclopediaofalabama.org.

England, Ann D. "A Compilation of Documented Information About the Confederate Hospital in Marion, Alabama, May 20, 1863–May 20, 1865." N.p.: Marion Military Institute, n.d.

English, Bertis. *Civil Wars, Civil Beings, and Civil Rights in Alabama's Black Belt: A History of Perry County.* Tuscaloosa: University of Alabama Press, 2020.

Finestein, Israel. "The Jews in Hull between 1766 and 1880." *Jewish Historical Studies* 35 (1996–98): 38–40.

Finney, Charles G. *The Memoirs of Charles G. Finney: Written by Himself.* New York: Fleming H. Revel Co., 1876.

Fleming, Walter. *Civil War and Reconstruction in Alabama.* New York: Peter Smith, 1949.

Flynt, Wayne. *Alabama Baptists: Southern Baptists in the Heart of Dixie.* Tuscaloosa: University of Alabama Press, 1998.

———, and Gerald W. Berkley-Coats. *Taking Christianity to China: Alabama Missionaries in the Middle Kingdom, 1850–1950.* Tuscaloosa: University of Alabama Press, 1997.

Foster, L. S. *Mississippi Baptist Preachers.* St. Louis, MO: National Baptist Publishing Co., 1895.

Fraser, Walter J., and Winfred B Moore. *From the Old South to the New: Essays on the Transitional South.* Westport, CT: Greenwood Press, 1981.

Frost, Dan R. *Thinking Confederates: Academia and the Idea of Progress in the New South.* Knoxville: University of Tennessee Press, 2010.

Fuller, A. James. *Chaplain to the Confederacy: Basil Manly and Baptist Life in the Old South.* Baton Rouge: Louisiana State University Press, 2000.

———. "'I Whipped Him a Second Time, Very Severely': Basil Manly, Honor, and Slavery at the University of Alabama." In *Slavery and the University*, ed. Harris, Campbell, and Brophy, 114–31.

Garrett, Mitchell B. "Sixty Years of Howard College." *Howard College Review* 85, no. 4 (October 1927): 1–167.

Glover, Lorri. *Southern Sons: Becoming Men in the New Nation*. Baltimore: Johns Hopkins University Press, 2010.

Guffin, R. L. *A Lasting Legacy: First Baptist Church, Tuscaloosa Alabama, 1818–2008*. Tuscaloosa: First Baptist Church, 2008.

Guy, Richard. "Architecture and the Reinterpretation of the Past in the American Renaissance." *Winterthur Portfolio* 18, no. 1 (Spring 1983): 69–87.

Harrell, David E., Jr., Edwin S. Gaustad, John B. Boles, and Sally Foreman Griffith. *Unto a Good Land: A History of the American People*. Grand Rapids, MI: William B. Eerdmans, 2005.

Harris, Leslie M., James T. Campbell, and Alfred L. Brophy, eds. *Slavery and the University: Histories and Legacies*. Athens: University of Georgia Press, 2019.

Harris, W. Stuart. *Perry County Heritage*. Marion, AL: Perry County Historical and Preservation Society, 1991.

———. "Rowdyism, Public Drunkenness, and Bloody Encounters in Early Perry County." *Alabama Review* 33, no. 1 (January 1980): 15–24.

Hayward, Edward Farwell. *Lyman Beecher*. Boston: Pilgrim Press, 1904.

Hawley, Thomas S. *This Terrible Struggle for Life: The Civil War Letters of a Union Regimental Surgeon*. Ed. Dennis W Belcher. Jefferson, NC: McFarland, 2013.

Himmelfarb, Gertrude. *The Roads to Modernity: The British, French, and American Enlightenments*. New York: Vintage, 2005.

Holcombe, Hosea. *A History of the Rise and Progress of the Baptists in Alabama. . . .* Philadelphia: King and Baird Printers, 1840.

Hoole, William Stanley. "Letters from Johnson's Island Prison." *Alabama Review* 12, no. 3 (July 1959): 222–25.

Hornaday, John R. *The Book of Birmingham*. New York: Dodd, Mead, and Co., 1921.

Huey, Thomas E. *Ruhama, the Story of a Church, 1819–1945*. Birmingham: Birmingham Printing Co., 1946.

Hundley, Daniel Robinson. *Social Relations in Our Southern States*. 1860. Baton Rouge: Louisiana State University Press, 1979.

Jamieson, Patrick C. "Making Their Case: Religion, Pedagogy, and the Slavery Question at Antebellum Emory College." In *Slavery and the University*, ed. Harris, Campbell, and Brophy, 99–113.

Janey, Caroline. "The Lost Cause." *Encyclopedia Virginia* (Virginia Humanities). Last modified December 7, 2020. encyclopediavirginia.org/entries/lost-cause-the/.

Jones, J. Williams. *Personal Reminiscences, Anecdotes, and Letters of Gen. Robert E. Lee.* New York: D. Appleton and Co., 1875.

Julian, John. *A Dictionary of Hymnology: Setting Forth the Origin and History of Christian Hymns of All Ages and Nations.* New York: Charles Scribner's Sons, 1892.

Kirby, Jack Temple. *Rural Worlds Lost: The American South 1920–1960.* Baton Rouge: Louisiana State University Press, 1995.

Leonard, Bill J. *Baptist Ways: A History.* Valley Forge, PA: Judson Press, 2003.

Lind, Michael. "Why the Liberal Arts Still Matter." *Wilson Quarterly* 30, no. 4 (Autumn 2006): 52–58.

Lockley, Timothy James. *Lines in the Sand: Race and Class in Lowcountry Georgia, 1750–1860.* Athens: University of Georgia Press, 2001.

Lundstrom, John B. *One Drop in a Sea of Blue: The Liberators of the Ninth Minnesota.* St. Paul: Minnesota Historical Society Press, 2012.

Mallory, James. *Fear God and Walk Humbly: The Agricultural Journal of James Mallory 1843–1877.* Tuscaloosa: University of Alabama Press, 2013.

Marsden, George. *The Evangelical Mind and the New School Presbyterian Experience: A Case Study of Thought and Theology in Nineteenth-Century America.* New Haven, CT: Yale University Press, 1970).

———. *Religion and American Culture.* New York: Harcourt, Brace, Jovanovich, 1990.

———. *The Soul of the American University: From Protestant Establishment to Established Nonbelief* (Oxford, UK: Oxford University Press, 1994.

McIlwain, Christopher Lyle. "Harry: Faithful unto Death." *Alabama Heritage* 116 (2015).

McKinley, Kevin O. *Shadows and Dust III: Legacies.* Morris, NC: Lulu Publications, 2018.

Memorial Record of Alabama: A Concise Account of the State's Political, Military, Professional and Industrial Progress, Together with the Personal Memoirs of Many of Its People. Vol. 2. Madison, WI: Brant & Fuller, 1893.

Miller, Perry. *The Life of the Mind in America, from the Revolution to the Civil War.* New York: Harcourt, Brace & World, 1965.

Minnesota Historical Society. *Minnesota in the Civil and Indian Wars, 1861–1865. Vol. 1.* St. Paul: Pioneer Press, 1890.

Morelock, Kolan Thomas. *Taking the Town: Collegiate and Community Culture in the Bluegrass, 1880–1917.* Lexington: University Press of Kentucky, 2008.

Moss, Florence Hawkins Wood. *Building Birmingham and Jefferson County.* Birmingham: Birmingham Printing Co., 1941.

Naylor, Natalie A. "The Ante-Bellum College Movement: A Reappraisal of Tewksbury's *Founding of American Colleges and Universities.*" *History of Education Quarterly* 13, no. 3 (Autumn 1973): 261–74.

Noll, Mark A. *America's God: From Jonathan Edwards to Abraham Lincoln.* Oxford, UK: Oxford University Press, 2005.

————, Nathan O. Hatch, George M. Marsden, David F. Wells, and John D. Wood-bridge, eds. *Eerdmans' Handbook to Christianity in America*. Grand Rapids, MI: Eerdmans, 1983.

Northern Alabama: Historical and Biographical. Birmingham: Smith & De Land, 1888.

Owen, Thomas McAdory. *History of Alabama and Dictionary of Alabama Biography*. Chicago: S. J. Clarke Publishing Co., 1921.

Ownby, Ted. *Subduing Satan: Religion, Recreation, and Manhood in the Rural South, 1865–1920*. Chapel Hill: University of North Carolina Press, 1993.

Ostander, Gilman M. "Review: Accreditations for the Old-Time American College." *Historical Reflections / Réflexions Historiques* 10, no. 3 (Fall 1983), 395–407.

Porch, Luther Quentin. *History of the First Baptist Church, Tuscaloosa, Alabama*. Tuscaloosa: Drake Printers, 1968.

Potts, David B. "American Colleges in the Nineteenth Century: From Localism to Denominationalism." *History of Education Quarterly* 11, no. 4 (Winter 1971): 363–80.

Ray, Louise Crenshaw. *The Color of Steel*. Chapel Hill: University of North Carolina Press, 1952.

Reid, Alvin. *Introduction to Evangelism*. Nashville: Broadman & Holman, 1998.

Reid, Avery Hamilton. *Baptists in Alabama: Their Organization and Witness*. Montgomery: Alabama Baptist State Convention, 1967.

Richard, Carl J. *The Golden Age of the Classics in America: Greece, Rome, and the Antebellum United States*. Cambridge, MA: Harvard University Press, 2009.

Riddle, Joseph Esmond. *A Complete English-Latin Dictionary: For Use of Colleges and Schools*. London: Longman, Ord, Brown et al., 1838.

Riley, Benjamin Franklin. *Alabama as It Is; Or, The Immigrant's and Capitalist's Guide Book to Alabama*. Atlanta: W. C. Holt, 1887.

————. *History of the Baptists of Alabama: From the Time of Their First Occupation of Alabama in 1808 until 1894*. Birmingham: Roberts & Son, 1895.

————. *Makers and Romance of Alabama History*. Birmingham: B. F. Riley, 1921.

————. *A Memorial History of the Baptists of Alabama*. Philadelphia: Judson Press, 1923.

Rogers, William Warren, Robert David Ward, Leah Rawls Atkins, and Wayne Flynt. *Alabama: The History of a Deep South State*. Tuscaloosa: University of Alabama Press, 1994.

Roosevelt, Theodore. *The Letters of Theodore Roosevelt: The Big Stick, 1905–1909*. Cambridge, MA: Harvard University Press, 1952.

Roth, Randolph A. "Can Faith Change the World? Religion and Society in Vermont's Age of Reform." *Vermont History* 69, Supplement (Winter 2001): 7–18.

————. *The Democratic Dilemma Religion, Reform, and the Social Order in the Connecticut River Valley of Vermont, 1791–1850*. Cambridge, UK: Cambridge University Press, 1987.

Rothman, Joshua D. *Flush Times and Fever Dreams: A Story of Capitalism and Slavery in the Age of Jackson*. Athens: University of Georgia Press, 2014.

Sellers, James. *History of the University of Alabama. Vol. 1: 1818–1902*. Tuscaloosa: University of Alabama Press, 2014.

Smith, Page. *Killing the Spirit: Higher Education in America*. New York: Penguin Books, 1991.

Spears, Ellen Griffith, and James C. Hall. "Engaging the Racial Landscape at the University of Alabama." In *Slavery and the University*, ed. Harris, Campbell, and Brophy, 298–314.

Stameshkin, David M. *The Strength of the Hills: Middlebury College, 1915–1990*. Hanover, NH: Middlebury College Press, 1995.

Stephenson, Wendell H. "William Garrott Brown: Literary Historian and Essayist." *Journal of Southern History* 12, no. 3 (August 1945): 313–44.

Sulzby, James Frederick. *Toward a History of Samford University*. Birmingham: Samford University Press, 1986.

Sydnor, Charles S. *The Development of Southern Sectionalism, 1819–1848*. Baton Rouge: Louisiana State University Press, 1948.

Taylor, George Braxton. *Virginia Baptist Ministers. 5th Series: 1902–1914*. Lynchburg, VA: J. P. Bell, 1915.

Tewksbury, Donald George. *The Founding of American Colleges and Universities before the Civil War. With Particular Reference to the Religious Influences Bearing upon the College Movement, Etc.* New York: Columbia University Teachers College, 1932.

Townes, Samuel A., and Lee N. Allen. *The History of Marion, Alabama*. Birmingham: A. H. Cather Publishing Co., 1985.

Trueblood, Elton. *The Idea of a College*. New York: Harper & Brothers, 1959.

The United States Biographical Dictionary and Portrait Gallery of Eminent and Self-Made Men: Missouri Volume. New York: United States Biographical Publishing Co., 1878.

Urofsky, Melvin I. "Reforms and Response: The Yale Report of 1828." *History of Education Quarterly* 5, no. 1 (March 1965): 53–67.

Wayland, Francis. *The Elements of Moral Science*. Boston: Gould, Kendall, and Lincoln, 1843.

Webb, Samuel L., and Margaret E. Armbrester. *Alabama Governors: A Political History of the State*. Tuscaloosa: University of Alabama Press, 2014.

Weishampel, John F., and George F. Adams. *History of Baptist Churches in Maryland Connected with the Maryland Baptist Union Association*. Baltimore: John F. Weishampel Jr., 1885.

Wiebe, Robert H. *The Search for Order: 1877–1920*. New York: Hill and Wang, 1966.

Williams, George Huntston, and Rodney L. Petersen. *Divinings: Religion at Harvard: From Its Origins in New England Ecclesiastical History to the 175th Anniversary of the Harvard Divinity School, 1636–1992*. Göttingen: Vandenhoeck Et Ruprecht, 2014.

Williams, Timothy J. *Intellectual Manhood: University, Self, and Society in the Antebellum South*. Chapel Hill: University of North Carolina Press, 2015.

Willis, Wayne. "Liberating the Liberal Arts: An Interpretation of Aristotle." *Journal of General Education* 39, no. 4 (1988): 193–205.

Wills, Gregory A. *Southern Baptist Theological Seminary, 1859–2009*. New York: Oxford University Press, 2009.

Wilson, Charles Reagan. *Baptized in Blood: The Religion of the Lost Cause, 1865–1920*. Athens: University of Georgia Press, 1980.

Winkler, E. T. *The Sacred Lute: A Collection of Popular Hymns, with Choruses and Forms for Special Occasions*. N.p.: Southern Baptist Publication Society, 1861.

Woodward, C. Vann. *Origins of the New South, 1877–1913*. 1951. Rpt., Baton Rouge: Louisiana State University Press, 1971.

Wyatt-Brown, Bertram. *Southern Honor: Ethics and Behavior in the Old South*. Ann Arbor: Scholarly Publishing Office, University of Michigan, 2010.

Dissertations and Theses

English, Bertis. "Civil Wars and Civil Beings: Violence, Religion, Race, Politics, Education, Culture, and Agrarianism in Perry County, Alabama, 1860–1875." PhD diss., Auburn University, 2006.

Jones, Terry Lawrence. "Benjamin Franklin Riley: A Story of His Life and Work." PhD diss., Vanderbilt University, 1974.

Pate, James A. "The Development of the Instructional Program at Howard College, 1842–1957." PhD diss., University of Alabama, 1959.

Peters, Chris. "James H. DeVotie, Leading the Transformation and Expansion of Baptists in Alabama and Georgia: 1830–1890." PhD diss., University of Alabama, 2014.

White, Walter Belt. "J. L. M. Curry—Alabamian." MA thesis, Samford University, 1971.

INDEX